*Protestant
Christianity*

JOHN DILLENBERGER
GRADUATE THEOLOGICAL UNION

CLAUDE WELCH
GRADUATE THEOLOGICAL UNION

Protestant Christianity

Interpreted Through Its Development

SECOND EDITION

MACMILLAN PUBLISHING COMPANY
NEW YORK
Collier Macmillan Publishers
LONDON

Macmillan Publishing Company
866 Third Avenue, New York, New York 10022

Collier Macmillan Canada, Inc.

LIBRARY OF CONGRESS CATALOGING-IN-PUBLICATION DATA

Dillenberger, John.
    Protestant Christianity interpreted through its development.

    Includes index.
    1. Protestantism — History. I. Welch, Claude.
II. Title.
BX4807.D5   1988   280'.4'09   87–11013
ISBN 0-02-329601-1

Printing: 1 2 3 4 5 6 7   Year: 8 9 0 1 2 3 4

ISBN 0-02-329601-1

Preface to the First Edition

This book is an essay in the interpretation of Protestant Christianity. It has grown out of the conviction that the nature and meaning of Protestantism can be seen only in the light of its historical development. We have, therefore, deliberately abandoned many of the usual patterns for interpreting Protestant life and thought. Survey descriptions of the various Protestant denominations almost invariably lack unity and historical depth and fail to disclose the spiritual dynamics which both cut across and give rise to denominational patterns. Interpretations which focus exclusively on the Reformation cannot give due weight either to the new impulses which have appeared in Protestant history or to the varying development of the Reformation principles. Efforts to develop independent statements of Protestant "principles" or "beliefs" tend to be so general and filled with all manner of qualifications as to be often meaningless, or they are sufficiently partisan as to exclude important motifs.

In view of these difficulties and of our conviction that Protestantism must be seen as an historical community of faith, by far the larger part of this book is devoted to historical development. The concluding chapter, "What is Protestantism?", is intended as a summary in retrospect. It is not a separate statement of principles, but an attempt to bring into focus the understanding of Protestantism which arises from the entirety of the historical analysis.

We do not suppose, of course, that history simply speaks for itself apart from the human beings who interpret it. We are quite aware that this book is throughout an interpretative study. It is intended as such. At the same time, we have sought to shape and test our interpretation by the historical materials which need to be interpreted. We hope that we have entered sufficiently into the perspectives of the people and movements studied as to communicate something of their spirit and self-understanding. We have also offered certain critical reactions which spring from our own perspectives as twentieth-century Protestant Christians. These are expressed in the conviction that Protestantism requires constant self-criticism, and that our views are in turn subject to criticism.

The content of the discussion is weighted on the side of Protestant thought. This is deliberate, for one of our prime concerns is to delineate the self-understanding of Protestant Christians. But we have tried always to set the development of theology in the context of the whole life of the religious community. Theology is only one way in which the vitality of faith is expressed, and we have sought to relate thought directly to the crucial events in church history. Moreover, we have tried to see the development of thought and institutions alike in their social and cultural settings. We reject the thesis that the life of the religious community is simply determined by social and cultural factors. But the notion that Protestantism can be understood apart from these is rejected with equal vigor. Of course, our concern is primarily with the Protestant story. We have, therefore, not attempted independent treatments of other modern currents of life and thought, even when these may have been more dominant in the Western world as a whole. Such movements are dealt with only as they have influenced the internal development of Protestantism.

In the organization of this book, certain further principles have guided us. First, we have emphasized those individuals and movements which seem to be of most significance for the understanding of the development as a whole, either in the expression of dominant themes and patterns or in the appearance of new life and thought. Needless to say, no attempt has been made to apportion space in relation to the number of adherents of a particular denomination. But we hope that in each case we have been true to the spiritual dynamic and the religious convictions of the various groups.

Second, we have followed the early movements in Protestantism only to the point where they achieved more or less classic expression, or where they became the occasion for reaction to themselves. There is, for example, no attempt to bring orthodox Lutheranism or Calvinism, or Anglican or Methodist patterns, up to the present, except through an occasional reference. Third, and this principle is related to the second, denominational lines and groupings have been followed only as, especially in their emergence, they developed distinctive religious ideas and new forms of church life. Where denominational distinctions became secondary to movements which cut through them —

and this has been generally true since the beginning of the nineteenth century — we have largely omitted them from consideration.

This project was undertaken at the request of the Committee on Projects and Research of the National Council on Religion in Higher Education. It was felt that there was a very serious need for a single book on Protestantism which could be used in college and university courses in religion, and which would in general make available to intelligent laypeople a deepened understanding of Protestant Christianity. It is this need that we have tried to meet.

In a venture as extensive as this, we have naturally drawn from a great many sources. Primarily, we have depended upon the major original writings which are a part of Protestant history. We have been guided also by numerous recent works on various aspects of Protestantism. The number and excellence of these works suggest a renaissance of Protestant studies. In the "Suggestions for Further Reading" we have listed both some of the most important original documents and some of the major recent interpretations in English.

This book also requires a rather special note of appreciation to those who helped by their criticism of early drafts of the manuscript. Professors William Christian and Seymour Smith of Yale University, E. Harris Harbison and Paul Ramsey of Princeton University, and Albert C. Outler of Perkins School of Theology have served as a subcommittee of the National Council on Religion in Higher Education to assist in our work. They helped in the planning of the project and rigorously scrutinized the initial drafts. Their comments were immensely valuable. We also owe much to our fellow members of the Society for Theological Discussion, who, in two series of weekend meetings, used our drafts of the manuscript as the basis for their discussions. To Professor H. Richard Niebuhr of Yale University, we are grateful for suggestions which resulted in a more radical recasting of parts of the manuscript than he knew.

We are grateful for the assistance of all of these persons. By their suggestions for refocusing, clarification, and outright correction in fact and interpretation, they have made this a far better book than it would otherwise have been. We are aware of many limitations, for Protestantism is a vast and intricate subject. But in conception and execution, this has been a common venture of the authors. While we divided the work of writing the initial drafts, the final text has been formulated by both of us, and for the whole we assume joint responsibility.

JOHN DILLENBERGER
CLAUDE WELCH

Preface to the
Second, Revised Edition

The first edition of *Protestant Christianity* was written over thirty years ago, when both of us were young teachers and scholars. Now, toward the end of our academic careers and when being in the same geographical location makes it easy for us to work together, we agreed to revise and expand, where appropriate, the original text. To be asked to revise a book after all these years means that it has continued to serve a purpose, one that may be better served by the changes that have been made for this edition. In addition to bringing the story up to date, especially by the incorporation of two wholly new chapters (XIV and XV) and the expansion of the treatment of the ecumenical movement (Ch. XIII), we have revised the text throughout by corrections, additions, reorientations of some interpretations in the light of new scholarship, and changes to the consistent use of inclusive language.

At least two developments have impressed themselves on us in the process of this revision. First, sound scholarship in the past three decades in all phases of religious history has been nothing less than astounding. In the 1950s we were able easily to add further suggested readings for each chapter. To do so now would require a whole catalogue of books and articles. Those who use the book for classroom purposes will be aware of the collateral literature, and those who read the text for their own instruction will hardly be helped by listing a multitude of books. So we have not included a formal listing of suggestions for further reading in this edition.

Second, the last thirty years have brought considerable diversity in outlook and a simultaneous widening of concerns, as Chapters XIV and XV show vividly. Social and political events have played an even greater role in relation to theological thinking. In addition, cultural phenomena (for example, music, literature, the visual arts, and architecture) have received more attention. New forms of Protestant life and thought have emerged in the Third World, especially in Asia — though we have not found it possible to survey these for fear of expanding the work inordinately. The Second Vatican Council, despite recent conservative tendencies, has fundamentally altered the ecumenical movement and set new agendas for the approaches between Catholics and Protestants, so that at some points there is great overlapping of thought (see especially Chs. XIII and XV), and the question of the distinctiveness of Protestant Christianity has to be looked at afresh (see Ch. XVI). Simultaneously, the dialogue with new and historic world religions is changing the shape and context of much religious reflection.

These developments have certainly made the task of interpreting in the 1980s more difficult than was the case when we were able to stop in the 1950s. For some people, the new diversity and the absence of reigning theologies have seemed like the demise of theology. On the other hand, and more correctly we think, one can argue that the new diversity, difficult as it appears on first viewing, provides new thresholds of understanding. Much of the thought of recent decades will fall by the wayside, as is usually the case. But the new perceptions may also be the basis for newly emergent theologies, more comprehensive than the special concerns of the present.

Berkeley, California   JOHN DILLENBERGER
                                                     CLAUDE WELCH

Contents

XII

Between the Wars   *233*

XIII

The Ecumenical Movement   *257*

XIV

Post-War Directions   *281*

XV

Toward the Future   *309*

XVI

What is Protestantism? *343*

Index *361*

CHAPTER I

A New Era Begins

Preliminary Notes on the Nature of Protestantism

Diversity in belief and practice is a striking part of the Protestant heritage. Individuals think differing thoughts even when they seek to witness to the same gospel. This may be due to human creativity and human finitude; even more it may be due to prideful individuals who think too highly of their own outlook upon life. This ambiguity is a part of the Protestant heritage, a sign both of health and of sickness. In the ecumenical movement, where individuals are keenly conscious of the broken and divided nature of the churches as the body of Christ, the fact of necessary difference is accepted. The hoped-for reunion of many of the churches of Christ will not and ought not bring people to one opinion, but it may provide a framework within which different nuances of life and thought may in effect be considered to strengthen rather than weaken the Christian cause. It may provide a place where differences are considered a sign of health and vitality as well as of pride and sin. Revitalization in the churches may conceivably be possible without the breaks in community which once seemed inevitable.

Moreover, diversity is peculiarly inevitable where a movement consciously assumes the burden of relating its message directly to the concerns and problems of people in particular historical periods. There may be a certain constancy in the problems that people face, but the particular questions which they ask are forged by the cultural outlook, expressed and unexpressed, of a period. Protestantism is, on principle, concerned with the relation of the gospel to such particular questions. The strength of such an approach lies in the bold attempt to relate the biblical message directly to the needs of a time. At its best, this means that certain aspects of the gospel are featured because of those particular needs. Luther emancipated people from the fear of God by stressing God's merciful acceptance apart from every concern of self; Wesley showed the warmth of the new life in Christ in a time when individuals verbally believed in the gospel but did not feel its power. Luther and Wesley do not essentially contradict each other, but the major emphases are different. To this day, these men disclose something about the respective character of Lutheranism and Methodism (though it must be recognized that today the differences between major Protestant denominations are far less clear-cut than at the time of their appearance).

The dangers in a movement which relates itself directly to the concerns of every period is that its message may be distorted and weakened because its problems and answers are forged too exclusively out of the historical context. It may lose its vitality in the very attempt to gain it. The great concern in nineteenth-century Liberal theology was a noble attempt to save human dignity in a period when the difference between humans and animals seemed small, but the partial deification of humanity by some theologians was a serious departure from the gospel which informs Christendom (see Chs. IX, X). Here liberalism's genius turned out to be its liability. But in spite of such problems, Protestants have generally felt that such difficulties were to be preferred to any imposition of uniformity upon culture.

In Protestantism we are involved not so much with a Church as with a movement made up of churches. Protestantism is a story to be told. One cannot define it by a single religious concept or by a combination of religious concepts. This, together with its diversity, accounts for the recurring false impression that Protestantism is synonymous with the right to think what one wishes in religious matters. Protestants do generally maintain that individuals must think their own thoughts and stand directly under God, but they have always maintained also that one's life and thinking take their cue from the message of the biblical tradition, however differently that message is understood. In fact, the striking thing about Protestantism is not its diversity, but its unity. Protestants claim that the vitality of their faith is nowhere more evident than in the stress upon each individual's own experience of the biblical faith which produces so many authentically similar expressions of faith. From this perspective, the differences which do exist are not as important as is sometimes assumed.[1]

Nevertheless, Protestantism is the story of individuals and groups

---

[1] Although Protestantism has proliferated into more than two hundred fifty separate bodies in America, approximately 85 percent of the individuals who constitute these groups belong to twelve major denominations, and many of the distinct organizations can be grouped into closely related families.

who have taken their understanding of the gospel so seriously that they have been willing to create new forms of the church. In so doing they have not been unaware of tradition or of church history, but have insisted that they were reforming or changing the form of the church in the light of the demands of the gospel. Historically, of course, Protestantism begins with the Reformation in the sixteenth century. Although the reformers reluctantly broke with the medieval church, they did not think that they were starting a new church. On the contrary, they maintained that they were calling the church back to its genuine basis. Spurred to action originally because of the abuses in the medieval period, they soon became conscious that their understanding of the gospel was fundamentally different from that of the existing church. Since they were frustrated in every attempt to renew the church from within, their only apparent recourse was to bring Christians together in new forms of church life.

The Protestant story must begin with an understanding of this attempt to recover the life and vitality of the church in the light of the gospel. Hence, it is necessary to give a picture of many currents within the medieval period and of the life of the medieval church as the background from which the work of the reformers is to be understood. We must begin by understanding Martin Luther in the context of his time.

Factors in Weakening the Medieval Synthesis

The period of the Middle Ages was far from uniform in thought or in life. But in contrast to other periods of history it is unsurpassed in the uniformity of its religious ethos. It was marked by a "religious culture" in which the life of the church was not separate from other activities, but rather pervaded all of them. Politics, economics, art, and philosophy were the direct concerns of the church. The papacy was a political as well as a spiritual power. Much of the economic life was organized around and controlled by the parish churches. Art was religious by definition. Painting and architecture alike reflected the concern with the transcendent. There is no clearer evidence of this than the self-conscious regard for the vertical thrust of the cathedrals. Even the rediscovery and acceptance of Aristotle did not disturb the total pattern, for the more earthbound character of Aristotle's philosophy only served, when slightly reinterpreted, to provide a picture of nature which longed for its completion by a more significant aspect of reality, the grace of God itself. It is no wonder that the culture was characterized as the *Corpus Christianum*, the body of Christendom.

That achievement had developed over centuries. After the collapse of the Roman Empire, the church had slowly conquered an alien and pagan world and fashioned it after its own designs. It had literally created a Christian culture in which many remnants of Graeco-Roman culture were baptized and reworked into a grand Christian scheme. This was indeed a tremendous and important achievement and upon its stability people felt able to depend.

But in this very culture forces were forming and discoveries were made which weakened its foundation and supplied the Reformation with the possibility of success which might otherwise have been denied to it. The Reformation cannot be explained as simply an aspect of the emergence of old and new forces in the Middle Ages; but it certainly cannot be understood apart from this. For example, would people have flocked to the new way of understanding the gospel if not for a pronounced anxiety engendered by the particular application of the penitential system in the later medieval period? One can ponder what might have happened had the printing press not appeared on the human stage in time to carry Luther's prophetic protest and provide wings for his positive gospel message.

Hence, in order to understand how the Reformation succeeded in gaining support for its message, we need to assess various ingredients in the late medieval world, some of which had a longer history than others. Among these movements are various forms of mysticism, nominalism, Renaissance humanism, conciliarism, national and economic changes, and the ecclesiastical practices of the church. We will briefly discuss each in this and the following section.

The first was mysticism. Mysticism had a long and glorious history ranging from the dubious Christian orientation of Dionysius the Areopagite (a fifth-century writer later confused with one of St. Paul's converts at Athens) through the classical figures of the medieval mystical tradition — Bernard, Bonaventure, Eckhart, Tauler, Ruysbroek — to groups such as the Brethren of the Common Life.

Common to the prominent individual Christian mystics was the conviction that God could be directly experienced, though in essence God remained incomprehensible. Most of the mystic's time and energy were spent in preparation and discipline, with the aim that God might enter the soul and lift it to ecstatic heights. Such experiences made life livable since they introduced one into the very presence of God. Sometimes the experience was that of the presence of Christ, at other times of Godhead apart from Christ. On the one hand, St. Bernard spoke with great warmth of the presence of the exalted Christ, nearer to himself than anything else, because Christ permeated and filled his being. On the other hand, Tauler's sermons describe God's direct presence almost without reference to the mediation of Christ. Indeed, the difference between St. Bernard and Tauler is a major one, the former being more in accord with the Franciscan ideal of conforming to Christ, and the latter with the Dominicans, among whom the fruits of contemplation were central.

Although the church insisted that God was known and mediated through the sacramental system, mystics, for all their emphasis on individual disciplines in order to know God, did not challenge the sacramental realities. Mystics were incorporated into the fold and constituted one component, though a subordinate one, of the medieval synthesis. Even Dionysius the Areopagite, influenced more by Greek than by Christian ideas, had been incorporated into the Christian framework because of his supposed connection with St. Paul. He was extensively quoted by Aquinas, the foremost theologian of the classical Middle Ages. Eckhart and Tauler in Strasbourg, Ruysbroek and à Kempis in the Netherlands, and Rolle and Julian of Norwich in England were powerful and recognized figures in the church. But individual mystics and their supporters, even when what they said seemed to subvert the church and in some instances led to condemnation, as in the case of Eckhart, were not sufficiently numerous to become a major problem.

Of a mystical bent but uninterested in the subtleties of theology were various associations of lay individuals, devoted to revitalizing the spiritual life of the church. Among such groups were the Friends of God in the Rhine Valley, the Brethren of the Common Life in Holland, and the Sisters of the Common Life, also in Holland. While these were lay groups, free of monastic vows, their ideal of life and conduct represented monastic goals as they applied to those outside the monastery. Some referred to the world as their monastery. Geert Groote, founder of the Brethren of the Common Life, also planned a model monastery, and upon his death the monastery of Windesheim was established. Thus the form and shape of life had a monastic cast for lay people and for those in monastic vows. Practically and theologically, such ideas were expressed in writings, chief of which were the *Imitation of Christ* by Thomas à Kempis and the *Theologia Germanica,* an anonymous mystical work which Luther initially praised.

Such groups, which continued well into the Reformation, were concerned with the revitalization of life in the Catholic church, and when Luther appeared, they rejected his approach. Nevertheless, individuals and groups which stressed the direct experience of God found themselves in a state of tension with the notion that God was known and mediated primarily through the church as a sacramental agent. They created a new climate, a soil out of which Reformation ideas could grow. Although Protestantism is not to be equated with the mystical groups or merely characterized by its emphasis upon direct accessibility to God (indeed, it can be said to be antithetical to such ideas), many recruits to Protestantism did come from people of mystical and similar

persuasions. Luther was quick to see that the gospel which he proclaimed spoke to these people, in contrast to those who accepted the
increasing authority of the church in life and in thought.

A second force leading to dissolution within the society of the church
was nominalism. According to an earlier medieval view, reality was
characterized by structure and order. Patterns of rational thought
were understood to be inherent in reality itself. Hence, language as
a medium of discourse expressed and reflected reality. Concepts expressed universal realities. Nominalists, on the other hand, maintained
that names, concepts, and generalizations were but tags used to talk
about individual things. Moreover, only individual things were real.

One consequence of the nominalist outlook was that even God could
not be described in terms of rational structure. In the older view,
God's will was always understood as an expression of God's being.
God willed in conformity with a nature appropriate to God and the
created order itself reflected the structure of this willing. But in the
nominalist view, God was understood as will, wholly free from humanly
conceivable structure or consistency. As a result, God's declared intent
to save sinners was not indicative of God's essential nature but of
God's resolve. For some of the nominalists, the appropriate word for
the relation between the Creator and the created order was not a
rational structure but a God initiated covenant, a concept more in
accord with subsequent Reformation ideas than with a world of rational
order.

In this new philosophy, humans felt unique. As self-conscious individuals, they formed and belonged to communities. Humanity and
community were not realities defining individuals. Rather, the relations
among individuals gave meaning and form to such words as humanity
and community.

The understanding of the church and society was also changed by
this new outlook. On the basis of nominalism, one could not speak
of the church and of society as corporate, organic bodies, or of the
body of Christendom, or of the church as the body of Christ. One
no longer belonged to a social body which sustained and carried;
the body now referred to an aggregate of individuals. The concept
of contract or covenant between individuals rather than that of organism was the new key to church and society.

In this new situation, the church assumed greater authority as it
took over domains formerly guaranteed through philosophy and a
sense of a natural community. In the earlier medieval period, reason
and revelation, philosophy and theology, fitted together hand-in-glove.
Reason could show God's existence and say something about God as
a consequence of God's existence. Reason was completed by revelation
which added that which was essential for a saving knowledge of God.
In the new situation, reason was incapable of giving knowledge of

God. Even knowledge of God's existence depended completely on revelation. Only the church as the authority which acted in God's name could guarantee the veracity of revelation.

Nominalism thus stood in an ambiguous relation to the late medieval church. On the one hand, it made room for, indeed required, greater authority on the part of the church. On the other hand, when nature and grace, reason and revelation, no longer stood in a supplemental relation with each other, the church was no longer understood as the natural end of nature and reason. Instead of reason requiring the church for its completion, now the church had no necessary basis in society for its own authority. Authority, no longer based in the natural or willing consent of society, eventually turned out to be precarious.

The third movement which was to effect a change was the Renaissance, particularly in its humanistic form. The Renaissance, too, was related to the church and not infrequently was sponsored by it. For most of the Middle Ages minimal classical learning had been preserved in the church, primarily in monasteries and in the rising universities. However, the Renaissance version of classical learning marked a new concern with the outlook upon life expressed in Greek and Roman literary and artistic mediums, appearing in the fifteenth century in the city-states of Italy. From there it permeated Europe and in the realm of art found its greatest protagonists among the "Renaissance popes." Pope Sixtus IV was interested in the arts and his name is perpetuated in the Sistine Chapel. It was Pope Julius II who commissioned the artists Raphael and Michelangelo.

The interest in classical learning demanded new and accurate texts of ancient writings. When the critical acumen acquired in this enterprise was turned toward a number of writings which affected the church, the result was indeed embarrassing. Lorenzo Valla, one of the great humanist scholars, turned his critical eye upon the "Donation of Constantine," reputedly a document in which the Emperor Constantine bequeathed his earthly power to the papacy. By analyzing style and content, he showed that this could not possibly be a fourth-century document and that therefore papal claims to temporal or political authority could not rest upon its contents. He described as legend the claim that the Apostles' Creed comprised twelve statements, one made by each apostle. He further applied his energies to the text of scripture, raising questions at points of the accuracy of the Vulgate as a translation of the Hebrew text of the Old Testament and of the Greek text of the New Testament. But it was Erasmus, the Christian humanist scholar, who pointed out not only more inaccuracies, but also some of the differences a more accurate text made in religious belief.

The impact of Renaissance humanism was greater than the attacks which some of its scholars made upon specific documents and claims of the church. It represented an outlook upon life which was essentially different from that represented by the medieval church. It created a view favorable to the concerns of this life in and for themselves. Renaissance humanists believed in God, and many, like Erasmus, remained faithful members of the church even in the period of the Reformation. But the accent had shifted. The stress of humanists was upon the greatness and nobility of humanity. They found this nobility particularly in works of Cicero and Plato, rather than in that of scholastic theology. Humanists, in fact, were for reform. They proposed that classical learning be substituted for scholastic theology in the educational curriculum and they attacked superstitions within the church.

On the one hand, mysticism, nominalism, and humanism were a natural part of the later Middle Ages; on the other hand, each had ingredients that could be used to challenge facets of that society. To these intellectual movements must be added a new interest in the thought of Augustine in the later Middle Ages, an interest which cut across the mystical, nominalist, and humanist heritage. Until Erasmus, who preferred Jerome and relegated Augustine to being but one of the church fathers, Augustine was considered the church father *par excellence.* While interpreters differed in their understanding of grace and predestination in Augustine, they agreed that these issues were central to the life of the church. Gregory of Rimini, Gabriel Biel, and at the time of the Reformation, Staupitz, were Augustinians who influenced Luther, though Luther's own interpretation of Augustine took a distinctive turn. Indeed, Augustine became of special importance to the major reformers.

Concurrent with these movements, there were developments in the social scene which created a new milieu and tended to undermine the culture which the church had created. In the medieval development the church had become the creator and custodian of social life. In the process, the church acquired half of the land in France and Germany and organized its use along the accepted hierarchical pattern of feudalism. Hence, it is easy to see that social as well as religious life belonged to the orbit of the church.

The breakdown of feudalism and the rise of a middle class preoccupied with trade and commerce created a new segment of society independent of direct influence by the church. Even the Crusades, organized with the prompting and blessing of the church to wrest the Holy Land from the Turks, accentuated an economic development which depended upon money and trade rather than directly upon land. Moreover, the contacts made by the Crusades facilitated the new interest in trade and commerce.

This development led to a different kind of culture. Small towns and cities now became urban centers in which people were free from direct dependence upon the surrounding land for their livelihood. Although the new members of this class usually felt themselves to be good church people, they did feel free from the church in matters which pertained to their vocational interests. They represented a new, independent force, forcefully expressed in the new slogan "City air is free air."

The new middle class was self-conscious of its position and encouraged new loyalties beyond those of church and empire. It fed and frequently supported ethnic groups. It was in part responsible for the waves of national feelings which in many instances eventuated in modern national states. The empire, whether controlled by church or emperor, was transformed and eventually gave way to new social and ethnic forces. This was true in the Germanic lands also, though statehood in the fullest sense came several centuries later.

By the time of the Reformation, the social scene had been so transformed that the effects were evident in a number of ways. There were already unfortunate victims who felt deprived of their dignity and rights under the emerging commercial situation. The new alignment of social forces had also made the peasants conscious of their status, and their discontent finally broke forth in Luther's own day in the Peasants' Revolt.

In many areas new things were happening. The printing press was invented in the latter half of the fifteenth century and in the last decade of the century Columbus discovered a new world. At the very time when Magellan was circumnavigating the globe (1519–1522), Luther wrote three famous treatises and engaged in debates which launched the Reformation. In Luther's own lifetime the astronomer Copernicus challenged the traditional view of the world by suggesting that the sun, not the earth, was the center around which the planets moved. Although the world was still one in which the church was dominant, many new forces, in addition to the efforts of the reformers, were beginning to undermine the church's hold upon the masses.

The Situation in the Church

Since the church was responsible for the political organization as well as the religious life during the early Middle Ages, it was only natural that it was in fact, if not yet in name, a temporal as well as a spiritual power. The church had won its position as a creative, functioning body in a disorganized world and, as new forms arose, its leaders naturally felt that only the continued exercise of the church's power would guarantee a Christian culture. But it was precisely the exercise of power that caused fissures and conflicts in the church itself, whether the conflict was between the papacy and the conciliarists or between the papacy and kings or emperors. In both situations, the papacy, in spite of temporary reversals, eventually triumphed. During the almost seventy-year period of the fourteenth century when the papacy was at Avignon (resulting primarily from the loss of estates in Italy and the consequent dictation by French monarchs that the papacy reside in France in return for financial support), the popes still found and perfected ways of raising revenue for maintaining their extensive empire and their many secular interests. Toward the end of the Avignon period, the papacy suffered a temporary setback, for there were two claimants to the papacy, and then after the Council of Pisa, three, the two former ones not capitulating to the one elected by the Council. Hence, there were claimants at Avignon, Rome, and Pisa. It was in this context that the reforming ideas of those who believed in the right of councils to define the future of the church suddenly seemed the only hope, in spite of the failure of the Council of Pisa. Pressured by the emperor Sigismund, the Pisan pope called the Council of Constance in 1414, where cardinals and theologians elected a new pope in place of the three, but also burned the reformer, John Hus of Bohemia, at the stake on the grounds of heresy. Hence, it was clear that the Council was more interested in defining authority than in reform, particularly if it involved differing theological ideas. Indeed, authority was the issue, and on that even the conciliarists were not in agreement. Generally, conciliarists believed in shared authority, either with the papacy preeminent, or the council dominant with considerable authority given to the papacy. More extreme were conciliarists who believed that a council was supreme, with the papacy acting in an executive capacity, and popes who believed that councils existed as extensions of their own views and powers. In spite of subsequent councils, the papal view largely prevailed. Nevertheless, in the Reformation, new appeals were made to the reforming role of councils in the life of the church.

Just as councils and the papacy were locked in struggle, so were kings and emperors with the papacy. Since a king or monarch was considered an arm of God, a divine appointment to serve God, it was understood that state and church went hand in hand. Without abandoning that attitude, subsequent conflicts between popes and monarchs effectively challenged the balance between the two. Since the state served only one's earthly pilgrimage and the church directed one's life with the aim of delivering one safely to another life, the church naturally felt that the more important function belonged to itself. Moreover, it also felt responsible for forming and directing the social life of society. In order to effect that transformation, sovereigns were to act in the church's behalf. On the question of entrance to God's kingdom, kings were impotent, while the ordinary priest, acting on the authority committed to him, was all-powerful. Kings might attempt to depose popes, but the real power was the papacy since it dealt with the destiny of every believer. As early as the thirteenth century, Innocent III was more powerful than any monarch.

The church's claim to control every aspect of life, with its attendant conflicts, made it almost inevitable that the church would over-extend itself, become secularized in the process, and fall victim of the problems of the world around it. Its very greatness turned into an Achilles' heel. In spite of notable exceptions, this was the case among popes and priests alike. This, coupled with the picture of rival claimants to the papacy at the end of the Avignon period, had the general effect of undermining the religious, though not the temporal, authority of the papacy. In fact, the effectiveness of the church's formal hold upon its constituents was temporarily increased by the techniques which came into prominence to meet the financial needs. For example, a newly appointed bishop's first year's income went to the papacy. To increase the income, bishops were frequently moved and sometimes vacancies were not immediately filled so that the papacy could claim the funds in the meantime. Such procedures made it possible for the papacy to maintain its control and to secure the necessary financial assistance for doing so.

The techniques developed by the papacy were used by bishops and priests as well. Frequently they were absorbed in offices of politics, holding dioceses or cathedrals which they seldom visited, but from which they collected revenue. In England, Cardinal Wolsey claimed partial support from the sees of Durham and Winchester successively, and from sees in France and Spain. Nor was the situation different in France, Italy, and Germany. A prince was sometimes a political ruler and absentee bishop. He collected funds from his bishopric and not infrequently shared them with the papacy in payment for the assignment of the bishopric to him.

Such practices were obviously not conducive to spirituality among popes or clergy. The general development was toward an excessively "worldly" church, and not infrequently to outright cases of immorality. There were reform movements within the monasteries; and the conciliar movement, however ill-fated, was an attempt to reform the church from the Pope down by a decentralization of its administrative machinery. Individuals like Wycliffe in England and Hus in Bohemia had vehemently objected to the low state of affairs in the church. Both religious and secular historians concede that on the eve of the Reformation, reform of the church and particularly of the clergy was indeed necessary.

The financial crisis within the church and the general decline in spirituality had their effects, too, upon the relation of the church to the average individual. The controversy over "indulgences" affected those in the parish more immediately and directly than any of the intellectual or social currents and thereby threatened the church at a very crucial point. To appreciate its full impact, it is necessary to see the problem of indulgences in the context of the developing penitential system. The church always claimed that salvation was grounded in the grace of Christ and quite early insisted that it was made available primarily through its commissioned agents, the priests. It was taken for granted in the Middle Ages that upon the confession of sins, the priest, if he considered the penitent worthy, would declare absolution of sins in the name of the triune God. This constituted the sacrament of penance and signified the imparting of grace and the restoration of oneself to a full religious position under God. Forgiveness was actual restoration. But the reconstitution of life was not considered complete until one had made amends, insofar as humanly possible, for the inescapable consequences of an act of sin. An act of sin offended God and humans alike. It violated an order of justice. Forgiveness or absolution saved one from eternal punishment; but punishment for sin still took its course and was completed in purgatory, prior to one's final entrance to the kingdom. By making temporal satisfaction, one could already now begin to mitigate and decrease subsequent punishment. Such temporal satisfaction took the form of specific acts (frequently prayers) assigned by the priest to the penitent, and tended to serve two functions. The performance of assigned acts of penance indicated that one was indeed contrite. But more important, the church declared that such activity would now begin to pay the penalty of sin, instead of postponing it all until after death. This claim rested in the notion that God had entrusted the work of redemption to the church and that what was "bound" or "loosed" on earth would be bound or loosed after one's death.

Initially, "indulgence" was merely a term for the cancellation under appropriate conditions of a part of this assigned special activity or work of penance. It was an instrument used by bishops in cases where assigned acts were a distinct hardship on the person, or where distinct service to the church, such as a gift of land or money, merited special consideration. The first extensive use of an indulgence for special meritorious service was Pope Urban II's promise of complete indulgence to all who joined the first Crusade. An indulgence, therefore, was usually the substitution of one kind of act or deed for another. It did not alter the fundamental conception that satisfaction must be made or that justice must run its course.

The full development of the idea of a "treasury of merit" considerably changed the initial use of indulgences. Surely Christ and the saints had done such good works that they accumulated merit far beyond their own needs. It was held that this superabundance constituted a "treasury of merit," from which under appropriate conditions the church could draw to meet the needs of the ordinary person in arrears in completing the assigned penance. Since it was also believed that the average person died before completing the necessary penance or satisfaction, the question arose whether the treasury of merit could be made beneficial to those in purgatory. In purgatory those who were destined eventually for God's kingdom suffered for their sins until final satisfaction was complete. If the merit could be made available to them, both the extent of their suffering and the length of their sojourn might be reduced. On the thesis that the church was the body of Christ, it was decided that the merits of Christ could definitely be made available to those in purgatory. In a healthy body, no part withholds its life and help to the rest.

The church drew from the treasury of merit by authorizing an indulgence. The visible side of an indulgence was a slip of paper upon which was noted its spiritual worth. These could therefore be sold like an article of trade. It was not unusual for the papacy to farm out the sale of indulgences to princes who aspired to ecclesiastical importance. They in turn would send an agreed-upon share of the proceeds to Rome.

The possibility of abuse was great. Any decent person desired that departed friends or relatives might be spared some of the pain and time in purgatory. Since most indulgences were proclaimed for just such relief, a ready market was at hand. Hence, the need for revenue on the part of the papacy became a temptation to issue one indulgence after another.

One of the great preachers of indulgences was a Dominican by the name of Tetzel. He traveled from town to town preaching an indulgence, the proceeds of which were to go to Rome for the completion of the new St. Peter's Church. Albert of Brandenburg had agreed to the sale of this indulgence in his territories in return for an appointment to the archbishopric of Mainz, a link which he needed in the chain he was forging to make himself master of the German lands. Since the stakes in this venture were high for both Albert and the papacy, this indulgence was pushed with all the force and pomp which could be mustered. An eloquent example of the type of preaching which accompanied the promotion of the sale of this particular indulgence is the following from one of Tetzel's sermons:

> Listen now, God and St. Peter call you. Consider the salvation of your souls and those of your loved ones departed. . . . Listen to the voices of your dear dead relatives and friends, beseeching you and saying, "Pity us, pity us. We are in dire torment from which you can redeem us with a pittance." Do you not wish to? Open your ears. Hear the father saying to his son, the mother to her daughter, "We bore you, nourished you, brought you up, left you our fortunes, and you are so cruel and hard that now you are not willing for so little to set us free.

Will you let us lie here in flames? Will you delay our promised glory?"

Remember that you are able to release them, for

> As soon as the coin in the coffer rings,
> The soul from purgatory springs.

Will you not then for a quarter of a florin receive these letters of indulgences through which you are able to lead a divine and immortal soul into the fatherland of paradise?[2]

Increasingly the careful distinction which had been drawn between forgiveness and temporal satisfaction was obscured. Many of the vendors of indulgences promised forgiveness and redemption on the basis of their purchase and paid scant attention to the fact that officially indulgences had always been confined only to the remission of penalties, whether here or in purgatory. In the confessional the average person, just as Luther, was told that the purchase of indulgences was effective also for salvation. This made them all the more attractive. It more effectively tied one's religious needs to the financial machinations of the hierarchy. It is apparent that financial interests, coupled with human foibles and ambitions, played a large part in corrupting the internal life of the church.

Faith Is Rediscovered

Long before Luther there were protests against the situation within the church. Among the most significant, as we have seen, were Wycliffe in England and John Hus in Bohemia. As did the Germans later, Wycliffe protested against the importation of Italian priests and the draining of wealth from the country. He railed against the corruption of papacy and clergy because of their seemingly exclusive preoccupation with wealth and power. He emphasized the directness of everyone's responsibility under God without the benefit or hindrance of any intermediate channel. Further, he protested against the concept of transubstantiation, the theory that in the consecration of the elements God performs the miracle of transforming the essence of the bread and wine into the actual body and blood of Christ. He objected that this placed a necessary and irreplaceable intermediary between God and humankind. Wycliffe's greatest impact upon the popular mind, however, came through his part in organizing and in sponsoring the translation of the entire Scripture into the English language. While accused of heresy, Wycliffe died before any official action was taken.

Of no small importance was the influence of Wycliffe's writings on

---

[2] Roland H. Bainton, *Here I Stand* (Nashville, 1950), p. 78.

John Hus in Bohemia, where there was also a reforming party. Hus attacked corruption in the church from clergy to papacy. He was outspoken against indulgences, though more conservative in his estimate of tradition than Wycliffe. A Hussite church was formed with emphasis upon Christ as its true head. The situation in Bohemia was complicated by the counter pressures of papacy and empire, each continually threatening the life of Hus. Actually, Hus, as already noted, was burned at the stake by a council of the church, not by papacy or empire. This was a shock, though not a fatal one, to those who placed their hopes upon the deliberations of councils as a means of checking abuses in the church.

When Luther issued his ninety-five theses in Wittenberg in 1517, he was only one of a series of individuals and groups which were already in protest against the practices and procedures of the church. Moreover, he was merely following the accepted custom of preparing propositions one was ready to debate. Little did he foresee that his actions would initiate a movement destined to redirect the understanding and visible practice of much of Christendom. Others, too, had repudiated the practice of purchasing and selling indulgences as a way of shortening the time of the departed in purgatory and had rejected the unauthorized claim of some that God's forgiveness could be made available through their purchase. Like them, Luther felt compelled to protest. Tetzel's preaching made him particularly indignant. It was as if one's relation to God was on the level of barter and trade.

In the ninety-five theses, Luther did not reject indulgences outright. He rejected only the abuses. The papacy, he declared, did not have the power to remit *guilt* in respect to the least of venial sins, nor could indulgences be said to have any effect on purgatory. The Pope could change or cancel only those penalties imposed by his own authority or by the canons of the church. Indulgences were valid only when confined to such human and organizational discipline and had no necessary relation to the final destiny of any individual believer.

Such was the specific religious protest of the ninety-five theses. Behind it lay the beginning of a new religious understanding, the significance of which became clear to Luther and his contemporaries only under the pressure of subsequent events. The roots of it went back to Luther's days as a young theological instructor. In his lectures on Psalms in the year 1513 and on Romans in the year 1515–1516, Luther began to discover a gospel which met the anxiety of his own soul. He had entered the monastery in order to find peace with God, to save his own soul. Having been nearly struck down by a bolt of lightning, he had resolved then and there to follow the noblest and most certain path. But the prescribed path did not bring the peace he sought. God was a righteous God who demanded one's unswerving obedience and destined one to salvation only if salvation was merited. To be sure, the church existed in part as a remedy for sins committed, and claimed that it had been established by God to act in God's name. In this way it always provided one with a new start. Moreover, it was the custodian of grace and merit which could help make one righteous.

But the church had a remedy only for sins confessed. If one confessed one's sins, one could be absolved and undertake to carry out the prescribed penance. Only so could one become righteous. It was exactly this which could not satisfy Luther's conscience. He suspected that there might be sins about which he did not even know or sins which he committed after leaving the confessional for which he might at any moment be held accountable. The uncharitable interpretation of his unrest is the suggestion that such concern is pathological. It is more constructive to understand Luther's unrest as the searching of a sensitive man for the proper relation to God. The burden of evidence points to the latter interpretation, for this zeal pervades every move he made as a monk. He could not put aside the question of certainty under God; in fact, this quest drove him to confess his sins so frequently to his fellow monks as to annoy them. The rule of the monastery, he confessed, was easy to perform, but it did not provide the peace of soul which one ought to have under God. The words of his saintly superior, Staupitz, advising Luther to relax and to trust in the grace of God, did not help. God's righteous demand was too serious to permit rest.

The impossibility of finding assurance drove Luther even to wonder whether God was just at all. Perhaps God was a tyrant who never gave peace and who was not even trustworthy. According to late medieval nominalism, God could act in opposition to God's declared intention. There were moments when Luther hated God, when he felt utterly frustrated and among the damned.

In this state of mind Luther was hardly fit to become a lecturer in Bible. But out of the necessity of lecturing came his answer. In the Psalms he discovered two important aspects of the Bible which shed light on his problem. In the first place, he was struck by the verse in the twenty-second Psalm, "My God, my God, why hast thou forsaken me?" In line with the prevailing opinion that the Old Testament foreshadowed or anticipated the new, this verse obviously could have reference only to Christ. But that Christ, the son of God, should be forsaken just as he, Luther, had been was incredible until it dawned upon him that this signified how Christ took upon himself the sins of the world. To redeem humankind, God in Christ took on one's lot, participating in one's despair and lostness. Christ might therefore be not only the righteous Judge, but also the merciful one.

In the second place, the phrase in Psalm 31, "Deliver me in thy righteousness", became a source of insight. The connection of righteousness and deliverance challenged the conception that the former always meant the demanding, judicial, fearful justice of God. If it were such, it could hardly be associated with deliverance.

But the decisive turn did not come until Luther understood the passage in Romans 1:17 which refers to the gospel as the disclosure of the justice or righteousness of God. In fact, this passage had rather kept him from stressing Paul's writings to which he was otherwise attracted. Now it became the basis of a new understanding, including that of Psalm 31. Speaking of this passage in Romans, Luther wrote:

> I had indeed been captivated with an extraordinary ardor for under-standing Paul in the Epistle to the Romans. But up till then it was not the cold blood about the heart, but a single word in Chapter 1:17, "In it the righteousness of God is revealed," that had stood in my way. For I hated that word *righteousness of God,* which, according to the use and custom of all the teachers, I had been taught to understand philo-sophically regarding the formal or active righteousness, as they called it, with which God is righteous and punishes the unrighteous sinner.
>
> Though I lived as a monk without reproach, I felt that I was a sinner before God with an extremely disturbed conscience. I could not believe that he was placated by my satisfaction. I did not love, yes, I hated the righteous God who punishes sinners. . . . Thus I raged with a fierce and troubled conscience. Nevertheless, I beat importunately upon Paul at that place, most ardently desiring to know what St. Paul wanted.
>
> At last, by the mercy of God, meditating day and night, I gave heed to the context of the words, namely, *In it the righteousness of God is revealed,* as it is written, "He who through faith is righteous shall live." There I began to understand that the righteousness of God is that by which the righteous lives by a gift of God, namely by faith. And this is the meaning: the righteousness of God is revealed by the gospel, namely, the passive righteousness with which merciful God justifies us by faith, as it is written, "He who through faith is righteous shall live." Here I felt that I was altogether born again and had entered paradise itself through open gates. There a totally other face of the entire Scripture showed itself to me. Thereupon I ran through the Scriptures from memory. . . . And I extolled my sweetest word with a love as great as the hatred with which I had before hated the word *righteousness of God.* Thus that place in Paul was for me truly the gate to paradise.[3]

Now Luther had discovered that the gospel spoke about a righteous God who indicated faithfulness, mercy, and love toward those who knew that they were not righteous. Here was disclosed a God who, without rescinding a demand, was righteous also in another way. With-out asking a sign of worth, God extended mercy to those who trusted,

---

[3] *Preface to the Complete Edition of Luther's Latin Writings, 1545,* in *Luther's Works* (Philadelphia, 1960), Vol. XXXIV, pp. 336–337.

not themselves and their activities, but God. Theologically this was expressed by the term "justification by faith."

To be justified, to be made right and just before God — this was the problem with which Luther started his religious pilgrimage. His life in the church had been geared to that problem, on the basis of the actual and calculable righteousness of humankind. But that he was really righteous was Luther's doubt, since the calculation of righteousness depended upon whether or not one had confessed all one's sins and received absolution. The injunction to disregard as irrelevant and not serious sins of which one was not aware might have been good counsel, but it did not help his uneasy feeling.

Now the accent shifted from the one who was actually righteous to the one "who through faith is righteous." The release was tremendous. Now one might be accepted as one was, since God justified those who came, not on their merit or righteousness, but on their trust in God for their life. One's status under God was no longer weighed in the scale. Rather, it was a position sustained by God and experienced directly by the believer. In short, the whole base of orientation was transformed. Instead of the question, how can one be righteous? the decisive point now was that God was righteous. God, without easing the demand upon us, had revealed righteousness as mercy and had thereby made it impossible to think of righteousness in respect to one's relation to God. Now the accent was upon the mercy which accepts, which is gracious, which is therefore grace. Where this is experienced, one need no longer be preoccupied with self; one is set free from oneself. But this is only possible if one abandons all calculation and measurability as a false notion in relation to God.

Justification by faith was thus a term for a religious experience whose primary characteristic was faith or trust springing from a direct encounter with the redeeming presence of Christ. Redemption centered in the life, death, and resurrection of Christ and was said to be experienced by those who found forgiveness and power in Christ's presence in their lives. This was the logic of righteousness proclaimed in the Bible.

> Now the righteousness of God has been manifested apart from the law, although the law and the prophets bear witness to it, the righteousness of God through faith in Jesus Christ for all who believe. For there is no distinction; since all have sinned and fall short of the glory of God, they are justified by his grace as a gift, through the redemption which is in Christ Jesus, whom God put forward as an expiation by his blood, to be received in faith. This was to show God's righteousness, because in his divine forbearance he had passed over former sins; it was to prove at the present time that he himself is righteous and that he justifies him who has faith in Jesus.[4]

---

[4] Romans 3:21–26 (Revised Standard Version).

Such was Luther's central discovery. Only in the controversy which ensued did it become clear to him that indulgences needed to be rejected outright and that his new comprehension of faith demanded a radical reforming of the church.

Faith Makes Its Protest

The formulation of the ninety-five theses did not issue in the debate Luther anticipated. At the request of the Pope, Luther was summoned to a meeting with Cardinal Cajetan. But instead of being invited to discussion, he was ordered to recant. This he refused to do. Even the subsequent discussions and debates, such as the Leipzig debate with Eck and those at the Diet of Worms, were aimed only at forcing Luther to retract. In 1520 the Pope issued a bill of excommunication against Luther.

In the meantime, Luther had seen that his protest meant not only a rejection of abuses, but also a change in the nature of the church itself. Three years after the posting of the theses, Luther rejected indulgences themselves as inconsistent with the gospel and referred to them as the "knavish trick of the Roman Sycophants." He was now calling for an outright reformation of the church in the light of the biblical faith. Since the church was unwilling to change, Luther called upon the nobles and princes to effect the reformation. (This, too, had been done by Wycliffe and Hus in their respective situations.) In *An Open Letter to the Christian nobility of the German nation concerning the Reform of the Christian Faith,* Luther charged these officers with the task of reformation because the church had built around itself three walls which prevented any far-reaching changes. The first wall, he declared, was the claim for supremacy of the spiritual over the temporal order. The church claimed exclusive and absolute authority over one's spiritual life. Such a unique position under God clearly argued for the church's supremacy over all earthly affairs and for the obedience of the temporal to the spiritual, or even for the spiritual to assume temporal power.

The second and third walls prevented reform which might come from appeal to scripture or to council. One could not utilize the Bible to correct the church since the final right to interpret scripture was in the hands of the papacy. Nor could one instigate proceedings for a council, since the Pope alone was authorized to call a council. Outright attack under the aegis of other constituted authorities remained the only recourse for breaking through the papal walls.

The prescription for the church which Luther had in mind was indeed fairly drastic. It was nothing less than the rejection of the entire sacramental system. Luther rejected the claim that the church was the custodian of God's activity on earth, and that to it had been entrusted the responsibility of doing God's work through the treasure of grace which Christ and the saints made and continued to make available to it. In such a system there was an experience of God, but one's status and relation to God was of necessity channeled through the agency of the church and assumed a quantitative character, becoming a question of the amount of merit. Emphasis was upon being made right and righteous through the sacraments, which were the agencies for the dispensation of God's grace. For example, baptism was the sacrament through which original sin was erased and grace restored: the moment of baptism was the moment of righteousness, and the sacrament of penance always restored the righteousness of the baptismal state.

Luther's insistence that the gospel of the New Testament was the account of an objective act of mercy to be subjectively appropriated in the church, and that grace was not confined to sacramental realities mediated by priests, challenged the very nature of the constituted church.

In *The Babylonian Captivity of the Church,* Luther appealed to the New Testament for the repudiation of many aspects of the development of the church. He considered the medieval mass as a violation rather than as an expression of the gospel. Just as there were three walls, so were there three captivities in conjunction with the mass. The first was the withholding of the cup from the laity. For this Luther could find no biblical basis and declared further that it served to accentuate the estrangement between clergy and laity. Luther rather cynically remarked that if it was a mortal sin for the priest not to take both elements, then it was also a sin for the laity.

The second captivity, said Luther, was the concept of transubstantiation. Luther's own understanding of the presence of Christ in the bread and wine will concern us in the next chapter. Here it is important to note that the miracle of transforming the bread and wine into the actual blood and body of Christ appeared magical to Luther, and again emphasized the distinction between clergy and laity.

The most basic captivity, however, was the idea that the mass was a good work in which, after the consecration of the elements, Christ was offered as a sacrifice to God each time the mass was said. Carried to its logical conclusion, this made the mass a worthy act quite apart from the presence of any believers, except for the priest whose intent, one could reasonably assume, was properly directed. Luther could find in the New Testament no grounds for declaring the sacrament a good work, since it had no efficacy apart from the believers who received it. Nor could he find any basis for the notion of sacrifice, since Christ was not offered to God but rather was given by God to us. In the theory of the mass, of course, Christ is sacrificed to God in order for us to receive Christ also. There is both an upward and a downward motion. For Luther there could be no upward motion. He writes:

> Therefore, just as distributing a testament or accepting a promise differs diametrically from offering a sacrifice, so it is a contradiction in terms to call the mass a sacrifice, for the former is something that we receive and the latter is something that we give. The same thing cannot be received and offered at the same time, nor can it be both given and accepted by the same person. . . . Hence the only worthy preparation and proper observance is faith, the faith by which we believe in the mass, that is, in the divine promise. . . . The safest course, therefore, will be to go to the mass in the same spirit in which you would go to hear any other promise of God, that is, prepared not to do or contribute much yourself, but to believe and accept all that is promised you there, or proclaimed as promises through the ministry of the priest.[5]

Not all Protestants agree with Luther's rigid rejection of sacrifice in connection with the mass. Those Anglicans who regard themselves as Protestants prefer to use the word sacrifice, but insist that the sacrificing of Christ to God is an event of the past and is not repeatable by priestly function. While the majority of Protestant bodies reject this also, they often use the term sacrifice in reference to offering the goods of life and themselves to God. Here it is not the word, but its underlying meaning, which is important.

While Luther singled out the mass as the pivotal point at which the church's orientation involved a violation of the New Testament, he eventually called all the traditional sacraments into question. Only baptism and the Lord's Supper were instituted in the New Testament as events in which act, word, and participation were involved. These three aspects, appearing together in the New Testament, implied that a sacrament had been instituted. Hence, penance, extreme unction, marriage, confirmation, and ordination were rejected as sacraments, though all of them were considered significant acts in the Christian life.

The impossibility of achieving a reconstitution of the church in the light of these biblical criteria made an outright break inevitable. Hence, there resulted the constitution of parishes independent of Rome. It should be evident that the basis of the Reformation was ultimately religious in nature. Even Wycliffe and Hus, however much they parallel Luther in some of his attacks, did not have the vision of justification by faith as the point around which the life of the Christian and the church must be understood. Here Luther broke through to a clarity of understanding and motivation which distinguished him from all his predecessors.

[5] Martin Luther, *The Babylonian Captivity of the Church, Luther's Works* (Philadelphia, 1959), Vol. XXXVI, pp. 52, 44.

Protestants affirm that this renewed religious outlook, for all its relation to contemporary social, economic, and political forces, can be finally explained only as an act of God in which, for better or worse, the burden of a message was laid upon a human being. Historical and cultural factors, many of them religious in nature, did provide the context in which the beginnings of the Reformation occurred. Without them Luther and his work could not have succeeded. Luther could be threatened, but his work could not be stopped. Thus, in the juncture of a revitalized faith and new historical forces, individuals may discern a genuine providential ordering.

CHAPTER 11

The Formation of a Reformation Theology

The main developments in the life and thought of the various Reformation bodies will be discussed in later chapters. In the present chapter, attention will be focused on the restatement of the faith in the first decades of the Reformation, focusing particularly on Martin Luther, the first of the reformers, and John Calvin, a second generation pastor and theologian. Other reformers, such as Andreas Karlstadt and Philip Melanchthon, originally from the Lutheran side, and Theodore Beza, Heinrich Bullinger, Martin Bucer, Johannes Oecolampadius, and Ulrich Zwingli from the reformed, will receive attention as they debated or influenced the direction of specific theological issues. Indeed, on many fronts these figures were historically more formative of the future than was Luther or Calvin. Nevertheless, Luther and Calvin provided restatements of faith that touched all facets of life and thought with a passion, thoroughness, and competence that makes their work classical.[1]

[1] Some attention was given to the life of Luther in the previous chapter. Now a brief word on John Calvin. He was born in Picardy in 1509 and educated in theology, law, and the humanities at Orleans, Bourges, and Paris. Classical studies under leading humanists bore fruit in his first published work, the *Commentary on Seneca's Treatise on Clemency*. His early contacts with the Reform and the time of his conversion to it are matters of dispute, but in 1533 he was among the Protestants forced to leave Paris. He settled finally in Basel. In 1536 he published the first edition of his major work, *Institutes of the Christian Religion*, which was revised and expanded in many editions over the next quarter century. Detained to aid reform in Geneva in 1536 by William Farel, and banished in 1538, Calvin spent three fruitful years of study, writing, and ecumenical activity in Strasbourg. He was persuaded to return to Geneva in 1541 where, with the aid of Protestant refugees from all over Europe, he undertook to make the city into a model Christian community. After the expulsion of his opponents from the city in 1555, Calvin was virtually master of the city (although officially only a pastor in the church) until his death in 1564.

Luther and Calvin are the theological giants who stand out in the Reformation above all other individuals and movements. This does not mean, of course, that everything which occurred is to be judged or understood by what these two men thought. Both the more radical groups of the continental Reformation, including the Anabaptists, and the English Reformation were movements nourished by roots partly independent of the work of Luther and Calvin. And the developments in Lutheranism and the Calvinistic (or Reformed) tradition cannot be measured simply by Luther and Calvin. But few individuals and movements, either of the Reformation or of later Western religious history, have been able to escape their influence. Their greatness is evident in the opposition to them as well as in attempts to follow them.

The point of departure in religious thinking is for both Luther and Calvin the same, namely, the concept of justification by faith. Moreover, the implications that they develop from this concept for all other areas of theology are surprisingly similar. There are some fundamental differences between Luther and Calvin and they will be noted, but the basic agreement is striking.

These reformers together represent the most radical and comprehensive recasting of religious understanding since the beginning of the Christian movement. Their thinking is radical in the sense that they directly challenged traditional developments in the light of a very simple but positive message of God's grace. It is comprehensive in that they rethought the major aspects of Christian faith in the light of the new criterion. This is true whether the theological writing is unsystematic, as in Luther, or systematic in the traditional sense, as in Calvin. Even Luther's unorganized and sometimes hastily conceived theological statements are informed by and frequently revised under the criterion of faith. Calvin's *Institutes* begins with the concept of God and only in Book Three does he deal directly with justification; nevertheless, the notion of faith is presupposed in the entire first part. Both Luther and Calvin knew that Christian thinking is a totality, that each affirmation is related to every other one. Faith was the burning problem of their time, and from this base they rethought the other problems.

God and the Human Situation

Sinful Humanity

"Nearly all the wisdom we possess, that is to say, true and sound wisdom, consists of two parts: the knowledge of God and of ourselves. But, while joined by many bonds, which one precedes and brings forth the other is not easy to discern."[2] So writes Calvin in the opening sentences of the *Institutes*. Here he reflects the temper of a time in which people still believe that knowledge of self and God are inseparable, but are no longer sure precisely how the two are to be understood or from which vantage point. Humans are a problem to themselves and they do not know themselves truly apart from God. In a sense, Calvin's theological enterprise is nothing else than an exposition of this polar relation in the light of his faith. Luther, too, knew the duality of this single problem. Only as he was able to comprehend both God and himself in a new light did he find the peace of a religious wisdom.

Both the medieval church and the reformers assumed that the problem of God and the self was one with which a human being could not adequately cope. However different the understanding of both God and self in the medieval church and in the reformers, they assumed that persons could not finally understand themselves apart from God's redemptive work. It went without saying that apart from God, humanity was lost.

But for the reformers, in contrast to the medieval church, this "lostness" was illumined only by justification as conceived in the biblical tradition. Only in the light of the answer to one's central problem, declared Luther, could one have the courage to see oneself as one is, a creature separated from God and disrupted from fellow human beings. For the reformers, this state of humanity is depicted in the Genesis story of the Fall — a story which they interpreted as historical — and can be characterized as "total depravity." Depravity, however, does not mean terrible acts which some people commit. Depravity concerns one's *acts* only as they reflect the broken character of one's relation to God and fellow humans. It refers to the inability to institute a relation with God on the basis of human activity. Depravity is considered "total" because no aspect of life or activity is exempt from the corruptions of self.

When Luther and Calvin consider a human being as sinner, they thus have in mind a state, a position, and every act of sin is but a reflection of this state. Sin is not to be equated with specific acts of sin. It can be described as the tendency of humans to build the world around themselves, to corrupt even their best achievements by being conscious that they are *their* achievements. It is the pride and self-concern which manifests itself even in our noblest deeds. It is the activity which is done apart from faith and which therefore is not done only for God and neighbor but also for self. This is why Luther spoke of sin as separation from God, or unbelief. It was not that the activity of the good pagans was bad. Their acts might even have been

---

[2] John Calvin, *Institutes of the Christian Religion*, I, i, 1, in *The Library of Christian Classics* (Philadelphia, 1960), Vol. XX, p. 35.

better than those of many Christians. The question is one of relation to God and of fundamental orientation and motivation. What is not of faith is sin. That is why Luther almost shockingly declares that "if a man were not first a believer and a Christian, all his work would amount to nothing at all and would be freely wicked and damnable sins." Or as Luther also declares, the heart of a human being is naturally curved within itself. As long as this is the case, sin is inevitable.

The reformers contended also that human beings continually attempt to cover up their true state. Part of sin is the unwillingness to accept oneself as sinner, as one who needs to be rescued by some reality other than oneself.

For both Luther and Calvin the "law," particularly in its Old Testament form, revealed our true situation. It was a preparation for the gospel, exactly because it made God's demand so crystal clear that one ought to see oneself as sinner and therefore turn to the mercies of Christ. It shows the demands of God's righteousness in a concreteness which leaves no doubt as to where one stands. For Luther and Calvin, the law is a problem, not because it destroys the spirit, but because it shows how far one is from the genuine spirituality which belongs to an adequate relation to God. The law convicts of sin.

For Luther and Calvin, the teachings of Jesus also belong to the level of law. They are the most concrete and graphic presentation of the kind of life required under God. Instead of joyfully accepting the teachings of Jesus as the new disclosure of God, Luther saw in them the last barrier which stood between God and ourselves. Even when the spirit and intent of the teachings were stressed, he found them no more tolerable, since that only focused the issue more clearly. Precisely because the crucial problem is not what is done, but how and why it is done, the teachings of Jesus were so depressing, apart from justifying faith, that they became a new source of despair. They exhibited a life in full relation to God and therefore one which fully expressed and lived out the teachings. Since the teachings represented the life, the last door to self-redemption was closed. Where sin is act, there is some hope of an act or acts which will turn the tide; but where sin is a state, a position, a disease, there a cure, not a new act, is essential.

That is why no one could speak of contributing to one's justification. The reformers believed that the relationship out of which came a life resembling Christ's was established only by God's initiative. This was exactly the message of the New Testament. Any insistence on the righteousness of one's activity, declared Calvin, itself furnishes grounds for inordinate pride and takes from God the glory which is appropriate to God. To believe even partly in the merit of one's works or righteousness is pride, i.e., sin. To insist upon contributing anything to one's justification is to invert and reject the gospel. It is itself an expression of sin. Justification is the declaration of God that the sinner is accepted, not that one is no longer sinner. For Luther and Calvin, one is inevitably sinner. One's refusal of faith, one's attempt to rely on some activity of one's own, is itself the final expression of a revolt against God. It is corruption at the point of one's noblest ambition, one's desire to be related to God.

Faith and Decision

This understanding of sin means that there is no final hope for one apart from God's redemptive activity. The goodness of the gospel is the acceptance of the sinner — the possibility, as Luther put it, of trusting God rather than oneself. It is the power in which the reformers saw an answer both to one's obvious sin and to one's more deceptive attempts to escape one's plight in a round of activity. Certainly, neither Luther nor Calvin counseled that one should sit by, with folded hands, waiting for something to happen. They merely asserted that activity in the world would not guarantee the reconstitution of a satisfactory relation to God, and that every activity which was predicated upon that could only spin the web around one more tightly than ever. They knew that probably only those who seek God would find God's presence (and primarily as they sought it through the Bible). They knew also that every finding was a gift, an actual experience of God's merciful, justifying presence.

Luther and Calvin affirmed that faith is both a gift and a decision. Without the gift, the decision is not related to the experience of God's forgiving love. Yet the experience of God's mercy, and the affirmation that God has led one to this experience, do not vitiate decision. Those who insist upon decision without ascribing the credit to God distort the meaning of faith by making it a work. On the other hand, those who stress the activity of God without reference to human decision make automatons and objects out of us.

The reformers followed St. Paul and St. Augustine in respect to this problem. St. Paul's eloquent declaration, "I, yet not I, but Christ who dwells within me," bears witness to individuality and decision which are based, supported, and understood from the standpoint of Christ's work. St. Augustine expressed the same conviction when he declared "I would not have found Thee, hadst Thou not first found me." Calvin, discussing the familiar medieval view that repentance came before faith (repentance was the medieval description of a decision), inverted the order, explaining that ". . . when we refer the origin of repentance to faith we do not imagine some space of time during which it brings it to birth; but we mean to show that a man cannot apply himself seriously to repentance without knowing himself to belong to God. But no one is truly persuaded that he belongs to God unless he has first recognized God's grace."[3]

The question at issue was not chronological or psychological precedence, but that of foundation in a specific reality, either divine or human. Obviously, faith is only experienced by the self and there is a decision of faith; nevertheless, the reformers insisted, faith cannot be manufactured by the self. It is based in the gracious activity of God. Faith is born; it is not made. When faith occurs, humans confess that not their own doing but God's work was responsible, regardless of how much they sought. The person who insists that faith is an individual decision to accept God's offer of mercy has not yet experienced its transforming presence. Those who have, know that faith's source is truly in God. God's offer of mercy is not like an object which one takes or leaves; God both confronts and is at work in the decision. Yet this does not exclude human responsibility and decision.

It is on this level that the debate on the "freedom of the will" can be understood. When Luther and Calvin denied freedom of the will, they were emphatically not interested in reducing the human will to a subpersonal object of mechanical determination. This is most clear in Luther's *Bondage of the Will*. Speaking of the scholastic problem of freedom, Luther, or someone expressing his views, wrote:

> I could wish indeed that another and a better word had been introduced into our discussion than this usual one, "necessity," which is not rightly applied either to the divine or the human will. It has too harsh and incongruous a meaning for this purpose, for it suggests a kind of compulsion, and the very opposite of willingness, although the subject under discussion implies no such thing. For neither the divine nor the human will does what it does, whether good or evil, under any compulsion, but from sheer pleasure or desire, as with true freedom; and yet the will of God is immutable and infallible, and it governs our mutable will, as Boethius sings: "Remaining fixed, Thou makest all things move"; and our will, especially when it is evil, cannot of itself do good. The reader's intelligence must therefore supply what the word "necessity" does not express, by the will of God and the impotence of our evil will or what some have called the necessity of immutability, though this is not very good either grammatically or theologically.[4]

The denial of freedom of the will (as well as the concept of total depravity) refers only to the inability of one as sinner to will oneself to faith. One can will and decide many things; but cannot give oneself faith. Even if this were possible, said Luther, he would gladly give

---

[3] *Ibid.*, III, iii, 2.
[4] Martin Luther, *The Bondage of the Will*, in *Luther's Works* (Philadelphia, 1972), Vol. XXXIII, p. 39.

up that "freedom" to take the burden of his salvation from the shaky reed, namely, himself, and rest it in God.

The decision of faith is rooted in the experience of the merciful presence of Christ. Faith as a decision has a plus side which ordinary decisions do not have. God lays hold of one, and one experiences this in faith. The inward experience refers to a ground outside itself. In the Reformation sense, faith can be said to be the subjective side of the objective reality of God in Christ which has grasped one. It is experienced as real and its reality is experienced.

The reformers, Luther in particular, also knew that this experience is not an enduring possession which one can claim as perpetually present. If it were, the mercy of God would be a possession rather than a promise. God's mercy may be consistently offered, and faith is sustained by the gracious activity of God. But sustaining does not mean that God will always be experienced or present, not even when one most desires this. In fact, Luther's darkest days were not those *before* he experienced God's righteousness as also God's mercy; they occurred when the mercy which he had experienced was no longer present, and came only in moments which could not be controlled as to time or place. Luther found peace only after he recognized that the merciful God whom he *had* experienced was also the God whom he might experience *again*.

If faith is the experience of God's mercy, it must therefore also be trust. In this sense, it is an attitude or a decision, based on the promise and hope of God's trustworthiness. The mistake of many in the sixteenth century was to assume that the experience brought and kept them so in the presence of God that they were above the necessity of trust. Against this, Luther contended vigorously. But he also insisted that trust must be anchored in a prior experience of God's mercy. The total dimension of faith includes both the mercy of God, rooted in God's activity, and trust in God when God is not experienced. The second is genuine only on the basis of the first, though it may occupy the moments of one's life more often than not. The one who has experienced God's gracious presence and who, frequently or infrequently, continues to do so, will at least know what is being trusted.

For Luther particularly, predestination must be understood in exactly this context. Predestination is a confession about the trustworthy character of God at two crucial points. First, one would not have become a believer unless in the mystery of God's activity one had been led to faith. Second, since one has been led to this destiny under God, one can trust God even when one's faith is at a low ebb. Predestination therefore has meaning only for believers and is not a concept for general speculation. And just because of this, Luther finally rejected the notion of "double" predestination (namely, that God wills the damnation of some as well as salvation of the elect) in favor of the concept of "single" predestination. God is to be held accountable only for salvation. Luther rejected double predestination because he could not make a statement about God's activity apart from faith, and faith can speak only of God's merciful choice. The most that Luther could say was that, apart from faith, people naturally excluded themselves from God's kingdom. (This did not solve the problem, of course, for it must be recalled that there is nothing one can do to change one's lot but to seek God with no guarantee of finding God.)

Calvin, who accepted the concept of double predestination, was equally certain about his starting point. The doctrine was meaningful for God's elect, those who found themselves as believers. Calvin moved from faith to an elaboration of predestination as a way of showing that God is wholly the author of our faith and that every notion of work or merit must be rejected. His motivating principle is most clearly expressed in a comment on St. Paul: "By saying that they were elected before the creation of the world, he [St. Paul] precludes every consideration of merit."[5] The notion of double predestination is a last drastic guarantee against any concept of merit and a final affirmation that our destiny is entirely in the hands of God. In the passages in which Calvin most vigorously defends double predestination, the exclusion of merit is central. God's gratuitous mercy operates in election irrespective of human merit, and in damnation by a just but incomprehensible judgment. In either case, human calculation is excluded.

On the basis of the opposition between faith and merit or work, Calvin elaborates a deterministic view of God's entire operation in the world. It may be necessary to reject his determinism, but it should also be remembered that he developed it in contrast to the concepts of fate and chance. Like the early church fathers, he found determination by God a liberating and meaningful destiny in contrast to the darkness of fate or the undependableness of fortune. So also, it is important to remember that Calvin moved from faith to predestination, not from predestination to faith.

Predestination as the basis of faith and as the expression of the sovereignty of God was elaborated by Theodore Beza, Calvin's successor in Geneva, and through him was mediated, as we see in Chapter IV, to the reformed tradition. Accent on the sovereignty of God as the expression of God's overarching plan and activity in the world was more characteristic of Beza than of Calvin, for whom sovereignty implied the reality of grace. For Beza, predestination and sovereignty meant God's plan for the world from all eternity, in which the Fall and the elect are embedded in God's determinate activity. The resolve of God is prior to the Fall; hence, it is called supralapsarian. In Beza's thought, all things happen as the result of God's will and purpose,

[5] *Institutes*, III, xxii, 2.

and are therefore equally accented. Election and damnation alike express God's sovereign nature, and the Fall and redemptive activities are part of what God has willed to come to pass. Sovereignty means that nothing accidental occurs, either in the Godhead or in history; all is under God's control. For Beza such thinking expressed the sovereign nature of God. That such a God could appear to be arbitrary did not occur in the matrix in which Beza worked.

The Life of the Christian as Saint and Sinner

The experience of the forgiving, accepting mercy of God, for both Luther and Calvin, is in reality the presence of the living Christ in the believer. The Christian, therefore, lives in the presence of Christ. Although this experience, as we noted in the previous section, may vary in intensity from time to time in any individual, it is of the essence of the Christian that one has the strength and motivation of one's life in the encounter with the living, transforming presence of God. The Christian lives by a power not one's own, because one lives by the power of Christ. Christ is experienced as both forgiveness and power. In moments of ecstatic utterance about the presence of Christ, Luther can even speak of being "one cake" with Christ. It is Christ who dwells within.

But neither Luther nor Calvin dwells on this experience as an end in itself. Christ drives one from self to neighbor. All activity is in fact the result of this relation to Christ. Therefore the reformers speak not against works, but against a false understanding of the place of works. "Our faith in Christ does not free us from works, but from false opinions concerning works, that is, from the foolish presumption that justification is acquired by works," wrote Luther in *The Freedom of a Christian*.[6] Calvin makes the same point many times in the *Institutes*. The following sentence is typical: "For justification is withdrawn from works, not that no good works may be done, or that what is done may be denied to be good, but that we may not rely upon them, glory in them or ascribe salvation to them."[7]

The Christian who experiences Christ may be said to be free from all works which enslave, but bound by the encounter to serve the neighbor. Luther eloquently expressed this in the paradox: "A Christian is a perfectly free lord of all, subject to none. A Christian is a perfectly dutiful servant of all, subject to all."[8] The first axiom is the expression of a faith set free from every demand, and gives joy and

---

[6] Martin Luther, *The Freedom of a Christian*, in *Luther's Works*, (Philadelphia, 1957), Vol. XXXI, pp. 372–373.

[7] *Institutes*, III, xvii, I.

[8] Martin Luther, *Freedom*, p. 344.

zest in living. One is no longer bound by rule or command. But freedom is not license. The Christian is the servant of all and the Christian's freedom is above, not beneath, the law. More often than not Luther assumes that the Christian is so directed by Christ as to do freely and naturally even more than the law required. A statement such as the following is not uncommon:

> Behold, from faith thus flows love and joy in the Lord, and from love a joyful, willing and free mind that serves one's neighbor willingly and takes no account of gratitude or ingratitude, of praise or blame, of gain or loss. For a man does not serve that he may put men under obligations. He does not distinguish between friends and enemies, or anticipate their thankfulness or unthankfulness, but he most freely and willingly spends himself and all that he has, whether he wastes all on the thankless or whether he gains a reward. . . . As our heavenly father has in Christ freely come to our aid, we also ought freely to help our neighbor through our body and its works, and each should become as it were a Christ to the other that we may be Christs to one another and Christ may be the same in all, that is, that we may be truly Christians.[9]

This is a picture of the grateful Christian whom Christ has made into a new person. Luther went so far as to say that Christians would not need the restraints of the state, since they would naturally live together in love and unity, but that they were obliged to obey the state out of love for the un-Christian neighbor who did need it. If this was an unwarranted assumption on the part of Luther, it nevertheless shows his confidence that the presence of God's mercy in Christ dramatically transforms life.

In his better moments, Luther knew that the Christian was not so Christian as to do naturally what was required and that more often one fell quite short of the mark. Where gratitude for redemption in Christ did not suffice, Luther was quick to point to the claim of God upon us. The Redeemer makes demands of those who belong to Christ and in this respect law necessarily enters the Christian life. Luther did not mean primarily the biblical law, but the law of the conscience captive to God and the law of society for justice and order. Law takes over whenever faith is weak, and its necessity is a reminder that the Christian remains a sinner who constantly stands in the need of forgiveness.

While Calvin's position on the transforming power of Christ is essentially the same, there are important nuances of difference that should be noted. Luther speaks with great exuberance about the presence of Christ and almost regrets the necessity of law within the Christian life. Calvin, too, stresses the new life in Christ, but he is sober rather than ecstatic in his account.

[9] *Ibid.*, pp. 367–368.

Whereas Luther spoke of the qualitatively new and decisive redirection of the Christian life, Calvin preferred usually to speak of the path in which the Christian walks, and in which, with diligence, one can make some progress.

> Let each one of us, then, proceed according to the measure of his puny capacity and set out upon the journey we have begun. No one shall set out so inauspiciously as not daily to make some headway, though it be slight. Therefore, let us not cease so to act that we may make some unceasing progress in the way of the Lord. And let us not despair at the slightness of our success; for even though attainment may not correspond to desire, when today outstrips yesterday the effort is not lost. Only let us look toward our mark with sincere simplicity and aspire to our goal; not fondly flattering ourselves, nor excusing our own evil deeds, but with continuous effort striving toward this end: that we may surpass ourselves in goodness until we attain to goodness itself. It is this, indeed, which through the whole course of life we seek and follow. But we shall attain it only when we have cast off the weakness of the body, and are received into full fellowship with him.[10]

In one passage Calvin even dares hope that the Christian will have nothing left but the most venial of sins if one keeps on the path toward righteousness.

On this path, Calvin sees a very positive role for biblical law (i.e., the moral law, including both the moral demand of the Old Testament and the teaching of Jesus). Not only does this law convict of sin and lead to Christ and preserve order in a world of sin; its most significant place is that it supplies the Christian with a better and more certain understanding of the divine will, and by meditation upon it, exhorts one to obedience and keeps one "untainted from the slippery path of transgression." Thus Calvin urged the preparation of a compendium of biblical texts which might serve as a guide for the Christian.

While Luther was concerned with the qualitative transformation of the Christian life and while Calvin emphasized the possibility of progress within it, both seriously affirmed that the Christian remains a sinner who needs God's justifying mercy at all times. "Even we who have the first fruits of the spirit, groan and travail within us," writes St. Paul in the eighth chapter of Romans. The Christian stands at every moment under a mercy which is more infinite than anything which one can accomplish in faith. That is why, in the estimation of Luther, the Christian is both sinner and not a sinner at the same time. Similarly, Calvin declares:

> I say that the best work that can be brought forward from them is still always spotted and corrupted with some impurity of the flesh, and

---

[10] *Institutes,* III, vi, 5.

has, so to speak, some dregs mixed with it. Let a holy servant to God, I say, choose from the whole course of life what of an especially noteworthy character he thinks he has done. Let him well turn over in his mind its several parts. Undoubtedly he will somewhere perceive that it savors of the rottenness of the flesh, since our eagerness for well-doing is never what it ought to be but our great weakness slows down our running in the race. . . . We have not a single work going forth from the saints that if it be judged in itself deserves not shame as its just reward.[11]

Calvin was clear that no works or activity could survive the scrutiny of the Almighty except in forgiveness, but he did believe that they could be a confirmation of faith. They could be a sign for the believer of faith and therefore of election. "Therefore, when we rule out reliance upon works," writes Calvin, "we mean only this: that the Christian mind may not be turned back to the merit of works as to a help toward salvation but should rely wholly on the free promise of righteousness. But we do not forbid him from undergirding and strengthening this faith by signs of the divine benevolence toward him."[12] Or again, Calvin, in reconciling James and Paul, states that it is as if James had said: "Those who by true faith are righteous prove their righteousness by obedience and good works, not by a bare and imaginary mask of faith."[13]

It is natural to expect that being a Christian makes a difference. It was Luther's genius which saw what the presence of Christ automatically does without reference to signs of any type. It was a liability that some of his successors interpreted this unconcern in the direction of license and freedom from all restraint. It was Calvin's greatness which saw that guidance and results both belong to the Christian life. But this could become a liability when individuals began to look at their works to discover whether or not they were truly of Christ's company. Such self-consciousness leads easily to self-righteousness. It is spiritually dangerous to look for signs of election.

In spite of the differences of emphasis, Luther and Calvin were in fundamental agreement on the place of works in the Christian life. These are not trustworthy in respect to salvation. Nevertheless, they belong to the life of faith. Granting this, however, there is no way of calculating to what extent works are essential. Any rigid definition could destroy the vitality of the Christian life in one of three directions — license, complacency, or self-righteousness produced by despair.

---

[11] *Ibid.*, III, xiv, 9.
[12] *Ibid.*, III, xiv, 18.
[13] *Ibid.*, III, xxvii, 12.

Luther's and Calvin's basic approach can perhaps best be expressed by speaking of "faith not without works." By way of contrast, this phrase may take a sharper meaning. It excludes both works plus faith, and faith plus works. The first was characteristic of the medieval views, in which the emphasis was upon worthiness, to which was added grace (though, e.g., for Aquinas, these works also spring from grace). The second represents a late nineteenth-century motif which still informs much of Protestantism. Sensing the essential priority of faith, exponents of this position stress that works are derivative, that one trusts God and does the best one can. The contrast to the reformers is in the "both and" character of the expressions. In Luther and Calvin, faith and works are included, but not as a matter of addition, from one side or the other. Such alternatives destroy the vitality which the reformers saw in the proper relation between faith and action.

In defining the proper relation, Luther and Calvin always began with justification, which stands over every human endeavor and over one in every moment. One is always related to God finally on the basis of faith, for without this one could not even begin. One can also trust that this faith is more trustworthy than actions or one's own nature. Forgiveness stands and needs to stand over the best of human hopes, aspirations, and activities. It is a continual necessity and a continual possibility. That is why the Christian makes no claims for works. The reformers would never say that the demands of God are easy as long as one's heart is in the right place (as some more recent generations have said); they emphasized that it is serious to fall into the hands of the living God even though God's mercy overrides every demand.

Where there are no works, there is no faith. But the place of works is relative. The biblical passages sometimes cited in support of a stress upon works actually places these in the context of faith. The injunction to "work out your own salvation with fear and trembling" needs to be quoted in its entirety, "for it is God who works in you both to will and to do." It is possible for Luther and Calvin to speak of working out one's own salvation when this is predicated upon the initiating and directing activity of God. Likewise, the biblical statement that "not every one who says unto me, Lord, Lord, shall enter into the kingdom of heaven, but he that does the will of my father who is in heaven" does not preclude but rather affirms the necessity of saying "Lord, Lord" — the equivalent of trusting the mercy of God — as the first word.

The phrase, faith not without works, expresses Luther's and Calvin's insistence upon the priority of the mercy of God at every point, and the necessity of works as a result. It carefully avoids making works the basis of redemption and takes away every quantitative calculation. The infinite patience and mercy of God, far surpassing that of humans, are expressed in the biblical affirmation that God will forgive not seven, but seventy times seven. This is not arithmetic, but the assertion that God's mercy is continuous and inexhaustible. At the same time, where forgiveness does not in some sense issue in new life, it is doubtful that it is actually forgiveness. Forgiveness itself directs and demands our responsibilities. But no one can simply add forgiveness and the results of forgiveness and expect to have the gospel. We are in both greater certainty and greater uncertainty. We are more certain because everything hinges on God's mercy. We are more uncertain because we do not have the possibility of resting assured that we have done all, or done it correctly. The gospel suspends us in the world, but gives us a point of security — God's abiding mercy and ultimate victory over the forces of evil. The Christian wrestles, seemingly at times in vain; but those who wait upon the Lord will renew their strength for the battle of life. They need not fear, because God's mercy is ample for every contingency.

It was from such a perspective that Luther asserted "sin bravely, yet more bravely still believe." This is not a counsel to sin; it is the recognition that life involves sin, that at no point can we completely escape it. It is a counsel against those who are so afraid of sin that they refuse to act or participate freely in the events of life. We can venture confidently, because our resource is not a state of sinlessness but the mercy of God. This faith is the emancipating power of the reformers' rediscovery of the Bible. Through God's unqualified acceptance of us, we are freed from calculation, terror, and self, and set free to love our neighbor and to work responsibly in the world. We are the continually forgiven ones who trust nothing else and whose earthly life is that of being simultaneously saint and sinner.

God and Christ

Luther and Calvin assumed the existence of God. This was not seriously challenged in their own time. Even Luther, who made very pointed remarks against reason as an avenue to knowledge of God, did not deny the possibility of such natural knowledge. He only denied its usefulness in respect to decisive issues. Calvin stated that all people are naturally endowed with the knowledge of God. They distort this knowledge, but only reality can be distorted. Calvin further spoke of natural impulses toward justice and goodness in people generally. But he understood these from the perspective of a believer analyzing the life of the unbeliever. He assumed that all people lived by the gifts of God even though they did not recognize them as such.

Genuine knowledge of God, in Luther and Calvin, is related to the meaning of life. To use a modern word, such knowledge is existential (i.e., related to one's very existence). The two opening chapters of Calvin's *Institutes* make the relation crystal clear. "Nearly all the wisdom we possess, that is to say, true and sound wisdom, consists of two parts: the knowledge of God and of ourselves. . . . The knowledge of ourselves not only arouses us to seek God, but also, as it were, leads us by the hand to find him. . . . It is certain that man never achieves a clear knowledge of himself unless he has first looked upon God's face, and then descends from contemplating him to scrutinize himself."[14] From this perspective, the question of God really matters only as God's existence has consequences for human existence.

Thus, while the two reformers accepted a natural knowledge of God, they immediately judged it from the standpoint of their faith and pushed beyond it to a genuine knowledge of God in Christ. They found much about God in the Bible apart from Christ, but when they spoke of God it was always with the revelation in Christ in mind. Calvin, who is known for stressing the glory and honor of God, emphasized particularly the grace of God in Christ as the expression of that glory. Luther, who had so much to say of the gracious presence of God in Christ, had startling things to say of God's majesty apart from Christ. He reiterated how terrifying it is to confront the terrible, naked majesty. But even this was considered a form of disclosure not unrelated to God's merciful presence. Luther and Calvin completely agreed that God is known adequately only in Christ.

The precise relation of Christ to the Godhead was not a problem of direct concern, as it had been in the early church. The issues of the sixteenth century concerned justification, and such doctrines as the Incarnation and the Trinity were largely taken as part of the received faith which needed no reformation or reformulation. Luther expressed some distaste for the formulations which emerged from the early controversies, but he accepted and expounded them. His battle was not on that level. Calvin wrote with greater detail than did Luther but also followed the lead of the earlier centuries.

Far more important for the reformers was the claim that God assumed the sins of humankind in the life, death, and resurrection of Christ. This was the question of Christ's "work" rather than his "person." "For our sake he made him to be sin who knew no sin," writes St. Paul. For Luther, Christ is the true sinner who never committed sin, and for Calvin, "the Son of God, though perfectly free from all sin, nevertheless assumed the disgrace and ignominy of our iniquities, and, on the other hand, arrayed us in his purity."[15] Calvin further declared that Christ is the "sacrifice" for our sins and that he has enough merit for us all. In one way or another the reformers claimed

---

[14] *Ibid.*, I, i, 1 and 2.
[15] *Ibid.*, II, xvi, 6.

that God took over the sin of the world, that it cost God something to overcome sin but not in such a way as to threaten or frustrate God's being. The glory of God's righteousness is that God did not ask us to assume the responsibility for unbelief and offenses, but took it over.

On the *way* in which God assumed our sin, Luther and Calvin differed. Stressing the titles *prophet, priest,* and *king,* Calvin described how Christ fits these categories more adequately than all predecessors. Taken together they point to the exalted majesty of Christ in roles which took him through suffering to glory. For Luther, however, the recurring theme is the majesty of God descending to the lowliness of a human form in which no titles of honor are implied. God's strength is hidden in weakness, and this marvel never ceased to fascinate Luther. In this form God outwitted even the devil. Recalling the early Greek Fathers, Luther declared Christ to be the bait with which God caught the devil, for the latter expected a display of power, not a power of weakness which was stronger than the strength of all other power. Luther did not mean that the weakness of Christ was weakness as usually understood, nor that weakness as such has particular strength. He was more interested in the form of apparent weakness through which God's power was manifest. Such power, whatever its form, was to be given its full weight as power.

Christ's redemptive power is particularly evident as power in view of the forces over and against which it is exercised. Luther, as St. Paul before him, said that we wrestle not only with flesh and blood (human beings), but also with principalities and powers (that is, structures of evil and sin which are more powerful than individuals and the sum of their evil activities). The words *sin, death, the devil, powers of darkness,* include the sins of individual men, but they represent forces which are a part of the structure of things. The sins of individuals belong to situations of evil which have a reality greater than the individuals involved. That is why they represent powers to be opposed and overcome by a strength not one's own. Christ is the sure conqueror of these forces. Christ's reign means that although the powers of evil are not yet subdued, their final subjugation is already assured. The clearest expression of this outlook is in Luther's hymn, "A Mighty Fortress is Our God."

The stark contrast between the forces of evil and the lowliness of Christ is one of the reasons for Luther's conviction that God's presence in Christ is not self-evident. God hides in Christ in order to become known. Faith must pierce the veil; it must be given to one to see the power and love of God in his lowliness. God for Luther is not self-evidently love. God's love is the miracle that human eyes are not able to see, unless it has been given to them to see through the providential activity of God. God is never apprehended directly. God is known as God through a veil. God's nature is to be found in Christ, but even in Christ, God cannot be possessed. God confronts us from out of the mystery of being genuine love. There is sufficient knowledge of God to exclude the plea that God is sheer mystery, attractive or unattractive; there is sufficient mystery so that we can never claim we have understood or fathomed the miracle of God's love and concern.

It is such faith also which lies behind the affirmations of creation and God's providential governance of the world. Both Luther and Calvin were convinced that the concept of God as the creator distinguishes the biblical idea of God from all other gods in the history of religion. Such a positive affirmation of the world is to be found nowhere else. As men of their time, the reformers accepted the Genesis story in its cosmological detail as well as in its meaning for faith. But they were not concerned with "scientific" proofs or disproofs. God as creator was an item of faith.

It was also affirmed that the God who made the world was still at work in it and exceedingly active in its history. This attestation, too, rested upon faith, not upon proof. Calvin was willing to offer some evidence of God's activity. But Luther, more often than not, could find no reason for believing in God on the basis of ordinary observation of the world. The world appeared to him as a spectacle of disorder rather than of order, of unreason rather than reason, of injustice rather than of justice. His faith triumphed over his inclinations, as in the famous assertion that the essence of faith is to believe God just though God looks so terribly unjust.

Bible, Church, and Tradition

Word Within the Bible

For Luther and Calvin, God can be known adequately only through the Bible. It was, after all, on the basis of the Bible that the Reformation was launched. But when the reformers referred to the Bible as the Word of God they did not in the first instance mean that the book and the revelation were the same. Calvin, more than Luther, insisted also upon the text of the Bible as itself the Word of God, but he did so on the basis of the word which spoke to us from the Bible. The Bible's authority as the Word rested upon its *content*, its central message. There was no acceptance of the Bible simply as "sacred book."

Even the content of the Bible must be *experienced* as the judging, forgiving presence of God in Christ for it to be the Word of God. The Word is discovered through the Bible, but it is Word because it is confirmed in the hearts of believers through the Holy Spirit. At the same time, that which the Spirit confirms corresponds to the Christ portrayed in the Bible. Calvin declared that

> . . . the Word itself is not quite certain for us unless it be confirmed by the testimony of the Spirit. . . . For by a kind of mutual bond the Lord has joined together the certainty of his Word and of his Spirit so that the perfect religion of the Word may abide in our minds when the Spirit, who causes us to contemplate God's face, shines; and that we in turn may embrace the Spirit with no fear of being deceived when we recognize him in his own image, namely, in the Word . . . God did not bring forth his Word among men for the sake of a momentary display, intending at the coming of his Spirit to abolish it. Rather, he sent down the same Spirit by whose power he had dispensed the World, to complete his work by the efficacious confirmation of the Word.[16]

This equally excludes all appeals either to the Scripture apart from the Spirit or to the Spirit apart from the Scripture. The Word must live through the Spirit, and the life in the Spirit must be checked by its correspondence to the content of Scripture. On this point, Luther and Calvin were in total agreement.

They differed in the understanding of the scope of the content. For Luther there is a Bible within the Bible. This inner Bible is Christ, and the whole Bible is characterized as the cradle in which Christ is laid. Only Christ is finally important; everything else in the Bible is important only as the matrix in which Christ is found. This implies that not everything in the Bible is of the same value. For instance, Luther once called the epistle of James a "right strawy epistle," since it did not conform to what he believed to be the central norm of the Bible, that is, Christ and Christ's redeeming activity. Instead of anchoring works in faith, it made works a clue to faith. Though a lofty document, he felt it missed the central point in an important problem. He further affirmed that anybody with sufficient inspiration could write biblical books, though he believed that inspiration had disappeared and therefore we are safe only if we confine ourselves to the present canon.

In the eyes of Luther, the emphasis upon the Bible within the Bible resulted neither in subjectivism (that is, taking what one wants and leaving the rest) nor in the inability to determine what is the core of the Bible. He was certain that there was a sufficiently clear and central body of material concerning Christ which would be common property to those who searched the Bible and had been grasped by God's redeeming work. He was convinced that a clear reading of

[16] *Ibid.*, I, ix, 3.

the Bible would result in the emergence of God's justifying work as the central point.[17]

Although Calvin, like Luther, emphasized that faith in Christ is the central part of the gospel and therefore of the Bible, his interpretation was distinctly different. Calvin insisted on the fundamental unity of the Bible and therefore on the validity of most everything within it. For example, in considering the relation of law and gospel, Calvin distinguished between the two but also insisted upon their unity. Word and Spirit are conjoined on every page of the Bible and, although Christ is the center of the gospel, God speaks through every page of the Bible. At times, this principle made it necessary for Calvin to devote pages to reconciling contradictory passages of Scripture. It should be made clear, however, that Calvin identified the Bible with the Word of God only in the sense that faith in Christ attested to its authenticity. He was not a literalist or fundamentalist in the twentieth-century sense (see Ch. X). He did not move from a conviction of verbal inspiration to faith, but from faith in Christ, grounded in the Bible, to a concept of total inspiration. In this sense, he was less free in dealing with the Bible than Luther was.

Both agreed that God can use any vehicle in addressing us. Luther declared that if God once spoke through Balaam's ass, God can speak through anything, whether stone, stick, thunder, or what not. Nevertheless, both agreed that we should look for God in the Bible, and primarily in the witness which the Bible makes to Christ. Every other disclosure of the divine ought to be checked by its correspondence with what is known of God through Christ, and that is mediated through the Bible.

Church and Sacraments

Since faith is born and based in a gospel indissolubly connected with the Bible, the Bible must stand over the church as the continual norm for its faith. Luther and Calvin were, of course, aware that the Bible was originally the product of the church, but they insisted that the

---

[17] This has always been the contention of Protestants and there is ample evidence of its validity. Protestants, as the following chapters show, have not always seen this as the central point nor understood it in the same way. But they have frequently been driven back to it. Even the many denominations and sects do not destroy this principle. This diversity is not considered too great a price for the freedom which each individual has of direct access through the Bible to God's disclosure. As a matter of fact, the stress on individual interpretation arose partly out of this Reformation emphasis, but partly also as a reaction to the fact that the original churches of the Reformation themselves did not permit the freedom which their principle of interpretation demanded.

gospel is nevertheless based in the inspired character of books which in a unique way become the means of faith. The church therefore is nourished by the Word of God, particularly as found in the Bible. The church is not the guardian of the Bible; rather the Bible is the guardian of the church because in it is the source of the Christian life. The gospel is associated with the Bible in a way it is not with the church. Through its impact on us, the Bible creates the church.

The church is the community or fellowship of believers, those who are committed to God in Christ and who live by God's mercy and power. Their community is anchored in a common faith in a common Lord; they meet together to hear God's Word preached and considered; they participate in the sacraments as particular and significant acts instituted in the time of the New Testament. In worship they give thanks for God's marvelous mercy, confess their sins, hope to be renewed in mind and spirit, hear the meaning of particular passages of Scripture interpreted by ministers — all in the faith that God will be made known for their daily existence.

Differences within the church are functional and vocational. There is no difference of status before God for clergy and for laity. The two reformers did not believe that everyone should function as clergy. They were much too insistent on order in the church to risk such apparent anarchy. The concept of the priesthood of all believers did not mean that the clergy are superfluous. But utilizing the medieval concept of priesthood as the necessary mediation of the presence of God in Christ, Luther graphically showed how each person confronts God and neighbor as priest or mediator. Before self and God, there can stand no priest. Here one is one's own priest. No one can have faith for another. It can only be one's own. Likewise in relation to neighbor, no persons or groups can claim to be special channels of grace. We are all priests in mediating Christ to our fellows, neighbors in the deepest sense of the term.

In the life of the Christian, the priesthood of all believers means being a witness to God's redeeming activity and presence in every circumstance. This is the theoretical base for the concept of "vocation," which Luther stripped of its medieval hierarchical distinctions. Now one can be equally a Christian in every decent calling; no calling is "higher" than another. The cobbler who exercises a calling with Christian responsibility is doing a task under God with the same significance as the minister who functions in the church. The difference between cobbler and minister is one of function. They stand equally under God, and both are called upon to think out their Christian faith, to nourish it, and to witness to others by being Christians in their tasks. The minister, to be sure, has a particular responsibility to expound the gospel and faithfulness to that task will be a sign of the fulfillment of a proper vocation. The minister may know more of the intricacies of the Bible and of its meaning, but this will provide neither more faith nor more certainty in what is believed.

Early in the Reformation, the church was described as the place where the Word is rightly preached and the sacraments rightly administered. Calvin very clearly uses this formulation in the fourth book of the *Institutes*. For Ulrich Zwingli in Zurich and Martin Bucer in Strasbourg, a third mark of the church was added, namely, discipline in the believing community. Whereas Calvin saw to it that discipline was exercised in the Genevan community, both he and Luther did not accept the third mark, lest accent on the life of the community shift from formal criteria to an evaluation of visible characteristics of the actual life of a community.

In the Reformation churches, preaching assumed an importance it did not have in churches that were primarily sacramental. The faithful exercise of expounding Scripture was a criterion for the adequacy of the minister, since the Word and its correlative, faith, were the basis of the life of the church. The minister was a steward of the mysteries of God. The minister could not give another person faith, but was responsible for the faithful setting forth of God's redemptive message and in this way indirectly responsible for the life and vitality of the flock entrusted to a pastor.

Neither the preached nor the written word was in itself the Word of God. They became the Word of God when they became alive in the heart and mind of people through the Spirit. One came to the faith either through the written or preached word, usually the latter. In this sense, preaching, as the explication of the biblical word, could be said to be more primary than sacraments.

Luther and Calvin insisted that the word be preached each time the sacrament was given. Preaching was for the imparting of faith, for instruction and for the confrontation with God's judging and redeeming word. The sacraments presupposed this faith. Therefore, one of the prerequisites of a proper sacrament was the faith of the believer. In addition, the criteria of a sacrament included an instituted sign or visible act (water in baptism and bread and wine in the Lord's Supper) and a spoken word of promise in connection with the acts (the forgiveness of sins) — these signs having been given in the New Testament. The application of these criteria required the reduction of the number of sacraments to two: baptism and the Lord's Supper.

Having rejected the medieval sacramental theories, Luther nevertheless found himself in controversy over the understanding of both sacraments. On the question of baptism, he found himself between the Anabaptists and the Roman Catholics. The Anabaptists (see Ch. III) rejected infant baptism because an infant could not be considered to have faith. It was believers who were to be baptized into the community. Luther was convinced, however, that faith is more than intellectual assent, and he felt that the Anabaptists had relegated it to that level. For him, faith includes a total commitment based upon the activity of God and cannot be confined to the age of reason or possible rational decision. Neither could he accept the view of baptism in the medieval church, according to which the act of baptism automatically restored the grace lost through original sin. Luther resorted to the idea of "infantile faith" as his way of stressing the importance of faith against all magical theories. At the same time, this provided him with a weapon against the Anabaptists, who in spite of their emphasis on Spirit seemed to him to rationalize the religious dimension by confusing it with consciousness. It is perhaps just as well that Luther did not explain the term "infantile faith"; one can, however, understand why he came to it.

For both Luther and Calvin, baptism is the sacrament in which, through God's promise and its acceptance in faith, one dies to sin and is reborn in faith. This symbolism is accepted even when faith is not a conscious possibility, and emphasis falls upon the faith of the congregation in initiating the individual into the Christian fold. It is the symbol and sign of the Christian's forgiveness.

Calvin and Zwingli particularly use the language of initiation and covenant in relation to baptism, and consider it to be the New Testament analogue to circumcision in the Old Testament. For Calvin, it is however an incorporation into the household of faith, for the seeds of future repentance and faith, while not fully formed, are already present in infants by the power of the Spirit.[18] For Zwingli, the initiatory sign represents but does not indicate an inward change in the one who receives it. He believes in the baptism of infants, not because something happens, but because infants belong to families, the unit by which we are especially related to God. Here, as in the Lord's Supper, to which we now turn, there is a gradation of views, with Luther and Zwingli at one end of the Lutheran and Reformed spectrum, and Calvin in between.

Emphasizing God's promise in connection with the Lord's Supper, Luther assumed that the words, "This is my body," surely meant no less than actual body. As a minimum he interpreted this to mean that in faith God in Christ is present, in, with, and under the elements, both in bodily and spiritual form. He did not accept the medieval notion that the bread and wine are changed into the body and blood of Christ, while remaining under the accidents of bread and wine. But he did insist that Christ is bodily present, even as he is spiritually present. Christ therefore is not bodily sitting on the right hand of God. His body or his spirit is potentially everywhere. Without this, Luther insisted, Christ is not fully present. Calvin, too, emphasized bodily as well as spiritual presence, but still maintained that Christ is

---

[18] *Institutes*, IV, xvi, 20.

seated at the right hand of the Father in glory. Like Luther, he insisted on the bodily presence as a way of affirming God's veritable presence to those who believe. Unlike Luther, he did not spell it out in a metaphysical way.

While Luther expressed the issue of presence in semiphilosophical categories, such as the ubiquity of Christ's body, Calvin believed that the Holy Spirit united what could not otherwise be comprehended. "Even though it seems unbelievable that Christ's flesh, separated from us by such great distance, penetrates to us, so that it becomes our food, let us remember how far the sacred power of the Holy Spirit towers above all our senses, and how foolish it is to wish to measure his immeasureableness by our measure. What, then, our mind does not comprehend, let faith conceive: that the Spirit truly unites things separated in space."[19] Calvin also suggested that the Spirit may lift us to Christ as well as Christ descending to us.[20] Hence, while Luther and Calvin differed on the mode of presence, they were united in the conviction that a form of presence was essential to an understanding of the Lord's Supper.

Debates over the Lord's Supper mainly stemmed from controversy with Luther, consisting of meetings and exchanges of tracts, particularly on the part of Luther, Karlstadt, and Zwingli. Luther returned from hiding in the Wartburg castle to confront Karlstadt on the issue of images, sacraments, church order, and the nature of reform. For Karlstadt, the sacrament has no relation to the forgiveness of sins. It is a rite in which we remember the meaning of Christ's death for us, the reality in which our forgiveness exists. Wrote Karlstadt: "The remembrance, however, is a passionate and loving knowledge or perception of the body and blood of Christ. For indeed no one can remember what he has not perceived. . . . Yes, if that is true, it is not a frozen or dead understanding, but rather an ardent, passionate, industrious, powerful knowledge of Christ which transforms the perceiver into the perceived life and death of Christ and desires to do or forsake for Christ's sake all that Christ wants."[21] The sacrament is a lively expression of faith, not of the possibility of faith.

While Zwingli's views are similar to Karlstadt's, he focuses more on an analysis of the biblical texts. The sixth chapter of John, which for Luther has nothing to do with the Lord's Supper, is critical for Zwingli, interpreting, as it does, Christ's presence in spiritual terms to those inclined to confuse the material and the spiritual. Eating

---

[19] *Ibid.*, IV, xvii, 10.
[20] *Ibid.*, IV, xvii, 31.
[21] "Concerning the Anti-Christian Misuse of the Lord's Bread and Cup . . .", in *Karlstadt's Battle with Luther, Documents in a Liberal-Radical Debate*, edited by Ronald J. Sider (Philadelphia, 1978), pp. 78–79.

and drinking are thus spiritual estates, in which there is no mastication of the body and blood of Christ. Moreover, eating and drinking in a literal sense is not possible, for Christ has ascended to heaven in a fleshly form not present there before. Indeed, Zwingli rejects Luther's view that what is said of the humanity of Christ must also be said of the divinity and vice versa. Rather, when we talk of suffering and ascension, we talk of Christ's humanity, for suffering is not characteristic of divinity, nor is ascension appropriate to humanity. Divinity's presence is spiritual, that is, presence after a divine nature. The "is" in *this is my body* or *this is my blood,* is to be understood as signifies, represents, as a sign, figure, or memorial. Hence, Zwingli, interpreting Augustine with approval, wrote:

> Briefly, then, . . . when you come to this thanksgiving you need neither teeth to press the body of Christ nor stomach to receive that which you have chewed, for if you believe in him you have already partaken of him, and when in the thanksgiving, in company with the congregation, you partake of the two elements of bread and wine, all that you do is to confess publicly that you believe in the Lord Jesus Christ. Therefore, when we take the signs of bread and wine the principal things to which we must look is to believe in Christ. For he who believes in him feeds on him. To feed on him is simply to believe in him.[22]

Hence, in eating and drinking, the believer is graphically reminded of and participates in the total drama of God's redeeming activity in Christ. One is nourished in faith as one engages in an act which vividly recalls the total meaning of the life, death, and resurrection of Christ. This act is a visible sign in which is telescoped the totality of the gospel in a way words alone could not achieve. The remembrance is a dramatic presentation of the whole of that which is at the basis of faith.

In these different delineations of the Lord's Supper, one factor remains constant, namely, the vital relation between the taking of the elements and faith. It was surely that recognition which led to the attempts to come to some unity among the Lutheran and Reformed groups, as at Marburg, and on the part of both, with the Roman Catholics, as at Augsburg and Regensburg. But both attempts came to naught, much to the disappointment of the reformer Martin Bucer, who had spent so much time in trying to find rapprochement, and to the Lutheran Philipp Melanchthon, who, like Bucer, had made reluctant accommodations that did not lead to unity. While formally all agreed on the relation of faith to the sacraments, it was precisely the differences in the understanding of faith that kept the groups apart. Humanist, mystical, and metaphysical ingredients in the under-

---

[22] "On the Lord's Supper," in *Zwingli and Bullinger,* Library of Christian Classics (Philadelphia, 1953), p. 198.

standing of faith could not be brought to a rubric of common under-standing. Indeed, there was a difference; and Luther was undoubtedly right, however intemperate it seemed, when he said of the Zwinglians that they were of a different spirit. In the subsequent Reformation history, the Lutheran tradition went its own way, not without great debates over Luther's views of bodily presence and Melanchthon's apparent drift toward a position close to that of Calvin, while the developing Reformed tradition followed the views of Zwingli much more than those of Calvin.

Word over Tradition

Such differences in theological formulation must be seen in the light of the reformers' insistence that the authority of the Word can be guaranteed neither by ecclesiastical authority nor by tradition. Neither Luther, Calvin, nor Zwingli accepted the notion that tradition is finally decisive. They were aware of the dangers in breaking with the past. The most difficult taunts Luther had to bear were those which sug-gested that he was going against the practice and wisdom of the ages and setting himself up as the interpreter and custodian of truth. He finally insisted that his conscience was captive to the Word of God and that this was his authority over against all tradition. The problem was more difficult for Luther than for Calvin, since by the time of the latter the initial break had already been made. By that time, too, many of the Protestants, not without help from humanist scholars generally, had come to a better understanding of the texts of the church fathers through fresh publications of the texts. Johannes Oeco-lampadius, the successor of Zwingli in Zurich, was a relentless publisher of the Greek fathers, while others had made many of the Latin fathers available.

Moreover, Luther and Calvin both studied and knew the church fathers. They quoted Augustine most. Ideally, the fathers were to be understood as those who expounded biblical truth, who led us to an understanding of the Bible. Actually, both of the reformers (Luther particularly) felt that the fathers generally led not to the clarity of the gospel, but away from it. Even the councils of the church could not be taken as finally authoritative or necessarily correct. Luther pointed out frequently that it was often a council which called the results of a previous council heretical. Calvin remarked that one ought to argue from Scripture and that from this perspective, "councils would come to have the majesty that is their due; yet in the meantime Scripture would stand out in the higher place, with everything subject to its standard."[23]

---

[23] *Institutes*, IV, ix, 8.

Tradition is not to be taken lightly, but it is to be corrected by biblical truth. That is why Luther, while reluctant, did not shrink from the *reforming* task. The reformers did not believe they were starting a new church. They believed that they were calling the church to a more adequate reflection of the gospel which was its base. Moreover, they believed this is a continual necessity. When, therefore, Rome would not reform, they felt that it was no longer the church. They felt their work to be in the tradition of the ages. But they were convinced that the life of the church in each age is nourished by the biblical faith, not tradition. The gospel itself is the only proper tradition, imperfectly but significantly reflected in a continuously reforming church.

The Christian, the State, and Culture

For Luther, Christians find their lives occupying two spheres — the spiritual and the temporal. Similarly, Calvin distinguishes between the inward and outward aspects of government, the former referring to the inner life of the soul in its earthly pilgrimage, and the latter to forms of external conduct. For both men, there is an individual and a corporate ethic.

We have discussed the nature of ethics insofar as it concerns the basis and direction of one's life (in the preceding section, "The Life of the Christian as Saint and Sinner"). Here it is important to recall that Luther had such confidence in Christians that he believed they do not need the state themselves, but obey it out of love for their neighbor. For Luther, the state is a remedy for sin, preventing disorder and anarchy. In accord with his own understanding that the Christian is still sinner, it would have been logical to assume that the state, too, would still be needed if all men were Christians. Luther's statement must, however, be understood in an ideal sense; he never anticipated that it would be realized in this life.

Calvin emphasized progress in the Christian life much more than did Luther, but he insisted that Christians, too, need the state for the welfare and ordering of their own lives. The state is a remedy for sin. But even more, it exists as a place of concord, order, and relative peace given by God for the well-being of the Christians in their earthly pilgrimage toward final redemption. Though related to sin, the state is a positive blessing of God. One of its tasks is to guarantee and protect pure religion. (Luther did not consider this a necessary function of the state, but he was willing to call upon Christian princes to reform a church which would not reform itself.)

For both reformers, the state is ordained of God and a gift for this life. Therefore, Christians are not to despise it but to accept it.

They are to obey it and not interfere with its functioning. Those in authority are like gods under God, given the responsibility of order and concord in the world and the suppression of disorder and anarchy. Rulers ought, to be sure, to govern justly, and if they do not they will ultimately pay the penalty before God. They can and must be called to account by the Word of God, even the preached Word of God. But, Luther held, they cannot be actively resisted. In the face of injustice, Christians can only suffer. They cannot rebel.

The difficulties of Luther's approach became apparent in the Peasants' Revolt (1524–1525). Although personally sympathetic to the cause of the peasants, Luther wrote vitriolic attacks against them when they revolted. In part, Luther acted out of religious conviction, but other important factors also played a role. Luther felt that the peasants were confusing their cause with the Reformation. Further, he lived in an explosive period and, as is usual in such times, had a much greater fear of anarchy than of tyranny. Authority must be preserved at all costs.

Yet Luther's claim of loyalty to God against every tyrant is unmistakable. One's obedience to God is more ultimate than one's duty to the state. Therefore God must be obeyed above all else. Perhaps because of the peculiar problems of his own situation, Luther did not see the full implications of this position. (It was just this claim of loyalty to God above all else which was used by Norwegian Lutherans as the basis for their valiant resistance against the Nazis.)

Calvin, no less than Luther, urged obedience to duly constituted authority, but he made at least two significant qualifying statements which became of fundamental importance for posterity. Speaking of obedience to parents enjoined by the fifth commandment, he stated that they are to be obeyed "in the Lord" — that is, as parents who do not demand what is contrary to God. ". . . if they [parents] spur us to transgress the law, we have a perfect right to regard them not as parents, but as strangers who are trying to lead us away from obedience to our true Father. So should we act toward princes, lords, and every kind of superiors."[24] Thus, if any superiors violate our religious obligations, we may refuse to regard them as representing constituted authority. In another passage, Calvin suggests, as others had done before him, how such an attitude might find implementation. Resistance to evil rulers is not the right of private persons but of lesser magistrates.

> For if there are now any magistrates of the people, appointed to restrain the willfulness of kings (as in ancient times the ephors were set against the Spartan kings, or the tribunes of the people against the Roman

[24] *Ibid.*, II, viii, 38.

consuls, or the demarchs against the senate of the Athenians; and perhaps, as things now are, such power as the three estates exercise in
every realm when they hold their chief assemblies), I am so far from
forbidding them to withstand, in accordance with their duty, the fierce
licentiousness of kings, that, if they wink at kings who violently fall
upon and assault the lowly common folk, I declare that their dissimula-
tion involves nefarious perfidy, because they dishonestly betray the freedom of the people, of which they know that they have been appointed
protectors by God's ordinance.[25]

Luther showed a similar understanding in changing his support
from the emperor to the princes in the struggle over Roman Catholicism. He shifted his support when a number of jurists declared that
the princes were the duly constituted authority since the emperor
no longer acted as such. Luther also suggested that in an extraordinary
situation, one like that which faced Samson, one needed to take things
in one's own hands. But he also knew how dangerous that was.

More important than such legal questions was the basic religious
affirmation that one's allegiance is to a sovereign God above all sover-
eignties. Under such a claim, princes, kings, and empires frequently
were both passively and actively resisted and not infrequently transformed. Political developments in England and America particularly
were related to this claim (see Chs. V, VII).

The state was never considered an end in itself, and just because
it served primarily as a means toward another end neither Luther
nor Calvin paid much attention to the form and structure of government. Yet there is a passage in Calvin's *Institutes* which may be more
related to subsequent constitutional developments of the distribution
of power, particularly the United States Constitution, than the usual
ascription of such developments solely to Montesquieu. "Men's fault
or failing causes it to be safer and more bearable for a number to
exercise government, so that they may help one another, teach and
admonish one another; and, if one asserts himself unfairly, there may
be a number of censors and masters to restrain his willfulness."[26]
Here the plea for the distribution of power is not that we are all
capable of its exercise, but that none of us is to be trusted with too
much power.

Yet Luther and Calvin did not see the responsibility of government
to extend to the creation of a Christian society as such. If they believed
that rulers should also be responsible for true religion, this did not
mean a religious society, ordered in every respect on the basis of
faith. They believed that Christians were still sufficiently un-Christian

[25] *Ibid.,* IV, xx, 31.
[26] *Ibid.,* IV, xx, 8.

so as not to trust impositions even of faith. By contrast, those who put more stress on the nature of the new life in Christ than did Luther and Calvin were inclined to believe that every aspect of society ought to be ordered in terms of faith. While Luther dealt with princes for the sake of the free life of the church and Calvin organized a city in the light of the gospel, others, such as the Strasbourg reformer, Martin Bucer, stressed the need for transformation of corporate life from top to bottom, a change in which monarchs were asked to play a major role. It is perhaps not by accident that, in addition to Bucer's personal destiny to spend the last years of his life in Cambridge, England, his ideas on the ordering of society were more nearly implemented in England than on the continent. The relation of faith to society has an ambience that is quite different in England than on the continent.

The "Last Things"

The reformers stressed obedience to the state, not for the sake of power or of absolutist claims, but because it served an interim purpose. All life is a pilgrimage destined to its final fulfillment in the kingdom of God. God's reign in the lives of individuals is the beginning of that kingdom and the basis for affirming its final consummation. Christians are pilgrims, but it is the faith of pilgrims which is the basis for the resurrection and kingdom hope. Because they know of the power of God now, they are able to affirm the eventual advent of the fullness of the kingdom. In Calvin's *Institutes,* the section on the resurrection stands at the end of the material on the Christian life. This is a reminder that it is the present faith of Christians which is related to the resurrection faith. Without the latter, faith would be in vain. But without present faith as its authentic basis, people believe in the kingdom because of fear. For Luther "the fear of the gallows" was an impossible reason for being a Christian. Only the one whose faith is meaningful in the present is safely permitted to think of the future life.

Neither Luther nor Calvin speculated on the nature of the future life. Luther believed that God's kingdom would soon be at hand. He interpreted the upheavals of his day to be the travail and tribulation before the end. This mistaken historical judgment does not, however, invalidate the affirmation of a kingdom which in its fullness depends wholly on the act of God, and certainly not upon our calculations.

The kingdom cannot be described.

> For though we very truly hear that the Kingdom of God will be filled with splendor, joy, happiness, and glory, yet when these things are spoken of, they remain utterly remote from our perception, and, as it

were, wrapped in obscurities, until that day comes when he will reveal to us his glory, that we may behold it face to face.[27]

It is more wonderful than the joy of present faith, yet that joy is sufficient for the present. Luther and Calvin believed in the future life, in the fullness of God's kingdom. But they were not obsessed with it. Because their hope in its final reality was grounded in faith itself, they confidently lived in the present world.

[27] *Ibid.,* III, xxv, 10.

CHAPTER III

Other Reformation Patterns

While Luther, Melanchthon, Calvin, Zwingli, Bucer, and others were laying the foundations for the development of the Lutheran and Reformed traditions (see Ch. IV), there were other Reformation developments in Germany, Switzerland, Holland, and England. Chief among these were the Anabaptist and related movements on the Continent and the English Reformation. Both of these were triggered by the work of the reformers we have discussed, but they also had independent roots. Their patterns of thought and institution were forged not only in opposition to the medieval church but also in contrast with the Lutheran and Reformed developments. For the Anabaptists, Luther, Calvin, and Zwingli had not gone far enough in the restoration of the New Testament church forms; for the Anglicans, they had departed too far from the historical traditions of the church. Both of these movements thus represent distinctive (though not wholly independent) Reformation traditions.

Radical Reformers and an Emerging Anabaptist Tradition

During the very period in which Luther was thinking through the implications of the newly rediscovered faith, there appeared other leaders and movements who thought of the reconstitution of the church in ways much more radical. Many of these groups arose independently of each other. But common to them was the conviction that the presence of the Spirit of God in the lives of believers called for a drastic change in belief and practice beyond anything envisaged by Luther, Calvin, or Zwingli. These movements were also linked by their repudiation of the sacramental understanding, whether that of Zwingli, Calvin, or Luther, and a clear demand, if baptism was at all to be practiced, for believer's baptism. Dividing the groups were such issues as whether the sword should be laid aside or used in the service of God, whether sacraments should be dramatically recast or abandoned entirely, whether Scripture was a normative pattern for life or an early infancy document of the church now to be abandoned, whether theological work was of the essence of faith or an impediment.

The phrase *radical Reformation* has rightly largely replaced the *left wing of the Reformation* in referring to these individuals and groups, for it combines the meaning of getting at the root of an issue with putting into operation what is discovered, no matter what the consequences. The result may be withdrawal or direct engagement with societal powers, in both cases posing a clear alternative to existing acceptable practices.

From the standpoint of the emerging Lutheran and Reformed traditions, as well as Roman Catholicism, such individuals and groups were indeed unacceptable, meaning, that they should have had no right to exist. This was an age in which toleration of fundamental differences was hardly on the horizon of consciousness. Hence, for the sake of the common order of society, one in which it was felt that truth and practice had to cohere, views outside certain parameters were outlawed, with governmental power as the executioner. Obversely, these individuals and groups had no power; hence, they were the victims, indeed to the extent that for some of them persecution was considered the concomitant of a true faith. The resultant situation was one in which those seizing political control in order to manifest the forming power of the gospel for society, and those wishing only to be left free to create societies of faith without relation to governmental structures, were equally the victims of persecution and death.

While scholars have differed in grouping the individuals and movements that fell outside of the then acceptable standards of those who held power, our purposes are served by making reference, first, to diverse activities that did not for long fit any of the existing movements (such as Karlstadt's pilgrimage through the Lutheran, Reformed, and Anabaptist alternatives, or Schwenkfeld's and Franck's individual spiritualism, or the anti-trinitarianism of Servetus); second, to individuals and movements that tried to create a new Kingdom (such as Thomas Münzer or the Münster episode); and third, to the formation of an Anabaptist tradition in its various forms. While the individuals and groups in the first and second categories affected the historical events of their time and were frequently quoted in subsequent movements, no organized religious movements stemmed directly from them. Inasmuch as identifiable churches stemmed from the third category, more attention will be given to the Anabaptist development than to the others.

Diverse Radical Approaches

One of the earliest manifestations of the radical Reformation spirit, to which reference has already been made, occurred in the city of Wittenberg while Luther was in seclusion at the Wartburg (1521). Here a group under the leadership of Andreas Karlstadt insisted that the reform of the church included the rejection of images and music as well as of the medieval understanding of the Mass. They believed that the former as well as the latter interfered with the worship of God through genuinely spiritual means. The stress upon the spiritual was carried further with the arrival of the Wittenberg "prophets" from the neighboring town of Zwickau. Insisting that God had spoken directly to them through the spirit, these individuals declared the Bible to be unnecessary. Moreover, they announced that God's kingdom was at hand in the reign of those who were genuinely spiritual. The ungodly would soon be destroyed.

Yet Karlstadt should not only be identified with the Zwickau prophets. He had been the dean of the theological faculty in Wittenberg, a man whose theological credentials were clear, and who himself based his insights on the understanding of Scripture, perhaps with some impatience in wanting to put them into practice. Karlstadt has the distinction of having performed the first evangelical eucharist, reading a simplified Latin mass with no reference to sacrifice, repeating the words of institution in German instead of Latin, and of having the lay people themselves take the bread and cup in their own hands. But Karlstadt, under pressure, removed himself from Wittenberg to a parish at Orlamunde, where he identified with the peasants, himself farming as one, and increasingly rejected the concept of presence in the Lord's Supper. Perhaps less deservedly than others, he became a symbol of the radical and was forced to flee from place to place, though in his last years he became a professor at Basel.

Of more radical temperament than either Andreas Karlstadt or the Zwickau prophets was Thomas Münzer. Like Karlstadt, he started with Luther but ended with a theology of a quite different order. His liturgical experiments in the city of Allstedt in 1523–1524 were widely hailed, even by traditional reformers, and his theological speculations and historical judgments were well informed. Apparently, he was among the first to date the "fall" of the church in the early centuries, basing his judgments on his reading of Eusebius. Münzer's theological assertions to the effect that God's spirit spoke directly to the human spirit — Scripture not being its source but merely its confirmation —

and that truth needed to be defended, indeed established, by the saints, using the sword if necessary, immediately placed him in jeopardy. Moreover, his various attempts to establish the rule of the saints, particularly in Allstedt and then in Mulhausen, sealed his destiny. While it is doubtful that Münzer had any direct responsibility for the revolt of the peasants in 1524–1525, he did identify with them, seeing their struggles as a medium through which the reign of the Spirit would be realized, firmly established, and the power of the saints used to destroy the ungodly. Thus, Münzer shared with the other reformers the idea that the ungodly should not be permitted; but his interpretation differed from theirs. While the other reformers felt that the rulers alone could exercise such power, Münzer firmly believed that it belonged to the saints. It was inevitable that such an outlook would conflict with the overwhelming power of the princes and the reformers.

Münzer was present at the decisive battle at Frankenhausen, in which the peasants were unequivocably routed. Münzer apparently encouraged them in battle, citing David and Gideon as heroes who had fought and won against insuperable odds. But when the bloody end was near, Münzer fled. He was found in hiding, identified, interrogated, and beheaded. It is no wonder that he became the symbol of all the evils of the peasants and the rule of the saints, even if he did have much less to do with them than the reformers and the political powers believed.

The best-known attempt to use force as a means of establishing the rule of the saints occurred a decade after the Peasants' Revolt in the city of Münster, which the leaders called the "New Jerusalem." The city, first under the sway of the preaching of Bernard Rothmann, soon found itself under the successive leadership of two lay Dutch individuals, Jan Matthijs and Jan van Leyden. Here, all books except the Bible were burned and those individuals who did not submit to baptism, though baptized already in infancy, were exiled from the city. The goods of life were shared in accord with the practice described in the book of Acts, and the motivation for this was both religious and social. The groups also instituted the practice of polygamy. (Luther, too, had not had a wholly good record on this problem, as his consent to the bigamy of Philip of Hesse indicates, though that consent was given grudgingly and under peculiar circumstances.) Aside from powerful sociological reasons for this brief venture into polygamy (notably the surplus of women over men in certain areas), two religious factors must also be noted. First, the reconstitution of the faith was so thoroughgoing that even the traditional ethic of monogamy had to be examined. Second, some felt that precedent was at hand in the example of some of the Old Testament patriarchs. Although the practice in Münster led to immorality, it must be kept in mind that in principle polygamy was intended as an answer to the temptation of immorality. Here is a case where practice had the opposite effect of the intention.

Münster was of course besieged and, eventually, through deceit, starvation, and the sheer power of the armies, the city fell, its principal leaders hung in cages as a gruesome reminder of the rule of the saints.

The militant activities of Thomas Münzer and the later events in the city of Münster were not typical of the outlook of countless individuals who rejected the Reformed and Lutheran developments. There were others who believed in the imminent end of the present stage of history and the advent of the reign of the saints. But in contrast to the revolutionaries, they counseled patient waiting for the end (e.g., Melchior Hofmann). There continued to be many also who believed in the direct accessibility of the Spirit apart from the Bible, and who considered the Scriptures unnecessary for salvation (e.g., Hans Denck). There were those who emphasized the individual relation to God without reference to the community, such as Caspar Schwenkfeld and Sebastian Franck. Franck had no interest in returning to the primitive Christian church, considering Scripture and the sacraments as necessary only for the infancy of faith. Hence, community was a name for the aggregate of free spirits under the sway of the Holy Spirit, not a group formed in a common ethos.

All of the preceding individuals shared with an emerging Anabaptist development an outlook which rejected the Reformed and Lutheran tradition and affirmed one or another tenet of faith with great vigor. This development contributed to the attendant confusion in which all radical groups were lumped together. Actually, however, the leaders of the Swiss radicals, while agreeing with much that Thomas Münzer said, rejected his claim for the sword on the part of Christians; others were far too much concerned with a truly visible Christian community to accept the views of Schwenkfeld or Franck, though they too stressed the intimate connection of faith and the Spirit.

The Formation of an Anabaptist Tradition

Establishing Christian community on the basis of and in accord with the descriptions of the church in the New Testament was the cardinal rock for the Anabaptists. The beginnings date from activities in the Swiss cantons, where there were such leaders as Michael Schlatter, the cultured Conrad Grebel, and the distinguished scholar Balthasar Hübmaier. Conflict early emerged with the Zwinglians in Zurich, perhaps particularly because the Anabaptist leaders, who shared much with Zwingli, believed that Zwingli's views demanded baptism of believers, not infants. In Zurich, the initially friendly disputations about the faith between Anabaptist and Reformed leaders turned into an outright campaign against the former, with the latter receiving the support of civil authorities.

Ostensibly, the point at which the Anabaptist New Testament views of the church most clearly and visibly were in conflict with the Reformed groups in Switzerland (and generally elsewhere) was the former's practice of baptizing persons who had already been baptized as infants. Hence the nickname Anabaptist (i.e., "rebaptizer"). Since the Anabaptists held that there could be no valid baptism apart from the faith of the believer, they rejected the notion that they "rebaptized." Infant baptism was no baptism at all. But this contention carried no weight with those who accepted infant baptism, and the latter were able to find legal basis for suppression of the Anabaptists in an ancient legal code of the Emperor Justinian, which forbade rebaptism.

At the heart of the conflict were different conceptions of the faith as expressed in the understanding of the church (these are discussed in the next section). However, the excesses of some Anabaptist groups unfortunately fed fuel to the fire of those who already feared the radical emphasis upon the spirit. They saw in this a source of a new disorder equal in danger to that of the medieval church. The good moral character of many of the Anabaptists, including their leaders, was conceded by the opposition. Nevertheless, it was felt that the implications of their position led to disorder and threatened the orderly affairs of the newly emerging Reformation churches. In the course of events, Anabaptist groups were banished and persecuted, while most of the leaders became martyrs through burning or drowning. (The latter was a particularly taunting form of death because of its associations with immersion in baptism.) Few of the leaders of the Anabaptist movement died in bed. But in spite of uprootings, sufferings, and the dangers of death, Anabaptist communities arose throughout north central Europe. In Bern, Basel, Strasbourg, Augsburg, Nuremberg, and Münster, there continued to be thriving communities, and numerous groups sprang up in south Germany.

But the core of the Anabaptist movement as it was destined to have its major impact upon posterity did not develop in either Switzerland or Germany. It came instead from Moravia and Holland, where the chief leaders respectively were Jakob Hutter and Menno Simons. The Hutterites, named after Jakob Hutter, became a disciplined and continuing Anabaptist community in Moravia. Menno Simons was undoubtedly the most outstanding figure in the Anabaptist tradition, and the Mennonites in Holland named after him contributed to the life of Protestantism in ways far beyond the confines of their own groups. Neither the English Baptists nor the Quakers can be traced directly to the Mennonites, but there were points of contact. It is not too much to say that these Anabaptists provided a type of spirituality that had its effects upon all those with whom they came into contact.

Later, the Mennonites in Holland surrendered much of their distinctive witness. The Anabaptist tradition continued with vitality in settlements in Poland, Russia, and Paraguay, but most of all in the Mennonite communities in Pennsylvania.

Tenets of Central Anabaptists

In the mainstream of Anabaptist life and thought there was agreement that a reconstitution of the church according to the pattern of the New Testament must be effected without compromise at any point. Luther, for example, allowed many existing practices having no basis in the New Testament, provided they did not contradict the essentials of the faith. Not so the Anabaptists. This only proved that Luther, as well as Zwingli, had not gone far enough. They were "halfway" thinkers who had made an excellent beginning but had not drawn the logical conclusion their positions demanded.

Actually it was not a matter of drawing a conclusion.[1] We have to do here with a fundamentally different understanding of the church and the Christian life. That is why the Anabaptists form an independent Reformation tradition. Basic to the Anabaptist view is the conviction that the church is a voluntary association of Christians patterned after the New Testament. For the reformers, as we noted in the previous chapter, the church, too, is a community of believers in which faith is related to every aspect of its life. But there is a difference between believing that faith is decisive for the church, and believing that the faith and life of Christians in themselves have a style demanding a particular form of the church. In the sense that the Anabaptists drew the latter conclusion, they could claim that they, rather than the reformers, were carrying out a Reformation only halfway completed by the reformers.

It is only as one understands the content of the statement that the church is a community of those who have experienced the living Christ that the genuine differences appear. Luther, Calvin, Zwingli, and the Anabaptists alike could make this statement. But the Anabaptists drew the further inference that a new pattern of life is at the heart of the New Testament, and that therefore the New Testament forms must be followed in every respect, including the order and practice of the church.

For the Anabaptists, then, the new life in Christ through the Spirit rather than justification by faith is the center of the New Testament

[1] One of the recurring sources of confusion in Protestantism is that those who stand in the Lutheran and Reformed tradition see only anarchy in the outlook of those who stress the Spirit and voluntary association, and that those who stand in the "free church" tradition prefer to view themselves as having carried the Reformation to its logical conclusion.

faith and therefore of the church. The life of the redeemed, the presence of the Spirit in believers, is foremost. Not the Word of God as found in the Bible, but the experience of Christ's presence is the foundation of the church. The Spirit of Christ spread abroad in the human heart is more important than any endeavor to understand the content of God's disclosure, whether found in the Bible or expressed in theological statements. The New Testament is a book of the Christian life, and authoritative in that sense.

The Anabaptists vigorously responded to all problems from the conviction that all that matters is the manifest vitality of Christian saints. That conviction provides the clue to what they rejected and what they affirmed. They were not interested in how individuals became saints, but in the life of people as they walked on a path leading toward perfection. That is why the struggle over justification was not central to their outlook and frequently appeared to them as theological bickering. They were interested in the "life" of the church rather than in its thought. Theology was considered a highly suspicious enterprise in which theologians spun out theses which were a stumbling block to those of simple but genuine faith. Anabaptists trusted farmers and craftsmen more than theologians. Those who were the regenerate constituted the church, quite apart from how they understood the relation of faith and works. Important was, not that God forgave sins, but the new life possible in Christ.

But theology was only one of the ways in which the Anabaptists saw the church as threatened by loss of its life. The church also lost its true nature when it was no longer confined to the regenerated and their own tests for membership in the community. For many Anabaptists, the adoption of Christianity as the religion of the empire (under Constantine) marked the "fall" of the church. Belonging to the church became no longer a matter of decision but of birth and social destiny. The vitality and very essence of the church as a voluntary association was destroyed. There were others who dated the fall of the church with the Council of Nicaea in 325. This represented the crystallization of trinitarian thought, precipitated by the intrigues of the powerful Roman empire and expressed through the speculation of philosophers. For others, it was the enforcement of infant baptism in 407 (with penalty for failure to comply).

Common to the different theories of the fall of the church was the contention that the true nature of the church as a voluntary, disciplined community of saints had been abandoned. To the Anabaptists, Luther and Calvin were not sufficiently clear on this point. The reformers' hopes of community or territorial churches, enforced through the arms of the state, were themselves considered a part of the pattern which characterized a fallen church.

Since the only possible church is a voluntary but disciplined community of saints patterned after the New Testament community, there is no distinction, not even of function, between clergy and laity. Those who have the Spirit are Christians and therefore equally a source of Christian truth and action. The priesthood of all believers refers not only to each person's relation to God and to one's priesthood to neighbor, as in Luther; it refers also to the equality of all people in the Christian community with respect to formal function. No person has any status not possessed by all. (Reluctantly, many of the Anabaptist communities did have to separate functions in such a way that some functioned as "clergy." But nowhere, except among the Quakers, has lay responsibility been greater.)

It was the community, chiefly through its leaders, which exercised the discipline required in the life of the church. The church was a voluntary and free association; but it implied a discipline and a way of life. Those who violated God's commands and did not exhibit the presence of the Spirit were warned, sometimes placed on probation, not infrequently punished, and occasionally barred from the community. But the church could maintain its discipline and life only by being a society "withdrawn." Therefore, Anabaptists were concerned primarily with fellow Christians, except in the case of missionary preaching (the object of which obviously was to bring others into the fold).

The purity of the community had to be maintained, both by internal discipline and by the inclusion only of those who are Christians by free decisions. Thus, the church must be a separate community, and in particular separate from the state. Most Anabaptists admitted that the state was a necessary institution for humankind and even for themselves, but they did not find it possible to assume any responsibility for it. For example, they felt that a Christian could not be a magistrate because that would contaminate and perhaps vitiate the witness one must make to the peace and order of the new life in Christ. Likewise, they refused to participate in war and to swear oaths of any kind. These acts violated the new life in Christ as exhibited in the injunctions of the New Testament.

It was the insistence upon the church as a community of the new life, patterned after the New Testament, which led to the Anabaptist view of baptism. Wrote Menno Simons:

> We are not regenerated because we have been baptized . . . but we are baptized because we have been regenerated by faith and the Word of God (I Pet. 1:23). Regeneration is not the result of baptism, but baptism the result of regeneration. This can indeed not be controverted by any man, or disproved by the Scriptures.[2]

---

[2] Harold S. Bender, *Menno Simons' Life and Writings* (Mennonite Publishing House, Scottdale, Pa., 1936), p. 78.

Baptism is the indication that one believes in the forgiveness of sins and the new life in Christ. It is not a medium for either, but rather an expression of the acceptance of both. It is not absolutely necessary, being one of the least of the commandments given by Christ.

Such a view of baptism demands believers who have reached some degree of consciousness and maturity. Simons rejected Luther's concept of infantile faith. By definition, infant baptism is meaningless. Moreover, the Anabaptists could find no basis whatsoever for infant baptism in the Bible. Infant baptism, therefore, violates the two criteria of the church, the voluntary nature of faith and the New Testament pattern. It places the cart before the horse; baptism must follow faith, not precede it. Baptism is not an instrument of grace; it is an expression of the fact of grace already visibly present.

The same logic applies to the Lord's Supper. In the words of Balthasar Hübmaier:

> That is the true communion of the saints, which is not a communion because the bread is broken; but where the bread is broken because the communion has preceded and been enclosed in the heart since Christ has come in the flesh. For not all who break the bread are partakers of the body and blood of Christ, which I prove by the traitor Judas. But those who are now in communion inwardly and in spirit, they may also use this bread and wine worthily in an outward way. . . .[3]

In no sense does anything special happen as the elements of the Lord's Supper are distributed. It is the outward expression of a communion and community which exists, the fellowship of forgiven sinners who are saints. It is a rite of fellowship inaugurated in the early church. There is no presence of Christ in the elements.

Such are the main tenets of this radical Reformation tradition. The church is a creation of the voluntary, free association of believers, uncoerced by either hierarchy or state. Everything which threatens this way of life of the church must be rejected; not violently, but through suffering if necessary. The faith of the Christian is nourished by the Bible. But more than that, the Bible provides a definite pattern for the expression of that faith through the discipline of the saints. In the Anabaptist tradition, the freedom of the Christian is combined with the utmost of discipline in community. While grace is affirmed, the freedom of the individual to both receive and live out the new life in Christ is accented. Hence, the sanctified rather than the justified life is featured. At the same time, that sanctified life, with its own discipline, represents a colony in the world, willing to accept the suffering that comes, a badge that one is truly a Christian.

[3] Balthasar Hübmaier, *A Form for the Celebration of the Lord's Supper*, in Harry Emerson Fosdick, *Great Voices of the Reformation* (New York, 1952), pp. 312–313.

The English Reformation and the Formation of Anglicanism

The Anglican tradition, which in the United States is known as the Episcopal church, was explicitly forged in the context of English history, so much so that it is necessary to speak of an "English Reformation." There were, to be sure, important influences from the Continent, but both in the break with Rome and in the pattern of reform, the English movement was distinctive. More than any other of the churches with a Reformation history, Anglicanism bears the marks of a national church. In order to understand the ethos and development characterized as central Anglicanism, it is necessary to look briefly at the events of the English Reformation, with its unique intertwining of affairs of state and church.

From Reforming Activities to the Elizabethan Settlement

In England, as on the Continent, there were signs of unrest before the Reformation. We have already noted the activities of Wycliffe (see Ch. I). While the Lollard tradition had been suppressed, much of its reforming spirit and outlook survived. There were other religious associations also, such as the "Christian brethren" or "known men." In addition, the Renaissance humanist tradition was strong. One need only recall the names of such men as John Colet, the dean of St. Paul's, and Sir Thomas More, author of the famous *Utopia*. Moreover, it was in England that the outlook of Erasmus was found to be most congenial.

More explosive than the foregoing was the relation of the English nation to both papacy and foreign political powers. The suppression by the papacy of some of the English monasteries (a practice later adopted by Henry VIII on a much wider scale and also mainly for financial reasons), with the revenue from sale of the properties going to Rome, raised the ire of many English on the scene. The assignment of Italian priests, many of whom were unable to speak English, was a further source of offense. In general, the English were tired of domination and interference by foreign power.

The spark which lit the fire was the refusal of the papacy to annul the marriage of Henry VIII and Catherine of Aragon. Although the papacy had waived canon law to permit Henry to marry the widow of his brother, it was unwilling to annul the marriage, primarily because of the risk of finally alienating the Holy Roman Emperor and King of Spain, Charles V (nephew of Catherine), upon whose good will the papacy had to depend at this time. Henry's concern for the continuation of his line and the stability of England had been expressed long before his fascination with Anne Boleyn. Since severe civil strife had been occasioned in an earlier time by lack of a male descendant for the throne, he was much exercised over the increasingly unlikely prospect of a male heir issuing from his marriage to Catherine. In order to effect an annulment, Henry broke the ties with Rome by a series of bold acts. Having deposed Cardinal Wolsey, he forbade appeals to Rome without the King's consent, and required through Parliamentary act that the clergy continue to function despite possible papal excommunication. In Thomas Cranmer, who had been sympathetic to the annulment and had suggested a university rather than canon law decision, the King found a ready Archbishop of Canterbury who might be the primate of all England. But the top position Henry reserved for himself. The Act of Supremacy (1534) declared: "The King's majesty justly and rightly is and ought to be and shall be reputed the only supreme head in earth of the Church of England called *"Anglicana Ecclesia."* Nevertheless, he was not a priest. He appointed, but could not consecrate, bishops; he could defend the faith, but he could not declare dogma. But he was head of a new national church.

Under Henry, however, "reformation" in practice or doctrine was not very extensive. He insisted on a Bible in every parish, with a chapter to be read each Sunday. The Ten Articles of Religion of 1536 made reference to the authority of the Bible and justification by faith, but made these no more central than in the medieval church generally. In fact, Henry himself approved of the use of images, invocations to the departed saints, the concept of purgatory and masses for those who still sojourned there, transubstantiation together with communion in one element only, celibacy for the clergy, private masses, and auricular confessions. With this outlook, it may seem startling that Henry destroyed images, turned into revenue those made of precious materials, and confiscated the properties of the monasteries. Given the aversion of the English to the alleged idleness and opulence of monastic life among those who lived with Lollard memories, Henry had little opposition to his practice of turning these assets to the advantage of the national treasury.

The views of Henry were not shared by the then Archbishop of Canterbury, Thomas Cranmer, whose influence reached its height in the reign of Edward VI, only son of Henry VIII. Edward was still a young boy at the time of his accession (1547), and the regime was first under the protectorate of the Duke of Somerset, and then of the Duke of Northumberland. In both instances, the affairs of church were dominated by Cranmer and his associates, including many of the Continental reformers who in this period found refuge in England. Among these were Martin Bucer, the Strasbourg reformer, and Peter Martyr, one of the early Lutheran theologians. It was during this period that the English Reformation was closest to that of the Continent. During the first protectorate, a general Lutheran outlook prevailed, and during the second, views reflecting the Reformed tradition. The two prayer books of Edward's reign represent the two traditions. Although these views did not prevail, permanent changes dating from this period center in the abolition of considerable medieval ceremony and liturgical practice. Rome was declared wrong in faith, transubstantiation was decisively rejected, marriage of the clergy was permitted, auricular confession was abolished, and communion was administered to the people with both bread and wine. But during this period when the continental influence was at its highest, the episcopacy was accepted without question and pains were taken to guarantee adequate succession.

Edward, always in poor health, died after only six years on the throne and was succeeded by his older sister Mary, the Roman Catholic daughter of Henry's first wife. It was only natural that policy should be reversed. Many who leaned toward the continental reforms, including Cranmer, were burned at the stake. A ruthless attempt was undertaken to reestablish Roman Catholicism. However, a full Roman Catholic approach to life no longer seemed possible for the English nation. But after five years, Mary died and was followed by Elizabeth, daughter of Henry and Anne Boleyn.

It was under Elizabeth's forty-five-year reign that a religious settlement was made which still gives form to Anglicanism today. Her motivations were undoubtedly colored as much by the desire for order and peace in the church as a way to political stability as by definite religious convictions. She decided against Roman Catholicism and for a broad Protestantism, far from the hopes of the Marian exiles who had returned from the Continent. The extremes of both Rome and the continental Reformation were rejected. While holding a firm grip, Elizabeth seemed even to relax control by the state by taking the title of "supreme governor" rather than "supreme head" of the Church of England.

Only in worship did uniformity appear essential, and that for the well-being of both church and state. Nevertheless, there was some demand for minimal doctrinal statements. The promulgation of the Thirty-nine Articles, which were accepted primarily as a guide rather than as a binding rule of faith, served this purpose. These are broadly Protestant in tenor, with stress at various points on the positive use of the tradition of the church. The sufficiency of Scripture for salvation and the authority of the church are equally stressed. The church has the duty of settling both ceremonial matters and controversies in faith, though in no case dare it decide upon a course contrary to

God's Word. The church, therefore, has a responsibility for the Bible and its proper interpretation. The papacy, purgatory, indulgences, and the veneration of the images and relics are rejected as unwarranted by Scripture and contrary to the Word of God. On the theological side, justification by faith is affirmed as against works, and the concept of single predestination is affirmed for the comfort of good persons and believers. On the Lord's Supper, transubstantiation is rejected, but the real presence of the body of Christ "after an heavenly and spiritual manner" is affirmed. The church is defined (as also by the continental reformers) as an institution in which the Word is properly preached and the sacraments rightly administered.

At the most, the Thirty-nine Articles have had a relative authority. Anglicanism has no doctrinal tests, and the Articles are viewed as but the setting forth of minimal aspects of the faith for the sake of direction in a period of history when foundations had to be laid. Even the enforced subscription to the Articles by clergy in the time of Elizabeth were based on this sort of consideration. The words of John Bramhall are instructive:

> We do not suffer any man 'to reject' the Thirty-nine articles of the Church of England 'at his pleasure'; yet neither do we look upon them as essentials of saving faith or 'legacies of Christ and of His Apostles'; but in a mean, as pious opinions fitted for the preservation of unity. Neither do we oblige any man to believe them, but only not to contradict them.[4]

Although the Articles are included in the Prayer Book and have been revised from time to time, Anglicans have thought of them as an adequate expression of the faith in the particular historical context rather than as a binding rule of faith for the church. The Nicene Creed and Apostles' Creed, which are affirmed in the Articles, are considered more truly normative. But even these are not thought of as complete and exclusive dogmatic statements. Rather they are accepted as precise and concise summaries of the broad dimensions of biblical faith, more adequately understood in intention through recitation or song than in exegesis or analysis.

And so the process continued even to the present. The revised Book of Common Prayer for the Episcopal Church in the United States, approved in 1979, includes the Thirty-nine Articles among Historical Documents of the Church, along with a section from the Council of Chalcedon on the union of the divine and human natures in the person of Christ, the Creed of Saint Athanasius, the Preface to the First Book of Common Prayer of 1549, statements adopted

---

[4] John Bramhall, *Schism Guarded*, in More and Cross, *Anglicanism* (London, 1935), p. 186.

by the House of Bishops in connection with the Chicago-Lambeth Quadrilateral of 1888, and Resolution ii of the Lambeth Conference, the latter dealing with the basis upon which reunion of the churches would be possible. This conference resolution, reflecting worldwide Anglicanism, states the basis as follows: "a) The Holy Scriptures of the Old and New Testaments, as 'containing all things necessary to salvation,' and as being the rule and ultimate standard of faith; b) The Apostles' Creed, as the Baptismal symbol; and the Nicene Creed, as the sufficient statement of the Christian faith; c) The two sacraments ordained by Christ Himself — Baptism and the Supper of the Lord — ministered with unfailing use of Christ's words of Institution, and of the elements ordained by Him; d) The Historic Episcopate, locally adapted in the methods of its administration to the varying needs of the nations and peoples called of God into the Unity of His Church." Hence, even in this 1979 collection of statements, the aim is to provide necessary benchmarks, but not to define them too scrupulously.

The Book of Common Prayer itself was of far greater significance than the Thirty-nine Articles, both for the Elizabethan settlement and for subsequent Anglicanism. Like the Articles, the Prayer Book was based on similar documents formulated under the previous reign but was given its distinctive form in the time of Elizabeth. It reflects the tendency to combine much of the ancient tradition of the church with some of the Reformation insights. Sometimes, the two aspects lie side by side, as in the following sentences from an early communion service: "The body of our Lord Jesus Christ, which was given for thee, preserve thy body and soul unto everlasting life. Take and eat this in remembrance that Christ died for thee, and feed on him in thy heart by faith, with thanksgiving." Nothing less than the genuine presence of Christ in the elements is combined with the Zwinglian concept of remembrance. The Communion service also retains the concept of sacrifice, but Christ is an oblation once offered.

The Prayer Book contains prayers and liturgical forms dating from the early history of the church. These were adapted to the new situation, and practices considered contrary to the Word were abandoned in true Reformation form. The whole work reflects an unmistakable biblical basis. Each service encompasses the full sweep of the gospel message. Moreover, through prescribed collects and Scripture readings for each service, full coverage of the various aspects of the faith is guaranteed year after year. In this way a prescribed form is combined with wholeness and variety of content. No single religious idea is singled out for emphasis. The totality of faith is represented in dramatic form.

Through the Thirty-nine Articles, the Prayer Book, and further steps taken by Elizabeth to insure the episcopal succession, the main lines for Anglicanism were definitely established. The Elizabethan settlement was in many ways the thought and practice of the Edwardian period, but modified in the direction of greater stress on the traditions and forms which had developed in the history of the church. It was a broad Catholicism, qualified by inclusion of central Reformation concerns. The settlement was formalized by the Act of Supremacy, which reaffirmed the place of the Crown in matters of state and church against all foreign pressures, and the Act of Uniformity, which assured uniformity of worship and practice.

Further Development of Anglican Self-Understanding

If the general direction of Anglicanism was settled during the early years of Elizabeth's reign, the full meaning of the new development had yet to be explored. Undoubtedly, Anglicans would have reflected on the implications of their distinctive community in any case, but this process was speeded by the appearance and rapid growth of a competing group, the Puritans (see Ch. V). The challenge of Puritanism, beginning during Elizabeth's time, led Anglican thinkers to an acute awareness that their new experiment was rooted in a very old tradition and could be justified on various grounds.

Foremost among such thinkers was Richard Hooker (d. 1600) whose *Ecclesiastical Polity* was written with the Puritans in mind. The immediate question at issue was the primacy of the episcopacy and episcopal succession. At first the episcopacy had more or less been taken for granted in the new English church. But the Puritans could find no basis for it in the Bible. Many Anglicans thought they could. Hooker, too, was convinced that a case could be made for the primacy of bishops in the New Testament; but he also admitted the possibility of reading the record in another way, as the Puritan Cartwright and his followers had done. In contrast to the Puritans, he did not rest his case upon the New Testament alone. Tradition and reason, too, were criteria for the church and when they were added to the New Testament, the argument seemed incontrovertible. For over fifteen hundred years, argued Hooker, episcopacy had been the dominant form of church government. Moreover, it was reasonable. It made for decent and proper order in the church, and what made good sense was worth having.

Behind the defense of the episcopacy lay more than immediately meets the eye. It involved a different understanding of the gospel and its relation to church than that held by either the Puritans or the reformed bodies on the Continent. But this was also quite different from the Roman views.

Hooker's concept of law and reason drew much from the medieval tradition, particularly Aquinas. The nature of God, the structure of the world, and the order of the church formed part of a single whole in which the church completed and fulfilled the natural order. Continuity, rather than discontinuity, marked the relation of God and the world. But Hooker's view of redemption in relation to the church was nearer to that of the Reformation bodies than to the Roman concept. Thus Hooker looked to an essential tradition of which neither the Reformation bodies nor the Roman church was the true descendant.

This general position was further elaborated in the seventeenth century by the group of distinguished preachers and writers known as the Caroline divines (e.g., Lancelot Andrewes, Thomas Barlow, William Beveridge, John Bramhall, Gilbert Burnet, William Laud, Robert Sanderson, Jeremy Taylor, John Wilkins, and John Woolton). These leaders considered themselves neither merely Protestant nor Roman Catholic, but those who held the "Middle Way," as John Donne expressed it, or those who held "the mean between two extremes," as Sanderson put it. Certainly the Caroline divines did not agree with each other on all points. But they represented a common perspective, and a faith in the distinctive character of Anglicanism as at once "Protestant and Reformed according to the Ancient Catholic Church." They denied the authority of Rome because they considered it tyrannical, and the emphasis on the Bible of the Puritans because they considered it bibliolatry and an offense against reason. Hence, like Hooker, they insisted upon scripture, tradition, and reason. They were united in a studied *via media*. Theologically, this meant an emphasis upon the early fathers of the church (and occasionally the implication that the early period was a kind of golden age of the church). Aquinas was quoted extensively and when stripped of the distinctively Roman aspects, he was considered more congenial than Luther or Calvin. But the reformers, too, were quoted. The Caroline divines were interested in a balanced religious outlook, related to the practical concerns of life. If they did not usually push any religious affirmation to its logical conclusion or always relate it successfully to others, this was a defect of their virtue of insisting that the totality of the life of the church was more important than great emphasis upon one religious concept. Their goal was a theology comprehensive in scope, conducive to morality, and always related to the life of the church.

For many, the Caroline divines represent the central stream of Anglicanism. This is perhaps easier to see in retrospect than it was in their own time, since most of the writers worked in a period of political and religious upheaval. In the civil strife of the mid-seventeenth century, the whole concept of the English church was threatened, though the restoration of the monarchy safely reestablished Anglicanism with greater strength than ever. This reestablishment was only slightly modified in the revolution of 1688 by the granting of greater privileges for dissenters.

The security of the restoration brought problems of its own, and first with the rise of the Latitudinarians. The term *Latitudinarian* was a nickname for theological liberals who emphasized tolerance and the primary role of reason in the theological enterprise. They were convinced that theology based upon reason could be demonstrated to be not at all contrary to revealed religion, and that, in fact, the religion of the Bible could be defended by appeal to reason.

The Latitudinarians made ascendant one element of the triumvirate of New Testament, tradition, and reason, thereby distorting the other two. The historical justification for their effort was the need to be creative in a period calling for readjustment. The new scientific discoveries demanded attention in the thinking of the churches and the Latitudinarians sought to relate the new knowledge to Christian faith by appeal to a common rational framework. They were liberals in a period when religion was not noted for that characteristic. They were among the first to advocate a genuine toleration which eventually triumphed in the English scene.

At the same time, however, men such as Stillingfleet and Tillotson reflected scarcely any of the evangelical outlook of the New Testament with its offer of mercy to sinful people. Both Latitudinarianism and the later more extreme accent upon the "reasonableness of religion," as presented by Locke, belong to a basic pattern in which the "rational" threatened the religious. By the second decade of the eighteenth century, the stress upon reason had made such inroads into Anglicanism that the Christian evangelical witness had all but disappeared. The fluid tradition had spread so thin that the waters no longer ran deep. Moreover, it appeared to many that the ecclesiastical machinery fostered rather than changed this situation. Thus, the eighteenth century saw the rise of the Wesleyan Movement as an attempt to recapture for the English church the living experience of redemption from sin (see Ch. VI). And in the nineteenth century, the Oxford Movement sought to recall the church to its Catholic heritage (in contrast both to an individualistic evangelicalism and a liberalism largely indifferent to the claims of gospel and church) while at the same time rejecting Roman interpretations of Catholicism.

In sum, Anglicanism is best understood as a broad stream, guided by a sense of order and tradition as guaranteed by the episcopacy and the Prayer Book. It asks no particular theological understanding, and has never been a theological church. Seldom has it had theological giants. It surmounted the crises of Reformation influences in its battles with Puritanism, and of Roman claims in connection with the Oxford Movement. It lost much of its vitality in the Latitudinarian Movement, but managed under pressure to regain it. For many, these three instances at least raise the question of how far the vitality of Anglicanism is dependent upon more tightly knit religious groups which basically challenge its interpretation of the role of the church.

In spite of this, Anglicanism can claim to represent a tattered but never broken tradition of the entire church. It reads its history as one which antedates the Reformation and preserves the significant elements in the life of the church since its inception. It claims, too, that in England the church was under the rule of Rome for a shorter period of time than on the Continent and that it stands, therefore, for the genuine tradition in contrast both to the Roman church, which distorted the tradition, and to the Protestants, who too rashly broke it.

For Anglicanism, the episcopal succession is the symbol and guarantee of the continuity of the faith in the life of the church. Anglicans differ as to whether the continuity is to be considered a continuity of the gospel symbolized by the line of bishops, or whether the succession of bishops is itself the continuity (through the laying on of hands since the time of the Apostles). The difference between the two ways of viewing succession is enormous. Nevertheless, the agreement that the church is one in its continuity makes it possible for individuals who so differ to remain together in a bond of fellowship. The sense of belonging to the communion of saints throughout the ages makes it possible for people of diverse outlook to live in the same church.

Anglicanism belongs to the history of the Reformation and to the history of Protestantism. But few Anglicans accept either the Reformation on the Continent or the English Reformation as normative. They prefer to think of themselves as belonging to a total history, purified from time to time through various reformations. Most think of themselves as Protestant and truly Catholic at the same time. In accord with the *via media,* they consider themselves Protestant in respect to continual *re*-formation and Catholic in the sense of the tradition and continuity of the church. Having ventured these general remarks, it is safest, nevertheless, to leave the question of whether Anglicanism is Protestant to the self-understanding of each Anglican, though for most Anglicans, the question is neither relevant nor vital.

CHAPTER IV

The Reformation Churches

The Lutheran and Reformed traditions are frequently called the Reformation churches, since they stem most directly from the activities of the major Continental reformers, Luther in the one case, Zwingli and Calvin in the other. Between them, they swept over most of Western Europe, and found their way to America, too. Here we can only outline the development, touching upon institutional and geographical expansion, and devoting most of our attention to the religious problems and outlooks of the two bodies.

The Lutheran Development

From the very beginning the Lutheran movement had the problem of determining its relations with the empire and princes on the one hand and of arbitrating differences of religious opinion within its own house, on the other. Precisely because the emperor had other urgent problems, he could not give time to stamping out the Lutheran "heresy." Lutheran churches prospered in this atmosphere to the point where they had to be accepted in one way or another. In 1524, the Diet of Nuremberg urged enforcing the decision of the Diet of Worms against Luther "insofar as possible." This qualification was itself a sign of the strength of the new movement. The second Diet of Speyer, in 1529, held at a time of a temporary setback for the Lutherans, accepted the principle of a territorial solution (see p. 74). Moreover, pending a final solution in a subsequent meeting, Lutheranism should be tolerated where it could not be suppressed. Catholic minorities in such Lutheran communities should be given religious liberty, but Lutheran minorities in Roman Catholic areas were not to be granted liberty of worship. Against this decision, the Lutherans declared "they must protest and testify publicly before God that they could do nothing contrary to His word." It was this witness and protest from which the name "Protestant" was first derived (see Ch. XIV).

The last attempts at reconciliation between Rome and the Lutheran group occurred in the Diet meeting at Augsburg in 1530, and in the ecclesiastical council at Regensburg in 1541. For the first meeting the Augsburg Confession was drafted by Philipp Melanchthon, who was the architect of the later Lutheran development. In the Confession, the common elements of the new group and Rome were featured, though the Lutheran view was frankly presented; justification by faith was affirmed and transubstantiation repudiated. The document did not bring unity nor did outright conflict result.

As at the Diet of Augsburg, the concept of transubstantiation proved to be a decisive dividing line in the Diet of Regensburg of 1541. In addition, some Protestants, such as Martin Bucer, would not grant papal dominion even if the other issues could have been resolved. The Inquisition followed, but it was impossible to stamp out the new movement. The only solution was the recognition of two faiths. This was accomplished through the principle of territorialism, viz., that the religion of a territory was to be that of its ruler. The two faiths were not to exist freely together. (In principle one could move to another territory if the religion where one lived turned out to be different from one's own.) Moreover, the Peace of Augsburg of 1555 recognized only Lutherans and Roman Catholics. The exclusion of other Protestant groups later became one of the contributory causes of the Thirty Years' War.

By 1555, Lutheranism had established itself in Germany as one of the two major groups. In the same century, Lutheran bodies were formed in East Prussia, Poland, Estonia, Hungary, and Transylvania. Directly to the north, Lutheranism became the established faith in Denmark and Norway. The Church of Sweden rejected the authority of Rome and adopted Luther's theology but did not take the name Lutheran and maintained the episcopal succession. A century later, in addition to the congregation in the Dutch settlement of New Amsterdam in America, Lutheran congregations were organized among the Swedes in Delaware. It was not until the eighteenth century, however, that a wave of German Lutherans settled in Pennsylvania, and it was this group which firmly planted Lutheranism in the new world.

Lutheranism spread rapidly and extensively. The controversies which beset it did not seriously hinder its early development, since the new religious movement met the religious aspirations of countless people. The controversies, in fact, manifest the exceeding vitality of the new movement, though in retrospect many think that the particular alternatives hardly left a real choice. Some of the issues came into focus through actual and assumed differences between the prophet of the Reformation, Luther, and its systematic exponent, Melanchthon. These differences, which were nuances rather than fundamental disagreements, grew partly out of misunderstanding and partly out of temperamental and cultural leanings. Luther met every new problem on the basis of the gospel message and never consciously wrote or thought in a systematic theological form. His consistency lay in a determined attempt to relate everything to the logic of faith. Melanchthon, a man of broad cultural, humanist, and classical interests, was more disposed to write self-contained tracts and to use the utmost of tact and mediation in every situation. The early edition of his *Loci Communes,* or "Common-Places in Theology," is a systematic discussion of the nature and implications of justification by faith. Although Luther rediscovered the power and meaning of the concept, he did not systematically discuss it as Melanchthon did.

The revision of the *Loci* and the Augsburg Confession give evidence that Melanchthon's formulations were phrased in such a way as to concurrently mediate differences and emphasize right doctrine and teaching. The latter could only be accomplished if the former was possible. In the controversies which developed later, the emphasis fell more upon correct doctrine, though not always in agreement with the views of Melanchthon. Not infrequently, occasional and almost offhand statements of Luther were tenaciously affirmed against Melanchthon. But whether in agreement or disagreement, the spirit of right thinking exemplified by Melanchthon increasingly formed a part of the Lutheran development. The seriousness of the demand for precise and rigorous thought is apparent in the renewed controversy over the physical presence of Christ in the elements and in the debates over various aspects of the Christian life.

1) The first controversy centered in the nature of Christ's presence in the elements of the Lord's Supper. Melanchthon, Calvin, and Luther rejected the Zwinglian conception of the Lord's Supper as a memorial or sign representing the drama of Christ's life and death. But on the nature of the presence of Christ in the sacrament, Melanchthon found himself nearer to Calvin than to Luther. All agreed that faith alone guarantees Christ's presence, but Luther also insisted upon the corporeal or physical presence of Christ in the elements (see Ch. II). He maintained that Christ was totally and genuinely present. He believed that a spiritual interpretation alone did not sufficiently take into account the total nature and activity of Christ and denied the bodily character of the risen Lord. It was therefore significant for the development of Lutheranism when Melanchthon rewrote the Augsburg Confession to permit just such an interpretation. In the conflict that ensued, the

conservative party won the victory over Melanchthon and believed that Luther's views had been vindicated. Actually, their literal understanding of the bodily presence of Christ in the elements led them to miss the point of Luther's insistence. They shifted the emphasis from the *meaning* of the bodily presence to a mere factual assertion of its necessity.

2) The second controversy dealt with the implications of the activity of the Spirit for the understanding of our humanity. It was agreed that God initiates and sustains faith. But what are we like in this process? Are we active or passive as the Spirit lays hold of us and directs us? The conservatives insisted that through the continuing presence of Christ in the believer, we are molded like a lump of clay. Melanchthon, however, contended that we are active and genuinely assert ourselves as ourselves even when God's power lays hold of us.

The issue was complicated in that the extreme conservatives overstated their case. Flacius, one of their representatives, used the concept of the lump of clay in a more than figurative sense. He defined total depravity as the complete loss of everything which makes us human, including every capacity for good. Regeneration then meant the creation of a new self, completely unrelated to the old self. In this analysis, one could only be said to be passive in respect to the activity of grace.

Flacius contended that he expressed Luther's views and quoted numerous passages in support. But it is doubtful that he was true to Luther's intent. Luther's statements on total depravity, one's inability to determine one's relation to God, and his accent upon the directing activity of the Spirit even in faith, reflect a religious confession based upon experience. He did not intend his statements to be understood as a doctrine simply of human nature, either before or in faith. He was concerned with the human situation before God.

The issue was further complicated because Melanchthon only partially understood Luther's views, and accepted the battle lines as drawn by the conservatives. Although Luther's main point about the bondage of the will referred to one's situation before God, Melanchthon, too, understood this as a statement about the nature of humanity. Melanchthon, therefore, insisted both upon the initiating and sustaining activity of God and upon human activity. God and human beings are co-workers. (Theologically, this is known as *synergism*.) By such phrasing, Melanchthon intended to safeguard the priority of grace while affirming a dignified concept of humanity. It is difficult to hold such a position, and some of Melanchthon's followers emphasized human activity so much that it was evident that they had shifted the accent too far in the direction of human striving. Such views were rejected, as were, on the other side, the views of Flacius.

Melanchthon's views were a compromise, designed to safeguard the gospel, rather than a creative solution. By accepting the problem as defined, Melanchthon lost the opportunity of confessing that one finds one's truest self, including one's activity and response, in the faith which lays hold of one. Instead, Melanchthon had to contend for a formal definition of human capacity, abstracted from the experience of faith.

3) A third controversy concerned the place of law and works in the context of faith. On the basis of justification by faith, Luther spoke in glowing terms of the new life in Christ, frequently without caution or careful definition. Sensing the need for careful thinking on this level, subsequent theologians took Luther's occasional and unguarded utterances at face value. Johann Agricola, for instance, rightly saw that Luther's understanding of the gospel demanded the abrogation of law. But he interpreted this to mean that one had no obligation to fulfill the requirements of God as laid down in the law and that good works were even detrimental to salvation. Such a position is called *antinomian,* since it emphasizes the life in the Spirit over against any stress upon law, commandment, or requirement. Although this interpretation arose from Luther's emphasis upon the freedom of the Christian man and the new life in the Spirit, it disregarded his concern that the law be fulfilled in the Spirit. The antinomians generally were people whose lives, lifted to new heights of achievement by the gospel, were examples of Christian grace. On the other hand, the lack of concern for standards occasionally led instead to acts of license.

In opposition to this, George Major insisted that good works were necessary for salvation. He did not state that we are saved by works. He insisted upon justification; he merely added that good works were necessary for salvation. Thus justification and merit together defined the Christian concept of salvation. This obviously contradicted Luther. Melanchthon, who acted as a mediator in the controversy, suggested that one could not say that good works were necessary for salvation, but one must say that good works were necessary.

As an attempt at mediation, this expressed Luther's general position with some cogency, but the difficulty was that the nuances of meaning were not the same. There is a difference between saying that the central emphasis is faith, not without works, and that works are necessary. The former places works in the context of faith at every point and leaves the definition of their "necessity" in unavoidable suspension. Melanchthon only verbally escaped the conclusion that if something is necessary in faith, it is necessary for salvation. Even without that conclusion, his statement distorted Luther's concern by considering works apart from a genuine relation to faith. At the most, Luther's writings ascribe relative necessity to works by casting every reference to human activity into the context of faith and the fruits of the Spirit.

4) The fourth controversy concerned the nature of the righteousness of the Christian. Generally, Saint Paul and Luther had declared that the righteousness of God is imputed to us, that is, ascribed to us though we do not actually possess it. Andreas Osiander insisted that we were genuinely made righteous in faith. In asserting that faith made a difference and that one entered into a new reality, Osiander was correct. But the insistence that even believers were unrighteous was so much a part of the Reformation that Osiander's view had no chance of success. As a believer, one may be more righteous than as an unbeliever. But in Luther's understanding, one is not yet righteous and needs to be covered by God's cloak of righteousness. He did not deny that the Christian was actually righteous *in contrast* to a former status. His main point, however, was that the unrighteousness which still characterized the believer made it impossible to think of righteousness or consider even degrees of righteousness. In the last analysis, we need God's righteousness ascribed to us if we are to stand before God.

The preceding issues were settled in the Formula of Concord in 1577 along the lines indicated above. In all cases, it was a victory for the conservative wing. The Augsburg Confession (and Melanchthon's defense of it), the Formula of Concord, and the catechisms of Luther were assembled and became the Book of Concord. This became the doctrinal standard for Lutheranism in Germany (and continues to have tremendous influence among conservative Lutheran groups; among other Lutherans, only the Augsburg Confession and Luther's Small Catechism are the generally accepted standards).

For many in the seventeenth and eighteenth centuries, the Book of Concord was a veritable textbook for the resolution of all problems. It was as indispensable as the Bible for being a Christian, since it contained the proper approach to, and the interpretation of, the Bible. Lutherans looked to it and to the Bible for all knowledge, including knowledge of the world. They built this wall around themselves in order to preserve the purity of Christian concepts.

In this development, Luther's stress upon the Spirit as the agent through which the Bible is and becomes the Word of God was considered too subjective. The Bible as Bible, understood through the Book of Concord, was synonymous with the Word of God. Faith in revelation meant assent to statements which had been given in an infallible form in a book. God's truth meant propositions about God. Thus the initial warmth and freedom of Lutheranism gave way to a stress upon statements derived from the Bible. And these were set forth with the rigor of a theological method in which sensitive spirituality was often lacking. Men were now more concerned with being correct than with the revivifying power of the Spirit. This kind of faith was subsequently challenged within the churches by the Pietist movement.

The Reformed Tradition

The Spread of the Reformed Movement

The Reformed groups early established themselves firmly in Zurich (where Zwingli was the leader) and the northern Swiss cantons. As a result the principle of territorialism was applied in Switzerland as well as in Germany. But in this situation the official recognition of the Protestant churches led to quite a different development from that in Lutheran Germany, and the contrast between the Reformed and Lutheran conceptions of the Christian life came clearly into view.

In Lutheranism, the individual in relation to God was the paramount concern. People expressed their faith in all their social relations, of course, but essentially through the existing social structures. In the "secular" realm, people continued to be subject to the ordinary demands of the community upon its citizens. But in the Reformed churches, there was a profound sense of the need for reordering the total life of the community into a truly Christian society. No activity was to be omitted; all were to be claimed as the domain of God's activity and as the area for special, collective Christian responsibility.

The Geneva community (under Calvin's leadership from 1541 to 1564) is the best-known example of an attempt in Protestant history to apply this principle in thoroughgoing fashion. As a Christian society, Geneva was to be governed by the community of the elect. By intent and design Geneva was democratic rather than authoritarian. Authority in the church was distributed among pastors, doctors, elders, and deacons. To the first belonged the ministry of the Word, preaching, and the administering of the sacraments. To the doctors belonged the teaching function of the church, a ministry particularly to the young as the future pillars of the church. Responsibility for the visitation of the sick and aid to the poor fell to the deacons. Elders made up a court of discipline, charged with the responsibility of seeing to it that all men obeyed the precepts of the gospel (willingly or unwillingly). The Consistory, which was made up of clergy and laity, but with lay members predominating, had the responsibility of supervising the corporate life of the community. Consequently, it was very important in the life of the city and not infrequently the subject of considerable debate. Whenever necessary, its decisions were enforced by the council of the city. This was in line with Calvin's notion that the state should not dictate to the church, but rather that the civil powers existed for the sake of maintaining and protecting the faith. The state must learn the true nature of the faith from the church, in order that life might be properly ordered. Being a magistrate was thus a Christian vocation and responsibility and included the responsibility not only for civil order but also for right religion.

The Geneva experiment is not easy for us of a later time to assess. The intolerance toward dissent (e.g., the execution of Servetus) and the rigid control through the Consistory over every detail of public and private life must be understood in their historical context (we are not speaking of justification or blame). The notorious execution of Michael Servetus does not tell us much about the uniqueness of Geneva — for this was not strange in a time when death was the accepted penalty for heretics who refused to recant, and when religious uniformity within a given territory was taken for granted (the affair of Servetus actually involved more than heresy; it was in fact a direct challenge to Calvin's leadership in Geneva). Geneva was also a haven for refugee Protestants, and it was partly through the training of such individuals that Calvin's influence spread so far. But central in the Geneva experiment was the vision of a city in every way dedicated to the glorification of God. It was this goal, together with the assumptions that total Christian patterns of life could be specified in detail and that the elect could safely be trusted to enforce such Christian standards, that led to the iron collectivism of Geneva.

The Geneva pattern could not be applied in the other areas in which the Reformed tradition arose and flourished. In fact, only in America was it possible to carry out a similar experiment, and then only for a time. In the other areas, there was considerable opposition on the part of constituted authorities and no possibility of taking over the control of affairs. This is partly why Geneva became such a symbol and why Calvinists in other lands looked half wistfully at Geneva. It was not that Geneva, under the leadership of John Calvin, was itself so important. Rather, Geneva seemed to represent the fullest expression of this type of reform movement. In many other places the drive for the manifestation of the Christian concern in all areas of life had to be content with personal morality and diligence and thrift in social and economic affairs, rather than in the direct control of all life through dedicated or friendly authority. The same drive which lay behind the Genevan community was involved in the support that industrious Calvinists gave to the new capitalist order.[1]

The most difficult place for the Reformed development was France. Initially, the "Huguenot" communities met little opposition, but as they grew they increasingly became a problem in a country which

[1] See Ch. V, and especially Ch. XI.

had accepted the principle of "one land, one religion." They were persecuted extensively, but in the Edict of January 1562 won limited toleration. Wars and intrigues followed, with the Massacre of St. Bartholomew's Day in 1572 acting as a call for the elimination of all Huguenots. Over ten thousand fell in Paris alone. As a result of revulsion to this act, but primarily because of changes in the crown, the Edict of Toleration in 1598 granted Calvinism full toleration. But this was revoked in 1685 under the reign of Louis XIV, who insisted on one faith, one king, one land. French Protestantism continued as a definite minority group.

In the Empire, the spread of the Reformed faith was limited by the strength of the Lutheran bodies. Nevertheless, Reformed churches emerged among the Magyars of Hungary, and even more in the valley of the Rhine, particularly in the Palatinate. Among the latter, a controversy concerning the Lord's Supper resulted in a notable document, the influence of which extended far beyond the immediate issue. This was the Heidelberg Catechism, written by Peter Ursinus and Caspar Olevianus, a balanced statement, admirably suited for purposes of instruction. It was accepted by nearly all of the Reformed churches.

In the Low Countries, the Reformed tradition did not have any strength until about 1560. Before that, this area had been a center for Anabaptists and Lutheran groups. For a period, there was considerable tension between the Protestant groups, though common fear of the Roman Catholic influence through the domination of Spain generally kept them from fighting each other. The Anabaptists, however, had been weakened by persecution and expulsion, and the Lutherans were not aggressive. In this situation the Calvinists won the ascendancy and also the favor of Prince William (probably because the concept of justifiable resistance by the lower magistrates appealed to him). Nevertheless, he was for some form of toleration. In the long run the territorial solution prevailed. In the southern regions (Belgium), Roman Catholicism became the established religion, while in the North (Holland), Calvinism was established.

Scotland, next to Geneva, presented a situation in which circumstances and the genius of the Reformed faith combined to shape and form a people. Here, largely through the energies of John Knox, a people sympathetic to reformation were welded into a religious society dominating the land. A man who had suffered under the Inquisition and who had drunk at the Reformation fountains of Zurich and Geneva, Knox feared nothing, and openly and successfully challenged the Roman Catholic queen, Mary Stuart. He was able to forge a church which for generations influenced the destiny of the nation.

The Puritan movement also belongs to the Reformed tradition. But because it has an outlook distinctive to itself, we consider it in the next chapter. Many of the national groups discussed here found their way to the New World and brought their respective traditions. Even the Huguenots made a settlement. The Dutch Reformed Church arose out of the Dutch Calvinist development and the first congregation in the New World was in New York, then New Amsterdam, in 1628. In the early eighteenth century, the Scotch-Irish migrated to the New World. From them came the Presbyterian churches. The German Reformed groups came in large numbers after the first quarter of the eighteenth century.

The Development of Orthodox Calvinism

Most of the Reformed groups in Europe formulated confessions of faith. The Second Helvetic or Swiss Confession of 1566, written by Bullinger, was a doctrinal statement of great influence throughout the Swiss cantons. The Gallican Confession in France reflected a strong emphasis on predestination. The Belgic Confession of 1561 in the Low Countries has the earmarks of the influence of Geneva. Initially, the Scottish faith found expression in the Confession of 1560, written largely by Knox. This Confession remained the standard of faith until the completion of the Westminster Confession in 1647, which, though prepared in England, had been written with the collaboration of Scottish delegates (see Ch. V).

The confessions of faith served originally as guides and often as dikes against distortion. But increasingly, in the midst of controversy, individuals pointed to the confessions as correct Christian thinking. People were asked to believe the confessions, and the faith these were meant to safeguard often took second place. That was the beginning of Protestant "orthodoxy," which not infrequently substituted right thinking for the experience which lay behind all thought. (This is one of the reasons why later generations find it hard to realize the power of the confessions in their original situations or to acknowledge the religious faith which initially informed them.)

The development toward orthodoxy was accelerated through theological controversies in which the conservative groups were consistently the victors. One of the earliest instances occurred in Holland in the early 1600's. Here controversy was provoked through the vocal doubts of a pious Christian by the name of Koornheert who, though he did not reject the idea, was perplexed by the claim that God damned individuals from all eternity. Arminius, who had been asked to refute Koornheert, instead became convinced that the traditional view must be rejected. He then became the leader of the group which now bears his name. The brunt of the controversy was borne by a disciple of Arminius named Bisschop. Another important supporter was the well-known jurist, Hugo Grotius.

The tenets of the Arminians were expressed in a series of articles

known as the *Remonstrance.* A *Counter-Remonstrance,* influenced largely
by the conservative Gomar, was then written. While the controversy
was settled in the Synod of Dort in Holland in the year 1618, an
examination of the issues will give us a picture of the theological
thinking of the period.

1) The first issue concerned the understanding of God's decree
in predestination. The Arminians rejected the now prevalent view of
predestination: that God decreed which individuals would be saved
and which would be damned. This repudiation applied equally to
what were later called "supralapsarian" and "infralapsarian" views of
predestination. Supralapsarianism, the view held by Gomar, was the
affirmation that before the creation of the world God had decreed
who would be saved and who would be damned. In fact, this decision
of God's was a reason for creation. God's decision concerning individuals had no reference to the Fall (lapsus). The infralapsarians, on the
other hand, related God's decrees to the Fall. In this view, God also
made the decision about every individual prior to creation. But in so
doing, he took into account the fact of the Fall before it happened.
This view provided a rationale for assigning individuals to hell and
put creation in a better light.

Having distinguished between the supralapsarians and the infralapsarians, we must now distinguish two types of infralapsarian thinkers.
The "double" predestinarians held that God had directly willed both
the salvation of elect individuals and the damnation of all others.
On the other hand, those who held the concept of "single" predestination contended that God had decided who should be saved but had
made no decision concerning those who did not belong to the pre-
destined. For all practical purposes, the latter were left to their
own devices (which was hardly more tolerable than to be among the
damned).

Brushing aside the preceding distinctions, the Arminians affirmed
instead that the idea of a decree has reference merely to the serious
nature of God's plan for the world. It is a statement of how God
works, without reference to the precise destiny of any particular individual. Defined in this way, the decree means no more than that God
has declared that whoever accepts Christ will be saved and whoever
does not will be excluded. It describes a general situation, the outcome
of which is to be determined by each in accordance with one's own
decisions in faith.

The Arminians anchored the concept of predestination in faith and
experience, but they reduced the decision of faith simply to a human,
rational possibility. The holders of lapsarian theories, on the other
hand, attempted to safeguard the priority of God's activity by ascribing
all events and happenings to God. They lost the experiential character

of faith and accepted a form of determinism as the basis of faith. Calvin, too, had had a deterministic understanding of the operation of God in relation to predestination. But he intended only one thing: the exclusion of works. His orientation definitely was from faith to predestination (see Ch. II). Now this was reversed. One moved from predestination to other problems, including those of faith. Whereas faith had once been the foundation of predestination, now predestination was the basis of faith, a view already expressed previously by John Farel.

The Synod of Dort did not transcend the choice between the rationalistic alternatives: either free decision to be a Christian or deterministic predestination. It adopted a view which was neither clearly supra nor infralapsarian, though definitely associated with a concept of single predestination.[2] God's decree before the foundation of the world was clearly affirmed. At the same time, the concept of single predestination took the onus of damnation out of the hands of God since God had not specifically ordained anyone for damnation. Actually, of course, the destiny of those apart from the elect was not affected by the affirmation of single rather than double predestination. In subsequent developments, double predestination was reaffirmed in spite of the Synod of Dort.

2) Closely allied with the preceding was the question whether Christ died only for the elect or for all persons. The Arminians, of course, insisted that Christ had died for all and obtained forgiveness for all, though forgiveness could be effective only as one accepted Christ. The orthodox party insisted that Christ died only for the elect. Convinced that what happens is what is willed by God and that whatever happens is determined by God, they insisted that Christ could have died only for the faithful. Otherwise God would be frustrated since what God intended did not happen. They gave expression to the universality and greatness of God, however, by declaring that God's grace would be adequate for all, though it was intended only for the elect.

The Synod of Dort sided with the orthodox party. As in the case of predestination, there was no sign of a new formulation of the problem which might have avoided these two alternatives, each of which leaves much to be desired.

3) Another issue concerned the understanding of faith in relation to the possibility or impossibility of rejecting God's grace. Both Armini-

---

[2] This is in contradistinction to the usually accepted opinion that the Synod took an infralapsarian position, a judgment based on the fact that historically the concept of single predestination had been associated only with the infralapsarian position.

ans and orthodox agreed that there is no salvation apart from faith. On one level, they even described faith in the same way. For the Arminians, faith was the acceptance of God's intention for human beings; for the conservatives, it was assent to what God had done. Thus both those who contended for human volition and those who insisted upon a rigid determination defined faith as a decision. From opposite positions, they came to deceptively similar affirmations of salvation by faith.

The problematic nature of this agreement became apparent in the discussion of whether a person could reject God's grace. The Arminians affirmed that one could, and if one could not, one was no more than a puppet. Their prime theological interest was to safeguard the meaningfulness of human decision. That of the conservatives, on the other hand, was to place the will of God above all else. The latter group naturally appeared in a better light, though not necessarily in a better theological position. The orthodox refused to distinguish between God's will to redeem and one's acceptance. If God willed faith for anyone, it happened.

Again, the Synod of Dort came down on the conservative side and declared that "faith is therefore a gift of God, not on account of its being offered for man's choice, but because it is in reality conferred, inspired, and infused into him. It is not that God confers the power to believe, and then awaits the concurrence or act of believing from the will of man; but he who works in man both to will and to do, and indeed all things in all, produces both the will to believe and the act of believing also." (From this passage it is clear that the conservatives should have disagreed with the Arminians on the nature of faith.) This statement is no longer a confessional statement of the overwhelming experience of grace; it is a metaphysical account, abstracted from faith, of the operation of God and of human impotence. It makes one into an object maneuvered by God.

4) Can the person in whom God's grace is operative possibly lose it? The Arminians tentatively answered "Yes," pending further study of Scripture. This was in accord with their concern for the volitional nature of the self. The conservatives insisted that one could not fall from grace. Just as one could not resist grace, so one could not lose it. To say that one could, would mean that God was defeated in specific instances. That was intolerable from the strict Calvinist position.

Again, the Synod of Dort took the conservative position. But the alternatives, as in the previous instances, confused the issue as the Reformers had seen it. No one deliberately departs from grace, and the one who stands under its power can reasonably expect to remain under it. But this hope is based in the sustaining and trustworthy activity of God. This was the truth in the orthodox system, though distorted by a deterministic view of God's nature and activity. Nevertheless, it does happen that individuals do not remain in the state of grace. This was the truth of the other side, in which the activity of God and of human beings were not simply identified.

On every level, the Synod of Dort defined the will of God in such a way that what God wills and what happens were virtually identified. Only the Fall as such was excluded from the divine decree; all else, including the results of the Fall for human life and destiny, was the outworking of God's immutable will.

It was this general outlook which dominated the Calvinist tradition for at least another century. There were significant developments on the problem of predestination, the interpretation of Scripture and miracles, found in the writings of such thinkers as Danaeus (1588), Dusanus (1599), Bucanus (1609), Polanus (1623), Crocius (1636), Martinius (1603), Cocceius (1648), Van Til (1704), and Heideggerus (1696). But in the general perspective we have outlined, we can see the basic concern of later Calvinist theologians. We suggested earlier that although the Synod of Dort affirmed single predestination, it was followed by a theological development in which double predestination was predominant. The rationale for this development lay in an increasing emphasis upon the glory, majesty, and honor of God. Others before, including Calvin, had stressed the majesty of God, but as grounded always in God's justifying activity. In the later tradition, God's honor and glory *per se* become the dominant motif of interpretation. The concern was to express this at every point.

At the root of the discussions of predestination was always the bewildering problem that the mercy of God becomes a reality for some, but not for others. It was assumed that all deserve nothing else than damnation, but the question remained of God's purpose in election and rejection. The later Calvinists' way of meeting the problem was through the concept of double predestination, understood as a declaration of the absolute sovereignty and glory of God. God is God. Since God sends some to eternal life and some to eternal damnation, God is a God of glory, majesty, and power. Heideggerus, for example, declared that God's glory is expressed more clearly through the concept of damnation than through the idea of a just death for human sins. "The supreme end is the glory of God reprobating; — the subordinate end is the righteous condemnation of the reprobated to death for their sins."[3]

This is a rigorous view of double predestination. It is infinitely different from the views of the mystics and of the early Luther, for whom

---

[3] Heinrich Heppe, *Reformed Dogmatics* (London, 1950), p. 187.

faith was so wonderful that they proclaimed their willingness to be
damned for God's sake; that is, to accept God's plan for them. That
was a declaration of faith in which the possibility of damnation is
overarched by the experience of faith. For the later Calvinists, double
predestination is considered without reference to the confession of
the believer. Calvin's movement always from faith to predestination
(in order to guard against a doctrine of works) has been lost. Now
rigid determinism is accepted as a doctrine in its own right.

In the interpretation of Scripture, Luther and Calvin in principle
distinguished between the Word of God and the Bible. Word and
Bible were brought together through the testimony of the Holy Spirit.
To later Calvinists, as to Lutherans, this opened the door to purely
subjective interpretations. Their fears had been partially fostered by
the extremes of some of the Anabaptist groups (see Ch. III), which
claimed the direct presence of God through the Spirit apart from
Bible. In reaction, the orthodox abandoned the notion that the Bible
contained or might become the Word of God in faith, in favor of an
unqualified identification of Word and Scripture. Already in the second
Helvetic Confession of 1566 it was declared that the "canonical Scriptures are the actual true word of God." Any question of the identification of the Bible and the Word of God was rejected outright. So
wrote Wolleb: "the query whether the Scriptures or sacred books are
the Word of God is unworthy of a Christian. As in a school we do
not dispute with one who denied first principles, so we ought to adjudge
a man unworthy to be listened to if he denied the first principles of
the Christian religion."[4]

The Calvinists did not reject the Holy Spirit; but the Spirit was
now the agent of God's authorship of the biblical record. Inspiration
no longer included participation in the reception and experience of
revelation. The book as such was revelation, because it was written
under the Spirit. Nevertheless, many disputes arose concerning the
relative activity or passivity of individuals in the actual writing. Those
who believed that the biblical writers were active could at least account
for the diversity of style in the Bible since if God simply dictated it,
one would expect the same style throughout. But even those who
pled that the biblical writers were active as well as passive never doubted
for a moment that the content of the Bible was literally the Word of
God. So the Bible was the Word of God from cover to cover.

Such an understanding of the Bible included literal acceptance of
miracles. These depicted God's activity in the world, and in debate
served as crucial evidence of the truth of Christianity. Miracles were
understood as acts of God which could not be accounted for in the
natural scheme of things. Their contrast to the natural order made

[4] *Ibid.*, p. 15.

them most important. Thus a miracle could be defined as "a singular work of God, beyond the order and above the power of the creatures, for confirming divine truth."[5] This view of miracle held sway among the conservative groups until such time as individuals could no longer find these Christian evidences in an ordered world, and until the whole concept of miracle was recast in the early nineteenth century, notably through the work of Schleiermacher (see Chs. IX and X).

The Spirit of Orthodoxy

The developments we have described in this chapter are generally characterized as "Protestant orthodoxy." The word *orthodox* means "correct belief," and as applied to individuals or groups usually denotes conformity to accepted standards. Thus where the goal is orthodoxy, the precise definition of truth is all important.

It is therefore understandable why the movements we have described are called orthodox. On many levels there was a discernible shift from religious thinking which always arises out of the experience of faith to a stress upon proper and right thinking. This is most clearly seen in the development of the understanding of predestination. The dynamic religious thinking of Luther and Calvin was arrested by a concern whether or not particular formulations were true to Luther or Calvin. Frequently, this concern led to statements which differed greatly from the spirit of Luther and Calvin.

This tendency was accentuated by the necessity of making statements in the midst of controversies. (We have already indicated that the alternatives in the controversies were so phrased as to make the problems incapable of solution.) Religious truth and propositions about religious problems were identified in such a way that the latter became the criteria for the former. People were asked to assent to statements of truth. Instead of statements reflecting an experience of encounter with truth, truth now was tantamount to the statement itself. Hence theological formulations became the norm of Christian truth, including that of the experience of God through the Bible. Whereas Roman Catholicism insisted that the church was the interpreter of the Bible, orthodox theology now tended to be the custodian of biblical truth. Theology came before the Bible, as the key to its interpretation, rather than after it, as its explication.

The spirit of this approach is reflected in the second term which is frequently applied to the movement as a whole, "Protestant scholasticism." The term *scholastic* is used because of definite analogies to medieval scholasticism. Assent to truth in propositional form marked both periods. There was similarity also in emphasis upon a natural knowl-

[5] *Ibid.*, p. 264.

edge of God, supplemented by revelation (and, in the case of Protestants, also corrected by revelation).

There is a contrast, however, between Protestant scholasticism and medieval scholasticism which is important for the understanding of the former. In the classical medieval period, rational propositions about God and rational discourse about revelation were in conformity with the climate of opinion of the period. Reason made room for revelation and revelation took account of reason. Theology stood in a positive and creative relation to the culture. In contrast, Protestant scholasticism had to argue its case. It was confronted by the shaping of a new "scientific" view of the world which stood in sharp contrast to the biblical scheme, and by a philosophical trend which was almost exclusively rationalistic. The orthodox theologians felt compelled to set themselves against these views, and could see no creative relation to them. But in this encounter, Protestant scholasticism did not escape the spirit of rationalism itself. It was, in fact, akin to the new rationalistic currents both in temper and in method. It was no wonder that the dissatisfaction with philosophical rationalism should also bring dissatisfaction with this type of theology.

Such dissatisfaction expressed itself in Pietism and in a kind of general revulsion against orthodoxy. The revulsion was accentuated by the impact of the Thirty Years' War, which to many appeared as a gross spectacle of religious groups pitted futilely against each other, fighting for particular theological interpretations unworthy of defense.

Nevertheless, the type of thinking which was represented in Protestant orthodoxy took seriously the nature of the theological task. It set for itself the rigorous discipline of trying to think from a Christian perspective at every point. Seldom has the task of saving the center of Christian theology against encroachment from outside been taken so seriously and so passionately. In this sense, such orthodoxy was part of a time in which there were few doubts about truth and its correct formulation. Moreover, they believed that an opponent could be convinced of truth by the sheer power of one's competent use of logic and metaphysics. Hence, Protestants and Catholics both believed in the possibility that the credibility of their theology should convince the other. Having no doubts about the truth of what they said, they felt free to elaborate its meaning on every side, always with the conviction that the total picture was irrefutable. In this sense, the emergent orthodox theology was like baroque art, a fully orbed expression of perceived truth. One may therefore also call it a baroque theology.

Hence, if one comes to the orthodox development from the standpoint of its own emergence, it is a vital, convincing enterprise. Seen in the light of its eventual inflexibility in a world in which many ideas were winning adherence, the creativity of the movement soon ended in ossified forms, uncongenial to the new springs of knowledge beginning to emerge in the world.

CHAPTER V

Puritanism and Related Movements

The Puritan Outlook

The term *Puritan* refers to a particular Protestant outlook expressed in the late sixteenth and seventeenth centuries in England and New England. Denominationally, the Puritans comprised primarily Presbyterian, Congregational, and Baptist groups. From a religious viewpoint, most of them represented a vital Calvinist tradition. But whether Calvinist or not, they were marked by an intense experience of the living God, nourished exclusively by the Bible and expressed in every thought and act.

Biblical Foundations

For the Puritans, the Elizabethan settlement appeared as a halfway house between Rome and Geneva. The appeal to tradition, church authority, and reason obscured the only proper basis for the life of church and society alike. Puritans believed in the sole sufficiency of the Bible. Only the Bible could be taken as a guide for faith and life. The biblical word, strictly adhered to, provided an adequate criterion for all problems.

The authority of the Bible had two facets. In the first place, it was only through the Bible that one obtained and experienced knowledge of the God who is related to every aspect of one's life. The Puritans did not mean that the Bible disclosed the inmost nature of God. This remained hidden. Even the Bible pointed to the incomprehensible being of God. But incomprehensibility did not mean unknowability.

In the faith nourished by the Bible one did know that God is in control of everything and predestines some to salvation and others to damnation. God's activity was known, but God's rationale was a mystery.

In the second place, the Bible was a document that reflected the organization of the early Christian community. There church order and the vitality of the faith went hand in hand. The organization of the church was not a hindrance to the depth of faith, as the Puritans suspected it had become in Anglicanism, but a natural manifestation of faith. Puritans were divided in their understanding of the constitution of the New Testament community. But they were agreed that the true order of the church was given in the biblical community of faith. Church order expressed faith and therefore no supplemental criteria, such as reason or tradition, could be used. (Later in the chapter we show in some detail how this understanding was expressed in English history.)

Election and Faith

The Puritans believed that God ordered everything in the world. At the same time they asked people to be active Christians whose lives would show forth the glory of God in the transformation of life and society. They were at once the most predestinarian and the most activistic of Christians. This paradoxical combination provides the clue to the understanding of the Puritan ethos.

Like Calvinists generally, Puritans believed that nature and history, the world and humankind, were governed by God. Providence, God's continual sustaining and ordering activity, and predestination, the governance of human destiny, were virtually identified as the determination of all things by God. God was behind everything which happened. Even sin could not be excluded from God's providential activity, though God was not held accountable for it. The guilt for sin was ours because of the Fall.

But such affirmations could only be made by those who were already believers called by God. Only the one who was a believer could say that God's predestining act was the cause of faith. Predestination was not a general proposition about all people. Determination by God made sense only to the believer. It was a category used by the faithful to account for their faith. It pointed to the mystery of election, grounded only in the God who controlled and ordered all. The view of God as the governor of all things belonged to the Puritans' experience and accorded with their understanding of the Bible. It was not strange or alien to their own existence. Although God controlled everything, God was not a tyrant. There was a profound difference between the majesty of God, however fearful, and tyranny. Only the one who had not taken God seriously could think of the latter. Moreover, the God of majesty had already been revealed as merciful. Hence God's activity, in which the concept of predestination was anchored, was already weighted, among the faithful, on the side of gracious activity. (As we saw, this had been the original basis for the declaration of God's predestining activity.)

The Puritans considered themselves among the faithful but emphasized the mystery of election. Hence they never questioned God's justice. Sometimes they rationalized it, as when with St. Augustine they stated that since no one deserved to be saved, there was no injustice in the election of some. At their best they insisted that the mystery of God would eventually be disclosed, but in the meantime one must simply accept it.

However much Puritans believed that God controlled all events, they never interpreted this as a sign for relinquishing the responsibilities they felt called upon to assume. If God had called them, they must do his work. God demanded things of the elect. To be called by God was serious and demanded the redoubling of one's activities. To relax would be not to be serious. Those who believe that a concept of predestination leads to quietism do not understand, as do believers, that it is God with whom they are dealing. Predestination means that God has laid a hand upon us for a purpose. Believing with all their being that God justified through faith, Puritans went on to assert that justification was but the first stage, followed by sanctification, or the new life in Christ.

As a result, many Puritans believed that the activity of Christians in the world was a mark of their election, a sign to themselves and to others that they were among God's chosen. The validity and certainty of faith was shown in the actuality of the new life, dedicated to doing everything under the rule and for the glory of God. "By their fruits you shall know them." This was a dictum which the Puritans applied to themselves. All things must be undertaken for God, and only in such activity could one gain reasonable certainty that one was not deluded in one's faith. Necessary as justification was, it alone did not give assurance of one's election. The believer's experience of justification must be followed by actual holiness. (It was the fear that one might not really be among the righteous which sometimes manifested itself in self-righteousness.)

The Puritans were aware of psychological issues at many levels. Often those outside the churches, with little or no experience of God, appeared more responsible and were better persons, judged by outward standards, than those who confessed that justification and sanctification came through the merciful activity of God. The problem was intensified because the Puritans had an uncanny sense that the outward was a sign of the inward. Could one be sure where one stood, particularly when some unbelievers did so well? The result of such questioning was only a more resolute attempt to live one's life as if only God mattered and as if one could not do enough in the world under God's rule. Thus predestination, which was such a comfort to Luther, became the most baffling problem for the individual Puritan. Although the Puritans never dreamt that one could be perfect, they nevertheless did expect clear signs of their election. And where signs are expected, one is never certain whether the signs which appear are clear enough.

The anxiety caused by this problem was eased in a later stage of Puritanism through the notion that one could not lose one's election. This did not mean that one could do as one pleased; it was a responsible statement made in the context of faith. This was a way of saying that God had an unending concern for humankind and that we need not be so preoccupied with ourselves. The impossibility of losing one's election should have been asserted when the faith was vigorous. It was actually suggested when Puritanism had lost much of its vitality.

More to the point for subsequent history was the continual assertion of the faithful that as long as one struggled under God as a believer, one could trust God to see one through. Many Puritans believed that whoever did not struggle or fight the battle of life was among the lost. Inactivity was a sure sign that one was not a believer, no matter what one's profession of faith. This is why the Puritans spoke of the warfare of life. If there was peace for them, it was in the midst of ceaseless activity under God. As long as one strove under God, there was some hope that one might be among the elect.

It was not easy to resolve the tension in the souls of those who believed in the all-determining nature of God's activity and yet saw their own activity as essential in relation to God. Indeed, this problem presented itself on several levels, both before and in the context of faith. First, while some believed that the advent of faith was the result of being vigorously and suddenly seized by God's judgment and grace, others saw that faith seemed more frequently to be the result of a process. Among both groups there was no doubt that God's activity was the source of faith. But could one, indeed must one, not do something to lay oneself open to the possibility of faith, to the discovery that one indeed might be one of God's elect? Both in England and New England, a group of individuals began to emphasize the preparation of the heart, citing passages of Scripture, such as I Samuel 7:3; Job 11:13,15; Psalm 10:17; Proverbs 16:1,9; or Luke 12:40. Conceivably, one could be one of the elect and never have any intimations of it, though that seemed unlikely. If one used the means God had provided, perhaps something of God's active presence might emerge. While not all Puritan divines — William Perkins, William Ames, Richard Sibbes, Thomas Hooker, Peter Bulkeley, to name but five — agreed on the steps one needed to take, there is a morphology of the conversion process, involving the debasement of the self in light of God's commandments, the desire for God's grace, the emergence of strivings of the heart which need to be tested to see if they may be of God, absolute assurance being impossible. Hence, the process was endless, for the discipline of examination, utilizing sermons, meditation, introspection, was essential both before and in the situation of faith. The mere statement that one was a believer was not enough. One needed to be able to give an account of one's faith, one's conversion, and its fruits. In early New England, a conversion narrative was considered essential to full participation in the life of the church, from sacraments to voting rights, for church and society were to be formed by visible saints, for the sake of God's church and kingdom.

Theologically, the Puritans also had resort to the concept of the covenant as a way of understanding both God's initiative and human responsibility. Whether grounded in English history or derived from Continental reformers, particularly Heinrich Bullinger, the covenant idea was congenial to the Puritans. But the concept was ambiguous, for it could be used by those who wished to accent God's initiative in electing a special people or by those who felt it necessary to assess the mutual obligations of God and humankind. It made it possible moreover to see the sacraments, particularly baptism, in a special light, for if baptism, in analogy with circumcision in the Old Testament, was the seal and sign of the covenant in the New Testament, infants were already a part of the new order of things. Hence, infant baptism stood for an order into which one had been launched; it represented a context God had prepared and in which one's subsequent preparation made sense.

While the Puritan idea of covenant was a way of maintaining great stress upon the will and responsibility of individuals without abandoning an equal stress upon the controlling and determining activity of God, it did not solve the problem of their relation. Some Puritans did stress activity so much that they shifted the emphasis to the point where it was felt that once the process of sanctification had started, one contributed to one's own salvation.

Ordering All Under God

The concept of covenant also focused the pervasive Puritan concern for ordering all life under God. This was the ethical side of the covenant, expressed in the Bible in both individual and social terms. Each individual had responsibility under God and no one could take another's place. But the covenant also involved a people meant to live in community under God. God's plan for the world had a social nature; it included the participation of individuals in a common unity which sustained and gave meaning to all. It involved a holy community sustained by

God but expressed by human beings dedicated to doing all things in accord with God's will and for God's glory.

We shall never be able to grasp the spirit of the Puritans unless we sympathetically try to enter into the perspective of people committed to the belief that everything is to be understood and ordered from the standpoint of the divine. This may be the aim of most Christians; but never before or after Puritanism has it been so consciously or self-consciously expressed. Self-consciousness frequently hindered the realization of the ideal. Nevertheless, the intense cultivation of that motif had important consequences for individual and social life of the time.

This dominant Puritan concern led to a high degree of sobriety and somberness toward life. But this was not a dour pessimism. It was rather a deliberate "sitting loose" to the things of this world. The Puritans believed that nothing in human existence held a meaning in its own right and continually sought for the meaning of existence under God. Since God had destined the elect for a life beyond, the achievements as well as the sorrows of this life were not ultimate. Loyalty to God meant that nothing in this life deserved final allegiance. Human existence was to be transformed insofar as possible by the might and power of Christians; beyond this was the assurance of a God who could be trusted to bring the history of the world to its fulfillment. Moreover, they expected that such an end was not too far away, for their reading of Scripture told them that they lived in the last times. They looked for and saw signs of that hastening of God's final activities.

Living in such a time, the faithful must be ready. Such readiness included a faithful church and a social setting in which visible saints could live. Some things were thus to be excluded from life and others included. Card playing was denounced not merely because it seemed to foster gambling, but primarily because it was a frivolous activity. The same could be said of the theater, though here it was also felt outright immorality was exhibited. All energies were to be directed to the service of God. Puritans read good literature, classical and secular as well as religious. Many were outstanding scholars and people of culture, enjoying good clothing, good food, good wine, and exquisite china and furniture, the visual arts alone having dropped out of their lives. But such possessions and pursuits must not be allowed to sidetrack people from the main business of life. They, too, must serve God. Joyful human associations, including the imbibing of wine (the teetotalism of a later generation should not be blamed on the Puritans) and dancing were accepted, provided they contributed to the well-being of the pilgrim traveling through this world under God. All such things were good, but they were not to be used for their own sake.

In economic life this outlook was conducive to the utmost thrift and industry. Money and goods were neither to be wasted nor trusted. When thrift was coupled with the zealous activity of Christians who saw in diligent performance of their work a service of God, and in success perhaps a sign of election, a combination was produced which could powerfully affect the economic developments of the age. Many Puritans belonged to the rising business class, and through their efforts and thrift undoubtedly accelerated the pace of the expanding capitalist development.[1] At the same time, the strong sense for responsible employment of all activity under God did much to check the most flagrant abuses of the emerging capitalist order.

Since no segment of life fell outside the purview of responsibility to God, the Puritans naturally hoped to organize all social and political life along Christian patterns. For this, Geneva remained a model. As we see in the following section, "The Major Puritan Bodies," such a dream was short lived in England and for that matter in New England, too, though it was more successful in the latter place.

Much more important for political development was the fact that the Puritans' faith led them to challenge tyranny and abuse of power, whether in state or church. God was sovereign and as members of God's legion they were unafraid of any earthly powers. When God alone is sovereign, all other powers are subject to restraint. Unrestricted power can be granted to no one. With this sense of responsibility to God alone, Puritans provided the spiritual foundation for a democratic society. This was the case even though many Puritans were so interested in establishing a society which reflected God from top to bottom that they did not see this implication of their faith, nor that their own lives frequently violated any semblance of democracy. Nevertheless, workable democratic structures have arisen primarily in lands influenced by Puritan traditions.

The Major Puritan Bodies

Puritans were by no means agreed on the proper pattern of church order. But they were agreed that such questions must be answered by a strict adherence to the biblical record. The Puritan religious outlook itself determined the understanding of the church. The issue with the Anglicans was not merely one of bishops versus presbyters in the church. The roots of the difference were as deep as the types of spirituality manifest in the respective traditions. It can be characterized as the difference between a rigorous adherence to the patterns

---

[1] The relation between Calvinism and the rising capitalist economy has been studied in detail in Max Weber, *The Protestant Ethic and the Spirit of Capitalism* (New York, 1930), and R. H. Tawney, *Religion and the Rise of Capitalism* (New York, 1926). See Ch. XI.

of the Bible on the one hand and, on the other, a more urbane and carefully considered view of the church as a part of the ongoing character of God's incarnation with historical and theological significance alongside of, though based upon, the Bible. Most Anglicans did not rest the case for bishops entirely upon the Bible, but also upon the dominant tradition of the church and upon its basic reasonableness. By contrast, the Puritans insisted that the Bible was the only place in which the norm for Christian living could be found, including church order. It was not enough to say that a church pattern does not contradict the Bible; rather, only that order is permissible when it is specifically founded in the Bible.

However differently they understood that order, even in the New Testament, Puritans were agreed that it was neither to be sought nor substantiated elsewhere. To their opponents this looked like a kind of biblicism, that is, an exclusive and narrow stress on the Bible; this, they felt, made the history of the church unimportant. The Puritans, on the other hand, insisted that they were returning to the church in its original state.

In spite of this common intention, the Puritan development was diverse. In the first place, there were differences of understanding and approach. In the second place, historical developments in England and New England were different and largely determined the respective patterns. In England, after the first major Anglican Puritan group, came the Presbyterians led by the Cambridge professor Thomas Cartwright. This group believed that the Genevan experiment and the Presbyterian pattern in Scotland represented the New Testament concept of the church. But the aim was not severance from the established Church of England. Rather, that church was to be purified and purged of the remnants of Roman corruption. These individuals believed that in the Church of England the ministry was neither rightly constituted nor properly educated, that medieval ceremonies still clustered around the sacraments, and that the prayer book had too many remnants of the Mass. In short, the church must abandon its halfway house between Geneva and Rome.

The Puritan Presbyterians called upon Parliament to change the Elizabethan settlement in order to make a truly reformed church. They, too, believed in a national church dominating the entire land. And if neither Queen nor bishops were ready to reform, then Parliament should. But the Queen insisted on keeping the religious settlement as it was. Thus, Presbyterians took other steps. They organized groups of ministers who met together to study and expound on the Bible. Sometimes laypeople were also included. Although the Queen insisted on the suppression of those groups, the Presbyterians actually took the additional step of trying to introduce their principles of church government from within the Church of England. Ministers of Presbyterian persuasion were ordained to episcopal orders, but would not accept a congregation without its express approval. They called themselves pastors rather than priests, and in various areas met together to exhort each other in faith and practice. They insisted upon regular ministers who preached, taught, administered the sacraments, and admonished and corrected believers whenever necessary.

Although the Presbyterians were the largest body of Puritan dissenters, there were other groups whose outlook was considerably different. Closest to the Presbyterians was a group of Independents or Congregationalists who also wanted to purify the church without separating from it. But their understanding of the church was characterized by an emphasis upon the local church as an independent body of believers, subject neither to a presbyterian nor episcopal system. Having a similar understanding of the church, but convinced that no good could come out of staying in the Church of England, was the group known as Separatists. They characterized the Presbyterians as those who tarried for the magistrates to undertake reformation. Their outlook was expressed in a tract by Robert Browne entitled "A Treatise of Reformation Without Tarrying for Any." The Separatist program defied church and state alike. It was a declaration that matters of church could not be dictated by magistrates. The church was not a church of the land or nation, including all who are born into it. It was truly the community of believers who entered into a covenant on the basis of their profession of faith.

Congregationalists and Separatists differed on the way the reformation of the church should proceed, whether from within or by separation. But on the nature of the church, they were mainly in agreement. Profession of faith was the *sine qua non* for church membership. Yet not everyone who decided to be a church member was permitted to be a part of the church in the fullest sense. Only those whose profession met the testing of members in good standing could be admitted to the full rites of the church. No accident of birth sufficed; not even one's own decision. The church was based on a covenant of believers, dedicated to making sure that the church expressed the spirit of its Lord. Hence, entrance into such a community required the approval of the other covenanted members.

Such communities of faith operate in particular places. By definition, in this way of thinking, the church is the local church. Hence the term *Congregationalists* — those who believed that the church is the local, functioning body. There is no church in the abstract, no such thing as a combination of churches forming the church. The church is always a concrete community and in the aggregate one can only speak of churches. This does not prevent a number of communities from undertaking joint projects; but in theory that would be only the concurrent action of individual churches. (In New England such common concern was expressed in the plans for an educated ministry and resulted in the founding of various educational institutions.)

Since the church was the local church and it was the believers who made the decisions, there was a tendency toward democracy in the congregations. But responsibility was still heavily focused on an educated clergy. Congregationalists were wary of untutored and untrained clergy. They distrusted emotion, though not vitality, and placed a premium upon learning. The polity (or church order) of Congregationalists, therefore, reflected an attempt to institute a structure in which all believers were on an equal footing, but which nevertheless placed particular responsibilities in the hands of a selected number. Such a particular procedure obviously made religious and practical sense. It took into account the fact that in Christ there are no essential distinctions, and yet there are differences in calling and training. The difficulty, however, for Congregationalists was that although this pattern might be in accord with the spirit of the Bible, it could not be found directly in Scripture.

In addition to the Congregationalists, Baptist churches also emerged out of the Separatist tradition. The first Baptist church was probably organized by John Smyth while in exile from England in Holland. This group migrated back to England under Thomas Helwys, a follower of Smyth. In spite of certain religious affinities and some possible direct relation with the Anabaptists in Holland, the Baptist movement was nourished primarily by the Separatist tradition in the English scene.

Generally, Baptists, in contrast to Congregationalists, were non-Calvinistic Puritans (though there were some Calvinistic Baptists, known as Particular Baptists). They preferred to steer a course between the concepts of free will and predestination, but were not interested in working out how this could be accomplished. Their strength did not lie in theological astuteness. Their interests were elsewhere. They were concerned with the church as a gathered community, with the corollary of believers' baptism, and with the separation of church and state. Like the Congregationalists, they believed that the church was a covenanted community in which all were on an equal footing, served each other, and assumed each other's burdens. For the Baptists, however, this implied a more rigid democratic structure. Among some Baptists anyone who had the Spirit could be the minister, provided one was called and elected; in other Baptist groups, minimal educational qualifications, as in Congregational groups, were required. Certainly democratic structures do not exclude the education of ministers. But many Baptist and sectarian groups insisted that education was wholly irrelevant to the operation of the Spirit. People were not only theoretically but actually equal in the Spirit. Baptists knew all too well that education has a way of producing class levels, even in a community of grace.

Many belonged to the lower economic strata of society and acutely sensed any drift toward social differentiation.

Like the Anabaptists, the Baptists came to the conviction that believers' baptism was essential. If the church was the community of those who were believers and had made a covenant together, then baptism must be at an age when one could enter the covenant by responsible decision. Certainly the form of baptism, immersion (which was not required originally), was less important than the emphasis on decision and faith as the key to the rite. Baptism was not a sacramental means of grace, but an "ordinance" symbolizing a regeneration which had already taken place.

Unlike the Anabaptists, the Baptists accommodated themselves to the demands of the state and supported it in the duties of citizenship up to the point where religious liberty was involved. Congregationalists, too, were for religious freedom, unhampered by magistrates in any way. But among English Congregationalists, this was not so much conviction as necessity. They had no other choice, with Anglicans on the one side and Presbyterians on the other, both determined that there must be a national church. For the Baptists, on the other hand, the separation of church and state was a matter of deep religious conviction. Since the church was a strictly voluntary association, its very nature was destroyed by any governmental decisions respecting its life. One danger of any alliance between the two was a loss of vitality in the church. This could only be maintained where the church itself was a "gathered" group of real Christians, as opposed to state churches which sought to include all, and by reason of accident of birth rather than Christian conviction.

While separation appeared essential for the sake of vitality, it seemed no less important for genuine liberty of conscience in matters of belief. Baptists were convinced that doctrinal tests violated the rights of those whose consciences under God led to different convictions. Perhaps this principle was partially reinforced by the fact that Baptists did not accept the prevailing Calvinism of Presbyterian and Congregationalist alike. But it was no more than reinforced, since freedom of religious belief and expression was a matter of fundamental conviction among Baptists. Their understanding of God and community demanded it.

In America, this faith first found expression in New England. Roger Williams, who came to New England as a Puritan turning Separatist, now became a Baptist in conviction and is credited with founding the first Baptist church in the New World in Providence. Essentially a searching man in religious matters, and banished from the New England Puritan community, he established religious toleration in his own area. He, too, believed in a Christian society, but one in which the church influenced the community through the quality of its life and not by means of laws. The separation of church and state, which is the heritage of America, was contributed to largely by Roger Williams and the Baptists. It obviously did not mean the separation of religion and culture.

For Baptists, the principle of individual decision in relation to God meant complete freedom for each individual with respect to faith. Because of this, church order belongs to the individuals who are Christians and not to clergy. Further, because the life of the church is the life of individual Christians, there can be no imposed liturgy. Prayers express a particular person's faith and therefore ought to be extemporaneous. But prayers are to be shared, for individuals covenant with God and each other for mutual edification.

Seventeenth-Century Developments in England

In England those of Presbyterian persuasion continued to hope that eventually their notions of reform would gradually be realized in the Church of England. Even some Congregational groups who did not believe in separation joined in this hope. When, with the execution of Mary Queen of Scots, it became clear that James of Scotland, king of a Presbyterian stronghold, would be the successor of Elizabeth, hopes ran high. Upon his ascension to the throne, the Presbyterian clergy sent a restrained petition to the king, calling for the reform of the church but carefully pointing out that they were not schismatics seeking the dissolution of the state church. To their great disappointment, the king decided in favor of the Anglicans. Not only were the dreams of the Presbyterians destroyed; they were to enter into a period of enforced uniformity and intense opposition. A group of Separatists migrated to Holland to escape persecution and to gain freedom, and some of them later sailed to America and founded the Plymouth Colony.

With the succession to the throne of Charles I and the increasing influence of William Laud, one of the most powerful and intensely Anglican of all English bishops, opposition to dissent expressed itself in an extremely vigorous policy on the part of both church and state. Complete conformity to Anglican practice was demanded, and countless Puritan preachers were deprived of position and not infrequently prosecuted. Because of this policy, many Puritans, most of whom were not Separatists but of Congregationalist leaning, left England and founded the Puritan settlement in Salem, Massachusetts.

In the immediately ensuing years, Anglicans sided with the king, even when he dismissed Parliament in 1629. But when the Long Parliament was convened in 1640, the Presbyterians were in the majority. Laud was cast into prison and the arbitrary actions of the king resulted in civil war two years later. Episcopacy was abolished and the Book of Common Prayer forbidden. Parliament called the Westminster Assembly for the purpose of effecting a new and proper church order. Under the influence of the Scots, whom Parliament definitely needed on its side in the war, it was insisted that the pattern for the new order be in line with that of the best Reformed churches. Present in the assembly were eight Scottish commissioners, lay members of both houses of Parliament, five Independent ministers, and a few of Anglican leaning. But dominating the entire assembly were the Presbyterian divines. Under their influence the Westminster Confession of Faith was formulated.

The Westminster Confession is both like and unlike the general Puritan understanding. While the particular affirmations are shared among Presbyterians and Puritans generally, the spirits of the two groups were different. When one reads Puritan writings, one catches a sense of vital and living faith. Earlier in this chapter, we noted the strong experiential quality of Puritan thinking. The Westminster Confession, which for a long time informed Presbyterian thinking and which still holds a prominent place in some segments of the Presbyterian church, is a concise and formal statement of points to be accepted. As an example of clarity and theological precision in confessions, it is a masterpiece. Yet it is a Puritan document curiously devoid of the usual vitality of Puritanism. Perhaps this was inevitable in the kind of semicreedal writing which characterized it. Like all such formulations, it suffers when the faith which underlies it is not evident to those who read it. In this instance, the situation is particularly telling, since the theology of Puritanism, apart from its experiential basis, is especially difficult. More than anything else, the Westminster Confession is responsible for later negative attitudes toward Calvinism.

The catechisms prepared by the assembly were in fact more representative of the Puritan spirit than was the Confession. The Directory for Public Worship likewise exhibited this spirit and hewed a path between a "prescribed liturgy and extemporaneous prayer." The schemes for church order, including ordination and discipline, had no chance of implementation because of the opposition of the non-Presbyterians who, in the changing political scene, became more influential.

Many Independents or Congregationalists (who had held a congregational understanding of the church combined with a Calvinistic view of the relation of religion to all of life) had not been Separatists but became so under Presbyterian pressure for uniformity. John Milton was convinced that the "new Presbyter is but old Priest writ large" and that out of Westminster one could not expect toleration. In the

Commonwealth and Protectorate under Oliver Cromwell, who had defeated Charles I, the Presbyterians were unable to assume control as they had expected. Cromwell himself was an Independent and insisted upon toleration for many of the religious groups. But he did not accept the principle of separation completely. Rejecting both Presbyterian and Anglican domination, he yet insisted upon some control of church order and payment of clergy by the state. Through local Committees of Ejectors, unfit clergy to the number of over six thousand were deprived of their positions, while through a national committee of Triers, the vacancies were filled from among Presbyterians, Independents, and Baptists. Since the primary criteria for incumbency were a godly life and trustworthy political opinions — obviously those which would not threaten the new regime — a considerable number of Anglicans remained. In this way, Cromwell worked out a system which comprehended diverse elements while maintaining national control. Although Quakers had no clergy and therefore did not fit into this scheme, they, too, were tolerated by Cromwell and were comparatively unmolested (see subsequent section "The Quakers").

This settlement lasted no longer than the life of Oliver Cromwell. His son Richard had neither the understanding nor forcefulness of his father. Presbyterians and Royalists alike longed for the restoration of the monarchy. In the Long Parliament and in the Convention Parliament, which was to work out the details of the recall of Charles II, the Presbyterians had a majority. Their intention was to work out a system which would include Presbyterians and Anglicans in one national church. Had they insisted upon this as the basis of the recall, rather than on subscription by Charles II to a nebulous statement granting liberty to tender consciences, they might have been more successful. As it was, the political settlement was made and the king, with the support of the Anglicans, dismissed the Convention Parliament, and the newly elected Cavalier Parliament, composed primarily of Royalists and Anglicans, reestablished Anglicanism more securely than ever. Exiles returned and suppressed Anglicans came back to life. As one writer has put it, Archbishop Laud was more successful in death than in life, for now his dreams were realized.

From this point on, the Presbyterian hope of belonging to a national church in England was completely shattered. Now Presbyterians shared the lot of Independents and Baptists. In the Act of Uniformity of 1662, episcopal ordination was required and all clergy had to subscribe to the revised Book of Common Prayer. It was a serious offense even to attend a service which was not conducted in accord with the Prayer Book. Now the Puritans were definitely forced out of the Anglican fold into the role of "Protestant" dissenters; and severe penalties were attached to dissent.

Not until the advent of William and Mary, who came to the throne partly through Protestant support, did the picture change. The Act of Toleration of 1689 was "An Act to exempt their magistrates' Protestant subjects dissenting from the Church of England from the penalties of certain laws." However, such Protestants had to be trinitarian, and their places of meeting had to be registered. Clergy had to subscribe to the doctrinal, though not liturgical, aspects of the Thirty-nine Articles. Not until 1779 was the authority of the Bible substituted for the Thirty-nine Articles, and not until 1813 were nontrinitarians tolerated. From the time of 1689, however, toleration of dissenters was never withdrawn. The Church of England was the established church, but the ideal of encompassing the diverse elements in one national church had been given up.

Puritanism in New England

In America, the goal of Puritanism was more nearly realized. Plymouth Colony had been founded by Separatists coming from England after a sojourn in Holland. Salem was established by Congregational groups who fled under the period of Laud. Within ten years' time over twenty thousand men and women came to the latter colony, including such distinguished divines as John Cotton, John Davenport, and Richard Mather.

The relations between Plymouth and Salem were friendly, but New England Puritanism was formed more by the latter than by the former. In the new situation in America, Puritans set out to do what had become impossible in England. The Puritan ideal of ordering all under God was combined with a congregational view of the church. Most of the New England Puritans were non-Separatist Congregationalists who had hoped to reform the Church of England from within. They felt that they were doing just this in America. The church was to be made up only of professed believers, covenanted together in local churches, but dominated by the Calvinistic ideal of a society ordered in worship and in all realms of life by a single religious understanding. This was a hope which emerged out of the English scene, but which became effective only in America.

The historic development in New England, however, manifested both variety and problems. The first generation, cast into a wilderness far from the life they had known, consoled themselves in having set up a true church, of which the chief characteristic was its vibrant purity. For such persons, proclamation of the Word and the rightful administration of the sacraments was not an adequate way to characterize the church. In addition, purity of worship and a visible Christian life needed to be guaranteed and tested through one's own conversion narrative if one was to be fully a member of the church.

Such visibility of life initially had no other rationale than to be the appropriate form of existence as one waited for the end time. But as the end did not come when expected — though it continued to be expected until well into the eighteenth century — and as events in England made the first generation's sojourn in New England a unique and lasting experience, new adaptations were necessary. In the second generation, the errand in the wilderness shifted from church to society in the sense that the religious dimensions took on social and political forms. There is a difference between structures that are provisional, as the first generation thought of their experiment, and those that result when one more permanently has to face the future. While the faith of the Old Testament had always been a paradigm or analogue to the Puritan consciousness, in the second and succeeding generations the religion of the Old Testament was supplemented by a regard for Israel as a total religious-political commonwealth. In that context, the Puritans could think of New England as the place which God had saved for the last, most complete manifestation of the divine purpose. Like Israel, they had a special destiny, the one standing at the beginning of God's plan, the other at the end, an end now differently comprehended, one slower in arrival and more social in character.

The arrival of settlers who had less interest in Christianity and more interest in social betterment coincided with the fact that some of the descendants of the first generation did not have the vibrancy of faith characteristic of their parents and grandparents. This created problems for those who had just redefined the goal of the errand in the wilderness. A Christian commonwealth could only be secured, it was felt, if voting and political rights were restricted to pure Christians, to those whose active faith had been tested and found adequate, who had the right of access to the sacraments.

It had perhaps been assumed too readily that the resources available would lead more people to be full communicants. It was widely assumed that preaching — that is, the laying open of the text, the elaboration of doctrine, demonstrating the truth thereof, and showing its application to life — would be more productive than indeed it was. A widely held assumption was that a severe declension had set in, that people did not adequately use the means available to them; the "the cannot" with which many described their inability to know the vibrancy of faith was indeed a "will not" for which one could be held responsible. In that situation of personal and social lukewarmness with respect to matters of faith, the jeremiad sermons became new lightning rods with which to prod the unwilling or the defected, joining understanding with strong emotional overtones.

But history was not on the side of the pure. For a time change could be avoided, largely through the fact that the churches were protected by the Charter which the Puritans had wrung from Charles I before leaving England. When those who are required to go to church but are excluded from full membership and the sacraments number more than the full communicants, a new reality is at hand which can hardly be ignored. Initially, the sacraments had been considered the seals of the covenant, or as the Westminster Confession of Faith put it, holy signs and seals of the covenant of grace. They thus belonged to those who know and who have experienced grace, who could provide the evidence that they indeed were true believers in thought and in deed. Sacraments thus were a sequel, a condescension to our corporeality in a situation in which religion was fundamentally spiritual. Or to put it another way, sacraments were visible sermons, though unlike sermons, not available to everyone.

Adaptation was inevitable as the problems could not be solved on the older basis. We noted previously that baptism was interpreted as a sign that you belonged to the covenant, not that one had been launched as an infant on a path one would oneself eventually appropriate, just as one's parents had done. But a situation arose in which the children of believers did not become full communicants, but still wanted their children baptized. Under the terms of the Halfway Covenant, such persons could be baptized. Moreover, all who believed in God but could not give the testimonies necessary for full membership, while barred from communion and voting on spiritual matters, were still considered members of the church and had the rights of citizenship.

A final blow to this way of understanding the life of the church occurred through the activities of Solomon Stoddard in Northampton, who saw the sacraments as themselves converting instruments. Hence, the communion, as the sermon, was available to all who believed in whatever gradations. While such an approach was widely resisted, including the resistance of Stoddard's own grandson, Jonathan Edwards (who for a period shared the parish with him), the two-tiered membership was doomed, including the rigors of church membership as originally understood.

Under the pressure of these and additional internal problems, it became necessary to modify the stress on the local church in the direction of some overall control. The local body remained the only true "church," but associations of clergy arose to deal with matters which affected the life of all the churches, such as education and the combating of divisions within the churches. For example, the Separatist views of Roger Williams, the remarks of Anne Hutchinson, and later still the coming of Quakers, demanded more than local treatment. Moreover, criticism from Puritans abroad concerning the exclusion of Presbyterians from full communion could not be answered by a local church. Nor could individual local bodies effectively protest against the Separatist views which came to dominate English Congregationalists after 1640. Further, the loss of the Charter in 1684 made it more important for the church to have an overall structure.

For a number of reasons, therefore, associations of churches and clergy developed early. Although the theory remained that such associations were merely consultative and practical, for all practical purposes they determined policy. While the Cambridge Platform of 1648 reaffirmed the congregational principle, it was itself the product of ecclesiastical forces which partly belied the principle. Thus New England Congregationalism, in order to maintain its Calvinistic ideals in relation to society, moved administratively closer to a Presbyterian conception of the ordering of the church by bodies more inclusive than the local church. But it never gave up its conception that the local church alone is the church. Indeed, that accent has continued to this day in the United Church of Christ, to the satisfaction of some, and the disaffection of others.

The Quakers

The Quakers were the most distinctive of the movements related to Puritanism. They arose out of the religious unrest of England during the period of Cromwell and stood for a radical kind of reform within Christendom which contrasted sharply with Protestant, Anglican, and Roman patterns alike. They preferred to think of themselves as the third way in Christendom, over against Roman Catholicism and Protestantism.

Small groups of "Friends" (as they called themselves) first met in the Lake District of England, and the movement spread throughout England. One of the foremost protagonists of the Friends was George Fox, who went up and down the length of England, disputing the beliefs of Christians, not infrequently interrupting sermons to challenge what was said and turning the challenge into a sermon itself. Fox felt called upon by God to gather people to the truth from out of the steeple-houses, as he called the churches:

> Now the Lord had shewed me, while I was in Derby prison, that I should speak in steeple-houses, to gather people from thence; and a concern sometimes would come upon my mind about the pulpits that the priests lolled in. For the steeple-houses and pulpits were offensive to my mind, because both priests and people called them the house of God, and idolised them; reckoning that God dwelt there in the outward house. Whereas they should have looked for God and Christ to dwell in their hearts, and their bodies to be made the temples of God; for the Apostle said, 'God dwelleth not in temples made with hands': but by reason of the people's idolising those places, it was counted a heinous thing to declare against them.[2]

Such conduct was hardly likely to be tolerated in a period not at all convinced of the value of tolerance. In spite of persecution, the move-

---

[2] George Fox, *Journal* (New York, 1948. Everyman's Library), p. 49.

ment grew. The essential seriousness of Quakers — so named because they quaked at the Word of God — soon won the respect of many and even a degree of toleration under Cromwell. In America, they suffered at the hands of the Puritans, but had freedom in Rhode Island (though Roger Williams considered them wrong) and in Pennsylvania, the colony started by Quaker William Penn with the principle of toleration as one of its cornerstones.

The fundamental tenet of the Quakers was that God is directly approachable and experienced within themselves. They spoke of the light within, or of Christ within, even of God within. God's spirit was immediately present and discernible to all who sought God in sincerity. God's truth and way of life could be directly apprehended.

To those Protestants who did not share this conviction, this appeared as a direct denial of everything biblical. The Puritans found sin rather than God within. Quakers, in contrast, insisted on the essential goodness of humanity. Puritans felt that the emphasis upon immediate revelation of the Spirit within led to uncertainty as to knowledge of the true God, disclosed in the Bible. They suspected that the Quakers belonged to the mystical tradition and had no adequate criterion of truth. (To be sure, the Quakers were in a heritage related to mysticism, though they were not directly its heirs.) Barclay in his *Apology* was quick to point out that "neither tradition nor the Scriptures, nor reason which the Papists, Protestants, and Socinians do respectively make the rule of their faith are in any whit more certain." Roman Catholics disagreed about tradition. The Protestants contended over the meaning of the Bible even as they idolized it. And the Socinians, a late-sixteenth-century rationalistic group, disagreed over the results obtained by reason. In contrast, Quakers felt that what emerged out of their own seeking was both more definite and consistent.

Early Quakers felt that they were carrying out the logical implications of the Reformation. Not infrequently, they quoted the reformers themselves. Both Jesus Christ and the Bible were important, but in no case should they be in the way of the believer's direct apprehension of God. In Jesus of Nazareth the love of God was historically manifest, and in the eternal Christ present in humanity, God is continually accessible and available. The Bible is an account of the historical manifestations of this love and it contains much truth which is important for us. But as such it is neither the word of God nor truth. Truth can be found directly by those who wait quietly for the Lord. The Bible itself bears witness to such truth discernible within. One needs to discover and rediscover this truth as the source of one's life, letting nothing else pull one aside.

The stringent emphasis upon the truth within gave discipline and order to the lives of Quakers. In this respect, they were a part of the Puritan ethos, in which life was ordered from top to bottom by the truth as perceived. For Quakers, a life, simple and elegant in its dignity, was more important than all thought. Plain speech and simple clothes were adopted. Integrity in all things was prized above all else. A life given in suffering was more important than all striving, since it witnessed to the truth and peace of God.

Since God was found directly within, it was the responsibility of each to discover and profess the truth. For Quakers, this implied a distinctive pattern of worship. The Quaker meeting was a place where each, in the presence of the others, meditated silently upon God's presence and spoke only as one felt called to do so, whether on God's presence itself or on the meaning of God's presence for some problem. Such directness excluded an organized ministry as well as a special church building, or a liturgical order of worship. Quaker organization existed only for the sake of convenience in coming together, in keeping records, and in taking care of other details of their common activity. All decisions involving action were jointly agreed upon, not by vote, but by a kind of consensus which the secretary recorded as the sense of the meeting. Until a consensus could be safely affirmed, nothing was recorded.

In the world at large, Quaker concern early manifested itself in the alleviation of suffering and in philanthropic works. Most Quakers have also believed in nonresistance, and have remained impartial in the conflicts between nations. Although this at times proved embarrassing, as in the Revolutionary War, it frequently made Quakers emissaries of relief and reconciliation across the chasms which have torn the rest of the world.

CHAPTER VI

Revival of the Evangelical Spirit

In Chapter IV we noted how the Lutheran churches increasingly emphasized right belief, and made assent to theological formulations central to the Christian life. They had unwittingly taken on the ethos and argumentative nature of rationalism. This made Christian faith exceedingly formal and aloof to those who rightly sensed that the New Testament emphasized justification and the new life in Christ as the basis for all Christian living and thinking.

In England, on the other hand, the vitality of faith was seriously weakened by the alliance with "natural religion," an attempt to ground faith in a universal knowledge of God through reason and nature. This led to formalism in the churches and to a partially "secularized" clergy. The net result was loss of the sense that religion touched the total human being. It appealed to the head without captivating the heart. The work of John Wesley and the Methodist movement successfully revived a faith which moved people's hearts.

The situation in America was similar. Puritanism had lost much of its religious power, while the form and structure of its theology remained intact. In the previous chapter, we noted that the theology of Puritanism at its height was undergirded by a profound and vibrant faith. With the partial loss of that faith, Puritan theology resembled the orthodox developments in Europe, against which Pietism reacted. Theological formulations which no longer reflected an experiential base might be correct: but they became odious when individuals who themselves had lost the power of faith continued to insist upon them. A contributory cause of decline was the Arminian influence which had also penetrated to America. It was part of a general tendency to stress reason above all else in matters of religious doctrine.

Pietism on the Continent, Methodism in England, and the great awakenings in America shared in a common pattern. Connections between them can be traced. Wesley visited a Pietist community on the Continent and read the Pietist writings. Whitefield, originally associated with Wesley, was the most noted preacher in the American awakenings. Interesting as these connections are, however, the movements were largely independent of each other in origin. The existence of the movements, rather than their derivation from each other, accounts for the connections. In their differing situations, they arose to arrest current developments by an emphasis upon the experience of the living Christ in people's hearts.

The Pietist Movement

The Pietist tradition began in German Lutheranism, through the work of Philipp Spener and his disciple, August Francke. Both were concerned to revitalize the Lutheran church, whose insistence on right doctrine seemed to make no place for experiential faith in the living Christ. Spener and Francke organized small groups of Lutherans who met together in private homes for the mutual enrichment of their faith. These were to be a leaven in the church, quietly bringing life into its structure. The *collegia pietatis* (associations of piety), as the little groups were called, nourished their faith especially in common study of the Bible. They dedicated themselves to the love of God in Jesus Christ, made known and experienced by the believer as one read and examined the New Testament. In this sense, they considered themselves the heirs of the Reformation. But in emphasizing the new life in Christ, they also felt they were bringing the Reformation understanding of justification to its fulfillment. The believer was not only justified; the believer lived a new life. One must be holy and as nearly perfect as possible. Perfection, however, was not interpreted as sinlessness; it meant definite progress in the Christian life. Such progress would be evidence of an undeviating allegiance to spiritual reality in contrast to the worldliness of the time, including that of the church and its clergy.

Pietists were under no illusions about how much they might accomplish. They did not expect much in this life. But the small communities in the midst of the churches were considered to represent the truly saved and redeemed community. As the redeemed, they did not pine for the end of the world, though many of them expected it momentarily. Rather, salvation was already present in their communities. Because of this the churches could be transformed, but the Pietists had no hope that the world as such would be changed. They were concerned with the living presence of Christ in the hearts and wills of individuals. Where two or three were gathered together in the Spirit, a community within the larger community of the church was born. In the terminology of a later time, the Pietists were disciplined "cell" groups who experienced and practiced the presence of Christ.

By intention, Pietism was lay minded. The concept of the priesthood of all believers now became a religious focus for insisting upon the responsibility of every person for the neighbor. Individuals not only studied the Word together, they exhorted each other toward faith and reminded each other of their responsibilities. They were examples to each other. Unfortunately, though they proclaimed the experience of forgiveness, they often were not themselves excellent examples of forgiveness. While insisting that the presence of Christ introduced warmth and feeling in life, they were nevertheless unbending toward those who had gone astray. Thus, Pietism was both personal and impersonal. It was personal in the sense of awakening each person to the unique and direct way in which the Spirit of Christ can transform human life. It was impersonal in that excessive emphasis upon the new life made many impatient of professions of piety which still exhibited marks of worldliness. To be in Christ meant to reject that which was not of Christ, and to have no traffic with it. It was inevitable that those not in sympathy with this outlook felt judged rather than exhorted, and suspected an element of unintended self-righteousness.

The genuine warmth of Pietism stemmed from the gospel itself. The movement should not finally be judged by how it reacted to what it disliked. Tired of the theological speculations of the Protestant scholastics, Pietists pointed to the practical and penetrating power of the gospel as it affected people's wills and hearts. Theological disputes were considered irrelevant and detrimental insofar as they were responsible for the loss of vitality within Christianity. From the standpoint of new life in Christ, doctrinal differences were unimportant.

The truth in this contention was that theology had lost its vitality and was no longer an adequate representation of the faith. It had become a substitute for faith. Nevertheless, every confession of the presence of Christ has theological implications, even when these are not explicitly stated. And this was no less true of Pietists. They tended to gloss over the depth of sin. Although they asserted that all needed to be justified, they quickly moved to sanctification, or the new life in Christ. The miracle and mystery of faith was sidestepped by an emphasis upon the availability of faith to all who would make the decision of faith. And those who could say that they had experienced Christ cultivated Christ's presence as if he could not and would not be absent from consciousness even for a moment.

The intention of Pietists was to revitalize Lutheranism without changing any of its religious conceptions or organizational structure. They did not realize how their own distinctive emphasis was often at variance with fundamental tenets of Lutheranism. This was sensed more by orthodox church leaders than by Pietists, and there was frequent opposition on the part of the former. Generally, however, Pietist groups remained in the churches. Usually, they thought of themselves as the leaven in the dough.

In one important instance, the Pietist movement did result in a separate religious body. Count Zinzendorf, a German nobleman whose pietistic tendencies were confirmed by contact with Francke, offered his estate at Herrnhut to the remnants of the Bohemian Hussites. The latter, suffering under persecution, gladly accepted. Originally, Zinzendorf paid little attention to the group from a religious viewpoint, but soon found himself both their patron and religious leader. The unwillingness of most of them to become members of the Lutheran church made it inevitable that they be consolidated into a distinct community. They became known as the Moravians, a name derived from the province of their origin.

Herrnhut became a center whose influence went far beyond its own confines. Christians from all over Europe visited the community to learn the secret of the Christian life in this community of grace. But even more important than this was the intense missionary consciousness of the community. Missionaries were sent throughout Europe, even to Greenland and the West Indies. Under the leadership of August Spangenberg, a settlement was made in Georgia. Several years later some of the Moravians in Georgia moved to Pennsylvania. Zinzendorf, on a visit to America, named this settlement Bethlehem, and it is still the center of Moravian influence in America.

The impact of the Pietist movement, both within the churches and in the Moravian communities, was extensive. The University of Halle and later the University of Tübingen became centers of Pietist influence. Through these universities, many of the promising minds of the future were shaped by the Pietist tradition and continued to exhibit many of its qualities even as they spoke against the movement. Individuals as diverse as the philosopher Immanuel Kant (see Ch. VII) and the theologian Friedrich Schleiermacher (see Ch. IX) bore the traces of Pietist upbringing and learning. For people disillusioned by theological bickering, religious wars, and rationalist patterns of thought, Pietism offered a religious dimension which touched the center of life. It provided a source of vitality in a period in which many were dissatisfied with old ways of thinking and were searching for new directions.

The Emergence of Methodism

The Cult of Reasonableness in England

After 1689 both the Church of England and the Protestant bodies settled down to a period of comparative security. The battles had been fought and a religious settlement had been reached. But the new and unchallenged stability in the church was itself open to the possibility of stagnation and loss of vitality. Within the Church of England a rationalistic form of religion increasingly manifested itself. This was already latent in the Caroline Divines, who had emphasized the role of reason and morality as a component of the religious life. It was more evident in the Latitudinarians, who had tried to reconcile the faith with broad philosophical and scientific assumptions by showing the reasonableness of faith. But in the case of the Caroline Divines and the Latitudinarians, the struggles with the Puritans over the nature of the church kept the rationalist elements from becoming dominant.

However, with this battle over, the forces whose motto was reasonableness came to the fore. To them the controversy between Puritans and the Anglicans was itself justification for a simple appeal to reason in settling religious disputes. As on the Continent, theological argument seemed like sterile and irrelevant bickering to those who believed that the fight was over nonessentials. They thought that an essential reasonableness ought to prevail in matters of religion and maintained that, after all, Christianity was essentially a reasonable religion.

The relation between the church and the new faith in reason had three important phases. In the first phase the supernatural character of the Christian revelation was maintained and declared to be in accord with reason. Prophecy and miracle were considered the two major supernatural and natural evidences of the truth of Christianity. Nothing was considered more reasonable than that Jesus was the Messiah, though the proof of this was found in prophecy and miracle rather than in reason by itself. The preeminence of Christianity over all other religious views was still assumed and proclaimed as being in line with both reason and revelation. Such an outlook found itself at home within the church.

The second phase was also characterized by the harmonizing of Christianity and reason. Christianity was seen as an instance or illustration of the "natural religion" of human beings. Natural religion meant simply those religious tenets justified by reason and found in religions generally. Almost a century earlier, Lord Herbert of Cherbury had announced five principal tenets of such a religion. They were: that there is a divine being, that this divine being is to be worshipped, that proper worship consists in moral obedience and piety, that obedience is to be rewarded and disobedience to be punished, and that reward and punishment continue after this life.

It was now declared that at heart Christianity was in accord with these tenets, though it had special forms of worship and practice. Moreover, since the beginning of time people have accepted these fundamental religious tenets. Thus Matthew Tindal could write a book called *Christianity as Old as Creation*. In essence, Christianity is older than Christ, since Christ recalls us to the religion which is as old as creation. The mission of Christianity is to republish the religion of nature, to call us back to a religion which had been obscured through sin.

A considerable number of Anglican clergy held this view even as they read the Book of Common Prayer and administered the rites of the church. But there were some who did not follow such views. Bishop Butler's *Analogy* was written particularly to refute the views of Tindal, by pointing out that there were as many difficulties and obscurities in natural religion as in revealed religion. But he did not succeed in winning adherents among those who were convinced that the way to true religion lay simply in reasonableness and clarity.

The third phase was testimony to the strength of those who believed that religion must be reasonable above all else. The second phase had already meant abandoning crucial points of the faith. Now there appeared outright opposition between Christianity and a form of natural religion called deism. In many respects, the antagonism centered in the understanding of the Bible. Those interested in reason attacked the miracles of the Bible, including the resurrection, as mythological. And by mythological, they meant fanciful and devoid of truth. (As we shall see, modern Protestants have to thank groups of this type for the early development of the biblical criticism which is now taken for granted.)

We need not concern ourselves with this third phase of the problem. Nor need we treat the first and second differently insofar as they relate to the spiritual life of the church. Whether certain religious affirmations were declared to be supernatural and defended essentially by reason, or whether certain supernatural aspects were shunted aside in favor of a fundamental core which Christianity and natural religion had in common, made little difference. Both promoted an attitude of indifference to what had been felt to be central and distinctive Christian affirmations. Certainly neither seriously touched people's hearts or lives. That had to happen apart from all arguments. The spirit of rationalism was met by another spirit, namely, the Holy Spirit, as it laid hold of people's lives.

The Nature of the New Spirit: John Wesley

The secure position of Anglicanism and the invasion of the rationalistic spirit combined to sap the spiritual life of the church. The resurgence of a vital Christianity resulted from the labors of a handful of individuals, chief among whom were John Wesley, Charles Wesley, and George Whitefield. The greatest preacher among them was undoubtedly Whitefield, noted for his preaching in both England and America. Charles Wesley is primarily known for the hymns which he bequeathed to a circle infinitely wider than the Methodists. But it is John Wesley who was responsible for creating the distinctive Methodist movement.

John Wesley was the son of a devout mother and of an Anglican priest of High Church leanings. He was a distinguished student and was elected a fellow at Oxford. There he became the leader of a group originally organized by his brother Charles, for the purpose of study and discipline so that the lives of the members might properly be directed to God and salvation. This group became known as the "Holy Club" or as the "Methodists," both originally being terms of derision.

Soon Wesley was sent to Georgia as a missionary. En route to America, he was much impressed by the faith of a band of Moravians in the midst of a terrible storm. In Georgia itself, things did not go as well as expected, though Wesley worked prodigiously. The natives were less prone to accept Christianity than the "noble savage" described in the literature of Europe. The settlers, on the other hand, found Wesley's High Churchmanship and rigorous demands not at all to their liking. His inability to decide between celibacy and marriage, though he had given a young lady some reason to believe his intentions were matrimony, did not help his situation.

The truth is that, although a priest of the Church of England, Wesley had not yet found himself. And he knew it. Upon his return to England, Wesley one evening reluctantly went to a religious meeting in Aldersgate Street. It turned out to be the event which changed his life. In Wesley's own words:

> In the evening I went very unwillingly to a society in Aldersgate Street, where one was reading Luther's preface to the *Epistle to the Romans.* About a quarter of nine, while he was describing the change which God works in the heart through faith in Christ, I felt my heart strangely warmed. I felt I did trust in Christ, Christ alone for my salvation; and an assurance was given me that He had taken away my sins, even mine, and saved me from the law of sin and of death.[1]

This was Wesley's surrender to the forgiving, revivifying power of God. Now he had experienced God's presence and power much as the Moravians whom he had so admired.

The significance of Wesley's conversion, as that of his brother Charles three days before him, was that now he had experienced in his heart what he had vaguely believed in his mind. He had known about God's grace and presence; but now he had experienced it. He had known that he could not come to God through work, but now he knew that he had been trying to do so nevertheless. From this he was now free; and he knew how free others might be who also shared this faith. Such persons under the power of God could transform a world and march on to perfection.

This experience, together with the faith that grew out of it, is the

[1] *John Wesley's Journal* (London, 1949), p. 51.

point for understanding Wesley's subsequent thinking and behavior. Wesley did not think new thoughts as a result of his conversion. He did not even let the old ones go. He related them to his new experience and transformed them in this way. The rigor of the Holy Club at Oxford was never lost. It became part of the intense ethical concern that all life be lived in the service of God, much as in Puritanism. Card playing and other amusements were rejected because they could not qualify under the rule of utilizing all one's time and energies under God. Drinking, which in the England of this period was an acute social problem, was particularly rejected. (It was perhaps inevitable that succeeding ages should forget the reason and only remember that certain acts were proscribed.)

The semimystical writings of individuals such as William Law and the Pietist tradition were also a definite part of the religious heritage of Wesley. But the nuances were distinctive. Wesley found Law's writings too mystical and not sufficiently based on Jesus Christ. But he was forever impressed by their depth and warmth of faith. The pietistic Moravians had attracted him ever since his trip to Georgia. Shortly after his conversion, he visited the Herrnhut community. It left an ineradicable impression upon him. Nevertheless, he found the members of the community, much as Law, too subjective in their faith and therefore not sufficiently based in Christ. Moreover, they appeared too complacent, assuming that piety would automatically produce fruit in personal and social life. For Wesley, faith must express itself in a definite pattern and direction. The difference can be illustrated by reference to the social scene. Neither Wesley nor the Pietists challenged the *status quo*. Economically and politically, they were conservative. But Wesley's sense for meaningful discipline and direction had tremendous social consequences. His dictum, "earn all you can, save all you can, give all you can," was formulated as a part of his faith, expressing the needful components of activity, honesty, frugality, and charity in the Christian life. It fostered economic development and supplied a conscience in the midst of it. Methodists as a result were often in the forefront of reform movements relating to the new industrialism.

Basically, the content of Wesley's newly discovered faith was the intimate experience of the empowering presence of Christ. Nothing else mattered. Wesley's singular devotion to Christ and what might be accomplished through Christ lay behind his concept of "Christian perfection." Perfection, for him, meant nothing else than full devotion to Christ, expressed in every act. It is important to stress the element of devotion rather than the acts. At times, Wesley did speak of perfection in terms of perfect acts or an achieved pattern of life. But when he did, he usually denied, as did Calvin, that perfection is a possibility for the Christian. Usually, Wesley referred to singular devotion to Christ as the essence of perfection. It is "simplicity of intention and purity of affection," guiding the life and work of women and men. If, as a result, the Christian's life is almost morally perfect, Wesley's real point was still that perfection refers to the power of the ever-present Christ so to transform our nature that we will do nothing but good and pure acts. Perfection is the state of being in Christ. Christ fills and permeates one's being, just as the bloodstream sends vitality through the human body. Perfect acts are but the consequence of this presence and are not to be considered apart from them. Where perfect acts are themselves the norm, living in Christ is secondary. That would have been utterly foreign to Wesley's intention.

Perfection is living in the presence of Christ and sin is failure to live in the fullness of that presence. At times Wesley's enthusiastic description of the life in Christ led him to make affirmations about moral perfection which appeared to shift the base from which he spoke. In the same way, his opposition to particular flagrant violations of God's will led him to denounce these in such a way that it sometimes seemed as if sin meant simply particular sins. Nevertheless, his fundamental orientation was clear.

Wesley's insistence that activity emerges out of grace was thoroughly in the Reformation tradition. But he gave this insight a distinctive turn by his emphasis on the life of experienced grace, zealous moral endeavor, and growth toward perfection. He considered the new life in grace so important that he relegated many other aspects of the faith to a peripheral position. It was not that he rejected these; on the contrary, Wesley was quite satisfied with the general theological tradition of the Thirty-nine Articles and the Prayer Book. He was simply concerned to emphasize certain elements in the tradition which had been neglected and were essential to a vital church. It was just this powerful concern with inward experience and moral living, however, which gave the Methodist movement its distinctive character — and this could and did often lead in later generations of Methodists to subjectivism and legalistic moralism, in which the larger theological background of Wesley's work was omitted.

Wesley did reject the concept of predestination. If God is just, individuals are not foreordained to damnation. The issue of their destiny must remain open. Anything less destroys the freedom of individuals, even the freedom which belongs to the sinner. We are not machines; we are essentially moral beings, whose activities have implications for the future.

Yet Wesley did not believe that we redeem ourselves. Although he believed in the uniqueness of every individual and insisted on safeguarding human freedom, he had a deep sense for the catastrophic and fateful character of the Fall. He insisted that nothing but God could rescue us. Apart from grace, we could do nothing good. But the Fall did not destroy our nature as responsible beings. And God's grace was continually given to sinful people, making it possible for them to respond to God's call. This was not the grace of faith, but the prior grace which enabled us to make the decision of faith. It was the ground of the freedom from which one might begin.

Wesley contended that those who nurtured this prior grace could expect God to respond in being present. Their seeking in grace was the precondition for God's full redeeming activity. But an individual was not justified, however, by this prior grace or by seeking. Anyone was redeemed through the empowering reality which came in the midst of one's search. One was justified by the fresh activity of God. But this came only to those who freely responded.

The advent of justifying grace could be sudden, but it could also be experienced as a moment in a gradual process of growth in grace. Justification was simply the forgiveness of sins. Sanctification, on the other hand, was the process of growth initiated by justification. It was the increasing presence of the grace of God in the human heart. But it was likewise the act of individuals expressing in works and discipline the new life which had come to them. Grace and works thus belonged together, mutually reinforcing each other. In fact, Wesley did not reject the notion of "saving works," provided they were understood as emerging from the regenerative power of the presence of Christ. Nothing was more characteristic of Methodism than the insistence that the Christian grows in grace and increasingly exhibits the perfect qualities of Christ.

Results of the New Spirit

In the power of such a message, Wesley found himself traveling the length and breadth of the English land, preaching whenever occasion presented itself. He declared: "I looked upon all the world as my parish; thus far I mean, that in whatever part of it I am, I judge it meet, right, and my bounden duty to declare unto all that are willing to hear, the glad tidings of salvation."[2] Nor was such preaching in vain. He, like George Whitefield, found ready audiences wherever he went. People were longing to hear a redemptive message which warmed the heart and imparted new life. They were ready for a religion which made a difference in their lives.

Whitefield was undoubtedly the greater preacher of the two. But it was Wesley's genius for "follow-up" and organization which created the Methodist movement. He established societies which met together separately to hear the Word and encourage a strict discipline. Wesley even issued tickets which needed renewal from time to time if one was to remain in good standing. In this way, he exercised control in order to increase genuine spirituality.

[2] Norman Sykes, *The English Religious Tradition* (London, 1953), p. 65.

Later he organized Methodist groups in "classes," each group consisting of twelve with a class leader. Aside from providing a convenient way to collect necessary funds, this device also helped to strengthen control over the societies. Increasingly, Wesley found himself not only preaching but also supervising the Methodist groups scattered throughout the country.

Contrary to his expectations, Wesley's work was not well received in the Anglican church. The clergy would neither cooperate nor participate. As a result, Wesley had to depend upon a number of lay preachers. Nevertheless, the work prospered and Wesley found it necessary to organize the societies in ways which made them virtually into a separate denomination. This was not his intention. Yet as the years went by, he had come to hold that in the New Testament, a presbyter was the same as a bishop, and because of the need of clergy, he began to ordain, first for America and then also for England. This made the position of Methodism within Anglicanism even more precarious.

The result of Wesley's work was that deism and natural religion were effectively challenged in the church. New vitality had entered into Anglicanism. But equally important, Wesley reached thousands of individuals who were never touched by the established church. In the increasing concentration of workers in towns as the industrial revolution progressed, Methodism was always near at hand, offering a spiritual experience and a new discipline, a source of hope and dignity for those of the lower levels of the new society. Unlike Anglicanism, Methodism did not have to wait for an act of Parliament. Nevertheless, Methodism in England remained within Anglicanism until after Wesley's death. By that time, it had prompted evangelical stirrings within the Church of England which continued to manifest themselves for some time in spite of the break with the Methodists.

Wesley had also sent missionaries to America. Some worked in the New York area, others in the South where they were greatly helped by the current awakenings. Greatest among the missionaries was undoubtedly Francis Asbury. During the Revolutionary War, Asbury favored the American cause while Wesley counseled neutrality. By the end of the war, American Methodists were restive and felt that the demands of the gospel in a new world needed greater zeal, flexibility, and mobility than associations with Anglicanism would allow. By this time Wesley was in agreement on the desirability of a separate American church. But both Asbury and Thomas Coke, set apart by Wesley to be superintendents in America, believed that they must also be independent of John Wesley. Out of this feeling, supported by Methodist groups, came the Methodist Episcopal Church in America. It began inauspiciously, but soon was one of the leading denominations in America.

The Great Awakenings

The "Great Awakening" is a term often used to describe the eighteenth-century rebirth of religious vitality which manifested itself in America in the Middle Colonies, in New England, and in the South, particularly in Virginia. Actually, there was no single great awakening, but a series of awakenings scattered in time and in space and relatively independent of each other.[3] It is more difficult to sift out the circumstances occasioning these than those of either Pietism in Germany or Methodism in England. But their situation was not dissimilar to that of the European movements. A theological formalism in the Reformed and Presbyterian churches in the Middle Colonies, and in Puritanism in New England, certainly played its part; outside the churches, a form of deism was widely prevalent.

The first stirrings of the awakenings occurred among the Dutch Reformed in the Middle Colonies in the 1720's. It was inspired by the emotional preaching of Theodore J. Frelinghuysen who demanded a conversion of the heart as the basis for life in the church in place of the formal piety of his listeners. It was not much later that similar manifestations of awakenings occurred in Northampton, Massachusetts, and from there spread sporadically throughout New England.

There were special factors in the New England scene. This was the home of the Puritan experiment. Increasingly, its vitality had disappeared while forms of orthodox views still persisted. Instead of fashioning a Christian society, Puritanism found itself surrounded more and more by the unfaithful. Within the churches themselves there was a spirit of indifference to vibrant religious passions, represented significantly in an increasing interest in Arminian views. Judging by the fact that Arminianism was so frequently attacked by the preachers of the awakening in New England, it was undoubtedly one of the chief occasions for the awakenings. But this was only part of a general development in the direction of stressing that which is "reasonable" in religious formulations. Predestination, the person of Christ, and the nature of redemption had been the central foci of orthodox formulations. A less rigid interpretation tended to make such doctrines more

---

[3] Because of this, we have accepted the term "great awakenings," which was first suggested to us by Professor Robert T. Handy. We are also indebted to him for the term "great revivals" to cover the various expressions of vitality in early-nineteenth-century America (see Ch. VII). This phrase, in contrast to the term "Second Awakening," suggests both the diversity of the movement and its greater stress on emotions. We are also indebted to Professor Handy for other suggestions concerning the American scene.

palatable, but both these and the orthodox formulations had become matters primarily for intellectual debate. They were articles to be believed rather than expressions of a living faith. A similar tendency manifested itself in stress on human decision and responsibility in the covenant relation, rather than on the initiating activity of God. The choice was either Puritanism devoid of much of its vitality or rationalized versions as a substitute. Neither touched the heart as well as the head.

Theologically, Jonathan Edwards represents the revitalization of Calvinism under the new conditions. He attempted to make Calvinism relevant again to the social forces of the time, but without its previous theocratic orientation. Moreover, his theological thinking was undertaken in the context of new philosophies in Europe, such as that of Locke (though he did not succumb to their religious presuppositions). In his battle with the Arminians, he attempted to recapture the living experience of God in Christ which had once informed Puritanism.

In these enterprises, Edwards showed intellectual acumen and considerable originality. He was a theologian for the time and probably the greatest theologian America has produced. But his effect on posterity was greater through his association with the awakening in New England than through his theology. His sermons on a judging, redeeming God, though read from manuscript and devoid of apparent passion, hit the hearts of people and not infrequently were received with great emotion. Edwards tried his best to distinguish between genuine and spurious conversions, and to guide those whom he could. As in Northampton, so in congregation after congregation in New England, people found themselves surrendering to the experience of the mercy of God in a new and intensely emotional way.

Among the Presbyterians in Pennsylvania, New Jersey, and New York, the awakening was spearheaded by the Tennents, father and son. But the person who did more than any other in spreading the awakenings throughout the colonies was George Whitefield, whom we mentioned in connection with the Methodist movement. He was virtually the only link between the awakenings. Both Edwards and the Tennents welcomed him.

Whitefield's tour of America was no less successful than his preaching in England. Even Franklin was forcibly impressed by him. Part of the secret of his success, apart from his own personal ability and charm, was his insistence that the power of the gospel was greater and more important than the traditional denominations. People redeemed by the activity and work of Christ are Christians without reference to their denominational affiliations. Preaching in Philadelphia, Whitefield declared: "Father Abraham, whom have you in Heaven? Any Episcopalians? 'No.' Any Presbyterians? 'No.' Have you any Independents or Seceders? 'No.' Have you any Methodists? 'No, no, no!' Whom have you there? 'We don't know those names here. All who are here are Christians — believers in Christ — men who have been overcome by the blood of the Lamb and the word of his testimony.' Oh, is this the case? Then God help us, God help us all, to forget party names, and to become Christians in deed and in truth."[4] With such eloquent and direct pleading, centered in the simple conviction that the experience of Christ would release one from one's afflictions and make one into a Christian, Whitefield affected the lives of thousands. It is estimated that thirty thousand people were brought into some form of Christian experience through the work of Whitefield and fellow evangelists.

But the awakening was not accepted everywhere with enthusiasm. In the Middle Colonies it became the occasion for a split between two factions which were already in disagreement. The Old Side Presbyterians felt that the confession of faith and appropriate actions by clergy and synods alone safeguarded the Church. They already distrusted the New Side Presbyterians, many of whom were trained either in New England or in the log college instituted by one of the Tennents. When the New Side joined in the awakening, the Old Side decided that this was the last straw. The New Side insisted that only a converted person was a true minister, no matter what education or credentials that person had. The Old Side responded by having the pro-awakening New Brunswick Presbytery forced out of the Synod. This split lasted only for the years 1741–1758.

In New England, too, opposition developed on the part of clergy who were appalled by the display of emotion in the awakening and by the impolite conduct of many revival preachers. A militant group formed under the leadership of Charles Chauncy. Over against the new movement, he defended sobriety and reason in matters of religion. Jonathan Edwards, admitting the excesses of the awakening, took issue with Chauncy and maintained that the whole person must be involved in the Christian experience. Unfortunately, his warning to the revivalists was not heeded. They went their way, the conservative theologians claimed Edwards as their spiritual leader, and the position maintained by Chauncy eventually developed in Unitarianism.

The awakening in the South was largely influenced by the North. Among Presbyterians who had settled in Hanover County, Virginia, the awakening had slowly begun under lay leadership through the reading of sermons of Whitefield and some of Luther's writings. But it came to prominence only after the arrival of William Robinson, sent to this area by the New Brunswick Presbytery of the New Side Presbyterians.

Although there were Baptist groups in the South early in the eigh-

---

[4] William W. Sweet, *The Story of Religion in America* (New York, 1939), p. 206.

teenth century, many came directly from New England under the impact of the awakening. The regular Baptists in New England had not been sympathetic to the awakenings, but many individuals and even Separatist churches became Baptist because the emphasis upon decision and voluntary association identified with the awakening made them feel most at home. Many migrated to the South where they carried on their interest in evangelism. Among the Baptist groups in the South, the awakening had a strong "revivalistic" tone and the enthusiasm engendered caused them to be the victims of persecution. Their calmness in the midst of attack, plus their growth in maturity under it, caused their numbers to increase and brought respect where there had been ridicule.

Thus the awakenings made their impact along the entire Eastern seaboard. The contributions which they made outlasted the awakenings themselves. In the long run, their effects were perhaps more indirect than direct. It was much to expect that the intensity of religious experience inaugurated by the awakenings could last more than a few decades.

The movement made a great contribution to education. Many of the colleges and universities grew out of the need to prepare clergy to serve a revitalized church. Princeton, Rutgers, Brown, and Dartmouth were some of the more significant universities created as a result of the religious impact of the awakenings.

Of greater importance still was the psychological impact of a religious movement which cut across denominational boundaries. In Europe, the Pietist movement and Methodism were more confined to special denominational groups. In America, geographical proximity and the intermixture of divergent groups were favorable to movements cutting through traditional lines. This tendency, so evident in the awakenings, was truly the beginning of a process which gave a distinctive character to American Protestantism.

CHAPTER VII

Trends in America and on the Continent

The Shaping of an American Tradition

Almost imperceptibly Protestantism in America lost its European stamp and assumed forms appropriate to the New World. In many cases, the early forms had differed from European patterns only because the new situation made possible the achievement of goals desired in the Old World, but frustrated there. New England Puritans after all wanted to institute an experiment denied them in England. Baptists in Rhode Island and Quakers in Pennsylvania had hopes that their religious convictions might find freer expression in America than in Europe.

It was inevitable that some of the clashes which occurred in Europe should also arise as the respective groups found themselves in the New World. The conflict between Puritan Congregationalists, Baptists, and Quakers in New England is but one example of this. Nevertheless, the resolution of such strife in America was different from Europe. In the New World a tradition eventually emerged in which the various churches were entirely on their own and free from governmental restriction or support. There was neither conflict nor union between state and church, yet the churches profoundly affected the society in which they lived. In Europe, on the other hand, the pattern continued to be that of a state church favored and supported by government. Adjustments were made which permitted other religious groups to function, though usually at a disadvantage.

It is our present task to delineate some of the religious and historical factors which went into the formation of this distinctive American

Protestant tradition. We have already mentioned the importance of Puritan theology in challenging all claims to absolute power and have hinted at the role this played in the revolution and in the formation of the American nation (see Ch. V, "The Puritan Outlook"). We have also mentioned the role of the Baptists, who in principle insisted upon the separation of church and state. The contact across denominational lines engendered by the great awakenings has also been noted. To these must be added deism, the impact of later revivals, the frontier situation, and the practical impossibility of a state church. These factors, when seen in the context of American history, produced free, national churches, but no national church.[1]

Protestantism and the Founding of the Nation

By the time of the crisis which led to the American Revolution, much of the enthusiasm of the awakenings was gone, except in the South where the awakening had begun somewhat later. In spite of this, the impact of the churches was not seriously diminished. Clergy of Congregational and Presbyterian persuasion in New England and the Middle Colonies were predominantly on the side of the colonies. Moreover, they had prepared the soil of resistance for many through their preaching of a sovereign God who stands over all other sovereigns. They were the heirs of a history in which individual people had defied magistrates before, because of the higher loyalty to God and sometimes for the sake of the liberty of conscience which they demanded for themselves and others. Governments, like individuals, served a higher law than themselves. When they did not do so, it was necessary to resist and replace them. Thus resistance was counseled, not on the basis of national feeling, but in the name of the liberty and justice demanded by a sovereign God.

Simultaneously, the impact of the awakenings on the psyches of the Americans must be taken into account. Both among the traditional churches and among the emergent evangelical groups, the awakenings, while not abandoning their accent on a sovereign God, fostered a spirit of equality among people. Before God, all were equal, sharing the decisions and vitalities of faith. Divided on whether or not an educated clergy was necessary or appropriate, the evangelical thrust leveled hierarchical tendencies, thereby diminishing the social standing of clergy and magistrates alike. Gone was the idea of a single covenanted community with political overtones. In its place stood countless individuals, secure in their personal faith before God, freed of all allegiances to social entities. Indeed, their social matrix was the common chord

---

[1] Toleration in Maryland was for a specific purpose and did not decidedly affect the American pattern.

of personal faith, a bond of faithful people concerned with political entities only when they interfered with their personal existence. Hence, such individuals no longer experienced a loyalty to England or to the original Puritan vision in New England. That psychic change opened them to the Revolution.

Methodists and Anglicans did experience difficulty during the Revolution. Their churches were dependent on the mother country. In New England the Anglican clergy had already pled for bishops from England. Fulfillment of this request would demand an act of Parliament. But to the other churches in New England, such an act was foreign interference which violated the spirit of the original charter. Nor had Presbyterians and Congregationalists forgotten the difficulties caused by Bishop Laud. It is clear why New England Anglicans vigorously favored the Royalist cause. In the South, on the other hand, Anglicans favored the Revolution. They considered the importation of bishops as an infringement of the rights of local vestries. Thus, the Anglicans were divided. Quakers and Moravians, traditionally pacifist groups, suffered most since they were distrusted by both sides.

The Declaration of Independence represented a current of thought derived largely from sources other than the churches. It affirmed certain natural rights, belonging to all people by virtue of their created being. It was essentially equalitarian. The views in the Declaration showed primarily the influence of French thought upon the more elite in American culture of this period. They were also derived partly from the writings of John Locke, whose political theories and views of humanity reflected a secularized Calvinistic background. People who held these views were generally religious, but mostly in a general, natural religion, or deist sense, with little concern for the churches' institutions and theologies, believing that all religions at heart affirmed the same truth, the existence of God and the goodness and equality of all. Jefferson, the writer of the Declaration, was such a person. Not infrequently, such individuals were also members of churches. This was especially true among Anglicans, who seemed to have no difficulty combining deism with the Prayer Book. Two-thirds of the signers of the Declaration of Independence were Anglican laymen, essentially deist in their outlook.

The churches supporting the Revolution had no difficulty accepting the Declaration of Independence. John Witherspoon, the Presbyterian divine who was president of the College of New Jersey, now Princeton University, signed it. To be sure, the churches were concerned with liberty and freedom under God, rather than with "natural equality." Moreover, their understanding of humanity was not that of the deists. Their arguments for equality took account of sin as well as dignity. For some, of course, the rationalist currents within the church made the document itself theologically correct. For different religious reasons people found themselves together in a common struggle, accepting a common declaration of independence. The roots of independence therefore were varied. Religious and so-called secular forces coalesced in the formation of the American nation. Although individuals often had different motivations and reasons for what they did, they found themselves united in common actions and plans.

With victory came the independence of all the churches. Methodists and Anglicans declared their freedom from the mother churches and proceeded to organize along lines which would fit into the new nation. The Methodist group, as we noted, declared its independence of John Wesley and organized itself as the Methodist Episcopal Church. The Anglicans had the problem of obtaining duly consecrated bishops, and when no one would ordain Samuel Seabury in England because he could not take the oath of loyalty to the crown, he was consecrated by three Scottish Anglican bishops. Later, Parliament authorized the consecration of bishops for America through the Church of England, and in 1789 the group in America was formally constituted as the Protestant Episcopal Church in the United States of America.

The independence of the American nation did not cut off associations with European churches. But it did definitely end a period in which connections and influences were sought, even if only to affirm that what had been hoped for in Europe had been accomplished in America. Henceforth, the churches in America were to set their minds and energies to the tasks at home.

The relations of the churches to each other and to the state awaited solution. In some of the colonies, one religious group was still favored and supported by taxes, usually either Puritan or Anglican churches. Although other groups could not be kept out, they had to pay taxes for the support of the group successful in being established in the state. Hence, toleration was at a price. In Pennsylvania there was the greatest freedom and liberty in religion from the beginning. In New Jersey, Delaware, and Rhode Island, toleration and freedom were widespread. There was neither establishment nor the payment of taxes for any religious groups.

In other areas, similar developments were less a matter of principle than of sheer expediency or necessity. Frequently the religious groups in the areas were diverse and no single group could gain control. In New York, for example, establishment did not succeed, and full toleration and freedom did develop eventually. In Virginia, a struggle for religious liberty was led by the Baptists, together with the Hanover Presbytery, against the tax-supported Church of England. We have already noted that for the Baptists as well as the Quakers, separation of church and state was a matter of religious principle. The Hanover Presbytery, a product of the awakenings, was sympathetic to the principle of the church as a voluntary association and thus was also opposed to all encroachments by the state. Most of the Presbyterians favored taxation for all religious groups. Jefferson and Madison agreed with the Baptists and fought against establishment of any kind. The battle was won. While Pennsylvania had not supported any religious group from the beginning, now the state of Virginia had actually cut off previous support, ruled out establishment, and made all churches equal before the law.

The Virginia enactment became a model for national policy. This was not by accident since James Madison had been so active in the Virginia fight. Included in the Constitution and the Bill of Rights were the following sentences: "No religious test shall ever be required as a qualification to any office or public trust under the United States . . . Congress shall make no law respecting an establishment of religion, or prohibiting the free exercise thereof." There was opposition to these clauses in the Constitution and several states continued to have established churches for some time (the constitutional statements, of course, did not refer to *state* actions).

Both Madison and Jefferson greatly influenced the religious outlook in the Constitution. But the roots of this separation between church and state were many. One important fact was the sheer religious diversity of the new country, with no church in a position to effectively assert a claim to establishment. Also significant was the influence of the Baptists, with their traditional strong opposition to the idea of a state church. The Quaker experiment in Pennsylvania also provided an important precedent. The great awakenings should not be overlooked, since they changed the complexion of many of the churches in such a way that voluntary association and free decision, rather than community inclusiveness, marked the essence of the church. The deists, too, played a significant role. Convinced that most of the difficulties between religious groups were petty, they were in favor of a solution which placed none of them in prominence. Again, non-Christian forces helped in the formation of a state of affairs beneficial to the churches themselves.

In other respects, too, the Constitution reflected the meeting of Christian and non-Christian forces. Unlike the Declaration of Independence, its argument for checks and balances and for equality was partly based on the dangers of misuse of power. It safeguarded liberty and equality through a system which presupposed the possibility of both baseness and dignity.

Historians will have to settle the question (if it can be settled) of whether the system of checks and balances came chiefly from Montesquieu or indirectly from John Calvin (see Chs. II and V), through the lineage of John Witherspoon and James Madison. Certainly at the time of the drafting of the Constitution, the Protestant influence on America was less than it was at the time of the Declaration of

Independence. Yet the Constitution accords more with the prevailing Protestant concept of humanity's nature. One cannot escape thinking that here, as in the Declaration of Independence and the struggle for religious liberty, Christian and non-Christian forces coalesced toward a common end.

For our purposes, the important point is that the conceptions of religious liberty and of the separation of church and state gave the theoretical base for a distinctive kind of Protestantism. It became actual for all the churches during the next half-century.

Through Infidelity to the Triumph of the Churches

A new nation had been formed. The exhilaration of achievement momentarily gave way to the letdown which almost invariably follows a newly won security. The spirit of the time was not favorable to expansion on the part of the churches. Moreover, in the last decades of the eighteenth century natural religion or deism, a form of the Enlightenment, had suddenly become a force in opposition to the churches.

By the middle of the eighteenth century, the tide of deism and natural religion had been effectively defeated in England by the Methodist movement. But it was only beginning to appear in the new world at this time. Only after the great awakenings did one find deists in America in appreciable numbers. They were neither antichurch nor aggressive in their outlook. Many of them belonged to the churches. They were what one might call gentle deists and came generally from the upper classes. They belonged to what Henry F. May has called the "moderate enlightenment."

In the period leading up to the Revolution and contemporaneous with it, two forms of enlightenment, which May has called the skeptical and revolutionary periods, can be noted. Different as they are, for our purposes they can be considered together, for both represent a departure from the easy alliance of church concerns and rational thought toward a more militant spirit which pressed for the victory of reason over the alleged superstitions of the churches. This movement became powerful after the founding of the nation and the publication of Thomas Paine's *The Age of Reason*. Such deism taught individuals to rely upon themselves instead of on the churches. God, it held, is the creator, and the author of the moral law in the universe. Individuals must obey this law: breaking it brings punishment. But the one who follows the moral law will discover the kindness and goodness of God, known directly in nature. The Bible, on the other hand, depicts a God of war and cruelty and caprice; even in the New Testament human dignity is degraded. Truly this was a religion of rational self-confidence.

Some of the milder deists were shocked by this outlook. But it was propounded by one who had himself participated in the glorious French Revolution, and this was the period of the height of influence of French culture and ideas upon the American scene. Deist literature was widely disseminated. Deist societies were founded, the first of which was under the leadership of a former Baptist minister, Elihu Palmer.

The deist outlook was influential even when it was not accepted outright. It appealed to self-reliant people who had just created a nation. It appealed to individuals on the frontier who daily had to depend on nothing else but themselves for food and security. For example, Lexington, Kentucky, became a center of deistic thinking. Deism appealed to many who had come to America for reasons of economic gain. It appealed to college students who were no longer impressed by theological thinking, whether Calvinist or not, and who found great difficulties in accepting the Bible as the Word of God.

This was a difficult period for the churches. While less than ten percent of Americans were church members, piety and evangelical dispositions had not disappeared among the population at large, as contrasted with some of the intellectual centers. Hence the new awakenings mainly built on a disposition that had never disappeared. Already in the last decade of the eighteenth century revivals were spreading through New England colleges and churches. Timothy Dwight, the new president of Yale, almost single-handedly stemmed the tide of "infidelity" in a university where there was hardly a theological student. But for the wider populace, Lyman Beecher and Nathaniel Taylor were the most prominent of the new revivalists. Aware that genuine faith touched the heart, Beecher had no fear of emotion as such, provided it was not too prominent and could be tested in terms of commitment toward the future, such as activity in missionary or reform movements. In order to make sure that things did not get out of hand, Beecher involved the regular parish clergy along with revivalist preachers in revivals in particular parishes. Hence, revivals were not merely the product of itinerant preachers invading the local parishes, but rather indigenous events, under local control. Thus, without the traditional fanfare of the revival circuits, the New England revival preachers effectively returned life to the churches and substantially increased their membership.

Beecher was aware that the new situation demanded new procedures, and adaptations in the current Calvinist theology. While fearful of the disestablishment of the Congregational church in Connecticut, Beecher quickly adapted to the new realities and within a few weeks saw new opportunities for the church as it worked out new procedures for evangelization and church organization. Theologically, this meant that Beecher and his associates adopted a voluntaristic conception of the church, and without abandoning their conception of God's sovereignty they stressed that God had provided "means" by which all of us were confronted and brought into the Christian orbit. Such means involved the eliciting of our true selves, our moral accountable nature. To what extent this was an abandonment or transformation of the Calvinist views need not concern us. What is apparent is that not easily reconcilable elements were affirmed side by side, such as the sovereignty of God and moral accountability even in matters of faith.

While this was happening in New England, the influence of the churches was weak on the frontier. Frontier towns were small and isolated. It was impossible to provide either clergy or churches for all of the communities. Congregationalists and Presbyterians, who insisted upon an educated clergy, were particularly hard pressed. In an effort to meet the need, they counseled communities where both Congregationalists and Presbyterians had settled, to form a single church and call a minister from either group. Methodists were generally more successful, since they organized small groups in "classes" with a lay leader in charge, just as Wesley had done. "Classes" and Methodist communities were then visited by a Methodist minister who traveled an extensive circuit of such groups. But Baptists were generally in the best position. In addition to having fought for political and religious freedom, they did not have the burden of a highly educated ministry. A Baptist preacher was one who felt the call. Once the decision had been made, preaching could begin. Moreover, such preachers usually were of the same social class as the people to whom they preached.

The preaching of most of these groups took on a "revivalistic" pattern. Individuals were confronted with God's terrible judgment upon the sins of indifference, infidelity, and immorality. These were painted in graphic pictures which brought fear and dread to the minds of listeners. When this was accomplished, the preacher pointed to the forgiveness of God for those who repented of their sins and were born anew by the spirit. This was a form of exposition uniquely effective in the life of the frontier.

At the turn of the century, such revival preaching was increasingly successful. But since families sometimes had to come from distances too great to permit them to return home on the same day, a new pattern of "camp meetings" developed in which the families brought provisions and stayed for several days of preaching and meetings. In such social settings, women and children participated and played a significant role. The most notable of such meetings were at Gasper River and Cain Ridge in Kentucky, the latter sponsored jointly by Methodists and Presbyterians. Among the most prominent of the preachers at such revivals was Peter Cartwright, a legendary figure in his own right.

Revivalism spread from Kentucky and Tennessee into the Northwest Territory. Its peak was reached by 1806. However, in the third decade of the nineteenth century, it sprang up again in the East, primarily in New York State through the preaching of Charles G. Finney. Indeed, it was Finney who introduced what were known as "new measures" in revival techniques and who gave the most systematic account of the revival theology in his lectures on revivals of religion. Central to Finney's strategy was unremitting pressure, such as all-night prayer meetings, reference to sinners by name, and the use of the "anxious seat," namely, a bench at the front of the church where those in distress were the subject of special prayers, exhortations, and convictions of sin and grace. Theologically, Finney believed that such measures made people confront themselves and make the appropriate decisions for God, decisions which God had given them the capacity to make.

However revivalists may be judged by a more sophisticated society, they did succeed in stemming the rationalist tide within and without the churches. It must not, of course, be forgotten that they were helped by a reaction to French influences after the excesses of the French Revolution. This did not, however, play a large part on the frontier. There the revivals alone won the victory.

The revivals had done much to revitalize and consolidate the life of the churches. They helped to establish the strength of the churches in a situation where there was neither state support nor interference. And churches generally now had the security to which free churches had been unaccustomed.

The American Church Tradition

Early in the nineteenth century, American Protestantism had thus worked out a distinctive pattern both in theory and in practice. Even the churches which had hoped for direct support from the state, or which hoped to dominate the life of the society through governmental recognition, either had voluntarily altered their position or had been forced to do so. There was to be no territorial or state church. This meant that even the traditional churches had become "sectarian" in the sense that each church now was composed only of those who freely professed their faith. Voluntary association had been a distinguishing mark of those groups sometimes called "sect-type" churches, in contrast to the churches which sought to be co-extensive with the community. Now all American churches were sectarian in the broad sense of the term. Religion was now a matter wholly of conscience and decision. One did not belong to a church simply by virtue of one's place of birth, though one might stay in the church in which one was nurtured. But one could also freely change denominations, as many did and continue to do.

This was a necessary solution in the American scene. But it was also in line with the spirit of the awakenings. There was a stress upon individual decision, an opposition to governmental influence, and a disregard for denominational lines. The individual's relation to God was the crucial point for religious thinking. This tended to make American Protestantism individualistic in its outlook.

The general pattern of American Protestantism had several corollaries. In the first place, denominational consciousness was never to be as great in America as in Europe. In spite of deep splits, some of which came out of the revivals themselves, denominations were generally not as isolated from one another as in Europe. Second, the stress upon individual decision under Christ provided an atmosphere which, connected with other factors, was not conducive to the development of theology. There was, in fact, a suspicion of theology. The revivals placed an emphasis upon "essentials," upon the presence of Christ, not upon theories about Christ.

Third, several new but related developments set a pattern for the future. Aware of the continual need for a trained and educated clergy, churches created a number of denominational colleges, chiefly west of the Appalachians. The need for Bibles and literature led to the formation of Bible societies dedicated to the distribution of Scripture. Tracts also appeared in increasing numbers, no doubt because they had been put to such good advantage in the propagation of deism. Sunday schools first made their appearance in this period. All of these agencies were directed to improving the understanding of a populace which was influenced by the religion of the heart. It is a credit to the awakenings that their more thoughtful adherents saw the necessity of directing this vitality and zeal into channels which would help preserve and consolidate the gains which had been made. Many of these developments are discussed in the next chapter. As we can see, they clearly testify that the separation of church and state had not meant the separation of religion and culture.

Europe: From Orthodoxy to Enlightenment

In the early decades of the eighteenth century, orthodoxy and Pietism were the two main Protestant currents on the Continent. Although Pietism represented a reaction against orthodoxy, it did not succeed in influencing or softening large sections of the churches. In some areas, both in Europe and America, orthodox developments continued well into the nineteenth and twentieth centuries. Charles Hodge, the most eminent professor of the newly organized Princeton Theological Seminary from 1825 on, was a follower of François Turretin, one of the foremost orthodox Swiss theologians of the seventeenth century. The older orthodoxy found perpetuation into the twentieth century, not through Princeton Theological Seminary, but through such groups as the Orthodox Presbyterian and the Bible Presbyterian churches. In Lutheranism, orthodox thought continued especially through the Missouri Synod Lutherans.

Predominantly, however, orthodox thought underwent changes, particularly on the Continent. In three phases of theological thinking, a general transition took place from orthodoxy to the Enlightenment. At first glance, one might think simply of contrast between these two, since orthodoxy was concerned with specifically Christian doctrine and the Enlightenment with religion in general. There was a kinship between the two, however, in the rationalistic spirit which dominated both; and as in philosophical thought generally, the rationalistic spirit gave way to a faith in an active, practical reason, so, too, there was a change in Protestant thinking which transformed and ended the orthodox development.[2]

From a New Scholasticism to a New Religion

Until the time of Christian Wolff (d. 1754), orthodox theologians reflected a rationalistic spirit but did not consciously relate their thinking to the new philosophical currents. Theirs was a scholasticism whose roots were planted more in medieval categories of thinking than in the newer state of opinion.

In Christian Wolff we see a man who considered himself quite orthodox and believed that the new philosophical outlook, particularly as seen in the philosopher Leibnitz, provided essentially the same truth as Christianity. Proper philosophy and theology lead to the same conclusions in most matters. Thus, following Leibnitz and the rationalist tradition, one can use the traditional proofs for the existence of God and ascribe attributes to God which are in accord with reason. Life itself is rational and ought to be directed toward virtue. Through virtue one's life is fulfilled and rewarded by God.

Wolff believed that the heart of orthodoxy was no different from this. To be sure, there were certain items not found in reason which were supplied by revelation, such as the Trinity, Christology, and Grace. But these were above reason, not contrary to it. Miracle may be possible. If so, it means the interruption and the restoration of a natural order created by God. The Bible is rational and rational criteria must be used to substantiate its claims. God is righteous, holy, and good. Nevertheless, sin is a fact. Therefore, atonement is both rational and necessary.

Wolff seriously attempted to safeguard the essentials of the Christian

---

[2] In certain respects the change was quite similar to the growth of natural religion and deism in England at a slightly earlier time.

faith. But the spirit of rationalism was so strong in his own approach that it, rather than the Christian substance, was determinative. Given the rubric under which he worked, it is remarkable how much of the traditional orthodox outlook he was able to maintain. To many in his own day, the enterprise appeared impossible. The Pietists were up in arms and had him removed from his professional position. And the philosopher Kant directed his attack against the rational proofs of God's existence as elaborated by Wolff.

The second stage in the movement from orthodoxy to Enlightenment was represented by what may be called the "transitional" theologians. Although they were not of the same mind on many points, they represented an attempt to improve the orthodox system by a new position which took seriously the new currents of thought but accepted neither Wolff nor the Pietists. Frequently, theirs was a position between Pietism and Rationalism. Included among such theologians were Buddeus, Walch, Mosheim, Baumgarten, and the illustrious son of François Turretin, Jean Alphonse Turretin.

Like Wolff, the theologians in this group believed that revelation does not contradict reason. But they did not accept the tight philosophical system of Wolff. They reflected a rational, but not a rationalistic, spirit. They were concerned with that which is reasonable. Some of them were influenced by English deist literature which had found its way into Germany. Like the deists, they were opposed to any system of thought which is essentially rigorous in what it asks people to accept, as in the systems of Wolff and of traditional orthodoxy.

Many of these individuals were intrigued, too, by the increased knowledge of other religious traditions, including those of the East. Convinced that Christianity in its Protestant form is preeminent, they nevertheless were searching for a rubric which encompassed the variety of religions and the natural religion of reason. Moreover, they were bothered by the divisions within Protestantism and by what they took to be quarrels about nonessentials.

Turretin's *Discourse on Fundamental Articles in Religion* represented one way taken by the transitional theologians in the light of these concerns. Turretin distinguished between that which is made known by the light of nature and that which is revealed. To the former belongs the knowledge that God is and that those who seek God are rewarded. From this statement, believed Turretin, other consequences could be drawn, none of which disagreed with revelation. As a Protestant, however, he believed that revelation is necessary for salvation, and that the implications of revelation are necessary articles of belief, if one is to escape damnation. But he immediately added that these are necessary only to those to whom the gospel is preached and who are endowed with sufficient faculties to receive them. Thus Turretin found a way to stress the distinctiveness of revelation, but escaped making it normative for everyone.

In Christian history, Turretin found many contradictory statements as to what is fundamental. He concluded that the fundamentals are few and that people have fought mainly over nonessentials, such as predestination. Let people confess that they are free, that God rewards according to works, and that God is in control of everything. But they need not make any of these points into a necessary article of belief. For Protestants, there are criteria. These consist in the Word and in prudence. In respect to the Word, individuals may err and therefore cannot claim complete truth for their own views. Individuals may hold convictions, but they must be tolerant. They must not confuse their interpretations with the total truth.

In this way, Turretin believed that he maintained Christian truth, while accepting the canons of tolerance and reasonableness. The Christian substance still had meaning for him, though its outmoded forms did not. He did not foresee that the canons of reasonableness which he proposed would not help to preserve a more thoughtful and convincing Protestantism, but would instead tend to become a substitute.

This happened in the third phase of the transition from orthodoxy to the Enlightenment through the "innovating" theologians. This group included such men as J. F. W. Jerusalem, J. J. Spalding, J. S. Semler, J. A. Ernesti, and Joh. David Michaelis. They believed that revelation was genuine, but that its content at no point was beyond that of definite accord with reason.

Reason, however, was not understood by these men in a wholly formal or rationalistic way. It referred rather to that which makes practical sense, reason as an internalized, functioning reason, genuine to oneself. Formerly, the activity of reason had been construed as the participation of thought in a universal rational structure in the nature of things. This had been the view of Wolff and of rationalism in general. Now reason was understood as personal and inner, functioning as an expression of the self, practical and partly expressed in moral terms.

Revelation had now been reduced to that which is comprehensible to such a reasoning self. It was no longer a mystery beyond reason. Hence a new criterion had been found for looking at Bible and church alike. For some in this group, the early church alone stood out as an example of revelation and reason unencumbered by accretions. The Roman Catholic and Protestant orthodox positions reflected the addition of incidentals which obscured the real center of the church. Some of the "innovators" pushed into the Bible itself, seeing there, too, beginnings of developments which betrayed reason and revelation in the practical sense. The genuine elements in the Bible, according to Semler, are the moral truths taught by Christ, through which we improve our lives. This is the Gospel behind the gospel. We must therefore return to the true revelation which is included in the Bible and which is essentially akin to natural religion. The world view or cosmology of the Bible was now no longer essential to the faith and could be laid aside in favor of its moral truths. Thus, the ordered Newtonian world no longer needed to be repaired or broken by a God of miracle. Evidences from miracle and prophecy, upon which unfortunately church leaders, philosophers, and scientists alike had depended, were now replaced by the self-evidence of reason. Moreover, such a procedure made it possible to maintain that there was truth in the Bible in spite of its contradictions. (Semler was one of the first to see the real implications of some of the contradictions and differences of viewpoint in the Bible. He suggested interpretations which became the basis for much of later biblical criticism. It must be recalled that he did this in a period in which such pursuits were extremely suspect. See the section, "Biblical Criticism," in Ch. IX.)

For the "innovators," revelation was still real and related to the Bible. But its content was not different from that of natural religion in general. What was said in the church was therefore not really different from that which thoughtful people were saying outside the church. Thus, in these theologians, Protestantism had moved from a new form of scholasticism to a new religion. The aim was understandable, but the distinctive substance of faith was gone. In these individuals, Protestantism had become the victim of the Enlightenment.

Enlightenment and the Need for New Directions

In the preceding section, we indicated how the Enlightenment moved into Protestant thinking and effectively ended orthodoxy. While we have delineated, in a series of steps, the influence of the Enlightenment on Continental theology, one could do the same for the English or American scene, as, for example, from Locke to Jefferson or Franklin. Because the new push toward a revitalized Christianity — which took the Enlightenment seriously and simultaneously set for itself the goal of overcoming it — occurred on the Continent, we chose to focus on the antecedents of Kant and Schleiermacher. Where the Enlightenment view was accepted, concern for revelation had ended. If revelation disclosed no more than we can naturally know of God and God's relation to the world, it was certainly dispensable. English writings on natural religion and deism were now read by German scholars, though their effectiveness in England was already being challenged by the Methodist movement. (The Scottish philosopher David Hume had also called natural religion into question by doubting that there was a stable human nature which was the same everywhere. Without a human nature which was constant, there could be no fixed truths of religion open to everyone. But Hume was not taken that seriously by the Enlightenment, except by Kant.)

Nevertheless, the German Enlightenment figures did not slavishly follow the dictates of natural religion. Natural religion was itself too formal in outlook and based on a fixed and static concept of reason. Thinkers such as Gotthold Lessing (1729–1781) were more concerned with a practical religion, grounded in virtue and the good life. All religions at heart, Lessing felt, were based on such practical interests. Their workability or helpfulness in the common good was the only criterion of their worth. That which helped humanity was enlightened, and that which hindered was superstition. Under the common God, all must reach forward toward a new humanity.

Enlightenment religion had cast off the "shackles" of the past. It no longer felt bound by theological or liturgical formulations of previous ages. These had enslaved people. Now they dared to think for themselves, to take the cue for life from what was directly observed and experienced about themselves and their world. This new feeling, apart from whatever content was applied by various individuals, was itself religious in nature. It was a devotion to truth wherever it might be found. But hand in hand with this concern went the conviction that such devotion would lead to the best of religion and humanity. Only among a limited number of French thinkers was there a strong antireligious protest. Essentially, the Enlightenment was religious, with great hopes for the present and the future. It declared its independence of what bound people in the past, though it had not always emancipated itself as much as was thought.

It is not difficult to see that such a spirit left no room for a distinctly Protestant outlook. In fact, Protestant thinking had lost whatever unique character it had. The transition from orthodoxy to the Enlightenment had been made within and without the churches. It was time for a new beginning.

This was made by the philosopher Immanuel Kant. It is not our task to go into his philosophy here, except insofar as it affects the Protestant development. Kant, too, rejected the orthodox development; he also rejected the Rationalism which paralleled and influenced it. Rationalism's claims to knowledge were too broad. Hence, Kant began, in the *Critique of Pure Reason,* by limiting *knowledge* to the experienced world. He did not deny the existence of "noumenal" reality, which lay behind the phenomena we experience directly; but this was not given to us in perception. Nor did he deny the reality of *a priori,* universal concepts of reason; but these were to be understood as patterns of the mind, brought by us to experience and used in organizing the data of perception. Therefore, claims to knowledge must be limited to the experienced world, shaped by the rational structures of mind. Within these proper limits, knowledge could be certain, philosophy could be rehabilitated (in spite of Hume's attack), and the scientific (i.e., Newtonian) picture of an orderly world could be given philosophical certification. Obviously, claims to knowledge of God through "pure reason" were quite impossible, and Kant systematically attacked the traditional proofs for God's existence (and in a way which many have felt conclusive).

Nevertheless, religion could yet be established on a sound basis. It, too, belongs to reason, but to a different kind than that which we employ in the domain of knowledge. Its ground is practical reason, in contrast to "pure" or theoretical reason. Practical reason apprehends the moral law within. A concept of duty or law is universal in all human beings, and therefore valid for all. Right action always proceeds from the motive of obedience to this law, rather than any desire for happiness or satisfaction. All activity ought then to be based on the universal law of duty and morality which is the law of self and of the universe.

Kant knew of the tensions which beset us and lead us to activity counter to our moral nature. In fact, Kant's description of radical evil was more penetrating than most theological analyses. But Kant found it impossible to believe that evil could not be broken by the deliberate act of individuals. He maintained that this must be possible by a herculean effort of will. Otherwise the world would not be moral and therefore would be meaningless. Above all else, Kant was convinced that this is a moral world.

Sensing, nevertheless, that we do not fully succeed in this world in living in accord with the moral law, Kant argued that we are justified in postulating immortality as the necessary extension of time requisite for the final perfection of virtue. Kant had rejected the idea that happiness could be a proper motive for action — duty was the only right motive. But he was still convinced that the virtuous individual must somehow be the happy one. Since one must not act from the desire for happiness, and since happiness and virtue do not seem to be commensurate in life, Kant concluded that we must postulate the existence of God to guarantee the proper correlation of virtue and happiness.

Such a reconstruction of the religious in connection with the ethical was more in line with the tradition of natural religion than with the prevailing currents of the Enlightenment. In some respects, Kant's views on religion were not so much an advance as a return to a tradition in which individuals insisted on establishing the religious by way of the moral.

More important for Protestant history was the influence Kant had on subsequent generations. The general outlook of the Enlightenment, including Kant's views on religion, convinced the Protestant theologian Friedrich Schleiermacher that a new start was necessary. But even his efforts at a new beginning, which we consider in Ch. IX, were partly determined by Kant's own attempt to overcome the Enlightenment. Instead of relating the domain of religion to the ethical realm of Kant's second critique, he drew from the *a priori* categories of the first. For Schleiermacher, religion itself was a unique realm of experience, related to but not determined by knowledge or ethics. Only in this way could Protestant theology begin again. Albrecht Ritschl, on the other hand (see Ch. IX), believed that Kant had begun a path in the second critique which opened the way for the revival of the Protestant Reformation.

Protestant theologians were to struggle for some time to conserve the gains of the Enlightenment, and at the same time recover the religious depths and particular Christian witness which they felt were lost in the Enlightenment. In the groping for new ways of thinking about the biblical message in relation to contemporary currents of thought, Kant's work played an important role. His distinction between knowledge and faith, however differently interpreted by theologians, continued to inform much of Protestant thinking.

CHAPTER VIII

A Century of Protestant Expansion

Characteristics of the Century

The beginning of the nineteenth century marks the onset of a new and formative period in the development of Protestant Christianity. This was an era of profound intellectual ferment, in which forces both within and outside the church combined to pose new problems for Christian thinking and to shape new perspectives for the understanding of the faith. We have already looked at one of the central features in the transition from eighteenth- to nineteenth-century modes of thought — viz., the critical philosophy of Kant (see Ch. VII). But equally important were the continuing influence of Pietism and Romanticism, the development of new tools for the study of the Bible, and the rapidly accelerating advances in the sciences of nature and society. The nineteenth century was also a period of striking institutional and geographical expansion in the Protestant churches. And this was a time of almost continual flux in the relations of church to society, brought on to some extent by the further growth of nationalism in Western Europe and America, but more especially by the social upheavals attendant upon the rise of an industrial society.

The overall significance of these nineteenth-century developments has been given the most diverse interpretations. Perhaps nowhere has the point of view of the historian been more influential in determining an understanding of history than in the estimate of the role of religion in the nineteenth century. For some, this is the time of the great decline in the influence of Christianity (and particularly of Protestantism) in the West, so that by the early part of the twentieth century the part played by religion in molding thought and action could safely be ignored. For others, the nineteenth century was a time of great advance for Protestant Christianity because of its remarkable numerical, institutional, and geographical expansion.

On the whole, most judgments on the nineteenth century have been less extreme than the two just mentioned. The importance of these extreme and contradictory views lies in their witness to the actual diversity in the religious trends of the century itself. On the one hand, there were important tendencies which seemed to indicate a serious weakening in the vitality and influence of the Protestant churches (and no less of Roman Catholicism and Eastern Orthodoxy). There was the powerful tendency toward formal separation of religious institutions from the political institutions. This trend was already apparent in the Bill of Rights of the Constitution of the United States, which forbade the federal government to make any church the official religion of the land (see Ch. VII). The trend was given impetus by the French Revolution (even though non-Roman Catholics were accorded new rights in France) and by the Napoleonic reforms, which among other things thoroughly reorganized the religious scene in Germany and brought to an end the 1648 settlement of the Peace of Westphalia, *cuius regio, eius religio*. Separationist tendencies were reflected in the English reforms of the 1830's which limited the traditional prerogatives of the Church of England. And through the first half of the century, partly as a result of the revivals stemming from British Evangelicalism and Moravian centers, there were pressures for (at least spiritual) independence from state establishments in the Reformed churches in Switzerland, France, Scotland, and Holland.

Generalized hostility to the church was represented in the revolutions of 1848, which were mostly met by negative reactions from Protestant and Catholic authorities alike (note, e.g., the turn to conservatism by Pope Pius IX and the Throne and Altar theology of German Lutheranism). The motifs of separation and hostility were also prominently expressed in a growing anticlericalism. That was most vividly seen in predominantly Roman Catholic countries (e.g., in the liquidation of papal states in Italy in 1870 and in the formal separation of church and state in France in 1905). Of course, it should be remembered that many Protestants have looked with grave suspicion upon any established church. Thus the trend toward separation of church and state is seen as a significant advance rather than a reverse for the church. But anticlericalism, in its nineteenth-century form of broad critique of institutional religion as such rather than mere suspicion of clergy (which certainly was not new), could be just as characteristic of Lutheran, Reformed, and Anglican settings as of Roman Catholic countries. Again, the support and control of education were taken over increasingly by the state and ceased to be primarily a function of the churches.

A less tangible though equally important development was the increasingly sharp distinction between the "religious" and the "secular," so that the life of faith became a thing apart from the world of government and of commerce, and the decisions of faith had little direct relevance to economic and political decisions. Formal "secular societies" appeared, whose goal was to emphasize the present world, whose values could be tested in this life, and thus to disentangle ethics from theology. Also, for many, the church seemed to be so tied to racial, economic, and national consciousnesses as to have no independent life of its own. Thus there arose charges that the church was simply the "opiate of the people" and the tool of class interests.

Particularly in the latter half of the century, the progress of science — notably biology, but also geology and anthropology, and later sociology and psychology — opened a veritable Pandora's box of questions as to the credibility of the traditional Christian worldview and of the biblical account of the origin of the world and of human life. Perhaps more important, the successes of the scientific method suggested that here at last was found the means to all truth, and religious claims to truth might now be left behind.

Moreover, the industrialization of the West, both by its successes and its failures, contributed to a sense of the irrelevance of religion. The new miracles of production and technology, together with the discoveries of science, led to the belief that the era of plenty was at hand and that human beings could be the masters of their environment without dependence upon divine assistance. At the same time, to the great and growing body of industrial workers, the message of the church seemed increasingly irrelevant, for it did not speak to the difficulties which had been created for them by the age of the machine.

These are only some indications of the unfavorable tendencies with which nineteenth-century Protestantism was confronted. And it is not altogether strange that some have thought that the church was simply waning in vitality, and that the adjustments in Protestant thinking toward the new sciences, the new philosophies, and a changing society were merely steps toward the ultimate dissolution of the faith itself.

But judgments of this sort rest upon only a portion of the evidence. For on many other counts, the nineteenth century was a time of the most vigorous activity and greatest growth in Protestant history. In terms of numbers and geographical extension, this century has not unjustly been called "the great century" of Christian expansion. This expansion was signalized particularly by the missionary movement, which we look at more carefully later in this chapter. Also, the religious revivals at the beginning of the century continued on the Continent, in the British Isles, and in America. As a concomitant of the westward growth of the United States, the percentage of church members in the American population rose from less than 10 percent in 1800 to over 40 percent in 1910 (and to a high point of 58 percent in 1951).

Methodist "circuit riders" and traveling Baptist evangelists had gone steadily westward with the frontier, and the success of their work accounts for the numerical preeminence of the Baptist and Methodist churches in the United States.

Moreover, if the development of institutional structures and the proliferation of new organizations are signs of life and strength, then the nineteenth century was a period of amazing Protestant vitality. This does not mean so much the appearance of new denominations — though in the United States that process continued apace in consequence of the revivals, of secessions from established denominations, of transplantation of European national churches through immigration, and of social cleavages (as in the division of several major bodies into Northern and Southern branches over the issue of slavery). More striking organizational developments are to be found in the church-sponsored or church-inspired movements which frequently cut across denominational lines and whose functions were supplementary to the work of the parish churches. This was peculiarly though not exclusively characteristic of Anglo-Saxon Protestantism, and was an expression of the vitality of the faith in establishing relevance to new situations.

Thus, a common characteristic of many of these movements was their direction toward particular groups and interests. Such were the student Christian societies, which grew rapidly toward the end of the century and joined in the World's Student Christian Federation. Similarly, in Germany, France, Britain, the United States, and Canada, such organizations as the YMCA and YWCA sought to provide new programs for spiritual, intellectual, social, and physical growth, free from the traditional church patterns and denominational differences. These groups were mainly concerned to work in urban areas in universities and colleges. Within the denominations, a host of young people's societies were formed (e.g., the Methodist Epworth League, the Baptist Young People's Union, and the Luther League).

The Sunday schools, as we saw earlier, made their first appearance in the late decades of the eighteenth century (in England), and were designed to give religious and moral instruction to the poor and to teach the young to read the Bible. As the movement spread, the Sunday School became the characteristic Protestant method of religious instruction. The concern for Christian education was further revealed in the scores of denominational colleges which were founded in the United States during the century, as well as in the establishment of theological seminaries for the further training of the ministry, as the universities ceased to be the primary places for clergy education (at least twenty-five seminaries were founded in the United States between 1808 and 1840 — and one should not ignore the creative role of the German theological faculties, especially at the new University of Berlin). Interdenominational Bible societies (such as the American Bible

Society, which has become increasingly important) had the dual aim of evangelism and religious instruction, gaining wide support in their efforts to make the Bible universally available.

We remarked earlier on the tendency toward the separation of the "religious" from the "secular" interests of life, and the separation of church and state. But there appeared also in this century a new and profound sense, on the part of the churches, of their responsibility for the well-being of the social whole. Evidence for this is found in the religiously inspired humanitarian and social reform movements, ranging from organizations concerned with particular social evils (such as the temperance and antislavery groups) to general philanthropic enterprises, and to efforts to Christianize the whole of the social and economic order (as in the Christian socialist programs or the "social gospel" movement).

Finally, the new vitality of nineteenth-century Protestantism is seen in the theological ferment of the period, beginning especially in Germany but spreading throughout the Protestant world. Measured simply in terms of sheer productivity and liveliness of debate, the century ranks with the most vigorous of Christian history. And for freedom and creativity of thought, it can be paralleled only by the early centuries of the church and by the Reformation.

What has now been said concerning the apparently contradictory trends in nineteenth-century Protestantism indicates something of the complexity of the century and the impossibility of simple generalizations regarding the development of Protestantism in the period. It also serves to suggest some of the central streams of development which must be examined in greater detail. Out of the variety of expressions of nineteenth-century Protestantism, we single out in succeeding chapters those broad trends which seem most significant for revealing the nature of Protestantism and the further development of its understanding of the Christian faith, and of that faith in relation to the world.

These general tendencies can be summarized under three main heads: 1) the growth of the Protestant missionary enterprise; 2) the rise of "liberal" theology; and 3) Protestant reactions to the social and economic changes of the century, particularly as these are seen in the rise of the "social gospel." These developments, which were going on more or less simultaneously, were closely interrelated; and while they will be treated separately, it should be remembered that they are but aspects which have to be taken together if we are to understand the total movement of Protestantism in the century.

Moreover, since we are not primarily concerned in this book with institutional developments, we need pay relatively little attention to denominational differences. The external forces which helped to shape Protestant thought and life in the nineteenth century were not respectful of traditional church divisions, and newer trends in Protestant thinking seem to have been quite independent of denominational emphases. Indeed, one of the most marked developments of the century was a decline in concern for theological differences among the denominations and the consequent cross-fertilization among Protestant theological systems. It is fair to say that by the beginning of the First World War, "liberal" Presbyterians, Methodists, Episcopalians, and Baptists in America, Lutheran and Reformed thinkers on the Continent, and Anglicans and Nonconformists in the United Kingdom, were much closer to each other in religious outlook than they were to the extreme conservative or "fundamentalist" Christians within their own denominations. We shall thus largely pass over intradenominational developments. These are no longer of primary importance for the understanding of the Protestant movement.

The Missionary Movement

The nineteenth century was the period of the greatest geographic spread of Christianity. The foremost American historian of the expansion of Christianity, Kenneth Scott Latourette, has asserted that, "Never had any other set of ideas, religious or secular, been propagated over so wide an area by so many professional agents maintained by the unconstrained donations of so many millions of individuals. . . . For sheer magnitude it has been without parallel in human history."[1] In this process, the Protestant churches, and especially the British and American churches, provided the chief impetus and the bulk of the resources.

The beginning of large-scale Protestant missionary activity is popularly dated from the publication in 1792 of a small book by a British shoemaker, schoolteacher, and preacher, William Carey, entitled *An Enquiry into the Obligations of Christians to Use Means for the Conversion of the Heathens*. Notice, in this title, the phrase "to use means." These words sum up Carey's opposition to a view that since God is omnipotent and has predetermined who are the elect, he will save whom he chooses without the assistance of human effort. Against this notion, Carey's view, which rapidly came to characterize nineteenth-century Protestantism and provided a primary stimulus to missionary activity, was that the New Testament command to "preach the Gospel to every creature" and to "make disciples of all nations" was directed to Christians of the present time as much as to the original apostles.

It would be quite incorrect to suppose that there had been no Protestant missionary work before the end of the eighteenth century. There

[1] K. S. Latourette, *Anno Domini* (New York, 1940), p. 169.

had been numerous earlier efforts, though mainly in colonial areas. Sir Walter Raleigh had been zealous for the introduction of Christianity in his colony. Wesley had in his early life gone out as a missionary to the Indians in Georgia. And among the Moravians, whole communities of families had devoted themselves to the propagation of the faith, chiefly in Greenland and the West Indies. Mainly because of the Moravians, Germany was the chief source of missionaries prior to 1800. An English missionary society was formed as early as 1649, and two other groups, which are still in existence, were organized at the beginning of the eighteenth century (the Society for Promoting Christian Knowledge, and the Society for the Propagation of the Gospel in Foreign Parts).

But in general, it must be concluded that before the nineteenth century, Protestantism was not characterized by very great concern for missionary work in foreign lands. The forerunners of the modern movement were few and ill-supported; they were largely confined to colonial areas; and they were often abortive because they accepted converts without adequate instruction and failed to develop native pastors and leaders. The early, scattered efforts are significant mainly as exceptions to the usual pattern. Of Protestant migration there was much, and of evangelistic effort where the church already existed there was much, but of attempts to transmit the gospel to those outside the Western European cultural milieu there were few.

The question arises, why was this so? And to this, several answers must be given. For one thing, most of the early Protestants had been indifferent or opposed to the idea of foreign missions. Often, it was held that the New Testament instruction to go to all nations applied only to the original disciples, and in the minds of some the doctrine of predestination seemed to make human efforts to convert the heathen both unnecessary and presumptuous. Moreover, the energies of the Reformers were wholly absorbed in the work of reforming the church; and in subsequent years, the intense theological disputes in Protestant scholasticism and the internal wars in nations which were part Protestant and part Roman Catholic (e.g., France, Germany, and the Netherlands) occupied the center of attention. Another deterrent was simply the lack of organization. For a thousand years the monastic orders had carried on the principal Christian missionary activity, and Protestants, opposed to the religious principle underlying monasticism, had no practical means of performing the missionary functions of the monks. Thus, for purely practical reasons, the idea of foreign missions seemed often to be extravagant, foolish, and hopeless. Anyway, there was enough to be done in converting those at home.

Another sort of factor was the economic and political context of the Protestant churches. During the first century of Protestant history, it was the Roman Catholic countries of Spain and Portugal which dominated the commercial and imperial expansion of the Western European peoples. This was the age of the great Roman Catholic missionary activity, symbolized especially by the work of Francis Xavier and Ignatius Loyola. Protestant peoples came less widely into contact with non-Christian cultures. Not until after the defeat of the Spanish Armada and the emergence of the British and the Dutch as colonial powers were the new continents open to Protestant missionaries. So also, there were specific elements in the nineteenth-century situation which contributed to the growth of Protestant missions: the general peace and prosperity of the century; the close relation of Protestantism to the economic and political liberalism of the period; the greater flexibility with which Protestantism was able to adjust to the changing intellectual climate; the important role played by Britain, and later the United States, in the commercial expansion of the time; and perhaps most important, the powerful spirit of optimism and confidence which was so deeply a part of the nineteenth-century temper.

These socio-economic elements are undoubtedly of great importance in understanding the rise of the Protestant missionary movement. It has even become quite common to interpret the missionary effort as a function of cultural imperialism, in which the religious motives were confused with bringing Western civilization to "backward and ignorant" people. Surely there were many such confusions. But it would be much too simple a reading of the evidence if we were to assume that this is all there was to it, that the inner movements of Protestantism simply reflected contemporary social changes, or that the missionary impulse was only the tail of the kite of economic and political expansion or cultural domination. Essentially the new concern for missions sprang from an impulse within the life of the church, and the correlation of cultural and religious factors in the nineteenth century was probably less close than in the preceding centuries.

As we noted earlier, previous Protestant evangelistic work had been largely confined to the sphere of Western cultural influences, but now an attempt was being made to carry the gospel to people of every land and every culture. And there was certainly no simple correlation of commercial and religious expansion. At the beginning of the nineteenth-century movement the East India Company, acting for the British government, vigorously opposed the entrance of missionaries into India. In the United States, the mushrooming of the missionary enterprise was all out of proportion to the relatively slower development of the commercial and political influence of the nation. It was not until after the First World War that the United States became a major power in world affairs, whereas in the nineteenth century it had already, with Great Britain, played the dominant role in the promotion of missionary work. In general, the growth of American foreign missions paralleled the rapid growth in wealth, population, and territory of the nation. And the idea of the kingdom of God in America could easily blend with the theme of manifest destiny. But one of the factors which most sharply distinguishes the missionary enterprise of the nineteenth century from that of the preceding centuries is the extension of the work beyond and quite independently of all direct commercial or political interests.

Here again, then, as in the case of the Reformation, we see a religious revolution in the midst of social change. The missionary movement can be accounted for only if we see in it a genuine rebirth of religious vitality, which we shall also find expressed in the theological vigor and the growing social concern of the century. It is this in which we are primarily interested, though we need to remember that the impulse to foreign missions would not have developed in the way it did apart from the general social and economic character of the time.

We see, then, at about the beginning of the nineteenth century the appearance in Protestantism of a new and pervasive impulse to carry the gospel to all humanity and of a new vision of the possibilities of such an effort. Whereas earlier the prevailing attitude of the major churches had been that missions were unnecessary and hopeless undertakings, voices were now heard on all sides proclaiming the duty of all Christians to share in the conversion of the peoples of the whole world. The Word of God spoken in Christ was a word addressed to all, and those who had heard the Word were to be the means by which it would reach the ears of the "heathen." The gospel was not the private possession of the European peoples. Nor was it proper to say, as the president of a Baptist conference told William Carey when he first made his proposal for a missionary society, that when it pleased God to convert the heathen, God would do it without Carey's help.

The tenor of the new movement is vividly expressed in many of the hymns of the period. For example, the following, by Reginald Heber (d. 1826):

> From Greenland's icy mountains,
> From India's coral strand,
> Where Afric's sunny fountains
> Roll down their golden sands;
> From many an ancient river,
> From many a palmy plain,
> They call us to deliver
> Their land from error's chain.
>
> Can we, whose souls are lighted
> With wisdom from on high;
> Can we to men benighted
> The lamp of life deny?

Salvation, O salvation!
The joyful sound proclaim,
Till earth's remotest nation
Has learnt Messiah's Name.

Waft, waft, ye winds, his story,
And you, ye waters, roll,
Till, like a sea of glory,
It spreads from pole to pole:
Till o'er our ransomed nature,
The Lamb for sinners slain,
Redeemer, King, Creator,
In bliss returns to reign.

A comparable assertion, not only of the responsibility of the believer but of the ultimate goal of the effort, is found in a sermon delivered in 1824 in which it was declared: "Our field is the world. Our object is to effect an entire moral revolution in the entire human race."[2] This was not felt to be an empty dream. The enthusiasm and devotion of the leaders of the movement, combined with the optimism and confident belief in progress which pervaded the West during this period, made the achievement of such a goal seem quite possible. Thus, the Student Volunteer Movement for Foreign Missions was able to take as its watchword for the early twentieth century, "the evangelization of the world in this generation."

In large part, the new religious understanding which lay behind the missionary impulse had its roots in the revivals of the eighteenth and early nineteenth centuries. The portions of Protestantism in which the missionary motive was the strongest were those which had been most affected by Pietism, by the Wesleyan revival, and by the awakenings (see Ch. VI). In these, the technical theological disputes over justification and predestination gave way to a living experience of God's gracious forgiveness in Jesus Christ. The rationalist reduction of religion to the following of simple moral rules was replaced by a new sense of the all-embracing demand of the Redeemer and of the power of liberation into a life of trust, obedience, and hope. And the absentee God of deism was supplanted by the sovereign presence of the Lord of history.

This renewal of the Protestant understanding was given expression in the complex of motifs which were the theological foundation of the missionary obligation. For many, the dominant impulse was found in the authority of the Scriptures, especially in the injunction of Jesus to preach the gospel to all the world, and in St. Paul's declaration of God's intention: "that at the name of Jesus every knee should bow,

---

[2] From an address by Francis Wayland to the Boston Missionary Society, later widely circulated.

in heaven and on earth and under the earth, and every tongue confess that Jesus Christ is Lord, to the glory of God the Father" (Phil. 2:10f.); and that through Christ God sought "to reconcile to himself all things" (Col. 1:20). For others, the call to spread the gospel through foreign missions was a call to be faithful to the example of the earliest Christians. For some, a heightened sense of the nearness of God's kingdom provided a note of special urgency. All three of these themes had been important motifs of the Reformation. Similarly, the Reformation doctrine of the "calling," particularly as interpreted in the Calvinist tradition, took on renewed meaning among those who became missionaries. Many felt impelled by a specific call of the Spirit to missionary fields. (This had been all along a characteristic feature of the Moravian communities.) Again, for some, the drive to present the gospel to all was an attempt to make actual the universality of the church, which was already in principle universal.

In sum, the concern for missionary work came increasingly to be seen as the natural and inevitable response of faith to the revelation of God in Christ. As the reformers had revived the New Testament witness that love for one's neighbor followed naturally from one's acknowledgment of God's love, so out of the revivals of the eighteenth and early nineteenth centuries — and out of the growing contacts with non-European peoples — it was seen that this love must be expressed in the preaching of the gospel to all. Whereas the former missionary societies mainly confined their interest to work in particular fields, especially the colonies, the new groups sought to lay comprehensive plans for reaching the entire world.

The new societies did not arise without considerable opposition, both from conservative elements within the churches and from commercial interests, but the movement spread rapidly. We cannot and need not here trace out the actual development in detail, but can only note a few of the hundreds of organizations and suggest some of their characteristic features.[3] A society later called the Baptist Missionary Society was organized in 1793 as a direct result of William Carey's *Enquiry* and his subsequent efforts. Three years later the Scottish Missionary Society and the Glasgow Missionary Society were organized, and the General Assembly of the Church of Scotland adopted an official policy for missionary work in India. Just before the turn of the century, the Church Missionary Society was formed as a channel for the work of members of the Church of England, and this eventually became the greatest of all the missionary societies in the extent of its work and the amount of its resources. Already, an interdenominational group, the London Missionary Society, had been organized by those

---

[3] An exhaustive history of the movement is to be found in K. S. Latourette, *A History of the Expansion of Christianity* (New York, 1941–1945), Vols. IV–VII.

of "evangelical sentiments" for the cooperative work of various denominations and with the resolution "not to send Presbyterianism
or any other form of church government, but the glorious Gospel of the Blessed God." The Methodists had begun actively to support foreign missions in the late eighteenth century, and an official
organ of the British Methodist Conference was established in 1817–
1818.

Protestant circles on the European continent also saw an awakening
of the missionary spirit. A society was founded in the Netherlands
in 1797, reflecting the influence of the work in Britain, and missionary
interest began to develop strongly in Germany and Switzerland after
1825. The movement in France did not arise until considerably later,
the Paris Evangelical Missionary Society beginning in 1882.

In America, interest in missions closely paralleled the development
in England, and eventually the United States supplied the majority
of the missionaries and over half the financial support for Protestant
missions. Much effort had been previously directed toward the conversion of the American Indians, and an earlier mission had been sent
to Africa, but it was with the founding of the American Board of
Commissioners for Foreign Missions (1810) that the American
churches began really to share in work outside North America. This
organization was begun at the initiative of a group of students at the
newly created Congregational Andover Theological Seminary. The
leader of the group was Samuel J. Mills, who while at Williams College
had led in the formation of a secret Society of the Brethren, in which
each member pledged to devote his life to missionary service. (It is
said that one of the landmarks in the formation of this group was a
meeting held in the shelter of a haystack near Williams.) At Andover,
the Society was joined by the later famous missionary to India and
Burma, Adoniram Judson. He and Mills were perhaps the leading
spirits in the early development of the missionary movement in the
United States. The American Board of Commissioners was shortly
followed by the Baptist Society for Propagating the Gospel in India
and other Foreign Parts, the United Christian Missionary Society (for
the work of Presbyterian and other Reformed churches), and other
societies within every major denomination.

The development of the missionary organizations was accompanied
by the rise of numerous Bible societies, whose aim was to make the
Scriptures everywhere available and who worked closely with the missionaries in translating the Bible into literally hundreds of native languages.

In addition to the comprehensive aims of the nineteenth-century
missionary movement, there were several other characteristics which
distinguished this movement from the efforts of the preceding centuries.

1) One was the relative lack of assistance by governments. Since the time of Constantine, when Christianity had become the established religion of the empire, the propagation of the faith had been actively sponsored by the rulers of Christian countries. This had continued to be true of the expansion in the sixteenth to eighteenth centuries, when the work of Roman Catholic missionaries was strongly supported by the governments of Spain and Portugal, and Orthodox missionaries by the Russian government. The former policy continued to some extent in the nineteenth century, but for the most part, and particularly in Protestant nations, the foreign missions received neither financial assistance from the governments, nor (and this is equally important) the state control over missionary activity which had often accompanied financial support. This change in the missionary movement was a part of the broader trend toward separation of church and state. As we saw earlier, the idea of a religiously uniform state was being given up in favor of a free society in which various religious groups might exist side by side. The ideal of religious freedom gradually dominated even the nominal state churches in Protestantism.

2) A second novel aspect of the movement, springing out of the new evangelical zeal, was a greatly increased participation of the rank and file of Protestant Christians. Instead of depending entirely upon the resources of a few benefactors, or of governments, or simply of the missionaries themselves, the new missionary societies were organized on the widest possible base. It was essentially and increasingly a popular movement. Not only did the support come entirely from private philanthropy, but it came from a growing minority of lay people of moderate or small incomes. (Carey, for example, had suggested in his *Enquiry* that subscriptions to the society range from a penny a week up, and it was finally decided that membership in the society should be accorded to those who contributed two and one-half pence weekly or ten pounds in a lump sum.)

3) A further distinctive development of nineteenth-century missions was a trend toward heightened requirements for baptism and admission to the mission churches. This was closely related to the decline of the practice of mass accessions to the faith, which had usually meant the conversion to Christianity of a particular ruler, who then made Christianity the official religion of the domain. That practice had been common in the Middle Ages and had made extremely difficult any substantial prebaptismal instruction. (Indeed, one of the major reasons for the medieval development of the penitential system was the necessity of providing a moral and spiritual educational program for those who had come into the church through the conversion of their sovereign.) Now, partly because of the Protestant emphasis

on the position of the individual before God and the disappearance of group conversions, partly because of earlier experiences of converts' abandoning the faith after baptism, the tendency was markedly toward more strict preparation for admission to the church, toward something of the severity of discipline and testing of faith which had marked the earliest centuries of the church's life.

Sometimes, indeed, the kind of requirements imposed on converts involved a confusion of Christian ethics with Western social customs, and such incidents have given rise to the picture of the missionary as a narrow bigot or prude, chiefly concerned with putting "Mother Hubbards" on "innocent savages." But this is at best a caricature. For the missionary was often keenly aware that the goal was not to make converts to European culture but to bring the promise and demand of the gospel to persons in many different social contexts. The difficulty of the missionary's work was really twofold: on one side was the danger that the message of the gospel might not be made relevant to the moral and social problems of the new Christians; on the other side was the peril of interpreting the implications of the faith simply in terms of Western patterns. But this was a problem of which the missionaries were increasingly conscious and which became, especially in the twentieth century, the subject of intensive study.

4) Another new feature of the movement was the wide variety of nonevangelistic humanitarian activities in which the missionaries engaged — the establishment of schools, hospitals, and centers for training nurses and doctors; the reduction of many languages and dialects to writing and the translation of not only the Bible but other Western writings into these languages; the introduction of public health measures and better agricultural techniques, social work, etc. In some cases these activities were closely related to the goal of conversion, as in the case of the schools, but much of this corollary development sprang simply out of the recognition of social and physical needs which no Christian could in good conscience ignore. The missionary's call was to serve humanity in the name of Christ. Particularly in medical work, the ideal of pure service irrespective of religious influence has been prominent. (Where this was not the case, incidentally, the missionaries were frequently plagued by the problem of "rice Christians," or persons who accepted baptism not out of conviction but in order to receive food, education, medical care, etc.)

We have seen something of the origin, the causes and motivation, and the distinctive characteristics of the nineteenth-century missionary movement. Now a final word must be said about the impact and significance of the movement.

In geographical terms, the result of the missionary endeavor has been a wide dissemination of the Christian faith. While centers of Christianity had already been established by 1800 in six of the continents, the past two centuries saw a vigorous growth from the previously established bases and the introduction of the faith to the large majority of the peoples of the world. The work was significantly successful in the islands of the Pacific, the East Indies, Ceylon, Burma, Korea, the coastal provinces and lower Yangtze in China, Japan (mainly in the intellectual and professional classes), India (especially among the lower castes and the hill tribes), Madagascar, and South and Central Africa. Anticlerical developments against Roman Catholicism in Meso- and South America helped to open the way for Protestant missions in those areas and numerous Protestant churches were established, mainly composed of converts from nominal Roman Catholicism.

The numerical expansion of Christianity resulting from the new missionary impulse should not, however, be exaggerated. The mission churches remained small in comparison with European and American churches, and Christians constituted a relatively small proportion of the population of the major non-Western nations. For example, though the percentage of Christians in non-Western nations more than doubled in the first half of the present century, the proportion of the population which is Christian had reached by the mid-1970s only about 3.5 percent in India, 3 percent in Japan, and 6.7 percent in Taiwan, though perhaps as much as 40 percent in parts of Africa. Christianity, whether Protestant, Catholic, or Orthodox, is still largely identified with the European peoples, as it had been since the fall of the Roman empire and the Moslem conquests of the early Middle Ages. The missionaries had least success in appealing to those from the highly developed Eastern religions and cultures, and almost no success among Moslems. Later, in the twentieth century, the new nationalisms tended to discourage missionary efforts.

Our concern, however, is not with the history of the expansion of Christianity, or of Protestant Christianity in particular, but with the significance of the missionary movement in the life of Protestantism as such. And here the most important fact is simply that beginning with the nineteenth century the Protestant churches became thoroughly committed to an effort to communicate the gospel of Christ to all the people of the world — and that in its intensity and zeal for the dissemination of the faith this movement can be compared only with the earliest centuries of the church.

Moreover, out of the missionary endeavor, particularly as it developed in the late nineteenth and early twentieth centuries, have come at least two major influences which bear strongly upon the contemporary Protestant scene. One of these was the development of indigenous leadership, self-support, and autonomy of control in the churches which had hitherto been largely dependent upon the paternalistic support and guidance of churches in the Western nations. This meant that in spite of the preponderance of numbers and material resources, Western Christians could no longer conceive of the Christian faith as peculiarly a religion of the "white man" or of the European.

Second, the missionary movement called for new and profound concern for the problem of Protestant divisions, as well as of the relation of Protestantism to Orthodoxy and Roman Catholicism. In its earliest stages, the missionary enterprise (like the early-nineteenth-century revivals) was marked by a spirit of common endeavor in the cause of Christ, and consequent cooperative work among the denominations. During the middle third of the last century, this spirit gave way to increasing denominational self-consciousness and competition. But denominational divisions and competition created a serious obstacle to the missionary's work. The non-Christian was not frequently attracted by the appalling variety of Protestant sects, whose divisions seemed largely meaningless and contrary to what Christians claimed about unity in Christ. What sense did it make for a North Chinese to be converted to the Southern Baptist Church? The recognition of this anomaly, and of the frequent duplication of effort and organization among the denominations, led, in the latter part of the century, to more cooperative and interdenominational activity, culminating in the International Missionary Council and successive international missionary conferences. Out of these, in part, came the modern "ecumenical movement," which we consider in a later chapter.

CHAPTER IX

The Formation of Liberal Theology

The history of Christian theology is always the record of a continuous conversation, carried on within the church and between the church and the world in which it lives. Thus the development of theology is always a dual movement, an expression of the inner life of the community of faith as it acknowledges the presence of God in Jesus Christ, and at the same time a reflection of the contemporary world. It is the effort of this community to understand itself and to make clear the nature of its faith — in relation to the thought and life of earlier generations, in relation to new insights into the meaning of the gospel, and in relation to the perspectives of the world to which the community proclaims the gospel. The faith is thus continually restated both as a function of the church's hearing of the Word of God and as a response to the problems of a new age.

From this perspective, we can understand the vigorous debate and theological ferment of the nineteenth century. For this century was not only a period of great institutional and geographical expansion in Protestantism, but also a time of intellectual vitality and reorientation of thought. In this and the succeeding chapter we seek to make clear the nature of the new trends of thinking and of the forces at work in them, especially as these gave rise to the complex movement commonly called "liberal theology."

The problem for Protestant thought at the opening of the nineteenth century can be summarized briefly in terms of the developments of the preceding two centuries. We recall the massive theological systems of the Protestant scholastics, with their concern for precision and subtlety of thought (see Ch. IV). But these had fallen into disrepute. Their gradual encasing of the vital religious themes of the reformers

161

in a hard shell of doctrines to be believed had meant not only the slow strangulation of the life which those themes expressed, but also the substitution of belief in correct articles of religion for faithful acknowledgment of the living God. And the seemingly endless disputes over theological minutiae had aroused feelings of boredom and disgust. Over against this scholasticism stood a nonreligious Rationalism which insisted on the full competence of human reason to solve all problems and to offer effective guidance for life, and which sharply attacked the claims of religion.

Deism and natural religion (see Chs. VI & VII) sought to work out various compromises between Rationalism and Christian faith by reducing religion to those "essentials" which could be "rationally" defended. The essentials were understood to be certain basic moral principles and a few "universally" held beliefs about God. All the other elements of traditional religion were merely ecclesiastical trappings and quite expendable. The Protestant scholastics, whatever their faults, had at least tried to preserve the distinctive features of the Christian message, the New Testament gospel of forgiveness and reconciliation, of incarnation, atonement, and resurrection. But in seventeenth- and eighteenth-century deism and natural religion these were abandoned in the drive for simplicity and economy of belief. Deists and proponents of natural religion were quite in accord with rationalists in the rejection of orthodoxy.

The living core of the Protestant understanding was not wholly snuffed out, of course, and we recall its reappearance with vibrant power in the evangelical revivals — in Pietism, in the Wesleyan movement, and in the awakenings (see Ch. VI). But this resurgence of religious vitality did not remove the difficulties which had been raised for Protestant thought. These movements were almost exclusively concerned with recalling people to an immediate personal experience of the working of God in Christ, and were generally indifferent or even hostile to theological endeavors. No real attempt was made to answer the questions posed by Rationalism and natural religion.

Finally, we recall the work of Immanuel Kant at the close of the eighteenth century (see Ch. VII). His "critical philosophy" not only worked a revolution in philosophy but also brought to a climax the Enlightenment attitude toward religion and symbolized the changed atmosphere in which the theologians of the nineteenth century had to work. Kant's sharp distinction between phenomena, which we know in our experience, and noumena, or things in themselves, which pure reason cannot know, was a severe blow to the traditional arguments for the existence of God, indeed to all claims to "knowledge" of God. Knowledge of the world could not lead to the knowledge of God.

Kant said that he destroyed speculative knowledge in order to make room for "faith." The affirmations of religion were to rest, not upon inference from our sensory experience (and certainly not upon revelation), but upon our apprehension of the moral law. God and immortality were to be accepted as necessary postulates of moral experience. Thus, Kant was squarely in the tradition of natural religion. Religion was still to be seen as a combination of beliefs and moral principles, only now morality was even more dominant, for religious beliefs were wholly dependent upon the dictates of the practical reason (moral experience). But at the same time Kant went quite beyond the perspective of natural religion in rejecting its view of nature as the prime datum for religious beliefs and in seeking to ground religion in another sphere of immediate experience. Both in his radical distinction between the knowledge of the world and the domain of religion and in his positive conception of religion, Kant was a source and a sign of the reordering of theology in the following century.

A Theology of Religious Experience: Schleiermacher

The man who, above all others, spoke to this problem was Friedrich Schleiermacher (1768–1834). His dealing with it was so significant that he has sometimes (though not altogether accurately) been called the father of modern liberal theology.[1]

Schleiermacher, like Kant, came out of a background of Moravian piety. In his early teens, he went to a German Moravian school and later to the theological seminary of the brotherhood. There, in spite of the opposition of his teachers, he came into contact with the thought of the Enlightenment. Subsequently, at the University of Halle, Schleiermacher made an intensive study of Kant and read widely in Greek philosophy. Both the deep and warm Moravian piety, and the critical philosophy of Kant, were major influences in Schleiermacher's constructive reorientation of theology. He later spoke of himself as "a Herrnhutter, only of a higher order" (Herrnhut was the famous Moravian community).

Perhaps the primary stimulus to Schleiermacher's new understand-

---

[1] In Britain, it was Schleiermacher's contemporary, Samuel Taylor Coleridge, who quite independently marked the transition to the new modes of thought. Though a most unsystematic theologian, Coleridge was concerned with the same central problems — the character of religious knowledge and authority. And he effected a similar reorientation of thought, freeing the Christian understanding from orthodox and Enlightenment molds, grounding belief in the living experience of faith, and paving the way for acceptance of biblical criticism and for a new relation to science.

Our discussion at this point is restricted to Schleiermacher for the sake of simplicity and because he was clearly the most influential figure in the total sweep of the movement.

ing of religion, however, came from a small circle of intimate friends who were caught up in the Romantic movement. The mood of Romanticism was one of reaction against the dry intellectualism of the rationalists; it pointed instead to imagination and to creative fancy, to freedom and individuality, and to the spontaneity and mystery of life (i.e., particularly to those dimensions of the life of the spirit for which Rationalism had no room). With the encouragement of this circle of friends, Schleiermacher wrote his first work on religion, which he called *Speeches on Religion to its Cultured Despisers* (1799). The "cultured despisers" were, of course, these same friends, and he begins by gently suggesting that despisers of religion should be sure that they know what religion really is. But do they? He writes:

> You are doubtless acquainted with the histories of human follies, and have reviewed the various structures of religious doctrine from the senseless fables of wanton peoples to the most refined Deism, from the rude superstition of human sacrifice to the ill put-together fragments of metaphysics and ethics now called purified Christianity, and you have found them all without rhyme or reason. *I am far from wishing to contradict you.*[2]

Doctrines, systems of theology, notions of the origin or end of the world, or "analyses of the nature of an incomprehensible Being, wherein everything runs to cold argument, and the highest can be treated in the tone of a common controversy" — these are not the true nature of religion.

In other words, Schleiermacher is saying to his friends, if dogmas and beliefs are what you are thinking of, then you do not really know religion and are despising something which it is not. Indeed, you are looking in the wrong place. The despised systems do not come from the heroes of religion. Why not look, therefore, at the religious life itself, at the inward emotions and dispositions, "and first those pious exaltations of the mind in which all other known activities are set aside or almost suppressed, and the whole soul is dissolved in the immediate feeling of the Infinite and the Eternal? . . . He only who has studied and truly known man in these emotions can rediscover religion in those outward manifestations."[3]

The Romantics, Schleiermacher is suggesting, have made the same mistake as the thinkers of the Enlightenment. They have identified religion with a way of thinking or a set of beliefs. Or they have confused religion with a way of acting, with ethics or art. Or they have thought of religion as a buttress of ethics, as necessary for maintaining the moral law. Or (as in the case of Kant) they have made religion merely

---

[2] *Speeches on Religion* (New York, 1958), p. 14 (Italics ours).
[3] *Ibid.*, pp. 15f.

an implication of ethics. But even those who have sought to defend religion in these ways have done it a grave disservice. Religion is neither metaphysics nor ethics, nor a combination of the two. It is some deeper, unique, special thing. Only when we see this can we account for the great appeal and pervasive expression of religion.

Where, then, is the heart of religion to be found if not in the human faculty of knowing (science, metaphysics) or acting (ethics, art)? Schleiermacher's answer is that religion belongs to the realm of "feeling" (*Gefühl*) or "affection." By these terms, Schleiermacher means a kind of primal and immediate self-awareness, a unique element in human experience which is really more basic than either ordinary knowing or acting. In both knowing and acting, I find myself over against the world as the object of my knowledge and action. But in the religious apprehension, I am immediately aware of the deeper unity of the whole. I know God, not indirectly by inference from the world of the senses or from morality, but directly, through a realm of my experience which is quite different from knowing and acting.

Religion, more precisely, is the immediate apprehension of the Infinite in the finite, of the unity in the diversity:

> The contemplation of the pious is the immediate consciousness of the universal existence of all finite things, in and through the Infinite, and of all temporal things in and through the Eternal. Religion is to seek this and find it in all that lives and moves, in all growth and change, in all doing and suffering. It is to have life and to know life in immediate feeling, only as such an existence in the Infinite and Eternal. Where this is found religion is satisfied, where it hides itself there is for [Religion] unrest and anguish, extremity and death. Wherefore it is a life in the infinite nature of the Whole, in the One and in the All, in God, having and possessing all things in God, and God in all. . . . In itself it is an affection, a revelation of the Infinite in the finite, God being seen in it and it in God.[4]

Religion is a sense and taste for the Infinite. It belongs to the sphere of "feeling," which is distinct from and really prior to knowing and doing.

Schleiermacher does not mean that religion is unrelated to morality and belief. Quite the contrary. Religion is the indispensable friend and advocate of morality, but where morality rests on the consciousness of freedom and seeks to manipulate, religion or piety begins in surrender and submission to the One. Like knowledge, religion is contemplative, but it is a contemplation (an immediate consciousness) of the Infinite and Eternal. Religious beliefs, doctrines, and dogmas come into existence as a result of reflection on this basic intuition, and are

[4] *Ibid.*, p. 36.

thus important. In his later work, Schleiermacher develops this point much more extensively, beginning with the proposition that "Christian doctrines are accounts of the Christian religious affections set forth in speech."[5] But here he is concerned to stress the primacy of the religious intuition. Though doctrines are unavoidable when feeling is made the subject of reflection, piety can exist without doctrines. Moreover, doctrines are not necessary for the communication of piety. In the language of a more recent time, religion is "caught," not "taught."

The gist of the reply, then, to the "despisers" of religion is that the institutions and dogmas which they criticize are only secondary manifestations of religion — reflections on religious affections which express the great variety of human awareness of the infinite (as well as the difficulties and errors of intellectual formulation), and institutions in which people associate together seeking religion. Religion can stand on its own feet. It is an experience that is *sui generis*. It can be understood only through itself and it needs no certification from "scientific knowledge," nor any justification by moral principles. In religion, "all is immediately true."

Here we are at the crux of the matter. Much that Schleiermacher says in the *Speeches* is open to serious question — the nature of God, the relation of the religions to each other, the significance of Christ, etc. — and much of this is changed in his later works. But these are not now our concern. The important point is that in his new understanding of the essential nature of religion, Schleiermacher has not only replied to the Romantics, but also has faced the difficulties raised by Kant's critique of knowledge. Schleiermacher can readily accept the destruction of the traditional arguments for the existence of God, for he sees that these are not at all the foundation of religion. Drawing on his Pietist heritage, he looks rather to the living experience, the immediate awareness, out of which religious beliefs and institutions spring. Moreover, Schleiermacher's understanding of the nature of religion provides a vehicle for expressing the vital dimensions of the Christian faith which had been nearly lost sight of in Protestant scholasticism and abandoned in Rationalism.

The systematic development of this latter theme is the task of Schleiermacher's greatest work, *The Christian Faith* (1821). That work begins with the same general conception of religion, but now more precisely formulated. The essence of religion, or the element which is common to *all* religion, Schleiermacher says, is the feeling (or immediate consciousness) of being absolutely dependent upon God. This awareness never appears in isolation or in pure form, but always as modified in various ways in the different religions. It is nonetheless

---

[5] *The Christian Faith,* § 15.

the presupposition of all religion and, though not all persons recognize it, is an essential element of human nature.

Concrete religions can therefore be understood as centering in particular modifications of the feeling of absolute dependence. Christianity is "a monotheistic faith, belonging to the teleological [i.e., ethical] type of religion, and is essentially distinguished from other such faiths by the fact that in it everything is related to the redemption accomplished by Jesus of Nazareth."[6] Note carefully the elements of this definition. In the first place, Christianity is centered unequivocally in Christ. This assertion stands in sharp contrast to the current Rationalism, for which Jesus had been important only as a teacher of moral principles, but not as in his person the redeeming act of God. Second, the work of Christ is redemption. The Christian faith is rooted not only in the experience of dependence upon God, but also in a further duality of experience: the consciousness of sin and the consciousness of grace. Sin means our lack of God-consciousness (i.e., "God-forgetfulness"), the hostility and alienation from God which is the failure to recognize our absolute dependence upon God. Redemption is the overcoming of sin, and transformation into full communion with God. This we cannot accomplish for ourselves. Redemption comes only by divine grace, and is communicated to us through the perfect God-consciousness of Christ.

All the Christian teachings, Schleiermacher says, are derived from reflection on this unique and complex experience. For example, the conceptions of God's eternity, omnipresence, omnipotence, and omniscience, and of creation, spring from the sense of absolute dependence on God. The conceptions of original sin, and of the holiness and justice of God, are elaborations of the consciousness of sin. And the doctrines of the love of God, of Christ as the redeemer, and of justification by faith, are all developed out of the awareness of grace.

There is neither space nor need here for a statement of Schleiermacher's detailed exposition of Christian doctrines in *The Christian Faith*. But several further comments may be made. First, in tracing out the relation of the various doctrines to their roots in Christian experience, Schleiermacher finds many traditional notions which need reinterpretation and some which do not seem at all justified. For example, "original sin" is not to be understood as referring to a first sin of the first human parents, but as an expression of the fact that the whole human race is involved in sin and in need of redemption. Such doctrines as the virgin birth and the second coming, and the traditional form of the doctrine of Christ's person (two "natures," divine and human), cannot be directly derived from our experience of redemption in Christ, though some of these may arise out of our doctrine of the

---

[6] *Ibid.*, § 11.

Scriptures. Moreover, the basis of our faith in Christ is not composed of the particular events of his life, or his miracles or teachings, but the total impression which he makes upon us.

Second, it is the doctrine of God which is all-determinative in Schleiermacher's understanding of the faith. This is seen not only in the emphasis upon *absolute* dependence but throughout *The Christian Faith*. Schleiermacher draws heavily upon the philosophy of Spinoza in working out his conception of God (especially in his identification of the "divine causality" with the total causal order of nature), but he stands equally in the tradition of the radical theocentricity of Luther and Calvin. Through the interpretation of religious experience, Schleiermacher was able to reassert the Reformed doctrine of God and to relate it to his audience.

Third, the religious life is essentially a social life. For the Enlightenment thinkers, and often for the Pietists, religion was primarily an individual matter. But for Schleiermacher (as for the New Testament and Christianity in general), to be a Christian is to share in an organic life which derives from Christ. As we are bound together in sin, so we are redeemed in a community. Finally, Schleiermacher ignores the differences between Protestant branches of Christianity. There is, he feels, an important difference between Protestant and Roman Catholic piety: in Protestantism an individual's relation to the church depends upon the relation to Christ; in Roman Catholicism the individual's relation to Christ depends upon the relation to the church. But no such differences exist between, for example, the Reformed and Lutheran traditions. They do not represent different types of piety, and their moral teachings and practice are not really different; hence, there is no finally valid reason for different theologies or even for continued separate existence of these Protestant denominations.

Enough has now been said to enable us to see the crucial place of Schleiermacher in the development of Protestant thought. Though Kant had anticipated the turn to a realm of subjective experience as the beginning point for theology, Schleiermacher first made explicit the understanding that the teachings of the church are really explanations or explications of Christian experience. By this means, the criticisms of the Rationalists and of the Romantics were held to be essentially beside the point. The affirmations of faith are not dependent upon the constructions of natural theology or ethics, nor are they simply deduced from an infallible Scripture or creed. The Bible and the creeds are important, but as records and interpretations of the experience of Christians. The Christian does not have faith in Christ because of the Bible; rather the Bible gains its authority from the believer's faith in Christ. The heart of Christianity, Schleiermacher had learned from the Moravians, is not doctrine or ethic, but a new life in Christ.

It was this new approach to the work of theology, and to the nature of the Scriptures and of doctrines, which more than anything else earned Schleiermacher the title of "father of modern theology." That view, and many of the implications which Schleiermacher drew from it, became central in Protestant "liberal theology" (sometimes also called "empirical theology," or the "theology of religious experience"). Much of Schleiermacher's understanding of the Christian affirmations, and indeed his whole approach, was later subjected to the severest kind of criticism (see Ch. XII). But even his sharpest critics are one with Schleiermacher in the recognition that God and faith belong together. We cannot speak significantly about God from a neutral corner. We know God only as we meet God in a venture of trust and obedience, as we respond in faith to the forgiving and liberating work in Christ. This was genuinely a renewal of the Reformation understanding of the gospel.

Biblical Criticism

At the same time that Schleiermacher was completing his work, there appeared another important movement which was to exert a powerful influence in the development of Protestantism — viz., the elaboration and growing acceptance of the methods of "biblical criticism," or "historical criticism" of the Bible.

The term *biblical criticism* must be properly understood, for confusion as to the meaning of the word "criticism" has often led to wholly misguided opposition to "critical" views of the Bible. In popular English usage, "to criticize" usually means "to find fault" or "to attack." But this is not at all the intent of the biblical scholars. They are critics simply in the sense of the Greek *kritikos,* which means "literary expert." In general, biblical criticism can be described as the application to the Bible of the same kind of analysis that is applied to the works of Homer, Virgil, Shakespeare, and to other forms of literature.

A somewhat different kind of critical study of the Bible had long been accepted in the church — viz., "textual criticism," or what was frequently called in the nineteenth century "lower criticism." This was a study of all available ancient manuscripts of the Bible for the purpose of determining, as nearly as possible, the original text of the biblical writings, thereby eliminating errors which had crept into the text in its transmission (e.g., through faulty copying). Such criticism had been given strong impetus by the Reformation, which challenged the authority of the Latin Vulgate (the official version in the Roman church) and stimulated the study of Hebrew and Greek texts. Thus, Luther used a Greek edition of the New Testament published in 1516 by the great Renaissance scholar Erasmus. Textual criticism also played an important part in the King James translation of the Bible (1611), in which a number of errors in the Vulgate version were corrected; and textual studies have continued to have a central role in subsequent translations, especially with the discovery of previously unknown and very early manuscripts.

The new criticism of the nineteenth century went far beyond the attempt to ascertain the original text of the Scriptures. Leaving aside, for the purposes of their study, traditional notions about the authorship or inspiration of the Scriptures, the critics now sought to answer afresh such questions as the following: what is the relation of the biblical books to each other? how were they written? by whom? when? what did the writers intend to say? were there historical causes which might account for the recorded developments in the Scriptures? what is the relation of the biblical record to other records of ancient times?

For the most part, answers to these questions were sought in an intensive study of the Scriptures themselves, using tools of analysis which were being developed in other literary study (though it should be noted that biblical scholars have contributed perhaps more than any other group to the origin and refinement of this kind of literary criticism). An example of such analysis is the work of the Italian Lorenzo Valla, who in 1440 had proved that the "Donation of Constantine" was a forgery (see Ch. I). The Donation was supposedly a decree of the Emperor Constantine, granting to the Pope temporal rule over the central states of Italy. Valla showed that the document referred to several events which had occurred centuries after the death of Constantine, and that therefore it must have been composed at a later time and attributed to the emperor.

Historical criticism of the Bible did not originate in the nineteenth century. It had been employed even in ancient times by some opponents of the church and by a small minority of Christian scholars. Moreover, developments in the Reformation and the Renaissance turned the study of the Bible increasingly in this direction. The reformers, especially Luther and Tyndale, had insisted on interpretation of the Bible according to the "plain meaning" of the text. This was in contrast to "allegorical interpretation" (i.e., the search for hidden or "spiritual" meanings), which had been a favorite method of dealing with apparent contradictions within the Bible. The reformers themselves did not altogether relinquish the method, but their stated opposition to allegory made it increasingly difficult to adopt this means of explaining the difficult passages. This insistence, together with the Protestant emphasis on the centrality of the Bible, helped to prepare the way for historical criticism.

Yet biblical studies in the church had continued to be largely insulated from literary criticism or defensive in reaction against it. There were important works of critics outside orthodox circles, such as Spinoza's study of the miracles and Old Testament sources (in the *Tractatus theologico-politicus,* 1670) and Thomas Hobbes's outline of methods for critical study of the Old Testament (in the *Leviathan,* 1651). But these began to receive sympathetic attention from Protestant scholars only in the late eighteenth century, in such men as Ernesti and Semler (see Ch. VII). Then in the nineteenth century, as theological leadership passed to the freer atmosphere of the German universities, historical criticism began to gain wide acceptance in the church and the methods of study were developed further. The goal of biblical study came to be historical objectivity: the task was to be purely factual and descriptive.

The method and significance of historical criticism can best be illustrated by some of the problems with which the scholars were concerned. One was the relation of the Synoptic Gospels (Matthew, Mark, Luke) to the Gospel of John. There are certain striking differences between the Synoptics and John which have to be accounted for in some way. The chronology of the life of Jesus is different. To cite only one example: according to John, Jesus twice celebrated the Passover in Jerusalem, the first being the occasion of the cleansing of the temple and early in Jesus' ministry (Jn 2:13ff.), the second at the time of the crucifixion (Jn 11:55ff.). The Synoptics record only one trip to Jerusalem for the Passover, at the end of Jesus' ministry, and the cleansing of the temple is placed there (see Mk 11:15ff.). Equally important is the remarkable difference between the Synoptics and John as to the form of Jesus' teaching. In the Synoptics we find Jesus speaking usually in short, pointed sayings or parables; in John we find him speaking in long, involved discourses. In the Synoptics, Jesus says very little about himself; in John he talks at length about his own person and his relation to the Father. Moreover, the latter gospel often seems confused about the geography of Palestine.

On the basis of these and many other considerations, the biblical critics concluded that the Gospel of John was a less reliable source than the Synoptics for accurate information about the events of Jesus' life or his actual teachings. It was rather a later theological interpretation, which sought to set forth the meaning of the events, without primary regard for historical accuracy, and which ascribed to Jesus much that he did not actually say (though the speeches recorded might be the author's expansion of certain of Jesus' sayings).

What then of the relation of the first three gospels to each other? A careful comparison of these gospels showed that nearly all of Mark, the shortest gospel, is included in Matthew and Luke — not only that the events and the sayings in Mark are related in the other gospels in the same way and order, but also that the language of the accounts is frequently identical. This was not a new discovery, but now a new interpretation was placed on the evidence. It was suggested, contrary to the tradition that Matthew was the earliest gospel, that in fact Mark was written first and the writers of Matthew and Luke had drawn on

Mark for their portraits of Jesus. This was the simplest explanation and the one which would be given for any other three documents which were similarly parallel.

When this relation of the first three gospels was accepted, a further question arose from the fact, that there are substantial portions (about 250 verses) of Matthew and Luke which are the same, and practically identical in language, but which do not appear in Mark. These parallels consist entirely of sayings of Jesus. The logical conclusion is that in addition to Mark, the writers of Matthew and Luke had another common source of information which each one incorporated into his gospel, together with the material from Mark and information which each had secured from other sources. As to what lay behind these written sources, subsequent analysis led to substantial agreement with a suggestion of Schleiermacher, that the gospels ultimately consist of a large number of fragments, more or less artificially connected.

Another closely related result of historical criticism was the conclusion that the various parts of the New Testament reveal distinctive "points of view," and that these show the particular background and interest of the writers and also indicate the existence in New Testament times of different and sometimes antagonistic wings or parties in the church. Thus the Gospel of Matthew emphasizes the continuity of Christianity with Judaism (Jesus as the fulfillment of the law) and this gospel is seen as a product of a Jewish Christian community. Luke, however, stresses the abrogation of the Jewish law, in line with Paul's view of Christ as superseding and making unnecessary obedience to the Jewish law; this was a gospel directed to the Gentiles.

So far, we have been speaking only of the study of the New Testament. Historical criticism had been applied even earlier to the Old Testament, and here there were some even more acute difficulties. If it was true that the gospels were composite writings (i.e., that they were not simply the products of individual writers but were compilations from various sources), this was even more true of the Old Testament. One important example is the book of Isaiah. By a thorough analysis of references in the book to the social and political environment, and to the religious situation of the Hebrews, it was concluded that the prophecies attributed to Isaiah were the work of at least two men, who lived centuries apart. Most of chapters 1 to 39 came from a man who prophesied in the kingdom of Judah between 740 and 700 B.C. Chapters 40ff. were largely the work of a prophet during the exile in Babylonia, specifically about 540 B.C. Moreover, Old Testament prophecy in general could no longer be understood as specific prediction of details in the life of Christ, but only as expressions of the general hope of the Hebrews for a Messiah, and thus perhaps as a general preparation for the revelation in Christ.

The most revolutionary conclusion of Old Testament criticism had to do with the composite character of the Pentateuch (the first five books of the Old Testament), which even before the time of Christ had been considered the work of Moses. This in spite of the fact that in one of these books, Deuteronomy, Ch. 34, the death and burial of Moses are described and it is stated that "no one knows the place of his burial to this day." The phrase "to this day" clearly suggests that it was written at a later time. Close analysis of the style of the writing, of the use of different names for God, of the duplication of narratives (e.g., two stories of creation and two interwoven accounts of the flood), of the variation in religious conceptions, etc., led to the theory that these five books of the Bible were the product of at least four different writers or schools of writers. The final form of the Pentateuch was held to be the work of a group of "editors" who, probably after 550 B.C., combined: 1) two ancient traditions about the origins of the world and of the Hebrew people — these were commonly called "J" and "E" writers, because they used the names Jahweh and Elohim, respectively, for God; 2) a law code, now comprising most of the book of Deuteronomy; 3) some other early snatches of poetry and legend; and 4) their own interpretative pattern and amplification of the laws. A similar composite character was discovered in other historical books of the Old Testament.

These illustrations make clear the crucial problems which biblical criticism introduced for Christian thought. The reliability of the Old Testament record was seriously questioned, not only as regards the stories of creation but even with respect to the history of the Hebrews. In some cases the traditional view of Israel's development was exactly reversed: the great law codes did not come before but after the prophets. Moses was not the author of the laws; indeed it was not clear that much of anything could be known for certain about Moses. In the case of the New Testament a similar embarrassment concerned the gospel records. Considering that the earliest was written a generation after Jesus' death, considering their uncertain authorship and the points of view or "biases" evident in the writings, could one be at all sure of their accuracy in reporting the life and teaching of Jesus?

In spite of these questions, most scholars at the end of the nineteenth century could speak of "the assured results of biblical criticism." The more extreme negative theories had been thoroughly discredited (such as the notion that Jesus never lived). The critics were confident that while many traditional conceptions of the Bible had to be given up, it was now possible to know truly the Jesus of history, to distinguish the words and character of Jesus from the interpretations that the church later placed on him and his work. It should be noted, however, that the confidence of the late nineteenth century in the success of the "quest for the historical Jesus" was due for some rude shocks.

By the turn of the century it was being seriously questioned whether the evidence is at all adequate to provide a biography of Jesus in the modern sense. As one scholar, Martin Kähler, put it, historical science uncovers only "a vast field strewn with the fragments of various traditions," out of which no sure account of the development of Jesus' life can come. Others, such as Johannes Weiss and Albert Schweitzer, were to contend that the authentic teaching of Jesus was not all that comfortable for modern minds to hear, because of its inseparable connection with his preaching of the imminent arrival of the kingdom of God. It became clear that in some cases the conclusions of historical criticism were shaped more by "scientific" assumptions or by cultural, philosophical, and theological presuppositions than by objective analysis. Thus, the miracle stories were often rejected as inauthentic or mythical simply because "miracles can't happen." Moreover, Jesus' teaching about the kingdom of God was frequently set aside as a later addition or an unessential element in his teaching that he merely took over from his contemporaries, or the idea of the kingdom was similarly construed more in terms of nineteenth-century thought than in the thought-forms of the first century. Further, at the very end of the nineteenth century, the so-called history of religions (*religionsge-schichtlich*) school of criticism began to show clearly how deeply imbedded were both the Old and New Testaments in the other religious traditions of the ancient Near East. The biblical stories of creation, for example, had to be seen in relation to Babylonian creation myths by which they were influenced. The New Testament affirmations about Christ had to be set in connection to other current kinds of ascriptions of deity and even to the ancient myths of dying and rising gods.

What is important here, however, is that in spite of uncertainties and debate, biblical criticism was in principle firmly and irrevocably established by the end of the nineteenth century and continued to flourish in new and sophisticated forms in the twentieth. The decisive issue was not the specific interpretations of historical criticism, but lay at a deeper level — viz., at the level of the *significance* and *authority* of the Bible as a whole (i.e., precisely in the giving up of traditional conceptions of biblical revelation). The acceptance of biblical criticism meant the abandonment of the belief that the Bible is an infallible record of divine revelation. There might be much in the Bible which is inspired, much that is divine, but there is also much that is human and even in error. The Bible is not a book delivered to us from on high and preserved from all error, so that we might trust it absolutely. It is instead a very human book, including widely differing understandings of God and of God's will, and including not only valuable historical documents, contemporary with the events they recorded, but also legends and even fiction, which often contradict each other and known historical facts.

In short, it was all up with the dogma of the inerrancy of Scripture. This was perhaps the most important development in nineteenth-century Protestant thought, even more far-reaching in its implications than the influence of the new scientific theories. The result of the new understanding of the Bible was a revolution in thought comparable to the Reformation itself. The reformers had challenged the absolute authority of the church and tradition and had insisted that final authority rested in the Scriptures alone. True, Luther had stoutly insisted that Christ is supreme over the Scriptures and could label some of the biblical writings as of lesser value than others; and by no means all of Protestantism had been committed to the rigid view of biblical inerrancy developed in Protestant scholasticism. The destruction of the notion that the Bible is from cover to cover a recording of divinely revealed truths was in part a return to the classical Protestant view. But none of the reformers had envisaged so radical a questioning of biblical authority as this.

It has often been said that biblical criticism was far more disturbing to Protestantism than to Roman Catholicism, because the former had relied exclusively on the Scriptures. This is true in the sense that biblical criticism came to be generally accepted in Protestantism and led to basic reorientations of thought. In Roman Catholicism, on the other hand, the authority of church and tradition could be appealed to in defense of the authority of Scripture, and the church steadfastly set its face against the new views, notably during the pontificate of Pius X, with the condemnation of "Modernism" in 1907.[7] Not until well into the twentieth century did biblical critical methods become commonplace in Roman Catholic scholarship.

We have spoken thus far of biblical criticism as posing certain problems for Christian thought. This does not mean, however, that the new conception of the Bible which came to characterize Protestant liberalism originated simply as a reaction to the discoveries of historical criticism. In fact, the situation was more nearly the reverse. It was new conceptions of religious authority and of the meaning of revelation which made possible the development of biblical criticism. One of these was the religious philosophy of Georg W. F. Hegel (1770–1831), which influenced several of the leading biblical critics of the first half of the century. According to this philosophy, the essence of Christianity lay in the great ideas which were enshrined in such doctrines as the Trinity and the Incarnation. The truth of these was not dependent upon the historical accuracy of the Bible; therefore the findings of

---

[7] In 1906 the Vatican Biblical Commission declared that the arguments against Moses' authorship of the Pentateuch were worthless, and later affirmed that the Gospel of John was equally reliable with the Synoptics as a historical source. Pius X specifically forbade Roman Catholic scholars to use the methods of "secular" historical analysis on the Bible.

the critics did not at all compromise the truth of the faith. The Hegelian interpretation was, however, relatively short-lived except in certain types of the philosophy of religion. It was quickly seen that Christian faith cannot be indifferent to the historical facts of its origin.

A far more important reinterpretation of religious authority had been suggested by Friedrich Schleiermacher — and it was along this line that there developed the characteristic view of liberal Protestantism which made possible a ready acceptance of historical criticism. Schleiermacher had insisted, we recall, that at its root religion is neither belief nor obedience to a moral code, but an immediately experienced relation to God. All Christian doctrines, creeds, and confessions are human interpretations of the experience of redemption through Jesus Christ. Not any external authority, Bible, or creed, or church, is finally normative, but only the living experience of Christians.

This insight led to a new understanding of the authority of the Bible — not the authority of a purely objective and external revelation, delivered by God for acceptance by believers, but rather the authority of a record of religious experience. As a product of the overwhelming experience of the earliest Christians, the New Testament has immense significance and authority for all subsequent understandings of the Christian gospel, and it serves to communicate the experience to later generations. But interpretations in the New Testament as to the meaning of Christ do not have to be taken as infallible divine deliverances. The central fact to which the New Testament points, the presence of God in Christ, is of all-embracing import, but differences in interpretation and in the reporting of events are to be expected. No longer is it necessary to tortuously explain away discrepancies in the accounts, or differences in point of view. The Bible is a human and fallible, albeit inspired and inspiring, record of the response of human beings to the revealing work of God. Biblical criticism does not destroy the religious value of the Bible; it enhances that value. In the New Testament it enables us to penetrate behind the documents to the central facts of the life of Christ. In the Old Testament, through the distinguishing of the various layers of tradition and their dates, it reveals to us the gradual development of Hebrew religion into the ethical monotheism of the great prophets.

Such was the general understanding of the Bible which emerged from the reinterpretation by Schleiermacher and his successors and from the new biblical research. Theological leadership was centered in Germany throughout the nineteenth century, but the movements which began there spread rapidly to France, Britain, and America, so that by the end of the century the new patterns of thought were rapidly becoming dominant throughout Protestantism.

A Theology of Moral Values: Ritschl

Before turning to a third major feature in the rise of Protestant liberalism and the changing attitudes toward science, we must look briefly at a German theologian of the latter half of the nineteenth century who also contributed much to the development of liberal theology.

Albrecht Ritschl (1822–1889) marked the confluence of several of the trends already described. He was an astute biblical critic, and his motto was "Back to the New Testament by way of the Reformation." He meant also "by way of the tools of biblical criticism," for these enable us to see clearly the historical facts and the original gospel at the heart of Christian faith. Above all else, Ritschl sought to restore the historical Jesus to the center of theology. Christ was the *punctum stans* for all Christian thinking. Thus Ritschl stood in the tradition of Schleiermacher, emphasizing the absolute centrality of Christ and seeking to ground all faith affirmations in Christian experience (though for Ritschl, religious experience was essentially *moral* in nature).

Moreover, Ritschl was deeply influenced by the critical philosophy of Kant. This is evident in two ways. First, Ritschl thoroughly agreed with Kant's limitation of theoretical "knowledge" of God. For Ritschl, this was a healthy step, for religion is not at all concerned with abstract and speculative assertions about God, but only with judgments made on the basis of living experience of Christ's work for and in us (i.e., with affirmations which spring from an appreciation of Christ's significance or value for us). Second, Ritschl accepted Kant's close identification of religion and morality. Religion is essentially a practical affair. It is concerned with winning the victory of spirit over nature in human life. Similarly, the judgments of faith are judgments of value or worth. We call Christ divine because he has the value of God for us and he does for us what only God can do.

Ritschl described the gospel as an ellipse with two foci: 1) Justification and Reconciliation, and 2) the kingdom of God. Justification and Reconciliation describe the redemptive work of Christ, which is mediated to the Christian through the church. This is the deliverance of personality from bondage to nature, so that the Christian enjoys dominion over the world, victory over sin. Christ, as the historical founder of Christianity, initiates this victory by his perfect identity of moral and religious purpose with the purpose of the Father. But the purpose of God is the establishment of a fellowship of redeemed persons. Thus we are led to the second focus of the ellipse: the kingdom of God. Reconciliation is for the sake of the kingdom, "the organization of humanity through action inspired by love."

Viewed in retrospect, Ritschl's conception of the kingdom of God is subject to serious attack. He misunderstood the New Testament view of the kingdom and too readily identified the ethical goals of Christianity with the cultural ideals of his time. The latter tendency led to the development of what the Germans call *Kulturprotestantismus* (i.e., the confusion of Protestantism with cultural faith and goals). At the same time, Ritschl's rediscovery of the central place of the idea of the kingdom of God in the New Testament gave powerful impetus to the development of the "social gospel" in Protestantism (see Ch. XI). Also, his stress on the practical nature of religion helped in the formation of the characteristic liberal concern for morality. Christianity, he insisted, is an absolutely ethical religion.

Closely related to the emphasis on ethics were two other aspects of Ritschl's teaching which became central in liberal theology. First, his insistence that God is love — not simply that love is one of the attributes of God, along with justice, power, etc., but that God *is* love. This is God's inmost nature, God's very being. Thus the notion of God's holiness and justice was suppressed (and the idea of God's wrath was denied). This teaching resulted in the practical abandonment of the traditional doctrines of punishment of the damned. Second, and connected with the former, was a qualification of classical doctrines of sin. Partly because of his notion of the religious problem as one of spirit versus nature, partly because of the prevailing mood of the late nineteenth century, partly because of his opposition to "theoretical" doctrines, Ritschl rejected the idea of "original sin." He was much more optimistic about the possibility of overcoming sin than either traditional Protestantism or Protestant thought since the First World War.

Religion and Science

Along with the historical criticism of the Bible and the theological reconstruction led by Schleiermacher and Ritschl, a third central feature in the rise of Protestant liberalism was the opening of a new phase in the relations of science and religion. At least since the time of the discoveries of Galileo and Kepler, which destroyed traditional conceptions of an earth-centered universe, the problem of the relation between the biblical conception of the world and the scientific conception of the world had been acute. But until the nineteenth century, the religious response to the problem had generally taken one of three directions. Protestant scholasticism had made its peace with the new astronomy, but with little effect upon its interpretation of the traditional religious views. The natural religion of the eighteenth century was the product of a Rationalism which abandoned the tradition in favor of a thoroughly "scientific" worldview — in this case, the machine-like world of Newtonian physics, in which all events were to be explained as parts of a network of natural causes. Thus Rationalism logically led to the superannuated deity of deism, whose function it was merely to start the machine, to guarantee the validity of moral laws, and to insure the rewards of heaven for the righteous. The Pietist and evangelical revivals, suspicious of Rationalism and scholasticism alike, had simply bypassed the question.

Now in the nineteenth century, the whole discussion took a significantly new turn. The new attitude was a result both of the rapid advance and expansion of science and of the religious developments already described in this chapter. If there was any single scientific event which brought the matter to a focus, it was the publication in 1859 of Charles Darwin's *Origin of Species*. Certainly this book, and the theory which it presented, evoked more intense discussion of the problem of religion and science than any other book in modern times. (It should also be noted that Darwin's theory provoked some sharp opposition in scientific circles.)

The idea of "evolution" was certainly not originated by Darwin. It had been suggested by early Greek philosophers and championed (in various forms) by Hegel and Comte earlier in the nineteenth century. The significance of Darwin's work was threefold.

1) He supplied a vast amount of data to show that, at least within certain areas of the biological world, there had been gradual evolution from simpler to more complex organisms. That is, he proved the notion of organic evolution to be true insofar as any scientific hypothesis is capable of such proof.
2) He offered a plausible suggestion as to how the development from simpler to more complex forms took place, viz., by "natural selection," by the survival of the best-adapted forms in the struggle for existence. Among the multitude of variations which appeared in the production of offspring, those strains persisted which were best suited for the struggle against the environment — these were "superior" strains which could successfully compete for existence with similar organisms. The gradual accumulation of such variations resulted in the appearance of new species.
3) Darwin used this theory to account for the origin of the human race.

It is easy to see why the intensified discussion of religion and science should have centered on Darwinism (rather than, for example, on the discoveries of geology). This theory seemed in direct conflict with Christian faith, and at a peculiarly vital spot. The assertion that the human species had gradually evolved from lower forms of life appeared to contradict the biblical story of human origins. It detracted from the dignity of being the "special creation" of God. (This was what gave such emotional force to the debates over "man or monkey".) And by setting back the date of the origin of the human race by countless thousands of years, it led to doubts as to the traditional view concerning the central place of Hebrew-Christian history in the history of humanity. Both by this and by its apparent conflict with the Genesis accounts of creation and the Fall, the theory of evolution seemed to strike a vital blow at the whole Christian conception of redemption.

Moreover, to some there now seemed to be no room for the working of a beneficent purpose in nature or in history. For the eighteenth century, the worlds of nature and of humanity obeyed the same inexorable laws, prescribed by a just and all-wise God. Now the natural law and the moral law were no longer in perfect harmony, but in harsh contradiction. Nature, "red in tooth and claw," dominated by the struggle for existence, was anything but moral. Here, then, was a vast magnification of the problem of evil: how to reconcile the terrible struggle and waste of the evolutionary process with the existence of a good and all-powerful Creator. (This was much less of a problem, of course, for the Calvinistic tradition, which acknowledged the inscrutability of God's ways and the radical corruption of the world.)

The initial reaction of the Christian community was mixed. There was bitter denunciation of Darwinism by many, especially in the English-speaking countries, who judged traditional Christianity and the theory of evolution to be irreconcilable. Others were prepared to wait and see what the theory would come to. Some Christians from the first saw the compatibility of evolution and Christianity, and it was in this direction that the central stream of Protestant thought was to move, toward a genuine partnership of science and religion, in which neither the essential witness of Christian faith nor the integrity of scientific investigation would be given up.

This movement was made possible by the developments which were already taking place in nineteenth-century Protestant thought. Biblical studies had shown that the Genesis stories of creation and the Fall could no longer be uncritically accepted as God's own description of human origins, but had to be understood rather as ancient Hebrew traditions. The theology of religious experience had taught that the doctrines of the church, including even the biblical statements, were not infallible revealed truths, but human interpretations of religious experience. All doctrinal formulations were thus subject to continual restatement. Moreover, the temper of the newer theological understanding was one of friendliness rather than hostility toward the scientific enterprise. Theologians and scientists alike were concerned to discern the truth, whether of the structure of the natural world or the verities of religious experience. Biblical criticism, after all, was intended to be scientific both in spirit and in method.

Thus the way was already opened for the acceptance of at least a modified Darwinism. There were, to be sure, certain types of evolutionary *theory* which could not be accepted without abandoning essential Christian affirmations. For example, the notion that the processes of natural selection provided a *complete* explanation of the origins of humanity, without any reference whatsoever to the external or internal workings of God, did stand in contradiction to the belief in creation. But the evidence did not, and in the nature of the case could not, compel the acceptance of this interpretation; for all purely "naturalistic" or "materialistic" explanations of the evolutionary process involved certain philosophical assumptions which were not necessitated by the evidence itself.

While it was often not Darwin's own theory that was accepted, or even understood, for many it was easy to view evolution as a process by which the creative activity of God was expressed. The discovery that the human species had come into being as a result of a very long process of development from lower forms of life did require a drastic alteration of the traditional views as to "how" God created, yet it did not affect at all the conviction that God is the creator (nor did it say anything as to the purpose, the "why" of creation).

Along this line, the new conception of the relation of religion and science developed. It is the province of science to tell us the *structure* of the physical universe and to describe the processes by which it has come to be what it is. But religion is concerned with more ultimate questions of origin and meaning, and from religious experience we know that God is the creator and sustainer of the universe and is continually at work in it, in the natural processes which science describes and in the lives of persons. The Bible is not a book of science, but a book of religion. The "science" of the Bible is the science of those who wrote it, and we should not expect that the biblical authors should have any more insight into the processes of nature than did their contemporaries. Indeed, the Bible itself shows no interest in natural processes for their own sake. It affirms that nature as well as history is ordered by the purpose of God, but its primary concern is with the redeeming work of God in human history. Modern interpreters cannot be satisfied with as simple a view of the physical universe as those of former times, and this means that the task of relating the insights of faith to the "secular" knowledge of the world becomes increasingly complex, but the witness of faith remains in substance the same.

It can hardly be said that the wholehearted acceptance of the work of science won immediate and universal acclaim among religious interpreters. The victory in Protestantism came only after prolonged and sometimes bitter controversy. And there were two groups of Protestants who did not finally accept the kind of adjustment which characterized Protestant liberalism: one, the ultraconservative wing, vigorously continued to defend the cosmology of the Bible against the "atheistic" attacks of science; the other, an extreme "liberal" or "modernist" wing, abandoned much of the Christian tradition in favor of a "scientific" worldview. These groups are described more fully in the next chapter. It is important to note here only that fundamentally they agreed on the incompatibility of science with the central affirmations of Christian faith. The main body of Protestant thought went in the other direction. Even in the United States, where the shift of opinion came somewhat more slowly, the tide was definitely turning by the time of the First World War. Determined efforts were made by "fundamentalists" in the 1920s to capture control of some of the major denominations, and the "controversy" over evolution caught the public eye because of the bizarre Scopes trial (1925). But generally speaking, it was only the sporadic outcries of a minority of extreme conservatives and the gross ignorance among some journalists and part of the public concerning what was being taught in the churches that made evolution persist as a live religious issue.

The most important influence of evolutionary theory on religious thought came from the application of the idea in fields other than biology, and especially in interpreting the development of religion. In the critical study of the Old Testament, for example, the concept provided a fruitful pattern for interpreting the great variety of religious insights there recorded. The history of Israel could be understood as the gradual evolving of the Hebrew religious consciousness, from the simple and crude conceptions of the earliest writings to the exalted ethical monotheism of the prophets. As God had brought humanity into existence through a long evolutionary process, so God was progressively revealed, with the climax being reached in Christ. A similar pattern of explanation was widely adopted in the study of the history of religions (or "comparative religions"), which came into prominence about the beginning of the twentieth century. Both in the interpretation of Christianity and in this general study of religions, increased emphasis was laid upon the influence of cultural environment in the development of religious thought and practice.

A comparable result of the adoption of evolutionary categories in religious thinking was the strong reinforcement of at least three trends in Protestant thought which may properly be associated with liberal theology. One was an increased emphasis on the "immanence" of God, that is, on the working of God *within* natural processes rather than by miraculous interruptions of the natural order. As one writer put it in a very influential book, *Lux Mundi,* published in England in 1889:

The one absolutely impossible conception of God in the present day is that which represents him as an occasional visitor. Science had pushed the Deists' God farther and farther away, and at the moment when it seemed as if he would be thrust out altogether, Darwinism appeared and under the guise of a foe did the work of a friend. It has conferred upon philosophy and religion an inestimable benefit by showing us that we must choose between two alternatives. Either God is everywhere present in nature, or he is nowhere. He cannot be here and not there. . . . It seems as if in the providence of God the mission of modern science was to bring home to our un-metaphysical ways of thinking the great truth of the divine immanence in creation, which is not less essential to the Christian idea of God than to a philosophical view of nature.[8]

This trend of thought had been given earlier impetus by Spinoza, by the Romantics, by Schleiermacher and Hegel, and by the nineteenth-century poets, but it was intensified by the acceptance of evolution.

The use of evolutionary patterns of thought also hastened the rein-terpretation of traditional conceptions of sin and redemption. The view that human beings had been created in a condition of perfect innocence and had then fallen into sinfulness from which they had to be redeemed, was exchanged for a view which put the golden age in the future. That we need to be redeemed from sin was not denied, but redemption was likened more to a process of gradual education from the state of the brute to the condition of an obedient child of God. Thus, in the "social gospel" movement (see Ch. XI) the pattern of evolutionary development in religion was extended to the expecta-tion that the work of redemption initiated in Christ would soon culmi-nate in the achievement of a truly Christian civilization.

Finally, the relation of Christianity to non-Christian religions was increasingly understood in evolutionary terms. The relation is not one of white and black, entire truth and utter falsity. Rather, the religions of mankind represent stages in the development of religious insight, Christianity being the highest and fullest revelation of God.

[8] Aubrey Moore, in *Lux Mundi* (London, 1889), p. 82.

CHAPTER **X**

Liberalism and Its Contexts

In the preceding chapter we described some of the principal forces at work in nineteenth-century religious thought. These forces converged in what is commonly called "liberalism" or "liberal theology," a movement which reached its zenith in the early decades of the twentieth century. Despite subsequent reaction against many of its tendencies, theological liberalism has left a permanent mark on the mood of Protestant thinking and on the interpretation of many central Christian affirmations. A more careful and systematic statement of its main features is therefore needed. There is no single definition that can be applied equally well to all who would call themselves "liberal" Protestants. But certain principles and motifs stand out as widely characteristic of the movement as it developed in Britain and America and on the Continent, and from these we can gain a relatively clear picture of what can properly be called the central stream of liberal Protestant theology.

It will be helpful to begin by looking at a small book which has often been hailed as one of the classic expressions of liberal Protestantism. This will be a "case study" in liberalism. Then we may broaden the scope of the description by setting forth some of the basic *principles* of liberalism. To this will be added an analysis of some of the more specific theological reinterpretations which have been typical of liberalism. Finally, we shall take account of several other trends in mid- and late-nineteenth-century Protestantism which stand in contrast to liberal theology and we shall note some internal tensions that began to emerge before the First World War.

What Is Christianity?

What Is Christianity? is the English title of a book by the Berlin professor, Adolph Harnack, often acknowledged as the greatest Protestant historian of the late nineteenth century. This book, called in German *Das Wesen des Christentums* (literally "The Essence of Christianity"), is a transcript of extemporaneous lectures delivered in the winter of 1899–1900 to a class of six hundred students from all parts of the university. The views Harnack expressed represent a relatively extreme form of liberal theology, and the book immediately called forth a whole literature of response, both Protestant and Catholic. But just this makes the book useful as an illustration of tendencies of thought that appeared in varying form elsewhere.

As the title of the work indicates, Harnack proposes to delineate what is truly essential in Christianity — to get behind the externals, to strip off the husks and lay bare the kernel. The gospel, he says, "contains something which, under differing historical forms, is of permanent validity." Behind the metamorphoses of Christianity, the changing formulations and expectations, the altering ways of feeling, behind even the form of the New Testament witness, there is that which is "really classical and valid for all time." Moreover, this "Gospel in the Gospel is something so simple, something that speaks to us with so much power, that it cannot easily be mistaken."

Where shall we look for this permanent and essentially simple gospel? Not in the dogmatic statements of a later time, nor in the ecclesiastical organization, nor in the ascetic morality of medieval Christendom. Not even in the formulas of the apostle Paul, for while it was his great work to free the original gospel from the bonds of a parochial Judaism, he also began that process whereby foreign and speculative ideas about the person of Christ came to obscure and even pervert the majesty and simplicity of the gospel. We must look, Harnack says, rather to the founder of Christianity himself, as he is known to us through the Synoptic Gospels. Those three gospels "offer us a plain picture of Jesus' teaching, in regard both to its main features and to its individual application; in the second place, they tell us how his life issued in the service of his vocation; and in the third place, they describe to us the impression which he made upon his disciples, and which they transmitted."

These facts are known to us through the critical understanding of the gospels. Harnack warns that we must not stumble over such matters as miracles, or belief in demons, or the apocalyptic element (i.e., the belief that the catastrophic end of the world is near). These are only part of the framework in which the gospel is presented; they are not essentially connected with it but merely belong to the age in which the gospels were written. We know that miracles do not happen, that there are no demons, and that the end of the world is not near; but the essential gospel is quite independent of these things.

The core of Christianity is to be found in the personality of Jesus and in his teaching. "He spoke like a prophet, and yet not like a prophet," for he impressed his followers as one having authority. "His words breathe peace, joy, and certainty. . . . He lived in the continual consciousness of God's presence. His food and drink was to do God's will. But . . . he did not speak like an heroic penitent, or like an ascetic who has turned his back upon the world. His eyes rested kindly upon the whole world. . . . He ennobled it in his parables . . . and he recognized everywhere the hand of the living God."

The teaching of Jesus, Harnack says, can be summarized under three heads:

> Firstly, the kingdom of God and its coming.
> Secondly, God the Father and the infinite value of the human soul.
> Thirdly, the higher righteousness and the commandment of love.

The simplicity of Jesus' message is found in the fact that each of these leading thoughts expresses, in a different way, the whole of the gospel; at the same time the message is so rich that each of these seems inexhaustible in meaning.

Jesus' teaching about the kingdom, according to Harnack, referred to the coming of the rule of God in the hearts of individuals. In the gospels, this thought of the kingdom is paralleled by an expectation of a dramatic, external, cataclysmic overthrow of the kingdom of the devil and the establishment of God's rule over the world. But that view of the kingdom, with its implicit Jewish nationalism, was part of the framework of ideas into which Jesus came, and though he did not dispute this idea, it was not his own. His concern was exclusively with the kingdom within, with the rule of God that is already present in the hearts of human beings, with the presence of God in power. This is the element which has permanent validity.

The second heading places Christ's message in the clearest light. Here is indeed the essence of religion: "God as the Father, and the human soul so ennobled that it can and does unite with him." God's fatherly providence and loving care extend to the whole world and is particularly directed to persons as God's children. Every human soul is of infinite value. Thus, the recognition of the Fatherhood of God leads to reverence for humanity. This is the religion which Jesus himself believed and taught. He did not desire his followers to worship him, but only the Father; "he desired no other belief in his person and no other attachment to it than is contained in the keeping of his commandments."

So we are led to the third inclusive summary of the gospel: the higher righteousness and the commandment of love. The gospel is uncompromisingly an ethical message, one which distinguishes the ethical from the ritualistic and which goes straight to the root of morality, to inner intention and disposition. This is the higher righteousness, the law of *love*. It is the practical proof of religion; without neighborly love and mercy, religion is but a vain pretense.

These three statements, then, which really coalesce with one another, constitute the heart of Jesus' teaching, and find expression in everything that he said. This is the gospel, and Jesus himself stands behind it, in perfect embodiment of his teaching. It was Harnack's belief that this gospel had again and again been lost sight of or distorted in the later development of the church and its dogmas. The Reformation was a recall to the essential gospel in its protest against all external authority in religion, whether of council, priest, or tradition. But Protestantism, too, has had its tendencies toward Catholicism; therefore, it is continually necessary to seek out the pure gospel, as found in the teachings of Jesus, and let it show its true authority.

It would not be fair to Protestant liberalism to say that Harnack was fully typical of the movement. Not only later interpreters, but most liberal thinkers of his own day saw that this was too simple a rendering even of the teaching of Jesus, and that Harnack had eliminated much that is essential to the Christian gospel. A more careful look at the fundamental principles and trends of liberal theology will give us a better perspective on both the virtues and defects of the movement.

Formative Principles of Liberalism[1]

The distinguishing features of liberal Protestantism can best be understood when we recognize that it rested on a duality of interest. On the one hand, this liberalism was open to all the prevailing thought currents of the nineteenth century. It was part of a broader development which affected not only religious but also scientific, philosophical, economic, and political thought as well. Liberalism in theology was thus a response and adjustment to nineteenth-century trends in all of these areas. On the other hand, liberal theology was the product of a resurgence of religious vitality which expressed itself in other ways as well, most prominently in the missionary movement (see Ch. VIII) and in the application of Christianity to social problems (see

---

[1] This summary of principles is in part developed from a statement by H. P. Van Dusen, in a classic twentieth-century product of the mainline liberal tradition, *The Vitality of the Christian Tradition*, ed. G. F. Thomas (New York, 1945), pp. 169–74.

Ch. XI). It grew out of a renewed and deepened insight into the Christian faith itself. It may be said, therefore, that the central principles of liberalism reflect a complex interweaving of interests from two sources: modern culture, or the general intellectual outlook of the nineteenth century, and the vitalities of specifically Christian experience. Thus the various liberal theologies in Europe and America are all to be understood as part of a pervasive pattern of adjustment or accommodation. And in viewing this accommodation, it is not fruitful to try to decide which of the two kinds of sources was dominant; that is, whether people influenced by the liberal tradition were being newly called back to the faith or whether they were being largely reassured that their modern beliefs reflected the essentials of Christianity. Both of these processes were going on.

Central among the presuppositions, or informing principles, of liberal Protestantism was *the liberal spirit* — the spirit of open-mindedness, of tolerance and humility, of devotion to truth wherever it might be found. This spirit can hardly be traced simply to the intellectual perspective of the nineteenth century. For such an attitude had from the beginning been present in Christian thinking (though, of course, in widely varying degree). It was represented in wholehearted commitment to the unity of truth, in the conviction that God is the source of all truth and that nothing that can be known by science or philosophy can ever finally be in contradiction to faith in him. The same respect for truth and honest inquiry is required of theologian and of nonbeliever. As Wilhelm Herrmann (see below) insisted: Christian faith can be nothing other than unreserved obedience to the truth, and an honest atheist is closer to Christian faith than a representative of a religion of wish, no matter how "Christian" the language of the latter. The prevailing mood of the Enlightenment and the nineteenth century, however, powerfully reinforced this tendency in Christian thinking, leading to markedly greater freedom in dealing with the historic affirmations and to new conceptions of the similarity of the search for truth in religion, philosophy, and science.

A classic expression of the liberal temper is found in Frederick D. Maurice, the most influential British theologian of the mid-nineteenth century. A biographer writes that "his whole sympathies lay with the scientific men when they were asserting what they had humbly, patiently investigated and found to be true. He was never tired of quoting the spirit of Mr. Darwin's investigations as a lesson and model for Churchmen."[2] The liberal spirit was neither that of defensiveness nor that of compromise. For the Christian faith, if true, did not need either to be compromised or to be preserved from attack. Thus Mau-

---

[2] *The Life of Frederick Denison Maurice*, edited by his son, Frederick Maurice (London, 1884), Vol. II, p. 608.

rice, like Coleridge before him, replied to the claim that biblical criticism was dangerous by insisting that the true danger — and impiety! — was in attempting to prevent criticism of the Bible. Opposition to biblical criticism implies "either that the Word of God is not really speaking to men in all ages as the Bible affirms; or else that the Bible is the one book in the world, which God does not care about, which is not safe under His protection, which we must patronize and watch over and keep from injuries. Priests and doctors in all ages . . . have looked upon the Bible as a feeble and tender plant, which was committed to their nursing, which they were not to let the winds of heaven visit too roughly."[3] But this is to make mockery of God and to doubt the truth of the Word declared to us in Christ.

The spirit of liberalism meant not only open-mindedness toward new modes of thought; it meant mutual sympathy and tolerance within the Christian community. This is one of the reasons why denominational differences became less important in nineteenth- and twentieth-century Protestant theology. Often, where the liberal spirit was combined with suspicion of theology in general, it was held that theological differences were insignificant. But even where this was not the case, the liberal temper induced a new attitude toward the discussion of differences — these were not to be grounds for mutual recrimination and excommunication, but occasions for mutual conversation in humility and in love, for the sake of deepened understanding of the fullness of the gospel.

Four other themes of liberal Protestantism were more definitely derivative from the nineteenth-century intellectual milieu. These were in part specific developments of the liberal spirit, but were also partly independent tendencies which gave to nineteenth-century theological thinking its distinctive character.

1) *Respect for science and the scientific method.* This was by no means a wholly new characteristic of religious thought, for the history of the church has been marked by recurrent endeavors to take account of the science of the time. But it is certainly true that in the nineteenth century the wealth of scientific discovery and the increasingly successful application of science to the practical mastery of nature led to new and overwhelming confidence in the scientific method as a means to truth. In liberal theology this meant not only the wholehearted acceptance of scientific study of the material world, but also the application of scientific methods of research in biblical criticism and the history of religion.

---

[3] From Maurice's *The Claims of the Bible and Science,* cited in W. L. Knox and Alec Vidler, *The Development of Modern Catholicism* (Milwaukee, 1933), p. 55.

2) *Tentativeness* or skepticism as to the possibility of achieving valid theoretical knowledge of ultimate reality. This uncertainty about metaphysical judgments, which stemmed especially from the critical philosophy of Kant, was often paralleled by a suspicion of theological formulations in general. Both of these tendencies were strongly reinforced by Schleiermacher's distinction between cognition or belief and "religious affections," according to which faith is prior to and independent of all theoretical formulations. Among theologians, the distinction between religious affirmations and metaphysical judgments came to sharpest expression in Ritschl's follower, Wilhelm Herrmann, for whom theology had nothing whatever to gain (and much to lose) from pursuing the goals of metaphysics, for the certainties of religious experience were wholly independent of the methods and conclusions of "science," whether natural or historical science. Each of these was true in its realm, but neither had the right to encroach on the other. In another vein, tentativeness in theological statements was represented by the argument of Horace Bushnell (the most interesting American theologian of the mid-nineteenth century) that all religious language is figurative in nature, therefore never wholly unambiguous and needing to be understood in relation to the personal history of each individual. No single creedal statement can be taken to be literally true. Similarly, F. D. Maurice, in a way that recalls John Stuart Mill's famous aphorism that people are most likely to be right in what they affirm and wrong in what they deny, insisted on the partiality and distortion that is present in every theological system.

3) *Emphasis upon the principle of continuity* (i.e., concern for similarity and likeness rather than difference and opposition). This was due, among other things, to belief in the unity of all truth, to the liberal spirit of tolerance, and especially to the evolutionary principle. Thus liberalism accepted the continuity of humanity with the rest of the natural world. It emphasized the common features of Christianity and non-Christian religions. In particular, it sought to bridge the gap between the natural and the supernatural, between human and divine personality, stressing the immanence rather than the transcendence of God. It questioned the traditional doctrines of Christ's person, which seemed to rest upon a too sharp disjunction of divinity and humanity. And it emphasized the similarity and even unity of all means of attaining truth: scientific research; artistic perception; the accumulated wisdom of experience; religious intuition; revelation — these being but varying aspects of the common quest for knowledge and understanding.

4) *Confidence in the future of humankind.* This is one of the points at which liberalism was most obviously under the spell of the late-nineteenth-century outlook. The whole course of Western history

seemed to conspire to promote a spirit of optimism: the relative peace of the century; rapid industrialization and growth of trade; a rising standard of living; political liberalism and steps toward more democratic structures of government; economic theories of a "harmony of interests"; the Romantic movement; the use of the idea of evolution in the interpretation of the course of history; and the new-found confidence in the scientific method. The age-long struggle against nature seemed almost ended. The final victory was not yet here, but the means for achieving it were, and the time when human beings could live in harmony and freedom from physical want was just around the corner. The achievements still left much to be desired, but the possibilities seemed unlimited. If humanity was not yet perfectly good, it was perfectible.

The optimism of the late nineteenth century appears strange and unreal to one who looks back through the agony of two world wars and a world depression, but at that time it seemed wholly justified. In religious thought, it nurtured the conviction that a truly Christian society could be achieved. (In Ch. XI, this hope is discussed at length.)

These are some of the major elements of the nineteenth-century spirit which went into the formation of the liberal movement in Protestant thought. We see in the next section how such presuppositions affected the understanding of particular Christian doctrines. But it should be noted in passing that these factors varied greatly in the permanence of their influence on Protestant thinking. The liberal spirit and the respect for science and scientific method became established features of Protestant thought. The tentativeness regarding metaphysical certainty and the emphasis on continuity persisted, but in modified form, in that liberalism which continues to play an important role in Protestant theology. The overwhelming optimism of the nineteenth century soon passed from the scene.

Together with these aspects of liberalism may be put four principles which were derived from its rooting in Christian tradition.

1) The first of these has already been noted: *the authority of Christian experience.* In place of the infallible Bible and the pronouncements of the church in its dogma, liberalism put the living witness of the religious life. This we saw was the new understanding of religion which made possible the acceptance of biblical criticism, the new sciences, and the philosophical criticism of the traditional arguments for the existence of God. It was given expression in Schleiermacher's appeal to the religious consciousness and in Ritschl's stress on the experience of reconciliation through Christ. It provided a new understanding of the significance of Bible, creed, and church, and of the development of Christian thought. A leading American liberal thus sounded the theme, asking:

Are the doctrines which form the subject matter of theology, dogmas to be received on authority, irrespective of their contents; or are they living convictions, born of experience, and maintaining themselves in spite of all opposition because of the response which they wake in the hearts and consciences of men?[4]

2) *The centrality of Jesus Christ.* In spite of all the questions which had later to be raised about the adequacy of the liberal's interpretation of Christ, it was the person of Christ which stood at the heart of the religious experience to which liberalism pointed. Here liberalism was true to its roots in the evangelical revivals. In Christ, Christians know the forgiveness of God and God's will for human beings. By reference to Christ and to his teaching all the doctrines of the church are to be judged: doctrines of God; of creation; of providence; of redemption. As Harnack put it, the essence of Christianity is nothing else than Jesus Christ and his gospel. The historical facts of his life and work are the touchstone from which all Christian faith springs. The goal of the "new theology," according to W. A. Brown, was in fact "the old cry, 'Back to Christ.' Let no theology call itself Christian which has not its center and source in Him."

3) *Criticism of the tradition from within.* This liberal Protestantism was consciously a movement within the Christian church. Its criticisms of the old orthodoxies were offered within the community of those who shared a common experience and a common loyalty to Christ and his church. However sharp might be the criticisms of orthodoxy, however much a break with tradition and a new start were demanded, this liberal Protestantism intended that its views should be expressions of the same truths which were encompassed by the orthodox statements. Much that earlier generations of Christians had affirmed was now thought to be not essential to the faith, much had to be adjusted and accommodated to new knowledge and new ways of thought, but the essentials remained the same — and this could be affirmed especially because the essentials were not external forms of dogma, but the religious experiences which lay behind the dogmas. The classic expression of this view is found in the phrase of Harry Emerson Fosdick, "abiding experiences in changing categories."

4) *Social idealism.* The new social idealism of the late nineteenth century is dealt with at length in the next chapter. It may simply be said here that this movement was closely interrelated with theological liberalism and grew in part from liberal emphases: renewed appreciation of the social or corporate nature of the Christian life (emphasized, for example, by Schleiermacher), of the uncompromisingly ethical

---

[4] W. A. Brown, in his inaugural address as Professor of Systematic Theology in Union Theological Seminary, 1898.

character of the gospel, and of the importance of the kingdom of God in Jesus' teaching (as, for example, in Ritschl and Harnack). These combined with a new sensitivity to the needs and injustices of industrial society to produce a profound sense of the church's responsibility for the righting of social wrongs and for bringing the social structure itself into harmony with the ideal of the kingdom of God on earth.

Some Specific Reinterpretations

Liberal Protestantism has now been described as a complex of principles or motifs of thought. But this liberalism was more than that. It was also a movement characterized by certain quite definite trends in the reinterpretation of specific Christian doctrines. The term *liberalism* refers to a theological position (or a pattern of doctrinal interpretation) as well as to a theological outlook. Of course, the very nature of liberalism makes generalization difficult at this point, but it is possible at least to mark out some basic lines of interpretation which were widely represented in liberal theology, and to indicate how these are related to the background and formative principles of liberalism. For convenience, these conceptions may be grouped under the headings of God, Christ, human dignity, and religious authority.

1) *The doctrine of God.* One major tenet of the liberal view of God, perhaps the most important, has already been suggested: the immanence of God. The Romantic stress on the inner divine spirit, Schleiermacher's conception of the identity of the working of God with the laws of nature, Hegel's philosophy of history and nature as the manifestation of the life of the universal Spirit, the theory of evolution — all these served to focus attention on the presence and working of God *within* the world rather than upon it. This was not a novel idea: early Christian thought had strongly emphasized the universal presence of the divine Word in the world process, and the doctrine of God's omnipresence had been consistently affirmed by Christian interpreters. But the older conceptions had almost uniformly taken for granted a radical distinction between the infinite, perfect, and immutable God and the finite and corruptible world. This distinction was now being severely modified. The new interpretations began, not with radical discontinuity, but with the assumption of a basic continuity, or even unity, of God with the world. Liberalism was more conscious of the nearness and "availability" of God than of the transcendence and holiness of God. This did not mean that God and the world are identical, but it did mean that God is somehow, in varying degrees, present everywhere *in* creation as well as active upon it.

The meaning of the doctrine of immanence can be seen most clearly in the understanding of the way in which God works in the world. God is not one who, existing wholly apart from the world, acts only occasionally, or interrupts the natural order of effecting events. God's providence is the guidance of the whole process by presence within all the processes of nature. "If God appears periodically, he disappears periodically. If he comes upon the scene at special crises he is absent from the scene in the intervals. Whether is all-God or occasional-God the nobler theory? Positively, the idea of an immanent God, which is the God of evolution, is infinitely grander than the occasional wonder-worker who is the God of an old theology."[5] The notion of a God who must break into the world process in order to act is not only discredited by science, but it is a less worthy conception than one that sees the whole natural order as the working of God.

In effect, the liberal doctrine of immanence involved the breaching of the traditional distinction between natural and supernatural. And this meant a profound change in the attitude toward miracles. Since the divine is present in all nature, there are no miracles in the sense of divine intrusions into the natural order. In another sense, everything can be said to be a miracle. As Schleiermacher had put it in his *Speeches:*

> Miracle is only the religious name for event. Every event, even the most natural and common, is a miracle if it lends itself to a controllingly religious interpretation. To me all is miracle.[6]

Thus, it is both futile and erroneous to appeal to miracles as proofs of God's activity, or of the divinity of Christ, or of the truth of Christianity. One does not believe in Christ because of "miracles" (as Protestant orthodoxy had supposed). It is the other way around. One sees events as miraculous because God is apprehended as working there, whether in ordinary and well-known natural processes or in strange and inexplicable events.

The emphasis on the immanence of God affected conceptions of revelation in a similar way. As God is present in all, so God is known in all. Thus, Elizabeth Barrett Browning expresses a favorite theme of liberalism:

> Earth's crammed with heaven,
> And every common bush afire with God,
> But only he who sees takes off his shoes.

This does not mean that God is equally revealed everywhere, for

---

[5] Henry Drummond, *Ascent of Man* (New York, 1894), p. 334. See also the quotation from Aubrey Moore, above, p. 183.

[6] F. Schleiermacher, *On Religion*, p. 88.

God is more clearly known in the insights of prophets and saints, and supremely seen in the life and teaching of Jesus Christ. But these are the "highest" points, the "fullest" revelations of a universal manifestation of God. God is most truly known in Christ, but this revelation is not different *in kind* from other knowledge of God. Moreover, because God is immanent, revelation comes from within; it is to be sought in religious experience, in mind and conscience, rather than in some special voice from without.

Finally, the liberal doctrine of divine immanence influenced the conceptions of Christ, of human nature, and of the church. The traditional doctrine of Christ's person had been formulated at the Council of Chalcedon in 451 A.D. It asserted that the one person, Jesus Christ, possessed two distinct "natures," divine and human, which were somehow united, but without destroying or altering either of the two. The theology of immanence seemed to provide a solution to the difficulties inherent in the traditional formula, for now it was not necessary to think of the divine and human natures as essentially opposed to each other. The perfection of humanity *is* the fullest embodiment of deity. The divine and the human in Christ are not alien to each other, but are one. Thus the notion of immanence also led to more optimistic conceptions of human nature. Humanity is not God, but the divine spark is present in all — in human reason and conscience. Human beings are essentially capable of conforming to the will of God. Similarly, the church as the sphere of divine redemptive activity came to be defined in more universal terms. The contrast between the church and the "world" became less sharp, and less importance was attached to the church as an ecclesiastical institution.

Two other characteristic elements in the liberal doctrine of God may be mentioned briefly. First, human personality is the best clue to the nature of God. God is a personal being, infinitely greater than human persons, but to be known by analogy from human personality. God's dealings with us are "like" relationships among persons; God does not treat us as "things," mechanically, but as persons, respecting human freedom and responsibility. Second, God is "Christlike." God is essentially loving, kind, merciful. God is just, upholding the moral order, but never in a cruel or arbitrary way. God is the divine Father, who ever seeks the good of the children. God's punishment is always corrective in purpose, never vengeful or retributive. This is not the kind of God who would condemn anyone to an eternity of punishment; God desires that eventually all shall be brought into full and perfect fellowship. Moreover, God does not impose the divine will arbitrarily. God seeks the salvation of persons, but does not deny their freedom to resist. The doctrines of predestination and irresistible grace must be given up as "immoral," for they violate human personality and contradict our highest insight into the character of God.

2) *The humanity of Christ.* We have already noted the influence of the idea of immanence on the understanding of Christ's nature. Related to this was another major development in liberal Protestantism: the rediscovery of the *humanity* of Christ. The traditional conceptions of Christ, according to liberalism, had almost invariably tended toward "docetism"; that is, they had so interpreted the divinity of Christ as to deny his real humanity. In appearance he was a man, but essentially he was God, all-knowing and all-powerful, having really none of the limitations of humanity. Biblical criticism, however, had shown unmistakably that the figure described in the gospels was most assuredly human — not just having a human body, but limited in knowledge, sharing the intellectual outlook of his contemporaries (including, for example, the mistaken belief that Moses was the author of the Pentateuch), knowing real temptation, despair, and even frustration. Whatever else Jesus was, he was man. The "orthodox" interpretations, which had infected Roman Catholicism and Protestantism alike, contradicted not only the New Testament but also the formula of Chalcedon.

By the rediscovery of the humanity of Christ, liberalism rendered a profound and lasting service to Christian thought. But the movement which accomplished this went further, and in directions of less permanent value. For having focused on the humanity of Christ, liberalism found it hard to say that Christ was anything more than a man — a man in whom God was supremely immanent, whose character and teaching was divine (or at any rate God-like), but this was only humanity raised to the highest power. Jesus was interpreted as teacher, leader, brother, source of power, morally unique, the fulfillment of the divine indwelling. It could be said that we see him as God, or that he shows us God, or has the value of God for us, but beyond this it was felt better not to go.

Moreover, liberalism drove a wedge between the "Jesus of history" and the "Christ of the creeds." It looked almost entirely to the "historical facts" which the Synoptic Gospels disclosed about the life and teachings of Jesus, and discounted as of secondary importance all theological interpretations. A sharp distinction was seen even in the New Testament, between the gospel of Jesus and the gospel of Paul, the "religion *of* Jesus" and the "religion *about* Jesus." Few would go as far as Harnack's assertion that "Jesus asks of us no belief in him other than obedience to his teachings"; but many agreed that there was a real cleavage between Jesus' message and the conceptions of Paul and the later church.

This distinction was thought to be the result of biblical criticism. Actually, however, it was as much the result of the grinding of theological axes. So also was the overly simple conception of the message of Jesus, which often overlooked or reinterpreted elements of his teaching which were out of harmony with fundamental tenets of liberalism.

There is real point, though exaggerated in its reference to liberalism as such, in the comment of a Roman Catholic critic of Harnack: "The Christ that Harnack sees, looking back through nineteen centuries of Catholic darkness, is only the reflection of a liberal Protestant face seen at the bottom of a deep well."

Concern for the humanity of Jesus, together with emphasis on human freedom, also led to altered interpretations of Christ's work of redemption. The influence of Jesus was seen in the power of his example, or the "potency of his God-consciousness" (Schleiermacher), or the identity of his moral and religious purpose with the purpose of God (Ritschl). Through these, followers are inspired to realize in their own lives that which Jesus embodied. This is his work of atonement (or "at-one-ment"), not some external or "magical" act whereby God is appeased and persons made righteous.

3) *Human dignity.* The dominant tendencies of the liberal conception are apparent from what has been said earlier. Liberalism emphasized the created dignity rather than the degradation, the ideal rather than the actual, the possibilities of human achievement rather than the present failures. This trend was fostered by the doctrine of divine immanence and had its strong roots in the Romantic humanitarianism of the preceding century. It was also a reaction against the deprecation of humanity which seemed implied in the worldview of nineteenth-century science, not only in the idea of evolutionary origins, but in the general tendency to reduce human existence to the interplay of brute natural forces. Thus Ritschl interpreted the religious goal as the victory of spirit over nature, and Henry Drummond proclaimed the "ascent of man." Personality was hailed as the supreme value.

The doctrines of the Fall and of an inherited guilt for original sin were rejected in favor of an appreciation of the natural goodness of the creature. The reality of sin was not denied, but its existence was often attributed to impulses of an animal nature, and traditional conceptions of the depth and extent of human sin were greatly modified. Emphasis was laid on the freedom and ability to respond to the commandments and proffered forgiveness of God, and on the cooperation of the human will with the divine will in the process of redemption, rather than on the radical perversion and corruption of human nature which had been stressed especially in traditional Protestant thought. The life after death became a relatively less central emphasis, attention being focused on the fulfillment of life here and now. The future life was increasingly interpreted as "immortality of the spirit" rather than as "resurrection of the body," and the idea of further growth and opportunity in the future life was attractive to many.

The view of humanity is summed up in such phrases, repeated countless times by liberal thinkers, as "the sacredness of personality" and the "infinite value" of human personality; and the conception typified by these phrases influenced the whole range of liberalism's interpretation of Christian doctrines. It can be argued with cogency that the heart of liberalism was its estimate of human nature.

4) *The nature of religious authority.* In the preceding chapter and in a previous section of this chapter, we examined the liberal appeal to religious experience as the ultimate authority. In one sense, this was an appeal, genuinely in the tradition of the Reformation, from all finite authorities (Bible, church, tradition) to the sole authority of God himself; and the Reformation perspective was reflected in the view that the Bible remained a unique record of the experience of the Hebrew-Christian community. But at the same time, the emphasis upon the inward (and individual) experience was often such as to make religious authority wholly subjective. Thus, the final court of appeal becomes one's own reason, conscience, and intuition; the witness of the Scriptures, of the creeds and traditions of the church, and of the existing Christian community, becomes subordinate to one's individual religious insight. Insofar as liberalism insisted that no religious claim can be finally valid for anyone until it has spoken directly and compellingly to that person, liberalism was true to the Protestant understanding. But the tendency was to go much further, rejecting the claim of any objective witness (e.g., Bible or creed) to be an authoritative or indispensable bearer of the word of truth. At this point, certainly, liberalism was primarily concerned with human dignity.

It is in doctrinal interpretations such as these that we see why liberalism was due for severe chastening at the hands of a later religious generation (see Ch. XII). Liberalism did represent, according to one of Protestantism's most perceptive interpreters, the renewal of "a dynamic element in religious life; it was a revolt against the fatalism into which the faith in divine sovereignty had been congealed, against the biblicism which made the Scriptures a book of laws for science and morals, against the revivalism which reduced regeneration to a method for drumming up church members, and against the otherworldliness which had made heaven and hell a reward and a punishment."[7] But, as the same writer goes on to show, liberalism also reflected a loss of the religious heritage — a dimming of the sense of divine sovereignty, a greater concern for religion than for God, an identification of human values with divine, a weakened sense of the estrangement from God and a corresponding view of the ease with which Jesus the teacher might bring about the full development of the spiritual capacities of humanity. In extreme form, liberalism

[7] H. R. Niebuhr, *The Kingdom of God in America* (New York, 1937), p. 185.

taught that "a God without wrath brought men without sin into a kingdom without judgment through the ministrations of a Christ without a cross."[8]

At the same time, the themes which liberalism stressed (and overstressed) were often those which had been traditionally neglected and were now brought clearly into focus. Moreover, liberalism meant the appearance of certain new features of Protestant thought (e.g., the liberal spirit, biblical criticism and the accompanying abandonment of the inerrancy of the Bible, a new social concern, and full recognition of the humanity of Jesus) which persist and have had a permanent effect on Protestant thinking.

Divergent and Parallel Trends

The dominant movement in the development of nineteenth-century Protestant thinking was the emergence of liberalism. To say this is not to make a social-survey judgment about the views of a majority of Protestants, but to identify the direction in which the theological leadership was rapidly moving, so that by the end of the century it could seem that liberal theology was sweeping everything before it. Roughly parallel to this stream, however, were other views and tendencies that provided context and reaction to liberalism's advance.

Continuing Conservatisms

If one were able to make a head count of individual Protestants through the nineteenth century, it would probably show that most popular religion remained largely traditional in its beliefs. That is to say, the theological notions of popular piety were those that had been given shape by the Reformation, by Protestant orthodoxy, and by Pietism, and that had been generally taken for granted in the missionary and revival movements of the century.

Along with this undercurrent of unreflective conservatism, moreover, there were some powerful and sophisticated efforts to reassert the traditional views. Immediately after the time of Schleiermacher, for example, a determined effort was made in Germany to replace the "Rationalists" on the theological faculties with professors committed to "believing theology." Here neo-Pietism and confessionalism made common cause. Traditional theologies generally received vigorous reinforcement from religious revival, particularly in Germany and America, but also in the Reformed churches of Switzerland, France, Scotland, and the Netherlands. Lutheran confessionalism, against which Ritschl protested so vigorously, remained strong in Germany and was exported

[8] *Ibid.*, p. 193.

to the United States with the German immigrations. Almost everywhere on the Continent and in Britain, the main ecclesiastical reactions to the revolution in 1848 were both religiously and politically conservative (witness the Throne and Altar motif of German Lutheranism). One could say that the major Protestant tendency was much like the "fortress mentality" that came to characterize the Roman Catholicism of Pope Pius IX. The ideas of the "confessional" church, of repristination or restorative theology, and of "biblical realism" as a way of reasserting the authority of Scripture, became stronger. The Tractarian movement in the Church of England had a sharply orthodox segment. In the United States, the foundation of such theological seminaries as Princeton (1812) and Andover (1834) was an explicit effort to preserve Calvinist orthodoxy, and Princeton in particular remained throughout the century as a strong bastion of conservatism. And by the mid-century there had been a resurgence of denominationalism — in contrast, for example, to the ecumenical spirit that characterized the early missionary movement.

In short, one may say that in Protestantism and Catholicism alike, the middle years of the nineteenth century were marked by the reassertion of the tradition. And in the latter years of the century, as liberal theology grew more and more powerful and widespread, the conservative motifs were still well represented.

Unitarianism

The Unitarian and Universalist movements of the nineteenth century (as well as the *freisinnige Theologie* of the Continent) may also properly be called trends within liberalism in the broad sense. At many points their critique of the tradition overlapped with the concerns of the liberal theology we have described earlier, and they are certainly not to be confused with such groups as the Secular Societies or the Rationalist Association in Britain. Yet in crucial ways the stance of these movements was different from that of the main stream of liberal theology and their position was more clearly at the edge of Christianity.

We may take Unitarianism as the most vivid illustration. Led initially in the United States by William Ellery Channing (1780–1842) and Theodore Parker (1810–1860) and in Britain by James Martineau (1805–1900), Unitarianism first appeared as a protest against objectionable features of early-nineteenth-century orthodoxies, particularly as found in the Calvinist churches. One central item of dispute between the Calvinists and the Unitarians was, of course, the doctrine of the Trinity, which the Unitarians thought incompatible with the unity of God (and certainly many current interpretations of the Trinity were guilty on this count, portraying the Father and the Son as separate personal beings, different even in character — the Father stern and forbidding, the Son merciful and pleading for the deliverance of humanity). But the Unitarians were equally concerned to protest against such doctrines as original sin, total depravity, infant damnation, the wrath of God, predestination, and traditional notions of the atonement. Such doctrines, they felt, made God immoral, violating conscience and every rational standard of morality, and were contrary to New Testament teaching. Christian doctrine ought instead to emphasize the moral perfection, the goodness and mercy of God, the work of Christ in leading us to a righteous life, human goodness, and the demand for true holiness of Christian living.

In the specific reinterpretations of orthodoxy which Unitarianism demanded, there were many points of agreement with the main body of liberal thought, and in many ways Unitarianism could be called an extreme form of liberalism. But a crucial difference lay in the principle behind the respective reinterpretations. Liberalism was essentially an attempt to recover the truth of the gospel as it spoke to the human heart and to present it in the thought forms of the modern world. It was a vital, existential, experiential recreation of theology which was not primarily concerned with creed or orthodoxy but with the living reality which lay behind these. This was also the spirit of Channing (even more of Martineau), but in Channing we also find a strong intellectualistic and rationalistic strain, which became dominant in later Unitarianism. Orthodoxy was to be rejected primarily because it seemed incompatible with the dictates of reason and rational morality — this had been the theme of seventeenth- and eighteenth-century Rationalism, and Unitarianism typified the continuation of this view in the nineteenth century. Thus, later Unitarianism came to be less and less concerned with the distinctively Christian witness and increasingly interested in general religious affirmations which would be wholly consistent with a "scientific worldview" and with a profound ethical concern. Unitarianism subsequently tended to split into two wings — one seeking to maintain essential connection with Christianity, the other abandoning any specifically Christian orientation in favor of an ethical humanism or some "general" religious view which serves as the basis for devotion to morality in individual and society.

The spirit which came to characterize Unitarianism, notably its rationalism and its attitude toward science, was not restricted to this particular religious group. Unitarianism rather symbolized a more general perspective that some have called "modernist" rather than "liberal." The term modernist is not helpful in this context, for there were many liberals in the United States and in Britain who preferred the word modernist to describe their theological efforts, and there was also an important "modernist" movement in the Roman Catholic church at the beginning of the twentieth century. The latter should not be confused with liberal Protestantism, for it sought to be explicitly

Catholic and was highly critical of liberalism, though it had strong affinities in the attitudes toward biblical criticism and toward traditionalism. (Modernism in the Roman church was condemned in 1907 by Pope Pius X and after the Anti-Modernist Oath of 1910 it ceased for a long time to be a live issue in the Catholic church.)

Yet, whatever terms we use, we can detect a clear difference in intention and emphasis between the perspective of what we have been calling liberal theology and the perspective for which we have used Unitarianism as an example. In the latter views, the central and overriding consideration was the relation of science and religion, and the validity of the scientific method was accepted as the starting point for all human investigation. That is, a stand was taken first of all with the presupposition of science and modern thought, and then an attempt was made to reclaim what could be maintained of the traditional faith. Liberalism, however, though equally concerned to relate Christianity to science and the new intellectual movements, was committed first and ultimately to the Christian tradition, and from that vantage point attempted effective adjustment to science and the changing world scene. Throughout the nineteenth century (and in the first quarter of the twentieth century), these two perspectives were in constant tension and struggle. But it was the latter view which was dominant in what we have called liberal theology and which made a permanent contribution to the Protestant understanding.

Rejections of Liberalism: Critical Orthodoxy and Fundamentalism

Stemming from the conservative tradition, but distinguished from it by highly self-conscious orientations to liberalism, were two kinds of protest that emerged in the late nineteenth and early twentieth centuries. One we may call "critical orthodoxy"; the other, in its American variety, is commonly named fundamentalism.

The most interesting illustrations of a critically orthodox view are provided by Martin Kähler (1835–1912) in Germany and Peter Taylor Forsyth (1848–1921) in Britain. Both these men shared liberalism's openness to biblical criticism and to science and the spirit of a critical appreciation and restatement of the tradition, but both protested strongly against such elements as the weakening of the classical notions of divine transcendence and of humanity's radical plight and need for redemption.

Kähler was particularly important in challenging the quest for the historical Jesus. Not only, as we noted earlier, did he reject the possibility of a real biography of Jesus, about whom historical science provides us with only scraps of information, he also attacked the principle of the quest as a notion governed just as much by theological presuppositions as had been the old Byzantine Christianity. The modern quest, for him, is interested in Jesus because he is like us and it seeks to distinguish the human characteristics from the overlay of ascriptions of divinity in the New Testament. But this is contrary to the biblical view as well as to the faith of the church, which is interested in Jesus precisely because he is unlike us, because he is revealed God and our savior. In the New Testament the genuinely human person and the resurrected Lord are inseparably one in a biblical picture that is authoritative for us. Hence in a historical view that is appropriate to the gospel witness, there can be no dichotomy between the Jesus of history and the Christ of faith.

Forsyth heartily approved the modern principles of freedom of the individual from external authority, the social idea of organic salvation, the stress on the moral dimension, the idea of historic evolution, and the passion for reality. But against liberalism's misuse of these principles, he wanted to insist on the objectivity and authority of the gospel, on something that is not derived from experience but given to experience. In particular, he emphasized the holiness of God and the reality of sin. God is not simply Father, but *holy* Father, who can be genuinely wrathful against sin; otherwise we could not ultimately trust God. The corporate reality of sin negates all ideas of inevitable progress or of the mere particularity and isolation of sins. In Forsyth's vivid images, sin means that the human race is not simply in arrears, but is infected by disease. The train of history is not merely late but has been involved in a terrible accident due to malice and crime. And this is something that has involved every aspect of human life, requiring a satisfaction of God's holy love by an act of reparation, a covering of sin that God performs in Christ.

In this critical orthodoxy, the voices of Kähler and Forsyth were largely lost in the chorus of late nineteenth-century liberalism, but they served as an important point of contact for the criticism of liberal theology that emerged after the First World War (see Ch. XII).

Fundamentalism also took its rise in self-conscious reaction to liberalism, but in a quite different sense, without the dialectical openness to liberal emphases that the critically orthodox possessed. In a strange way, fundamentalism shared the view of Rationalism and scientism, all assuming that Christianity is essentially incompatible with modern thought. Instead of giving up the tradition, however, fundamentalism sought to preserve Christian doctrine intact from all the attacks of science and modernity. It set itself consciously and rigidly against the spirit of compromise and adjustment that prevailed in liberal theology. In this respect, the fundamentalist attitude needs to be sharply distinguished from that of other conservative Protestants. Apart from the critically conservative, there were many Protestant thinkers of the late nineteenth century who sought to maintain the classical tradition and were not basically affected by the liberal theological formulations, but who had no fear of the liberal spirit or of science and modern thought generally. Also, we should recall the conservatism of the common people (the nontheologians), which was only very gradually influenced by the spread of liberalism. In sheer numbers, this was probably the most important nineteenth-century viewpoint. But it was not a self-conscious theological movement.

Fundamentalism is to be distinguished from these other forms of conservatism by its self-conscious and inflexible resistance to the entire liberal development. It took its stand on certain specific doctrinal formulations (and on a legalistic view of Christian ethics), insisting that without these Christianity could not be true to the Bible or to the historic faith. The name *fundamentalism* is taken from a series of tracts published in 1910–1915, called *The Fundamentals,* which sought to state these fundamental truths essential to Christianity.

At the center of the fundamentalist opposition to liberalism was the question of the authority and inspiration of the Bible. For the fundamentalist, Christianity is irrevocably committed to the inerrancy of the Bible. Of course, it may be allowed that there have been certain minor errors in the process of transmission of the Scriptures, but no such concession can be made regarding the "original autographs." The writers of the Bible were inspired by God in such manner that they were preserved from any distortion or error whatsoever in recording the divine Word. Therefore the Bible is in detail an absolutely reliable and authoritative source of knowledge of God and God's activity. To admit even the slightest amount of "higher criticism" is to cast doubt on everything in the Bible. (To say that we can have only a little bit of criticism, which will leave intact the essentials, would be to the fundamentalist mind like saying that a woman can be "just a wee bit pregnant.") As soon as we have questioned the authenticity of any of the recorded sayings of Jesus, or the validity of Paul's theology; as soon as we have said that the Bible is in part a result of the natural working of the human mind, without the full inspiration of the Holy Spirit; then we have left the solid rock of truth and embarked upon a hopeless sea of uncertainty. Either the words of the Bible are infallibly the words of God or we have no basis for our faith. It is all or none.

Moreover, the fundamentalist saw in biblical criticism a denial of the uniqueness of Christianity, for the indisputable proof of Christianity lies in the miracles and the fulfillment of prophecy as recorded in the Bible. To deny that the prophets foretold in detail the coming of Christ, or to deny the historicity of the biblical miracles, is to reject the signs by which God's activity is recognized. If these be not accepted, then Christianity has no claim to final truth.

This line of argument reveals a basic cleavage between the fundamentalist and the liberal conception of divine activity. For the liberal, God works primarily through natural processes; for the fundamentalist, God acts by supernatural intervention in nature. This is most vividly seen in another of the "fundamentals," the virgin birth of Christ. To deny the virgin birth, or to say that it is unimportant, is, according to the fundamentalist, to deny the incarnation and the deity of Christ. The virgin birth (no less than Christ's miracles and his resurrection) is the necessary proof that Christ was the Son of God.

At least two other fundamentals were of primary importance: the "deity" of Christ, and the atonement for sin by his crucifixion. By the deity of Christ was meant his divine (i.e., complete and infallible) knowledge and his divine power as shown in the miracles (as well as, of course, his moral perfection). With this was associated an insistence upon the physical resurrection and the ultimate return of Christ in the flesh to judge the world. The doctrine of atonement, as understood by fundamentalism, meant Christ's offering of himself on the cross as a sacrifice in place of sinners, substituting for humanity in receiving punishment for sin, thereby making it possible for God to forgive without compromising justice (which demands that sin be punished).

Together with the assertion of these "essentials" of Christianity, fundamentalism was characterized by vigorous opposition to the theory of evolution because of its conflict with the Genesis story of creation. It was the questions of evolution, biblical criticism, and the deity of Christ which occupied the center of the conflict between liberals and fundamentalists. This debate, which was particularly vigorous in the United States, was carried on mainly in the early twentieth century. Properly speaking, fundamentalism as a definite and self-conscious movement appeared first in the last quarter of the nineteenth century. During the early years of the present century, fundamentalist groups in each of the major denominations made determined efforts to stop the tide of liberalism in their respective churches, whether by securing positions of administrative leadership, or by the elimination of "liberal" professors from the seminaries, or by the adoption of doctrinal tests for ministers. By about 1925, however, the height of the controversy had passed in most of the denominations, and thereafter the influence of the fundamentalist wing declined markedly.

We are not suggesting that fundamentalism is dead. Far from it. On the European continent, some Protestant churches have seen a resurgence of uncritical biblicism and "orthodoxy" which has much in common with American fundamentalism. Some of the most rapidly growing American sects are fundamentalist. In these groups, characteristic fundamentalist tenets are often bound up with the expectation of the imminent return of Christ (the "premillennial" sects) or with the insistence on radical and overt signs of the working of the Holy Spirit, especially in conversion (the "Pentecostal" sects). Even within the "liberal" denominations, significant minorities continued to be fundamentalist in outlook. The cleavage between liberalism and fundamentalism (with a correlative division between social liberalism and social conservatism) is still in numerical terms the basic division in Protestant thinking in America, though such judgments must be qualified by recognition of the large numbers of "conservatives" who ought not to be considered fundamentalist.

The strength of the fundamentalist refusal to compromise with liberalism was not simply a resistance to change. It lay also in a valid apprehension of the difficulties which the liberal views created (and at this point fundamentalism had much in common with more moderate conservatism). For it was certainly true that liberalism involved fundamental alterations in the form at least of traditional Christian doctrines, and it was a valid question whether it had not also violated the intention of the classical affirmations. Even more important, by giving up the infallibility of the Bible, liberalism did seem to abandon all except the most subjective claims to religious certainty; nothing was absolute, all dogmas, all Scripture, and even the gospel itself were made relative. No sure, objective ground for faith seemed left. And liberalism was indeed to lead to other vigorous reaction (which, however, took quite different lines from fundamentalism — see Ch. XII).

But at the same time, fundamentalism was from the beginning a lost cause, theologically speaking. It was an intellectual rearguard action. It was not simply an attempt to be faithful to the Christian tradition; it was an effort, in the face of the perplexities and shifting currents of a changing world, to fix Christianity in the mold of a particular doctrinal complex and worldview. The doctrinal complex to which fundamentalism clung so tenaciously was not that of the ancient church, or of the Reformation, or of the Protestant development in general. It was essentially akin to the hardened framework of Lutheran and especially Calvinistic scholasticism of the seventeenth and eighteenth centuries (see Ch. IV). Only in that scholasticism had the doctrine of the inerrancy of Scripture been carried to such extremes; and in such doctrines as the atonement and the deity of Christ, fundamentalism (often unconsciously) assumed that the Protestant scholastics spoke for the entire tradition. Moreover, in its insistence that doctrine is irreformable, fundamentalism shared the scholastic equation of "faith" with "correct articles of belief." And especially in its notion of "miracle," fundamentalism took over the seventeenth-century view of the relation of Christian faith to science and philosophy. In its own day that view represented a significant attempt to bring religious, philosophical, and scientific thought into harmony; but the effort to perpetuate that adjustment in the world of the nineteenth and twentieth centuries was not only hopeless but violated the intent of scholasticism itself.

At root, fundamentalism sought to preserve a kind of certainty in a world of apparent confusion and flux — a kind of certainty which was simply no longer possible. The movement was part of a general resistance to social change. This was particularly evident in fundamentalism's commitment to legalistic views of personal morality (mostly of the nineteenth-century pattern) and its hostility to the "social gospel." The fundamentalists' bitter opposition to the Federal Council of Churches (and subsequently to the National Council of Churches) was focused as much on the social as on the theological liberalism of those organizations. And the extreme social conservatism was often paralleled by a suspicion of modern education because of its "scientific, sceptical, and secular influences." Here, too, was an attempt to hold on to the familiar, the simple and safe patterns, in the face of new and bewildering problems which the old patterns were not designed to meet.

Insofar as fundamentalism is committed to this sort of program, it is hard to see how the movement can claim the allegiance of thoughtful persons. In the post-World War II period, however, there emerged important signs that in some quarters the fundamentalist position was being modified — by reinterpretations of biblical infallibility, by a more liberal social outlook, and by a more ecumenical attitude (see Ch. XIV).

Inner Tensions of Liberalism: Ernst Troeltsch

Even before the cataclysmic blow of World War I to the Western self-confidence, there were clear signs of uneasiness and tension within the liberal tradition. Both on the Continent and in Britain, though much less in America, foreboding intimations of disruption of the peace and of the social order generally began to challenge optimistic assumptions about social progress. Even the possibility of the collapse of Western civilization was envisaged by some. And intrinsic to the liberal theology, the question of certainty in faith had become an acute preoccupation. One writer spoke for many when he said that a faith that has no certainty is not worth talking about. Yet how could confidence in the self-validating nature of faith, or religious experience, be maintained?

Wilhelm Herrmann (1846–1922) of Marburg, who was the teacher of a generation of British and American students, as well as of theologians like Karl Barth and Rudolf Bultmann, offered an extreme answer. Churchly authority, creed and doctrines, scriptural propositions, even Jesus' own teaching, are finally for Herrmann only shifting sands as a foundation for faith. They are all inadequate as merely external authorities, and as called into question by scientific historical investigation, which gives us nothing but probable results. The only secure foundation is to be found in our immediate apprehension of the inner life of the person of Jesus, which lays claim to us as the indubitable communion with God. This, for Herrmann, is a kind of historical encounter that is not subject to the uncertainties of scientific history. But, we must add, what a slender reed for support, in view of the growing awareness of the impossibility of a biography for Jesus, the questions raised by Weiss and Schweitzer about the usefulness for the modern world of Jesus' teaching of the kingdom of God, and the new understanding of the extent to which the entire biblical history was enmeshed in the world of the ancient Near Eastern religion!

The critical tensions for liberal theology, and indeed for Protestant thought as a whole at the end of the nineteenth century, were brought into sharp focus in the work of Ernst Troeltsch (1865–1923), whose stature has only in the mid-twentieth century been rediscovered. More than any other thinker of his time, he perceived the depth of the problem posed by the explosion of comparative religious studies. For the most part, theologians of the late nineteenth century either assumed that Christianity was a special case and did not worry about comparison with other religious traditions, or, under the dominance of the evolutionary idea, they judged that the evidence of the history of religions showed Christianity to be the supreme religious development. But Troeltsch, on the premise that Christianity must be treated according to the same canons that apply to the study of any other religion, came to doubt increasingly whether even the idea of a *relative* absoluteness as the culmination of religious history could be defended. Given the thoroughgoing individuality of every historical religion, the naive claims for absolute validity of the Buddhist and the Hindu religious experience (and these are undeniably humane and spiritual religions) cannot be denied the same genuineness that is accorded to Christian claims. And given the way in which Christianity has been inseparably bound up with Western culture, the most we can say is that Christianity is true "for us." It is undoubtedly a powerful spiritual force, and since it has shaped our being, it may be the only religion we can endure, but this certifies only its validity for us.

With respect to the question of the historical Jesus, Troeltsch perceived the crucial matter to be the necessity of the historical figure to the faith of the church. He himself was fairly comfortable in judging that historical research gives us a generally reliable picture of Jesus. But even if that is so, the question remains of a valid way of saying *how* Jesus is necessary to modern faith. A few thinkers, indeed, were prepared to say that Jesus is not absolutely necessary: if there had been no historical figure, that would be a loss, but not a fatal one, for the ideal of his filial relationship to God would still be valid. For Troeltsch, on the other hand, it continues to be important to speak of an essential significance of Jesus for faith. With the traditional ideas of the supernatural authority of Bible and church, and the christological dogmas, an inner, rationally, necessary connection was easy to affirm. But we can no longer accept that standpoint. Therefore the necessity must be restated in terms of social psychology, which shows how Christianity, like any other religious community, requires a support, center, and symbol for its religious life.

Troeltsch's best-known work was a massive and pioneering social history of Christianity, *The Social Teachings of the Christian Churches and Groups* (1912), in which he set out to examine the entire history of the church (through the Reformation) in the light of the varied interrelationships within its social contexts. The result was not only an influential account of religious community types ("church" and "sect" types, along with mysticism), it was also a detailed demonstration that the whole history of Christian social ethics was a series of adjustments or compromises in relation to the general society or societies of which the church had been a part. Christian ethics as well as theology is therefore relative (i.e., essentially related) to historical situations. The question is thus raised whether Christianity is a religion or a congerie of religions. And to the recognition of a genuine pluralism of religion is added the acknowledgment of pluralism within Christianity.

The purpose of the *Social Teachings* was to pose the problem of Christian ethics in contemporary life. For Troeltsch, the traditional types of social philosophy, Protestant and Catholic, had lost their power through the emergence of modern political, economic, and social conditions, as well as the necessity of the historical point of view (he thought the Enlightenment, rather than the Reformation, to have been the real turning point to the modern world), and he had little enthusiasm for the social gospels of recent times (see Ch. XI). Nowhere does there exist an absolute Christian ethic. Rather, there can be only continual readjustment, creative compromises within a world situation. Christian faith and ethics are still possible, but only in constantly renewed and relative forms.

CHAPTER XI

The Christian Criticism of Society

The internal vigor which gave rise to the missionary movement and to liberal theology in nineteenth-century Protestantism was expressed in yet another major direction, viz., in a movement dedicated to the reconstruction of society in accord with the ideal of the kingdom of God. In its peculiarly American form, the movement was called the "social gospel"; but this was only one manifestation of an impulse which appeared also with great intensity in Great Britain and on the Continent of Europe. The tenor of the movement is revealed in a declaration by one of the early leaders of the social gospel, Richard T. Ely: "Christianity is primarily concerned with this world, and it is the mission of Christianity to bring to pass here a kingdom of righteousness and to rescue from the evil one and redeem all our social relations." It marked a profound alteration in the understanding of the relation of Protestantism to its environing social structure, and in particular to the economic order.

Religion and Culture

In order to set the social gospel and its parallels in perspective, several aspects of the relation of Protestantism to society in the preceding centuries may be called briefly to mind.

1) The first is a shift in attitude toward "the world" which became prominent in Protestant thinking roughly during the period of the Enlightenment. This change has been aptly described in very general

terms as "the acceptance of a positive attitude toward political and economic and cultural achievements for their own sake."[1]

The center of attention in the medieval church and largely also in the Reformation had often been the "other world" rather than "this world." People's minds were directed primarily above and beyond the satisfactions of earthly life. In popular conception, this usually meant that religious interest was focused on the "hereafter." This world was conceived as a place of preparation, a place of pilgrimage in which one journeyed for a time but always, if one be a Christian, with the whole gaze directed toward the world to come (*Pilgrim's Progress*, by John Bunyan, is a vivid portrayal of this view of the world). The institutions of this world were important and necessary — they were ordained by God — but only as they could be used to further the religious life. Thus, the frequent hostility toward the arts and the theater, for which the Puritans are so commonly blamed, is to be understood as a rejection of things that did not seem to contribute directly to the main purpose of human life.

The roots of the new attitude may be found partly in the spirit of the Renaissance. Here was a "humanism" which called attention to the glories of humanity and its achievements without much reference to supernatural destiny. It was confident of the goodness of the natural and prized culture for its own sake. At the same time, the more positive Christian attitude toward the world reflected a recalling of the biblical sense of creation. The world, though distorted by evil, was nonetheless created good and intended to be the proper sphere of service to God. This biblical view found expression especially in the more activistic and "this-worldly" side of Calvinism (see subsequent paragraphs; also Ch. V), and in the natural religion of the Enlightenment.

Such factors as these, together with the development of science and the growth of commerce, converged to bring about in religious thinking a greater emphasis on the achievement of happiness in this present life and a growing optimism regarding human accomplishments.

2) The changing Protestant attitude toward the world may also be seen in the light of the post-Reformation development of the idea of the "calling" or "vocation" which symbolized the role of the Christian in the "secular" world. The primary import of this Reformation doctrine was its rejection of the superiority of "religious" or priestly vocations over lay or secular vocations. The distinction between priest and farmer was one of function only, not of significance; priest and farmer were equally charged with the responsibility of serving God in their respective ways.

[1] James H. Nichols, *Primer for Protestants* (New York, 1947), p. 79.

In the thought of Luther, the new understanding of vocation was expressed in the view that we are called to serve God in whatever situation we find ourselves. In Calvinism, however, the idea was given a slightly different, more "activist" turn. The all-controlling purpose and duty of the elect is to glorify God. Every aspect of individual and social life must be brought into line with this aim. Conversely, every aspect of life can be the means of exhibiting the glory of God. And the elect individual will glorify God in daily work precisely by honesty, diligence, moderation, sobriety, and thrift.

It was in this latter application that Calvin's doctrine of the calling is important for our present purpose. For coupled with the demand for actively glorifying God in one's daily occupation was a new openness toward the world of commerce and finance. The medieval feudal economy was rapidly giving way to embryonic capitalistic forms of economic organization, particularly in the areas in which Calvinism appeared. Calvin's sympathy with the new forces was indicated by his willingness to permit, with strict qualifications, the charging of interest (a practice uniformly prohibited, though also widely practiced, by the medieval church; it was also frowned upon by Luther). This concession, and the attitude which it symbolized, meant that commercial enterprise was no longer to be suspected as inherently evil, but was properly a field for the fulfillment of one's religious duty.

The studies of Max Weber and R. H. Tawney have suggested a close correlation between Calvinism and the growth of capitalism. It was precisely in the Protestant (and especially Calvinist) countries that capitalism developed most strongly. This does not mean that Calvinism was the cause of capitalism. But Calvin was at least less opposed to the incipient capitalism of his day than other religious leaders, and the virtues which the Calvinists preached provided a powerful impetus for the growing spirit of economic enterprise. "What in Calvin had been a qualified concession to practical exigencies appeared in some of his later followers as a frank idealization of the life of the trader, as the service of God and the training-ground of the soul."[2] In the process, religious ideas were both active and acted upon.

In the time of Calvin, when the city of Geneva was rigidly organized as a society in every particular directed to the glorification of God, the economic activities of the individual had been subjected to sharp control by the community. But this iron collectivism could not be exported, whereas the "economic virtues" of industry, sobriety, and thrift as means of glorifying God went everywhere that Calvinism spread. Thus later, particularly in English Puritanism of the seventeenth century and following, a further development of the ethic occurred, in which collective restraints upon the economic activity of

[2] R. H. Tawney, *Religion and the Rise of Capitalism* (New York, 1926), p. 199.

the individual were given up. This did not yet mean the abandonment of morality in economic life, but that the individual alone, under God, was to be the judge of the justice of business dealings. We must not underestimate the effect which the sense of responsibility to God had in moderating some of the more flagrant abuses of emerging capitalism. But the responsible employment of time and energy in one's work was a religious duty second only to worship, and in such a view, if duty seemed to be profitable, then perhaps profit-making was a duty. There seemed to be a remarkable coincidence between the service of God and the pursuit of private economic interest. In this situation, the strain upon conscience is evident. Appetite for gain might readily be transformed into resplendent virtue. Duty to oneself and to God could merge, the world being so ordered that one might, after all, serve two masters, being paid by one while working for the other.

From this point on, it became increasingly difficult to maintain effectively the sense of direct religious responsibility and moral restraint upon economic activity, particularly in the face of purely secular versions of economic "ethics." The Calvinistic ideal of a total society oriented toward the glorification of God had been dimmed to the point of invisibility. In its place appeared a sharp distinction between the specifically "religious" and the secular. Religion is concerned with a private relation to the creator and is publicly expressed in the worship of the church. The world of economic activity is left to its own immutable laws, and in this world the law for individual action is the pursuit of self-interest. The way is open, then, to economic individualism and self-aggrandizement pure and undiluted. But not undisguised! For the semblance of morality was given to the pursuit of self-interest by the theory of the harmony of interests. By this theory, which was at the root of free enterprise economics (given classical expression in Adam Smith's *Wealth of Nations,* 1776), the laws of the economic world were given divine sanction. The laws of society and the laws of nature alike were held to be unchanging expressions of the will of God, the divine ordering of the world in the best interest of the whole. Therefore, if we pursue our own economic interest, it will be for the good of all.

This is roughly the situation which obtained in the late eighteenth and early nineteenth centuries. The Protestant ethos had been gradually accommodated to the demands of the prevailing economic trends. In the area of politics, the Reformed and Free Church influence had been an important factor in the development of democratic structures of government (see Chs. V, VII), and perhaps here there persisted more of a sense of religious judgment upon social activities. But certainly in the economic realm, the capitulation had gone far.

We may speak of this process as a partial abandonment of the religious claim to govern the "secular" life, when economic activity for the sake of the glory of God becomes simply the good of production for its own sake. Or we may speak of the process as the synthesis of Christianity and civilization, based on a faith in the harmony of interests, and issuing in the identification of Christian goals for society with free enterprise, democracy, and patriotism (as in the case of the pervasive "American faith"). In either case the result was the implicit and often explicit sanctioning by Protestantism of the social, political, and (particularly) economic status quo.

3) It would be grossly unjust to suggest that the Protestant ethic had simply ceased to impose any restraints upon economic activity. What we have said is that there was no effective rethinking of fundamental economic relationships in the light of the gospel. The growth of commerce and the beginnings of the industrial revolution presented problems for which the religious community was as yet unprepared. Still the ethical dimension of faith could find expression in various ways. Within those relationships (debtor-creditor, employer-employee, buyer-seller, getting and spending), Christians did feel and exercise responsibilities as Christians.

One of the ways of exercising Christian responsibility was through individual "stewardship." It was hardly possible to take literally Jesus' extreme condemnation of wealth. But Jesus had also spoken of the faithful steward, the man who had used wisely — and profitably — the money entrusted to him. Here was an appropriate ideal for the growing Protestant middle class! The Christian was to be bound by moral principles in the acquiring of wealth and was to use well that which providence had given him. Stewardship was crowned by philanthropy. The prosperous person could express love for neighbor by giving wealth to the less fortunate (though poverty was like as not the result of sloth or bad management). This might not help to improve the fundamental economic position of the poor, but it could make their lot more bearable.

Also, the ethical demand could and did find expression in noble attempts at the correction of abuses in the working of the system. From the seventeenth-century Quakers through the nineteenth century, profound Christian concern for the welfare of human beings led to many important reforms. One might refer to the work of Elizabeth Fry and John Howard in prison reform, John Woolman and William Wilberforce in the abolition of the slave trade, or Lord Shaftesbury in the improvement of factory conditions and the fight against child labor.

These reforms had great significance, and their leaders were devoted and sincere. But this being accepted, it is still noteworthy that such reforms were conceived largely within the context of the prevailing economic patterns. It was not the system which had to be changed; it was specific abuses which needed alleviation.[3] And "social reform" was to be accomplished by the action of individuals as part of their stewardship.

Moreover, the concern for the reform of abuses was for the most part still associated with belief in the overwhelming priority of the life to come and the relative unimportance of the inequalities and hardships of the present world. The purpose of religion was to make less intolerable the burdens of economic and social inequality. Thus, even Wilberforce, in his *Practical View of the System of Christianity,* could explain that Christianity makes social inequality less galling to the lower classes. It counsels for them a life of diligence, humility, and patience. It explains

> that their more lowly path has been allotted to them by the hand of God; that it is their part faithfully to discharge its duties, and contentedly to bear its inconveniences; that the present state of things is very short; that the objects about which worldly men conflict so eagerly are not worth the contest; that the peace of mind which Religion offers indiscriminately to all ranks, affords more true satisfaction than all the expensive pleasures which are beyond the poor man's reach; that in this view the poor have the advantage; that, if their superiors enjoy more abundant comforts, they are also exposed to many temptations from which the inferior classes are happily exempted; that, "having food and raiment, they should be therewith content," since their situation in life, with all its evils, is better than they have deserved at the hand of God; finally, that all human distinctions will soon be done away, and the true followers of Christ will all, as children of the same Father, be alike admitted to the possession of the same heavenly inheritance.[4]

In sum, the Reformation doctrine of vocation had given a new dignity to common labor, and the spirit of the seventeenth and eighteenth centuries had made for a more positive acceptance of cultural, political, and economic achievements for their own sake, thus also greater concern for happiness in this life. At the same time, in the face of a new economic situation, the more activist form of the doctrine of vocation had been transmuted into a glorification of economic enterprise and a merging of Christian ideals for civilization with the prevailing patterns of the economic and political order. With the sanction of religion thus placed upon the existing order, even the programs for reform were palliative, and apart from these the effective role of

---

[3] There were important exceptions to this generalization: for instance, in the opposition to slavery (as in Woolman, Wilberforce, and Samuel Hopkins), and in Woolman's views on property.

[4] Quoted in J. W. and B. Hammond, *The Town Labourer* (New York, 1920), pp. 231–32.

religion was limited to the privacy of one's relation to God and to concern for the "spiritual" rather than the "secular" life. It was this kind of uncritical acceptance of the social order as a whole (particularly the economic order) which was to call forth most vigorous criticism in the nineteenth century. The objection came from two quite different directions, one outside the church, the other within.

The Challenge of Marxism

The most trenchant external attack on the church's position came from Marxist socialism, notably as expressed in the *Communist Manifesto* (1848) and Marx's *Das Kapital* (1867). According to Marx, history moves irresistibly along a path dictated by economic forces and marked by continual class conflict. All human institutions and ideas are to be understood as direct or indirect products of the economic struggle.

The historical pattern which Marx saw developing in his own day was this: capitalism by its nature required continual expansion, concentration, and centralization, and was predicated upon the exploitation of the workers for the sake of owners. Thus, capital and labor, whose interests were in principle contradictory, grew steadily further apart and all society was being sharply divided into the exploiting capitalist class versus the exploited proletariat. The conflict between the two groups could only grow in intensity, and the resolution of the conflict would come through revolution by the working classes, leading to the establishment of a communistic society in which everyone would produce according to ability and share in the goods of society according to need.

What is the significance of religion according to this understanding of history? It is of great importance indeed, not in the way its proponents have thought, but as an epiphenomenon, a reflection of human nature. Thus the criticism of religion is the premise of all criticism. The course of modern philosophy, through Feuerbach and Bauer, has shown that in reality religious beliefs are illusory, a function of a kind of self-alienation in which elements of human existence are projected into an imaginary world. Once this is seen, religion is done for; Christianity, if not dead, is *in extremis*. But the chief task is not to interpret but to act, to change the world that produces the self-estrangements, to give up the illusory happiness of religion in favor of real happiness. Thus in one sense, religion need not be combatted, for social action eliminates the need to think about it any more. It will simply vanish. Yet in another sense, particularly among Marx's followers, because religion was not dying as rapidly as expected and continued as a brake against the predicted course of history, the church could become an enemy to be opposed.

Thus religion is ultimately a product of economic forces, one of the alienations produced by private property and modern industry. It is antirevolutionary, an instrument whereby the dominant capitalist class is able to maintain its power to exploit the workers. It is the "opiate of the people" (Marx was not the first to use this language). It anesthetizes the sensitivity of the oppressed by holding before them the prospect of reward in the hereafter.

This was not an empty charge. Much evidence can be adduced to support the assertion of a recent interpreter that "no slave or servile class was ever more brutally exploited than the industrial proletariat" during the industrial revolution in England in the latter eighteenth century, and "in no age perhaps was the use of Christianity as an antidote to social unrest more blatant" than during this period.[5] Marx's accusation can be matched by only slightly less extreme statements by defenders of religion. The comments of Wilberforce, cited above, are one example. Another writer urged in 1798 that concrete steps be taken to bring the "lower classes" into the churches, in order that they may "learn the doctrines of that truly excellent religion which exhorts to content and to submission to the higher powers." And critics before Marx had insisted that "what the millions should generally know is this: that no rich man believes in religion of any sort except as a political engine to keep the useful classes in subjection to the rich."[6]

In Protestant countries the Marxist critique had more appeal to the disinherited on the Continent than in the Anglo-Saxon world. Virulent hostility to the church was much less common in the latter countries. But quite apart from the variations in direct impact, the appearance of Marxism was of the greatest importance as a symbol in at least two respects. First, Marxism represented the judgment which Christianity had not effectively pronounced upon the injustice and exploitation of the industrial revolution. It was a voice of protest against a system which seemed inevitably to lead to enslavement. But this was a word hardly heard from within the churches for the clamor of "the harmony of interests" and the loud enthusiasm for middle-class culture. Therefore, it appeared as judgment upon the churches.[7]

Second, the Marxist vision of a perfect society corresponded to (and had some roots in) the Christian hope for the kingdom of God on earth. In this respect particularly, Marxism has often been called a "Christian heresy." Like the idea of progress, the Marxist view of history as moving toward the final climax of judgment and fulfillment

---

[5] W. D. Morris, *The Christian Origins of Social Revolt* (London, 1949), p. 153.

[6] Bronterre O'Brien, in the *Poor Man's Guardian*, Dec. 12, 1835.

[7] There had been earlier Christian parallels to the Marxist critique (e.g., the writings of Gerrard Winstanley), but these had been largely ineffective.

was ultimately derived from the Christian theology of history. In Marxism, this hope was stripped of its religious foundation, historical necessity was substituted for the will of God, and judgment and fulfillment were translated into economic terms. But even this secularized version of the hope for the kingdom symbolized clarity in the recognition of social evil, confidence that the movement of history was toward the establishment of justice, and a prophetic denunciation of the idols of free enterprise. This in a time when the churches, to put it mildly, were confused and hesitant.

The Marxist dream was far more, of course, than a symbol of hope and prophetic criticism. It was also an utter disregard of the Christian view of the worth of persons, and it was to have terrible historical consequences as developed in modern Russia. These horrors are perhaps also partly a judgment upon failures to deal adequately with the problems of industrial society.

Social Gospels

At the time that Marxism appeared, however, there were already stirrings within the church of a powerful movement to overthrow the uncritical identification of Christianity with the existing order. Moreover, while the philanthropists and reformers of the early nineteenth century had not often envisaged radical transformation of society as such, their concern for the correction of social abuses did affect profoundly the tone of industrial society and paved a way both for the more incisive and trenchant criticism which was to follow, and for more radical proposals for reform.

One major sign of the changing attitude of Protestantism may be seen in the Christian Socialist movement in Britain, led by F. D. Maurice (theologian), Charles Kingsley (pastor and novelist), and J. M. Ludlow (lawyer). The movement began in 1848, the year in which the *Communist Manifesto* appeared and popular insurrections swept over continental Europe. Christian Socialism was explicitly an effort to provide a Christian method of social reform as an alternative to class struggle. The Christian Socialists recognized the failings of the churches. "We have," wrote Kingsley, "used the Bible as if it were a mere special constable's handbook, an opium dose for keeping beasts of burden patient while they are being overloaded." They sought to improve working-class conditions through religious regeneration, the formation of producers' cooperatives in which people might be their own employers, the encouragement of trade unions which would work peacefully for better conditions of their members, and the promotion of popular education.

The Christian Socialists of the mid-century were still, however, thoroughly middle class and had much of the attitude of a condescending,

though genuinely benevolent, philanthropy. They deplored suggestions of class militancy. Yet they were more realistic than most of
their contemporaries in assessing the depths of the evils of modern
society, and while their influence was relatively slight in their own
day, it was immense in the later development of social concern in
England. They marked a definite recognition of the church's duty to
work for the creation of a more just social order. And they saw that
this might require more than stewardship, philanthropy, and the regu-
lation of abuses. The spirit of Maurice and his associates influenced
both the Anglican church and the various nonconformist churches.
Partly under this influence, as well as the impact of Henry George's
Progress and Poverty, the late-nineteenth century in England saw the
growth of a whole flock of social movements, from the moderate Christian Social Union to the more radical Church Socialist League, the
Socialist Quaker Society, the League of Progressive Thought and Social
Service, and kindred groups. And this spirit was partly responsible
for moderating in England the opposition between organized labor
and the church that appeared almost everywhere on the European
continent, as well as being responsible for the profound religious ani-
mation of later British socialism and the Labor party.

The revolutions of 1848 also stimulated reform efforts in Germany,
though the main response of Protestantism there was an even closer
association of the church with political and economic conservatism.
The *Kirchentag* and the *Innere Mission,* founded by J. H. Wichern (1808–
1881), were attempts to give a positive answer to communism by apply-
ing Christianity to social and industrial life, particularly in the cities.
Unfortunately, these and successor movements in Germany hardly
went beyond the level of philanthropic and palliative measures, and
with the exception of isolated individuals the church social movements
maintained a steady opposition to the socialism of the Social Democrats.
There was little support for any major political or economic reordering.
For example, Adolph Harnack, who at the turn of the century was a
leader in the Evangelical Social Congresses, explicitly denied that the
church had any right to take positions with respect to economic questions.

It was among the liberal Swiss Protestants, particularly in the religious
socialism of Hermann Kutter (1863–1931) and Leonhard Ragaz (1868–
1945) at the beginning of the twentieth century, that the most dramatic
proposals were made. The impulse was comparable to that of British
Christian socialism and of the social gospel in America; namely, for
a radically new stance on the part of the church. The church must
be socialist in the deepest sense, and it must make common cause
with the Social Democrats, who are in fact doing what the church
ought to have been doing. They are revolutionary, but they are doing
the work of God, the great disturber, whose revolution is announced

in the New Testament. The church talks about sin, but the Social Democrats are actually fighting against evil. The Social Democrats are charged with atheism, but the church is worshipping mammon. A divine power is compelling the Social Democrats to do the work for which Christianity was called into existence. Hence they must go forward — and if the church is genuinely to look forward in hope for the kingdom of God, it must support them.[8]

The American movement distinctively known as the "social gospel" came into being in the last quarter of the nineteenth century and reached its height in the optimistic years just prior to the First World War. Here as strongly as anywhere else was sounded the theme that the thoroughgoing reconstruction of society was both imperative and possible. Here, too, was clearly expressed the primary difference between the new social concern and the older humanitarianism, viz., the conviction that the well-being of humanity required the transformation of the social environment as well as the changing of individuals.

The social gospel had unique roots in the American heritage. The dream of a kingdom of God on earth had long been a part of the American ethos (though the goal of the kingdom was often confused with the more immediate achievements of society). The Puritans had come in hope of the creation of "a new Heaven, and a new Earth in new Churches, and a new Commonwealth together." The hope of the kingdom had blended with the democratic ideal in the foundation of the republic and its later equalitarian aspirations. That hope was nourished in the evangelical revivals and accounted in no small measure for the fervor devoted to missions and against slavery (thus Edward Beecher wrote: "Now that God has smitten slavery to death, he has opened the way for the redemption and sanctification of our whole social system"). Moreover, the United States, with its rapid growth in size, population, industry, and wealth, was notably receptive to the spirit of progress and indefinite perfectibility of society which was current in eighteenth-century literature.

The birth of the social gospel was also assisted by a variety of distinctively nineteenth-century forces. One was the challenge of socialism and the rising labor unions. The American labor leader, Samuel Gompers, wrote in 1898, explaining the absence of workers from the church: "My associates have come to look upon the church and the ministry as the apologists and defenders of the wrong committed against the interests of the people, simply because the perpetrators

---

[8] It should be recalled in connection with the Protestant movements that in the late nineteenth century official Roman Catholic approval and encouragement also were being given to religious activities for social reform. These were marked especially by Pope Leo XIII's encyclical *Rerum Novarum* (1891) on capital and labor — though the proposals there were far more cautious than the programs of the British Christian socialists, the Swiss religious socialists, or the American social gospellers.

are possessors of wealth . . . whose real God is the almighty dollar, and who contribute a few of their idols to suborn the intellect and eloquence of the divines. . . ."

A second force was liberal theology. The moral idealism of liberalism, and its insistence on practical fruits of religion, intensified the sense of Christian responsibility for doing something about the evils of society. Liberalism's view of the sacredness of human personality and its optimism about human virtue were primary assumptions of the new social emphasis. Conceptions of the immanence of God and of evolutionary progress in history buttressed the faith that the transformation of society was possible.

Liberalism also contributed by helping to break down the extreme individualism which had entered the Protestant understanding of sin and redemption. Horace Bushnell (1802–1876), who did more than anyone else to further the liberalization of American theology, had emphasized the overwhelming importance of social environment in the development of character. Human beings are indeed united in sin, he asserted, not in some formal legal sense or through biological inheritance, but through their common involvement in the social texture in which personality is formed. And if sin is social, so is virtue. Individuals cannot be redeemed in isolation from society but only in and with it. There is social solidarity both in sin and in salvation.

Moreover, the liberal approach to the Bible was instrumental 1) in the renewed appreciation of the demand for social justice by the Hebrew prophets (notably Amos and Micah); 2) in the application of the teachings of Jesus regarding wealth, the family, the state, and nonresistance to problems of the industrial and political orders; and especially 3) in the rediscovery of the centrality of the kingdom of God in Jesus' message and the interpretation of the kingdom as a real ideal for the present world.

A third major nineteenth-century force which helped to call forth the social gospel was the intensity of the social problems themselves. By 1880, the United States was rapidly becoming a closely knit industrial society, and it was the problems of this society that the social gospel sought to meet. The new economic interdependence, the maladjustments attendant upon the growth of industry and the cities, the disruptions of social and family life, the failure of the new technology to fulfill the promise of plenty for all, mass unemployment and unprecedented poverty, growing labor discontent, the exaggerated individualism of the capitalist, the disregard of human rights — all these showed clearly that the neighbor could not be served in isolation. The social gospel was a new application of the Christian ethic in response to the demands of a new historical situation. Conscience had to become "social conscience."

From its birth (about 1870), the social gospel was marked by a twofold emphasis: a broader conception of the church's function, and a nascent critique of the patterns and ideology of the existing order. Penetrating criticism was directed against the theory of the harmony of interests, especially against the supposition that private gain always makes for public good. On such a view, it was suggested, the greatest public benevolence would be the most unrestrained, comprehensive self-seeking! Examination of the facts showed that unrestricted competition was leading directly to the most inhuman treatment of human beings in arrogant denial of Christian ethics and of the dignity of human personality. The good of all did *not* come simply as a by-product of the pursuit of self-interest.

Moreover, the early proponents of the social gospel saw (quite correctly, as later experience showed) that the crux of industrial maladjustment lay in the conflict between capital and labor. They insisted that the relations of capital and labor constitute a moral issue. It is, they said, not only inadequate but perverse to relegate these matters to the class of purely "economic" problems. The Christian law of love must be considered as well as the law of supply and demand. Thus Washington Gladden, often called the "father of the social gospel," wrote in 1876:

> Now that slavery is out of the way, the questions that concern our free laborers are coming forward; and no intelligent man needs to be admonished of their urgency. They are not only questions of economy, they are in a large sense moral questions; nay, they touch the very marrow of that religion of good-will of which Christ was the founder. It is plain that the pulpit must have something to say about them.[9]

Such a view required an enlarged conception of the church's function. It must speak not only of "honesty" in acquiring wealth, and "generosity" once it is acquired, it must speak also of "justice" to those who labor in the production of wealth. It must be concerned with the *patterns* of economic enterprise. There must be "new applications of the truth and the adoption of methods unknown to former times." The church can, if it will, provide these! So wrote Josiah Strong: "The world in this sociological age needs a new social ideal to direct the progress of civilization. Let the church fully accept her mission and she will furnish this needed ideal, viz., her Master's conception of the kingdom of God come upon earth." The church is to be the source of self-giving love to take the place of selfish competition.

The demand that the church assume an active role in the establishment of social justice, and that Christian ethics be applied to every aspect of social life, was voiced not only by individuals but by dozens

[9] Cited in H. Hopkins, *The Rise of the Social Gospel* (New Haven, 1940), p. 24.

of new journals and organizations. The social gospel was celebrated in popular hymns, such as Frank Mason North's "Where Cross the Crowded Ways of Life," Washington Gladden's "O Master, Let Me Walk with Thee," Clifford Box's "Turn Back, O Man," and Ernest Shurtleff's "Lead on, O King Eternal." The most distinctive literary production of the movement was the social gospel novel, which dramatized the possibilities of reforming society through the application of Christian principles in business and politics. The best known of these novels, a story by Charles M. Sheldon called *In His Steps: What Would Jesus Do?*, probably did more than any other medium to make people aware of the claims of the social gospel. In the generation after its publication (1896), this book sold an estimated twenty-three million copies in English and had been translated into twenty-one other languages. As a social tract, *In His Steps* ranks with such other American classics as *Uncle Tom's Cabin* and *Ten Nights in a Bar Room*. In spite of the fact that *In His Steps* is still relatively individualistic in its conception of methods of social reform, a comparison of this book with *Pilgrim's Progress* shows vividly how far Protestant thinking had changed in two centuries in its view of the role of the Christian in society.

The American Social Gospel's Greatest Prophet: Rauschenbusch

In 1917 Walter Rauschenbusch, professor of church history at Rochester Theological Seminary (New York), could say:

> The social gospel . . . is no longer a prophetic and occasional note. It is a novelty only in backward social or religious communities. The social gospel has become orthodox. It is not only preached. It has set new problems for local church work, and has turned the pastoral and organizing work of the ministry into new and constructive directions. It has imparted a wider vision and a more statesmanlike grasp to the foreign mission enterprise. . . . Conservative denominations have formally committed themselves to the fundamental ideas of the social gospel and their practical application. The plans of great interdenominational organizations are inspired by it. It has become a constructive force in American politics.[10]

This assertion may suggest a wider popular acceptance of the social gospel than a more sober judgment would allow, either for Protestantism in 1917 or a generation later. But certainly no one person

[10] *A Theology for the Social Gospel* (New York, 1917), pp. 2f.

was more responsible for gaining popular response and official recognition for the social gospel than Rauschenbusch himself.

The son of a German Baptist pastor and professor, Rauschenbusch served for eleven years a congregation of German immigrant workers in "Hell's Kitchen," the tough West End of New York City. There he found problems of human misery and economic maladjustment to which the inherited forms of his faith seemed to have little to say. A reexamination of the faith and of the Bible led to new convictions which were expressed first in a periodical, *For The Right* (1889ff.), published with the help of several friends for the discussion of the "interests of the working class." Shortly afterward, Rauschenbusch and a few other young pastors formed the Brotherhood of the Kingdom, meeting for a week every summer until 1914 to examine and to promote "the ethical and spiritual principles of Jesus, both in their individual and their social aspects." Rauschenbusch became the acknowledged leader of the social gospel movement with the publication of *Christianity and the Social Crisis* (1907). His writings gave mature expression to the purpose and program of the movement, as well as to some of the assumptions which a later generation was to find of dubious significance (see Ch. XII).

In a summary statement of the meaning of the social gospel, Rauschenbusch makes explicit the self-understanding which had characterized the movement from its beginning: the social gospel is new in its emphasis and broader in its scope, but it springs from the old evangelical faith.

> The social gospel is the old message of salvation, but enlarged and intensified. The individualistic gospel has taught us to see the sinfulness of every human heart and has inspired us with faith in the willingness and power of God to save every soul that comes to him. But it has not given us an adequate understanding of the sinfulness of the social order and its share in the sins of all individuals within it. It has not evoked faith in the will and power of God to redeem the permanent institutions of human society from their inherited guilt of oppression and extortion. Both our sense of sin and our faith in salvation have fallen short of the realities under its teaching. The social gospel seeks to bring men under repentance for their collective sins and to create a more sensitive and more modern conscience. It calls on us for the faith of the old prophets who believed in the salvation of nations.[11]

The underlying principle of this new understanding of the gospel was the explicit and consistent recognition of the social nature of personal existence. Society was seen as an organism rather than as a mere collection of individual units, and human interrelationships as "vital" and "solidaristic." This theme had been sounded vigorously

---

[11] *Ibid.*, pp. 5f.

by Bushnell and had been instrumental in the creation of the social gospel. With the full elaboration of the new gospel, as seen in Rauschenbusch's thought, that crucial insight was carried further in several directions: 1) in relation to the idea of the kingdom of God; 2) in a more thoroughgoing demand for reorganization of the economic *system;* 3) in a more scientific approach to the study of social problems; and 4) in an attempt to restate Christian theology so as to take fuller account of the social gospel.

1) The concept of the kingdom of God was for Rauschenbusch the focus of the original gospel and ought always therefore to be the center of the Christian message. Study of the New Testament was showing with increasing definiteness that the heart of Jesus' teaching was his proclamation of the coming kingdom. The social gospel, therefore, meant to Rauschenbusch and his associates the reestablishment of the ideal of the kingdom of God in the place it occupied in the message of Jesus. They (quite rightly) insisted upon the intimate connection between the ethical teachings of Jesus and his preaching of the kingdom. Moreover, though here they wrongly interpreted Jesus' teaching, they believed that the kingdom was to grow out of the existing institutions of society. The kingdom would come not with the destruction of the present social order, but with the redemption of the "permanent institutions of human society." The kingdom is not an otherworldly hope, but a goal for this world, the end toward which all the divine activity is leading, viz., the organization of humanity according to the will of God.

Rauschenbusch never supposed, as some of his lesser followers seem to have done, that the kingdom could be established simply or even primarily by human effort. For him, it is *God's* kingdom:

> The Kingdom of God is divine in its origin, progress, and consummation. It was initiated by Jesus Christ, in whom the prophetic spirit came to consummation, it is sustained by the Holy Spirit, and it will be brought to its fulfillment by the power of God in his own time. . . . The Kingdom of God, therefore, is miraculous all the way. . . .[12]

Nor did Rauschenbusch suppose that the kingdom could come without great struggle against the kingdom of evil (i.e., organized sin, evil which has become entrenched in the patterns of society). Nevertheless, the kingdom is in part already present and comes by slow growth; it is possible for us to help it along. "Every human life is so placed that it can share with God in the creation of the Kingdom, or can

---

[12] *Ibid.,* p. 139.

resist and retard its progress. The Kingdom is for each of us the supreme task and the supreme gift of God."[13] It is not to be expected that society will ever fully achieve perfection; but it is possible and a duty to move along the path of approximation to a perfect social order. "The Kingdom of God is always but coming," but it is also true that the kingdom of God is always coming.

2) In some respects, Rauschenbusch and others felt Western society was relatively far along on the way toward the kingdom (e.g., in education and in democratic government). These agencies, then, could be means for promotion of the kingdom in that area in which least progress had been made, viz., in the economic order. From the first, the social gospel had been particularly concerned with problems of economic justice; nowhere was the power of organized sin more apparent than in the cruelties of industrial society. The beginning of the twentieth century, however, revealed a trend toward a more radical approach to economic problems and their solution. Appeals to individual regeneration, and to love as the means to establishing industrial harmony, were definitely recognized as quite inadequate apart from social reorganization.

As early as 1890, this tendency appeared in a greater friendliness toward socialism, particularly in the demand of the latter for fundamental social reorganization. For the most part, however, those who sought to make common cause with socialism refused to identify the Christian social ideal with any specific "socialist" programs, and socialism was approved as a means to a social and religious end rather than as an end in itself. It was at the point of the *criticism* of the competitive and predatory features of unregulated capitalism that Christian ethics and the socialist critique seemed to have the most in common.

3) The scientific note was prominent in multiplied efforts to accumulate accurate and complete information regarding social problems and to incorporate this into programs of religious education. More objective studies were made of the function of religion in society. The role of the church was reconceived as in part that of a social service agency, and such institutional organizations as the religious social settlement and the "labor church" were accepted as essential elements in the church's ministry. The study of sociology and social problems became an integral part of the curriculum of theological seminaries. A correlative form of the emphasis on social science was the entrance of numerous Protestant ministers into professional social service work and into research and teaching in sociology.

[13] *Ibid.*, p. 141.

4) A final direction of the developed thought of the social gospel was the attempt to restate Christian doctrine in terms of the new social vision. The classic expression of this effort was the work already cited, lectures delivered by Rauschenbusch at Yale University under the title *A Theology for the Social Gospel.* In these lectures, Rauschenbusch explicitly undertook to formulate "a systematic theology large enough to match [the social gospel] and vital enough to back it," to show "how some of the most important sections of doctrinal theology may be expanded and readjusted to make room for the religious convictions summed up in 'the social gospel' "[14]

Rauschenbusch's own theological perspective was largely free from the sentimental optimism of much of the social gospel thought of his day and of the 1920s; and many of his deepest convictions ran counter to the prevailing liberal theology. Yet Rauschenbusch's concern to emphasize the distinction between the old theology and the theology for the social gospel made it inevitable that primary attention should be given to those aspects of his reinterpretation which seemed most in accord with liberalism. His keen sense of the kingdom of God as judgment, and of the deepening of the burden of guilt through the recognition of social sin; the new validity which he found in the doctrine of original sin through the recognition of the social transmission of sin; the sense of crisis in individual and social life, and the demand for repentance and rebirth; and the desperateness of the struggle against the "kingdom of evil" (the superindividual forces of evil infecting the whole social organism) — these elements of Rauschenbusch's theology were less influential than those which reinforced the characteristic liberal tenets.

With the liberals, Rauschenbusch defined sin as selfishness. The conception of God was to be freed of all despotic and monarchial elements, and "democratized" by reappropriation of Jesus' teaching of the Fatherhood of God: "the worst thing that could happen to God would be to remain an autocrat while the world is moving toward democracy." The immanence of God should be recognized as the basis of social solidarity: "the all-pervading life of God is the ground of the spiritual oneness of the race and of our hope for its closer fellowship." Conceptions of revelation and inspiration were to receive new meaning, and the spirit of prophecy (in its vision of the kingdom) would once more become central in the work of redemption. The redeeming work of Christ's life was seen as the battle against religious bigotry, graft and political power, corruption of justice, mob spirit and mob action, militarism, and class contempt (i.e., precisely those universal social sins which conspired to kill him). His death supremely

[14] *Ibid.*, p. 1.

revealed the power of sin and of the love of God, and strengthened "the power of prophetic religion and therewith the redemptive forces of the Kingdom of God."

Acceptance and Modification of the Social Gospel

Rauschenbusch's declaration that "the social gospel has become orthodox," if it implied full popular acceptance, was an exaggeration. But during the first decade of the twentieth century, the Presbyterian, Protestant Episcopal, Congregational, Methodist, and Northern Baptist churches had begun the establishment of official agencies for study and recommendation in the area of social problems; and by 1912 eleven other denominations had pledged themselves to carry out social service programs through existing church agencies. The official recognition of the social gospel was symbolized by the organization in 1908 of the Federal Council of the Churches of Christ in America (later merged into the National Council of the Churches of Christ in the U.S.A.). The Council was formed partly for the specific purpose of providing a centralized organ for the expression of Protestant concern in every area of social problems, and after a difficult struggle against elements both within and without the churches, it became a prominent force in the American scene. It continued to provide an effective framework for Protestant social action.

In similar fashion, the acknowledgment of the church's social responsibility became a prime factor in the movement for interdenominational cooperation on a worldwide scale (see Ch. XIII). This concern was focused in the "ecumenical" conferences at Stockholm (1925) and Oxford (1937) and in the Universal Christian Council for Life and Work (formed in 1929). The Life and Work movement became in turn a part of the program of the World Council of Churches. The World Council took as the theme for its first meeting (Amsterdam, 1948) "Man's Disorder and God's Design," dealing specifically with the problem of the church's relation to social and international disorders. Among the fruits of this study was the much-publicized criticism by the Council of both communism and laissez-faire capitalism.[15]

---

[15] This appeared in the report of Section III, on "The Church and the Disorder of Society." The relevant paragraph reads as follows: "The Christian churches should reject the ideologies of both communism and laissez-faire capitalism, and should seek to draw men away from the false assumption that these extremes are the only alternatives. Each has made promises which it could not redeem. Communist ideology puts the emphasis upon economic justice, and promises that freedom will come automatically after the completion of the revolution. Capitalism puts the em-

(Continued)

Since the middle 1930s, the Christian social movement has undergone important reorientation. As liberal theology has come under severe criticism in the light of a renewed appreciation of many classical Christian insights, the social concern of the church has been increasingly freed from dependence on the theological patterns of liberalism. The buoyant and often sentimental optimism of the "social gospel," in spite of Rauschenbusch's warnings, had continued unabated through the 1920s in such leaders as Shailer Mathews and Francis J. McConnell. But this has given way to soberer views of human virtue and a more radical understanding of the divine judgment upon human society and schemes for its redemption. The concern for peace, prominent even before World War I, had led in the 1920s to the channelling of much of the enthusiasm for the social gospel into uncritical pacifist positions. Subsequent thought took more positive account of the necessity of restraint of evil, even through war. (Perhaps the best expression in America of this changing perspective is to be found in the report of the commission chaired by Robert L. Calhoun on "The Relation of the Church to the War in the Light of the Christian Faith," 1944.) The frequent tendency of many social gospel proponents to rely simply on church pronouncements has been counterbalanced by more serious study of the processes of social change, of the role of the church in relation to legislative processes, and of the technical problems of the economic and political orders. The hope of "bringing in the kingdom" has been replaced by more concrete attempts to find proximate and viable solutions to social problems which continually recur in new forms.

Nonetheless, the ethical imperative of the social gospel, the emphasis on Christian social responsibility, the sharp criticism of any Christian ethics which deals only with "individual morality," the primary concern for the welfare of oppressed classes and races — these remain from the social gospel as an integral part of the Protestant witness, and this in spite of recent (often violent) criticism from ultraconservative groups. Most important, the social gospel both symbolized and popularized an apparently permanent shift in the Christian attitude toward social institutions in relation to man's salvation. Earlier it had been assumed that the patterns of the social orders were fixed, and that the quality of the spiritual life was essentially separable from the quality

phasis upon freedom, and promises that justice will follow as a by-product of free enterprise; that, too, is an ideology which has been proved false. It is the responsibility of Christians to seek new, creative solutions which never allow either justice or freedom to destroy the other."

The study papers prepared for the Amsterdam meeting, and the official reports of the four sections, were published in *The Amsterdam Assembly Series,* "Man's Disorder and God's Design," 4 vols.

of social life. Now, however, social institutions themselves were seen to be malleable, and both redemptive and restrictive in relation to the spiritual life. Thus, where prior to the social gospel, the influence of Christianity on social structures had been largely indirect and unconscious, now it became conscious and explicit. Now Christians felt required, as part of their witness, to conceive of the transformation of social structures as such.

CHAPTER XII

Between the Wars

The pattern of Protestant theological development has been one of recurrent reinterpretation of Christian faith in response to new needs and situations — of reaction and revival in the midst of fundamental continuity. This was true of the origin of Protestantism. The reformers were in revolt against serious perversions of the gospel which they thought had come to dominate the medieval church, and they sought to recall the church to its task of proclaiming the gospel of God's graciousness in Jesus Christ, as that gospel was set forth in the New Testament and as it spoke to the religious situation of the sixteenth century. At the same time, the reformers were speaking to the church from within, and the understanding of the gospel which they revived had never been wholly lost. A similar pattern was evident in the evangelical revivals and in the growth of the Free Church tradition. Liberalism, too, was marked by a breaking down of false and dated idols of creed and confession and a reappropriation of crucial facets of the Christian witness which had been abused, neglected, or forgotten.

Another in this series of renewed apprehensions and interpretations may be said to begin with the publication in 1919 of a commentary by Karl Barth (1886–1968) on Paul's Epistle to the Romans. Completed in the closing days of World War I, this was a book of violent protest, which became even sharper in the second edition of 1922, against the fundamental premises of "liberal" theology, and it called for a radical reexamination of the basis of Christian thinking.

Barth had himself been trained in the German liberal tradition of Ritschl and Harnack, especially under Herrmann at Marburg. But he had been dismayed by the fact that nearly all of the liberal theologians had joined in signing the 1914 manifesto of support for Kaiser Wilhelm. And as he sought to work out the implications of his early views, particularly as a young Swiss pastor faced Sunday after Sunday with the task of declaring the Christian message to his congregation, Barth felt with growing keenness that liberalism had really no *gospel* to offer at all, but only an attempted sharing of personal religious experience. As he later put it, his teacher Herrmann could state beautifully where the basis of proclamations was *not* to be found — in traditionalism, in Rationalism, or in mysticism. But Herrmann erred in reserving one little area, the inner experience of the individual. Jesus is human, the Scriptures are human, doctrines are human, yet in religious experience the inner life of Jesus can have authority for us. That, however, Barth came to see, is a wholly inadequate and unbiblical foundation.

Thus Barth reported a "joyful sense of discovery" with which he found, through renewed study of the Bible and especially of St. Paul, a radically different perspective for Christian faith. It was this new insight that Barth sought to develop in his *Romans* (1919, 1921). The biblical message, he affirmed, is not concerned with our discovery of God, or "religious experience," but with *God's Word* to us. This is a Word that comes to us in judgment on all our pretensions, including our religious pretensions. It is a Word about God's faithfulness, which reveals our utter faithlessness and rebellion. The divine Yea comes to us as an uncompromising No. It reveals, not a fundamental continuity between human and divine, but distance and estrangement. "God is in heaven and thou art on earth." The confidence of faith can, therefore, never rest in human religiousness or claim to goodness or social progress. Faith can only refer to the strange and unexpected Word from above. In an early essay, Barth wrote of the new perspective as the discovery of a "strange new world within the Bible":

> It is not the right human thoughts about God which form the content of the Bible, but the right divine thoughts about men. The Bible tells us not how we should talk with God but what he says to us; not how we find the way to him, but he has sought and found the way to us; not the right relation in which we must place ourselves to him, but the covenant which he has made with all who are Abraham's spiritual children and which he has sealed once and for all in Jesus Christ. . . . We have found in the Bible a new world, God, God's sovereignty, God's glory, God's incomprehensible love. Not the history of man but the history of God! Not the virtues of men but the virtues of him who hath called us out of the darkness into his marvelous light! Not human standpoints but the standpoint of God![1]

The reception with which Barth's commentary was greeted was one for which he was quite unprepared. He compared his experience to that of a man climbing in a church steeple in the middle of the night, who reaching out for support discovers to his dismay that he has

[1] Barth, *The Word of God and the Word of Man* (London, 1928), pp. 43, 45.

seized the bell rope and awakened the whole town. Barth immediately became the center of a storm of discussion and he continued for more than thirty years to be the leading and most controversial prophet of Protestantism. Protestant and Catholic thinkers both have had to take account of his work.

We should not suppose, of course, that a new mood and direction in religious thought is ever simply the result of one man's work. Rather, Barth's dramatic protest and polemic were the focus of a widely felt need for a new look at the gospel and all theological formulations. Powerful forces were already at work, both within the church's understanding of its message and within the world to which the church sought to speak, which necessitated theological reconstruction. The time was ripe for a thorough reassessment of both liberal and traditional forms for the understanding of the gospel.

Karl Barth's work was a noteworthy impetus and the twelve big volumes of his *Church Dogmatics,* published over a period of three decades from 1932, remain a monument and a touchstone for the new directions. Barth was of course not alone in his concerns. From an early time he was closely linked with Eduard Thurneysen, Friedrich Gogarten, and Emil Brunner (whose work was especially important in mediating the new perspectives in Britain and the United States). Barth was slavishly followed by few, and in the 1930s he broke sharply with Gogarten and Brunner over the issue of natural theology (or general revelation), which seemed to him to open the door to the terrible distortions of the German Christian party, with its support of Hitler's blood and soil religion. Others followed relatively independent lines: Paul Tillich, who in Germany in the 1920s was already developing an alternative, a theology of correlation; Reinhold and H. Richard Niebuhr in America, and the Marburg New Testament scholar Rudolf Bultmann, who was early on much influenced by Barth but who from the 1940s proposed a quite different sort of approach (see following section, "The New Theological Situation").

In the United States it was Reinhold Niebuhr who became the chief proponent for the new theological perspective. His *Moral Man and Immoral Society* (1933) had the same sort of "shock value" for America which Barth's *Romans* had for Germany. And Niebuhr was led to a similar recovery of the Reformation doctrine of justification by faith (and also the Augustinian-Lutheran analysis of sin) by the pressure of social and economic issues. It was the abysmal problems of human nature, which Niebuhr began to see in the intensive industrialization of Detroit during the years of his pastorate there (1915–1928), that required the rejection of the liberal dogmas. The doctrines of justification by faith and original sin had to be reasserted as indispensable for the interpretation of human history (and therefore just as relevant for sociology and the philosophy of history as for theology).

The purpose of this chapter is to sketch the broad outlines of the

theological tendencies of which Barth and Niebuhr have been important (and sometimes extreme) representatives. Other thinkers will be
noted at relevant points. This is not intended as an all-inclusive account
of the Protestant scene in the four decades following the First World
War. Such a survey would have to include the "ecumenical movement,"
which has indeed exerted a profound influence on recent theology
(see Ch. XIII). It would have to recognize the persistence of both
liberal and fundamentalist (or evangelical) thought. At the same time,
the impulses and patterns of thought described below were not limited
to any single theological school. They represented a mood and direction
in theology which permeated Protestant thinking until well into the
1950s, not only in Europe and America but also in Japan and Korea.

The New Theological Situation

One patent characteristic of the new mood of Protestant thinking
was the reaction against liberal theology. It demanded reexamination
of the fundamental premises of liberalism in the light of the Christian
tradition, and the place of honor was given to some elements of the
tradition with which liberalism had been most sharply at odds. Yet
the new theology (unlike fundamentalism, which had sought to bypass
the liberal challenge; see Ch. X) was unquestionably a "post-liberal"
theology. It came out of the midst of liberalism and its perspective
was shaped by the problems with which liberalism had to deal. The
revolt against liberalism was the revolt of a child against its parent, a
conflict required by the new situation in which the child must live,
by the deficiencies that new experience and reflection revealed in
the outlook of the parent, and by the desire to be loyal to the entire
tradition of which the immediate parent was but one representative.

At its center, then, the new theology was an attempt to exhibit
anew the realities to which Christian faith attests, with relevance to
the situation of the twentieth century. This Protestant thinking involved
both a continuation of liberal developments and a hammering out
of new insights in opposition to many liberal tendencies. The new
patterns showed both a reappropriation and a reinterpretation of classical Christian doctrines. They sprang both from renewed insight into
the Christian witness and from the necessity of newly interpreting
that gospel to a contemporary world.

1) One aspect of the new situation, certainly the most obvious
one, which called for renewed appraisal of the Protestant understanding of the gospel, was the dramatic alteration in the world scene. In
the nineteenth century it was possible to speak of a harmony of interests, based on faith in a good Creator and the order of the universe,
because there did seem to be a rough sort of harmony among the

various human activities. It was possible to believe in the progressive realization of a world of justice and plenty, because the relative peace and prosperity of the nineteenth century seemed amply to justify such a hope. But after a world war, the fatuous and irresponsible 1920s, a great depression, and the rise of National Socialism, this kind of outlook was simply out of the question. The problem was no longer one of a Christian understanding of the gradual perfecting of man and society. It became instead a problem of understanding human misery, tragedy, and bestiality. The word of the gospel had to be interpreted to a world of disorder and conflict, in which the whole fabric of society appeared to be rotting away, a world in which hope had been swallowed up by despair and a sense of futility. The Second World War accentuated this attitude and brought with it the fear of imminent and ultimate doom for all human achievements. The optimism of liberalism seemed naive and superficial, and the question had to be asked whether Christian insight really warranted liberalism's supreme confidence in human response to reason and ideals. Thus, Reinhold Niebuhr could write in 1934:

> The liberal culture of modernity is defective in both religious profundity and political sagacity. . . . [It] understands neither the heights to which life may rise nor the depths to which it may sink. . . . It is quite unable to give guidance and direction to a confused generation which faces the disintegration of a social system and the task of building a new one.[2]

Much more dramatic, also in 1934, was the formation in Germany of the Confessing Church and the issuing of the famous Barmen declaration. The Evangelical Church of Germany had seemed to become almost a tool of Nazism (including its antisemitism), and the Confessing Church, under the leadership of Barth and Martin Niemöller (and later Dietrich Bonhoeffer, who was finally executed for his part in the plot on Hitler's life), aimed to free the church from this idolatrous ideology. As the Barmen declaration, in which Karl Barth was the chief voice, put it, Christ is the sole authority over the church:

> Jesus Christ, as he is attested to us in the Holy Scripture, is the one Word of God which we have to hear and which we have to trust and obey in life and in death.
> We reject the false doctrine [that] the Church could and would have to acknowledge as a source of its proclamation, apart from and besides this one Word of God, still other events and powers, figures and truths, as God's revelation.[3]

---

[2] *Reflections on the End of an Era* (New York, 1934), pp. 14, ix.
[3] See Arthur C. Cochrane, *The Church's Confession Under Hitler* (Philadelphia, 1962), pp. 239–40.

2) A second feature of the new situation was the further development of biblical criticism. At the end of the nineteenth century some scholars were speaking of the "assured results" of criticism and were quite confident that the "historical Jesus" could be distinguished from the layers of "later" theological interpretation which were present in the New Testament record. It was thought that the "permanently valid" elements of Jesus' teaching and example could be lifted directly out of their context and presented as a universal claim upon humanity. But this assurance was quickly and rudely shaken by further New Testament study. For one thing, largely as a result of the writings of Albert Schweitzer, who was later to become the most famous missionary of the twentieth century, it now appeared that the expectation of an imminent, catastrophic establishment of the kingdom of God on earth was central to Jesus' teaching. Jesus believed that the kingdom would come soon, perhaps even in his own lifetime and certainly within his generation; his own mission was to call people to be prepared for its advent. Thus, it was not possible for modern interpreters to say that Jesus' followers had misunderstood him and had transformed his message of an inner spiritual kingdom into the hope of the overthrow of the external social order. Nor was it possible to say (with Harnack) that the external elements in the hope of the kingdom were merely the Jewish framework in which Jesus cast his message and were not really significant for his teaching. It was also impossible simply to separate Jesus' teaching about the Fatherhood of God or his ethical demands from the belief in the kingdom. All of Jesus' teaching had to be reexamined.

This new understanding of the nature and importance of Jesus' message about the kingdom therefore raised new questions about the permanent validity of Jesus' teaching. It was not simply a question whether Jesus was mistaken about the time of the coming of the kingdom, for liberalism had long since recognized that the gospels portrayed a truly human person, sharing in the limitations of finite existence. The problem was now deepened and broadened by new understanding of the extent to which even the most central elements of Jesus' teaching were bound up with the perspectives of his time. It was no longer possible to separate the "historical Jesus" from his social environment and to make of him a "modern" teacher. Few interpreters accepted Schweitzer's judgment that Jesus viewed the kingdom as purely a future event, or that the ethical demands referred only to the brief "interim" between Jesus' preaching and the coming of the kingdom. But Schweitzer's summary (in 1906) of the results of biblical criticism remains a classic expression of the kind of problem which now appeared:

> The study of the Life of Jesus has had a curious history. It set out in quest of the historical Jesus, believing that when it had found Him it

could bring Him straight into our time as a Teacher and Savior. It loosed the bands by which He had been riveted for centuries to the stony rocks of ecclesiastical doctrine, and rejoiced to see the life and movement coming into the figure once more, and the historical Jesus advancing, as it seemed, to meet it. But He does not stay; He passes by our time and returns to His own. What surprised and dismayed the theology of the last forty years was that, despite all forced and arbitrary interpretations, it could not keep Him in our time, but had to let Him go.[4]

On the one side, then, it was discovered that the historical Jesus could not be sundered from the world of first-century Judaism. But on the other side, it was seen that he could not be separated from the early Christian community and its faith. A better understanding of the process by which the gospels came into existence revealed that none of them could be considered "biographies" in the modern sense. They were documents written from the point of view of faith. This does not mean that the gospels were fictional creations, though there are clearly elements of legend in them, but rather that the writers of the gospels were not concerned simply with recording "facts" about the life of Jesus. They were interested in these facts because of their conviction that in this man God had wrought a mighty work of redemption. The Passion was the focus of the story. Jesus' deeds and sayings were significant only because of his death and resurrection, which disclosed him to be the Christ, the Son of the living God. Thus, the gospels are just that: "gospels," the good news of the work of God in Christ. They are from beginning to end colored by the faith of the church, and any attempt *finally* to distinguish the "facts" of the life of Jesus from the interpretations of the early believers is foredoomed to failure. Not only the Gospel of John, but also the Synoptics are *interpretations* of Jesus, though the Synoptics are relatively more accurate in their historical detail.

Further, the recognition that liberalism had erred in stripping away from the picture of the "historical Jesus" those elements which seemed foreign to the modern mind, and the appreciation of the characteristics of the gospels, led to new understandings of both the unity and the plurality of the New Testament witness. On the one side, it was no longer possible to say that Paul distorted the simplicity of the original gospel by the interjection of "theological" interpretations foreign to it. The gospel of Jesus was in fact not so simple. The Jesus of history is no less distant from modern human beings (and no less relevant to them!) than the faith of Paul. Moreover, as Martin Kähler (and P. T. Forsyth in England) had earlier contended, the faith in Jesus as the Christ is so integral to the entirety of the New Testament that none of his teaching (whether about God, the kingdom, or the ethical

[4] Albert Schweitzer *The Quest of the Historical Jesus* (New York, 1948), p. 397.

demand) can be lifted out of the context of faith in his person. The New Testament has to be considered as a whole, and the point from which Christian thinking begins is the Jesus Christ whose life, death, resurrection, and redemptive power are realities to which the whole of the New Testament attests. On the other side, the distinctive points of view of the several gospels and the other writings had to be recognized more explicitly, so that the New Testament could be seen to contain several Christologies, not just one.

Another major step in biblical interpretation came with the proposal of Rudolf Bultmann, first made in 1941 but considered to be a matter of general debate only after the war, that the New Testament must be "demythologized." This did not mean, as liberal theology had assumed, that the mythological elements in the New Testament picture could be set aside. On the contrary, the truth is to be seen precisely *in* the mythological statements. We cannot accept the mythological worldview of the Bible, with its three-story universe and its depiction of God as a supernatural being intervening in natural processes. Our science cannot be primitive science. But we can understand the purpose and meaning of the myth if we ask the right questions, which are not questions about an objective picture of the world but questions about the nature and meaning of human existence. "The real purpose of myth is . . . to express man's understanding of himself in the world in which he lives." The kerygma is an assertion that God has acted decisively in Christ and that a decision of faith is called for. But this proclamation must be interpreted existentially. The gospel message is one of a decisive change, in response to God's act, from inauthentic to authentic existence. That is the transition from life in sin to life in faith under God. Thus demythologizing, a process that already began in the writings of Paul and in the Fourth Gospel, is in fact existentialist interpretation; we need consciously to use existentialist categories in understanding the meaning of the biblical myths. (Here Bultmann found the philosophy of Heidegger of special value in analyzing the categories of existence, and it was the explicit appeal to such categories that offended Karl Barth and led to intense debate in the 1950s.)

3) This further development of biblical interpretation was closely related to a wider appreciation of the extent to which all human knowing is colored by the point of view, the location in time and space, of the knower. All institutions and ideas — political, economic, scientific, moral, and religious — are influenced by their particular historical and social environments. All visions of truth are the apprehensions of persons in definite historical situations and are in part shaped by the perspectives of those situations.

One aspect of this problem we saw in the failure of the liberal attempt to portray Jesus in the categories of the nineteenth century, for liberalism had overlooked the significance of the vast difference of perspective between a Jew of the first century and a Western European of the nineteenth. Jesus' teachings could not simply be abstracted from their context, for to understand the content of his message one had to see it from the standpoint of his own time, to think in the same historically conditioned terms in which he thought. Similarly, the creeds of the church could be understood only in the terms of their historical backgrounds and contexts. So also, the religious intuitions of nineteenth- and twentieth-century Christians could not be taken as complete and finally valid interpretations of Christian truth, but rather as views determined in part by the outlook of contemporary Western civilization.

Thus, the question of authority and finality in Christian faith had to be reexamined at every level. On one level, this concerned the claim of Christianity to be the final or highest religion. Liberalism had destroyed the appeal to miracles and to prophecy as "proofs" of the truth of Christianity, but had found the superiority of Christianity in its higher ethical ideals and the nobility of its conception of God. Now, however, it had to be recognized that even these ethical criteria were peculiarly part of a Western tradition strongly influenced by Christian contexts.

At the level of the statement of the Christian faith itself, however, the problem was no less acute, particularly with respect to liberalism's appeal to religious experience as the ultimate authority. In turning to the "Christian consciousness" or "value judgments" or "abiding experiences" as the norm of religious truth, liberalism had tended to lose the sense of an objectively "given" Christian message. And what liberalism placed at the center of attention and tried to make the foundation of Christian thought was precisely the subjective element which is most obviously conditioned by its cultural context. "Religious experience" could have even less claim to objectivity and permanence than Bible or creed.

Yet the church has lived by the conviction that it has indeed a gospel, a word which is not simply the voice of present consciences or the consciences and beliefs of past ages, but a word of truth and deliverance from One who transcends the relativities of time and space. The question then is: What is it that the church has to preach which is not simply bound to particular historical and social perspectives of past and present times? If the gospel cannot be identified with Bible or creed or religious experience, what is it? And if all human conceptions and experience are historically conditioned, how can Christians of one generation share in the convictions and experiences of those of an earlier generation? How can the gospel be communicated from one social context to another? Clearly, the problem of stating and transmitting the gospel has become infinitely more complex and requires a more profound understanding of the meaning of revelation.

4) A fourth feature of the new theological situation was the renewed study of the Protestant Reformation. This was stimulated especially by the German (and later Scandinavian) "Luther-research" of the early twentieth century. Luther had commonly been interpreted through the eyes of the later Lutheran scholasticism (see Ch. IV), but now it was seen that Luther was a far more lively and diverse thinker than his Lutheran commentators, and at many points they had gravely distorted his teaching. Central in the reinterpretation of Luther was the recognition of his utter theocentricity (God-centeredness), of his conception of faith as free communion with God rather than a religious quality of the believer, and of his appreciation that evil originates at a deeper level than the psychological or sociological. These aspects of Luther's thought were particularly important in revealing the profound relevance of the classical Protestant understanding of the gospel to the religious situation of the twentieth century. Thus, the study of Luther directed attention also to the whole of the Reformation and to the distinctive character of the Protestant witness.

5) Similarly, the twentieth-century theological situation has been affected by a more vivid awareness of the numerous voices in the nineteenth century which had spoken out against the prevailing trends of the time. There were those conservative strains of thought which, while they did not go the way of American fundamentalism, were yet severely critical of liberalism. This was particularly important in Germany and Scandinavia, where parallel to the liberal trend there was a less obvious but nevertheless active resurgence of biblical and pietistic Protestantism. In this movement there was a vigorous protest against the "subjectivism" and optimism of liberal theology, together with an insistence upon the essential unity of the New Testament witness, upon the validity of classical Christian affirmations, and upon the objective reality of a revelation and redemption which came to sinful humanity from the transcendent, holy, and merciful God. When the structure of liberalism began to totter, this conservative line of thought helped to provide the basis for a more sober reappraisal of the Christian tradition.

There were also throughout the nineteenth century occasional prophetic voices which anticipated (and influenced) the later critique of liberalism. The Danish writer Søren Kierkegaard (d. 1855), for example, protested vehemently against the identification of Christianity with "Christendom," against the easy assumptions that a culture could become Christian or that an individual could become a Christian simply by growing up in a "Christian" culture, against the reduction of Christian truth to "rational" systems, and against the philosophies of immanence. Christianity, he insisted, teaches an "infinite qualitative distinction between time and eternity," a paradoxical gospel of divine love and incarnation before which the human mind can only confess its utter inadequacy; a radical, even impossible demand for love of the neighbor; the utter precariousness of the human situation, which inevitably leads to anxiety over one's life and destiny and thence to self-centered rebellion against God; the absolute necessity for radical decision in the transition (the "leap") from sin and unfaith to faith; and the paradoxical nature of faith as a wholly God-given "comforted despair."

The recovery of Kierkegaard had much to do with the emergence of a variety of "existentialisms," which focused attention on the nature of personal existence as the prime philosophical question. Here the question of truth is a question of the meaning of life. It is a religious and ethical question, a question of freedom and destiny. One is concerned with truth that makes a difference. One cannot be a neutral, uncommitted spectator. One must think as an "existing individual" who is directly involved in the question. And this kind of thinking always involves decision, a choosing in the face of all the possibilities that the future continually presents. Thinking and acting are inseparable. We must decide what is true for us; our own destiny is at stake, for by choosing we make ourselves what we are. Thus the question of "time" takes on a special significance. Each moment is fraught with significance, as the point of decision. At every moment we are confronted by the question of our own being, of our relation to others, of future possibilities and the eternal. In some cases (e.g., in Tillich and Bultmann, though in differing ways), existentialist categories were taken up formally and explicitly into the fabric of theology. Much more broadly, however, existentialist themes were taken up in theological reflection on the meaning of faith, on the nature of human goodness and evil, and on eschatology.

A vivid sense of tragedy and estrangement in life was reflected also in the novels of the Russian Fyodor Dostoyevsky. In contrast to the dominant nineteenth-century appeal to the indefinite perfectibility of man, he pointed graphically to the actual and patent cruelty, torment, and pathos of life, to the suffering and humiliation as well as the exaltation of the human spirit. Both Dostoyevsky and Kierkegaard wrote as Christians. Friedrich Nietzsche, though wholly antagonistic to Christianity, whose ethic he condemned as a morality of weakness and pity, and whose influence he thought to be degrading, nonetheless saw more clearly than the liberal theologians the extreme character of the Christian ethic. As against the easy compromise of liberalism with the ethos of the nineteenth century, he emphasized the stark contrast between the Christian demand for compassion and self-sacri-

ficing love, and the ethic of self-affirmation and will to power which
he thought to be both appropriate to the ennobling of human existence
and the proper outcome of an evolutionary outlook. And while he
opposed it utterly, he showed the entire "transvaluation" of values
which Christianity had effected in ancient modes of thought.

6) Finally, the theological situation between the wars was beginning
to be altered by other trends in philosophy and psychology (e.g., the
philosophy of process, the growing interest in the analysis of language
and symbol, and the emergence of depth psychology as a dominant
force in culture). We need to return, in Chapter XIV, to the consequences of some of these phenomena.

Theological Reconstruction

As we have indicated earlier, a prominent motif in the Protestant
thought that emerged in the decades following World War I was a
renewed appreciation of traditional Christian modes of thinking. There
was a mood of increased sympathy with the biblical point of view,
with the creeds and doctrines of the church, and with the principles
of the Protestant reformers. Thus in an important sense the theological
emphases that came to occupy the center of the stage well into the
1950s can be described as a return to the past, a reaction against
liberal interpretations and a revival of "classical" patterns of thought.
Hence such terms as "neo-orthodoxy" and "neo-Protestantism" have
often been used to refer to the new theologies. "Dialectical theology"
has been another frequent designation, and it may help to suggest
that the spirit of the new movements was not simply a study of the
past for its own sake, or a kind of conservatism that sought to preserve
the stable and "secure" patterns of the past in the flux of present. It
was rather a revolutionary spirit that recalled the past because it found
there, precisely in those elements of the tradition that were minimized
or nearly forgotten by liberalism, principles that are relevant to the
problems of the present. The new theologies returned to Paul, Augustine, Luther, and Calvin because they found in them the means to
renewed understanding and appreciation of the gospel.

In the following summary of characteristic themes of Protestant
thought "between the wars," therefore, it will be convenient to focus
on distinctive motifs that represent reactions to liberal tendencies and
the reappropriation of classical Christian categories. But it must always
be kept in mind that the purpose of this rethinking of Christian faith
was neither that of simple attack on liberalism nor that of a return
to traditional views, but rather of renewed understanding of the relevance of the Christian message to the human situation. Thus, the

revival of traditional categories also meant their reinterpretation, and to this process the insights of liberalism contributed much.

The Sovereignty of God

If the divine immanence was a primary concern of the liberal conception of God, the newer Protestant thought emphasized the transcendence, the otherness, the sovereignty of God. The nineteenth-century doctrine of immanence emphasized the presence of God "in us," the identification of God with the goodness of the world, and of the divine activity with the progressive realization of human goals. But such a view was possible only in the context of the nineteenth-century outlook, and with the sobering realization of the falsity of the nineteenth century's optimism and confidence in humanity, renewed validity was seen in the traditional conceptions of God's transcendence over and judgment upon all finite existence. The limitations of all human perspectives and ideals were brought sharply into view. The liberal doctrine of immanence was seen to be, not simply a recognition of the divine working in the world process, but also a subtle self-worship through the identification of human ideals and plans with God's good.

The new emphasis on transcendence could be expressed in many ways. In Karl Barth's early work, God could be described as "totally other." In his more mature thinking, Barth came to speak of God's utter freedom in loving, so that God always remains the Subject in the action and only becomes "object" as the gracious divine act allows (or better, invites) the human creature to know God and to be free for God in the revelation and reconciliation in Jesus Christ. Paul Tillich could speak of "God beyond God" (i.e., beyond the finite deity of popular religion), and insist that God is never to be thought of as "a being" but rather as the ground and depth of being, or "being itself." H. Richard Niebuhr could write of a radical monotheism, in which God is the ultimate center of being and value, in contrast to all henotheisms in which something partial and finite is made the object of devotion and loyalty. Rudolf Bultmann could speak of the radical dependence of all history and nature on the transcendent God, but in such a way that God's action is never directly identical with worldly events but always paradoxical and hidden, known only in faith's response to the kerygma.

The rejection of "immanentism" did not mean the denial of God's active and continuous relation to the world. On the contrary, it was emphasized even more strongly that God's activity enters into the determination of all existence, life, and action. God acts not simply as one inward working power among others, but as One who is the Lord of history and nature, the source and ground of all that is. But God is eternally God — radically distinct from all creaturely existence, the free and living Lord. This means that God's goodness cannot be known simply by inspection of human goodness, but is always judgment upon finite goodness. Though there is no moment of history in which God is not active, that being and action are never exhausted in history. God transcends the whole of history, as known but also hidden.

The liberal view, in other words, had tended to bind God's activity to an immanent working in the orderly processes of history and nature. It had enclosed God in the "one-story" world of natural law which modern science had created. The ancient "three-story" universe, in which the world of history and nature was encompassed by heaven and hell, and thus controlled by forces from above and below, had been contracted by a scientific picture which explained the entire universe as ordered by a single pattern of natural process. Liberalism had sought to find room for God simply within this flattened world and had lost the dimensions both of height and of depth. But the God of Christian faith could not be contained in such a perspective. Liberalism had been right in denying that God works only in the gaps of natural process, or only occasionally, but it had failed to give due recognition to the transcendence and freedom of the Creator in acting in and upon creation.

The problem may be put in a different way by reference to the appeal to religious experience. For liberalism, God became essentially the counterpart of religious experience, and revelation tended to become identical with history (Ritschl) or religious experience (Schleiermacher). The primary reality, the one directly known, was religious experience. Of course, religious experience involved an objective ground or source of the subjective experience, viz., God. But God then is defined simply as the source of religious experience, and the reality of God is logically dependent upon the reality of religion. The existence of God is argued from the existence of religion, and the nature of God is discovered from the nature of religious experience.

The point of this is that, as it seemed to more recent thought, a terrible inversion had taken place. Religion had been substituted for God. The process was similar to the later development of Lutheranism, in which the doctrine of justification by faith in God had been subtly transformed into faith in faith itself (i.e., into a confidence in the saving power of faith rather than of the God of faith). Now liberalism had fallen before the same temptation by putting the emphasis on religion rather than on God. As H. R. Niebuhr wrote,

> Religion became . . . the enhancer of life, the creator of spiritual and social energy, the redeemer of man from evil, the builder of the beloved community, the integrator of the great spiritual values; the God of religion, however, came to be a necessary auxiliary, though it could be questioned whether a real God was necessary to religion or only a vivid

idea of God. The term "religionist" which has been invented in modern times applies aptly to those who follow the tendency inaugurated in part by Schleiermacher, for religion is the object of concern and the source of strength for them rather than the God whom an active faith regards as alone worthy of supreme devotion.[5]

(The accuracy of this statement can be tested by anyone who will note how frequently "religion" or "faith" has been appealed to as the way out of social crises, not only by ministers, but by countless "religiously minded" journalists and even politicians.)

Here, then, is the aim of the emphasis on the sovereignty of God. It is to be true to the Christian witness to the absolute primacy of God, to rebut again the perennial tendency to the "inversion of faith whereby man puts himself into the center, constructs an anthropocentric universe and makes confidence in his own value rather than faith in God his beginning."[6] Christian faith does not point primarily to Christianity, it points to God. At the center is not faith or religious experience (or church or creed) but only the God of Jesus Christ. And it is impossible to speak of God simply by speaking of humanity in a very loud voice.

From this perspective, the function of the church is clarified. The church exists for the purpose of bearing single-minded witness to the God of Christian faith. It is neither an association for the cultivation of pious feelings nor a society for the promotion of culture. Indeed, in directing attention to the God of faith, Christian faith declares the falsity of all idolatry, which would put anything other than God at the center, whether faith, or religious institution, or nation, or culture. It points to the finitude and relativity of human insights and ideals, and to the estrangement from God which is sin, but first and finally to God.

This stress on the primacy of God over all religion and culture was in no small measure a reappropriation of the radical theocentricity of Luther and Calvin. It also involved a deeper appreciation of the biblical perspective. Thus Karl Barth could speak of the discovery of a "strange new world within the Bible," the world of God. The biblical perspective was also evident in a recognition that Christian faith must speak of God's wrath and judgment as well as mercy and love — not in the sense of capricious or vengeful judgment, but the inevitable judgment of love itself upon the denials of love which haunt all human achievements. It is a judgment upon pretension and pride, upon all efforts to make absolutes out of the finite and relative (i.e., upon the modern idolatries of self and society). Therefore, God's love is seen, as the reformers also understood it, as paradoxical and strange by

---

[5] H. R. Niebuhr, *The Meaning of Revelation* (New York, 1941), p. 28.

[6] *Ibid.,* p. 31.

ordinary standards, given quite without regard for "merit," given freely not because of what human beings are but in spite of what they are.

Revelation

The renewed emphasis on the sovereignty and transcendence of God was intimately related to a profound concern for *revelation* as a source of the knowledge of God and the basis for Christian thinking.

This concern came to be widely expressed in stress on the "I-Thou" character of the relationship to God (i.e., the exclusively personal nature of the relation of God and self). Here the Jewish philosopher Martin Buber's famous book, *I and Thou* (1923), was of much influence (much more on Protestant than on Jewish thought). The contrast is between an I-It relationship, which is analytical, objective, and instrumental, and an I-Thou relationship, which is distinctively human and personal, involving genuine encounter and mutuality. The relation to God must be of the latter sort. God is not neuter, an It, an object about which one may speak as if its presence or absence were a matter of indifference. God is not known by argument about an ultimate cause, but as the eternally present Thou who meets us as a personal subject. God "confronts" us, comes to us as One who is over-against us and lays claim upon us. God meets us with the demand for acceptance or rejection, the demand for faith. Faith is therefore always *decision*. In the personal encounter with God, a decision must be made — for or against obedience or rebellion, faith or unfaith.[7]

In the new reassertion that revelation is the ground of all Christian affirmations, there is no return to the view that God has revealed certain truths or propositions which could be called "revealed truth" and identified with the words of the Bible or the creeds. The work of historical criticism cannot be undone. The fundamentalist notion of an inerrant Bible is not only untenable; it is a form of idolatry, a kind of perversion that exalts the finite and fallible to a place of authority belonging to God alone. In contrast, the new view insisted that the content of revelation is *God*, not Scripture or creed or tradition. Revelation means, simply, God personally present, God's self-disclosure.

So far, the understanding or revelation was not all that different from the liberal stress on religious experience. Liberalism, and before it Pietism and the Reformation, had seen that God and faith belong together, that God is known only as one responds in faith, and that God is wholly personal. Many in the nineteenth century had distinguished between revelation *about* God and revelation *of* God. But the connotation of the new emphasis was quite different from that of

[7] These themes are sharply expressed, for example, in Emil Brunner, *The Divine-Human Encounter* (Philadelphia, 1943).

liberalism. For now the stress was not on the human discovery of
the divine, but on God's act of self-manifestation; not on the continuity
of the human and the divine, which makes easy the ascent to God,
but on the distance and the estrangement of humanity from God,
which makes God's coming in revelation and reconciliation a radical
and paradoxical event. *God* reveals to faith. As Karl Barth most dramatically put it, only from the standpoint of God's self-disclosure can we
learn that any other attempt to know God is false and impossible.
God's Word stands in judgment of all human words and conceptions.
The final court of appeal is not rational norms, nor conscience nor
experience, but the self-revelation of God, and there is a "given-ness"
in this act that makes it always "over-against" the human subject.

Another frequent way of expressing the centrality of revelation was
in the language of the divine act. God reveals in act or deed, rather
than in the form of propositions or truths. The Bible is the book of
the acts of God. God works in historical events, being thus present
to human beings in judgment and redemption. All statements or propositions are statements about God's activity and are human, fallible
assertions that can never be adequate to express the reality to which
they point. Revelation is thus an event, though it is only *in faith* that
God is known in the event. There is revelation in Jesus Christ as
human beings are enabled to see in him "God reconciling the world
to himself." The facts about Jesus' teaching and life are inseparable
from faith's witness to incarnation and resurrection, to reconciliation
or the overcoming of estrangement (i.e., from faith's witness to the
activity of God of which the words and deeds of Jesus are a part) or,
in Tillich's language, from the acknowledgment of Jesus as the Christ.

Such a view of revelation tends to stress the absolute centrality of
Jesus Christ, the once-for-allness (*Einmaligkeit*) of this event. Christ
is, uniquely, the revelation. Not many were to go so far as Barth's
insistence on the exclusive nature of the revelation in Christ (i.e.,
that all theological truth derives simply from the knowledge of God
in Christ). Indeed, the issue of a natural theology or a "general" revelation to which the revelation in Christ could be positively related became
a center of controversy in which Barth dissociated himself from Brunner and other of his early associates. But it was insisted on all sides
that all Christian thought of revelation finds its norm in Christ. He
is the decisive event, and Christian faith is unequivocally faith in him.

Other distinctive formulations may be noted. For Paul Tillich, in
the language of his method of correlation, in which "answers" from
the kerygma are seen to correspond to the "questions" of the human
situation, revelation is the answer to the deepest questions of reason.
And Christ as the New Being is the answer to the question of the
overcoming of estrangement in existence. For H. R. Niebuhr, revelation is not so much a content as the giving of a point of view from
which interpretation begins.

Throughout, the renewed emphasis on revelation gave a far more important place to the Bible than was characteristic of liberalism and involved at least a partial return to the classical Protestant norm, *sola scriptura*. For liberal theology, the Bible was important as a record of developing religious experience, and especially as a record of the experience of the earliest Christians — but in the last analysis the Bible tended to be judged by modern religious experience. The final test of religious truth was always the reason, conscience, and experience of the believer. Subsequent theology tended to reverse this order of priority. As more than one writer put it, the conceptions of the Bible are to be taken at least as seriously as our own conceptions. For the Bible is related to the revelation of God in a unique and authoritative way.

It needs repeating that this does not make the Bible an inerrant collection of religious truths. Throughout, the Bible must be understood to be conditioned by the relative historical situations of those whose words appear in it. Nevertheless, the witness of Scripture is crucial and indispensable; it is authoritative for Christian thought and life. For one thing, it speaks uniquely of the utter priority of God. More particularly, it is the testimony to the revelation of God in Jesus Christ — and not only in the events of his life, death, and resurrection, but also in the dealings of God with humanity in the history of the Hebrews in anticipation of the coming of the Messiah, in the fulfillment of reconciliation and revelation in the community of faith, and in the final fulfillment of history. The revelation of God is Jesus Christ, but that revelation is mediated to us through the Scriptures. At this point, one recalls Luther's view that the Bible is the cradle in which Christ is laid.

Moreover, the Bible is not simply the record of revelation; it is itself part of the event of revelation, both as a human response to the divine act and as a medium of communication of revelation. The act of revelation is complete only as it is received by human beings. Thus, in Barth's language, every word of the Bible is a human word, yet every word of Scripture can *become* the Word of God as it speaks to the heart of the believer. Or, in Tillich's words, "the Bible is both original event and original document; it witnesses to that of which it is a part."[8] While the Bible accepted as such cannot be as *absolute* authority (this belongs only to God), it does have *relative* authority over the preaching of the church and individual experience. It provides the norm by which both personal experience and the teachings of the church are to be judged. To put it another way, the biblical symbols have a permanent significance for the understanding and communication of the gospel. They cannot be simply discarded for more "modern" conceptions. In Reinhold Niebuhr's language, such symbols as the

---

[8] Paul Tillich, *Systematic Theology* (Chicago, 1951) Vol. I, p. 35.

creation story, the story of the Fall, and the last judgment are not to be taken literally (as simple historical accounts), but they must be taken seriously, for they point to realities that can be described only in symbolic language.

The Person of Christ

One of the great gains of liberal theology was its rediscovery of the humanity of Jesus. From the point of view of subsequent Protestant thought, however, the liberal concern with the "historical Jesus" left little room for the recognition that he is also more than a man. Thus it was felt that liberalism departed both from the Christian tradition and from the biblical witness at a crucial point. For if we are to be fair to the New Testament, we must see that at its very center is the confession that Jesus is the Lord, that God was truly in him. Whatever is said about his life and his teaching is there only because of the faith that in him God was present, and that in his life and death and resurrection God was "reconciling the world to himself" (II Cor. 5:19)." Jesus as man is significant for the New Testament writers just because in this man "all the fullness of God was pleased to dwell" (Col. I:19).

This, then, is the center of the Christian faith. However much liberalism was right in insisting on the genuine humanity of Jesus, Christianity cannot be content with any view of Jesus Christ which does not make explicit his "uniqueness." Uniqueness here is not a matter of degree; it means radical difference, real discontinuity. Such terms as "religious genius," teacher, and prophet, are not at all adequate to express what Christian faith sees in Christ. He is more than a prophet, for a prophet is a bearer of the Word of God and has no authority in himself but only in the Word which he bears. But Jesus is himself the Word. He is the revelation of God not because of what he says about the nature of God but because God is personally present there, seeking the response of faith. It is not enough to say that Jesus teaches and exemplifies the mercy and forgiveness of God; he *is* the mercy and forgiveness of God. He is in himself — in his coming, his life, his death, his resurrection — the divine act of forgiveness. Thus, Christian faith is not essentially a matter of believing *with* Christ, it is believing *in* Christ.

The real humanity of Christ is to be maintained rigorously. Jesus was a man, a Jew of the first century, and to the "disinterested" or neutral observer he may appear as no more than a moral and religious teacher who lived a good life, collected a group of followers, and was put to death for his pains. But Christian faith sees in these events the presence and action of God and therefore acknowledges Jesus Christ as Lord. It perceives that hidden in this historically conditioned life is none other than the Lord of history, come in the form of a servant, disclosing incomprehensible love and redeeming power in the self-giving, the authoritative demand for repentance and faith, the suffering, dying and rising again, of the man Jesus of Nazareth.

Thus came a renewed appreciation of the relevance of the traditional doctrines about Christ as the Godman, truly God and truly human. The creeds do not explain this fact, and were not intended to do so. They were intended to express a mystery which is finally beyond human understanding, for God is ever beyond our comprehension. But the classical affirmations of the church, even though subject to frequent misinterpretation, nonetheless gave explicit expression to the central confession that in Jesus Christ we have to do not only with a man but with God, with eternity as well as time, the infinite as well as the finite — and this cannot be abandoned without falsifying the revelation itself.

Similarly, the doctrine of the Trinity returned to occupy a more vital place in Protestant thinking. For it is seen that if Christ is indeed the revelation of God, then Christian thinking about God must always start with that revelation. Belief in Christ is not something merely added to a previously held belief in God. Rather, belief in Christ involves a startlingly new apprehension of God. God is the same Lord of Old Testament faith, but now revealed in a new and fuller way. The Christian speaks of "God" as the One who has come in the Incarnation and the Holy Spirit, and therefore One who must be called Father, Son, and Holy Spirit.

Human Nature and Sin

The most hotly debated aspect of Protestant thinking in the decades following the First World War was doubtless the conception of human sin. Here the revolt against liberalism was most obvious and was reinforced by the course of historical events and the discoveries of modern psychology. The result was a quite conclusive repudiation of the optimism of the late nineteenth century, and an explicit and thoroughgoing recognition of the tragic aspects of human existence, of the precariousness of human achievements, and of the depths to which human action can and does descend. Even language about "total depravity" and an "obliteration" of the image of God could be revived.

This new emphasis did not mean a rejection of the liberal insistence on the goodness of the human being as a creature of God, or of human dignity and worth. The nineteenth century, in accord with the basic Christian tradition, was quite correct in asserting that human existence is neither "innately" nor "by nature" evil. The human creature is indeed made "in the image of God," and the limits of human capacity for goodness and creativity are indeterminate. So far, the new theology could go with the nineteenth century. But in two respects it insisted that the classical doctrines of the human condition (especially as understood by the reformers) were more adequate than the liberal notions.

First, human beings are creatures; they are not divine nor do they become divine — this some liberal thinkers occasionally forgot. Second, history is characterized throughout by a profound and tragic denial of the purpose of human existence. That was the lesson driven home by two world wars, by the rise of Nazism and Fascism, and (though not appreciated fully until later) by the horror of the Holocaust. There one could see demonstrated anew what was meant by sin, and it had to be defined as rebellion against God (see the English title of one of Brunner's major works, *Man in Revolt,* 1937), a distortion and estrangement so deeply rooted in the human self that it can be overcome only by the redeeming activity of God. Thus Reinhold Niebuhr, the most prominent American writer on the theme, described the Christian view as involving a "high estimate of human nature" (i.e., as created in the image of God) and a "low estimate of human virtue."[9]

The new analysis of sin also revived the notion of "original sin." That doctrine had been quite consistently rejected by nineteenth-century liberalism as both a slur on human dignity and a relic of the outworn idea of the infallibility of Scripture, for traditionally the basis of the doctrine had been found in the story of the "Fall" in Genesis 3. Together with liberalism, more recent Protestant thought rejected the ideas of a "historical fall" and of a biological inheritance of sin and guilt. But it judged that the concept of original sin points to a reality which is independent of both these ideas, viz., the fact that all are sinners and that every aspect of human life is involved in sin. The "Fall" is not an event which occurred in the far distant past; it is the turning away from God which is characteristic of every human life and action. In Niebuhr's provocative language, sin is not *necessary* (i.e., there is nothing in human nature that requires it) but sin is *inevitable* (i.e., it always occurs).

Sin is not to be identified with "wrong acts"; it is rather a distortion and perversion which exists at the center of the self. Nor is sin to be identified with the body, for the body is good and all sin has its origin in the spirit. ("Sensuality" is the self's denial of its own freedom and responsibility by an attempt to lose itself in physical nature.) Sin is the opposite of faith (i.e., it is the placing of ultimate trust in anything less than God). It is the opposite of love, it is the self turned inward. Essentially, sin may be defined as self-centered denial of responsibility to God, and it appears most universally and subtly — and most dangerously — in the various forms of pride (i.e., in the assertion of self by the denial of creaturely limitation). This may be the pride of power,

---

[9] *The Nature and Destiny of Man* (New York, 1941), Vol. I, p. 16. Chapters 7 and 8 of that volume constitute one of the powerful analyses of the dynamics of sin in modern literature. We have drawn on Niebuhr's description in the following summary.

which imagines itself completely master of its own existence and destiny. It may be the frantic will-to-power which seeks final security in itself by mastery over others. It may be the pride of intellect, or moral or spiritual pride, which imagines its own conceptions and values to be free from all taint of self-interest and thereby arrogates to itself divine authority. No aspect of life is free from such perversion — certainly not religion, where the temptation to prideful self-assertion is peculiarly subtle and dangerous. Every claim to infallibility or perfection is a form of self-righteousness and self-deification which leads to the attempt at mastery over others. Even the highest idealism is subject to transformation into an instrument of self-will and thereby injustice. And so every pursuit of self-interest cloaks itself in the guise of moral idealism. Moreover, egoism may be both individual and collective (i.e., it may be expressed by societies as well as individuals). Thus, all human achievements — moral, religious, political, economic, cultural — are involved in the corruption of sin. And the revelation of God in Jesus Christ is a judgment upon self-will and pretension.

Here is explicitly recalled the tradition of the Reformation: sin is universal, and it is total in the sense that no area of human life is exempt from the perversion of pride and self-centeredness and that all human actions involve at least a partial betrayal of responsibility to God (see Ch. II). One important qualification must be added: *the standard by which all are judged to be sinners is Jesus Christ.* It is not asserted that human life is simply or wholly without goodness. Indeed, no arbitrary limits can be placed on human capacity for good, and some actions are vastly better than others. But when individuals measure themselves by their obligation to God as revealed in Christ, they confess their continual betrayal of that responsibility.

History and the Kingdom of God

The chastening of the liberal faith in humanity inevitably had a profound effect on the social gospel, particularly as regards its confidence in the possibility of "building the kingdom of God on earth." This has not meant a denial of the church's obligation to speak to the social orders as well as to individuals. That central concern of the social gospel has continued. But the confident assumption that the social order might be progressively transformed into the kingdom of God had to be rejected. Its place was taken by a more vivid sense of divine judgment upon all human history and by a new understanding of the hope of the kingdom of God.

God's judgment is acknowledged to apply to all social structures and programs. (And this includes the church, which is involved both in religious pretension and in the economic, social, and racial injustice of society as a whole.) No social institution is free from the limitations

of human finitude or the temptations of self-justification and rational-
ization. Therefore, all utopian hopes and schemes are naive and self-
deceived — whether these be the programs of Marxist communism
or evolutionary socialism or free enterprise. Every scheme for the
solution of humanity's ills is subject to transformation into an instrument of power for the sake of the dominant groups, whether capital
or labor or bureaucracy. This fact, and the growing complexity of
social problems which requires vastly increased technical knowledge
in sociology and economics, means that no social order or proposal
for reform can be simply identified with the will of God. The responsibility of the church is therefore constantly to confront the existing
order (including itself) with the judgment of the law of love and to
seek positive ways for the establishment of relatively more just relations
among individuals and groups. It is to work for "proximate solutions"
to problems which continually recur in new forms, for every creative
achievement brings new possibilities of injustice. A full recognition
of the depth and power of evil requires a more sober estimate than
that of the earlier social gospel regarding the possibilities of achieving
a just social order. "Christian realism" requires more explicit recognition of the use of economic and political power as instruments of
love and as means of restraining evil.[10]

Let us repeat, the renewed appreciation of traditional Christian
insights into the depth of sin, and the consequent rejection of nineteenth-century optimism about social progress, has not meant a return
to a gospel for individuals only. The concern of the Christian faith
with the structures of society is firmly maintained. But the hope of
Christians is seen to point beyond history.

[10] At this point, we must note the vigorous discussion of the extent to which the
church ought to ally itself with particular social programs. It came to be generally
agreed that the church must proclaim the judgment of the gospel upon all forms
of injustice. It was also agreed that the church cannot accept any social program
or institution as a pure expression of the will of God and the solution of human
problems; every program remains under judgment. But there remained sharp disagreement concerning the church's responsibility to give qualified support to political
and economic patterns which seem to give relatively better expression to the Christian
demand for love and justice.

In part, this reflected a difference between Continental European and American
thought. It came to expression particularly in discussions within the "ecumenical"
movement (see Ch. XIII), in relation to the question of the nature of the Christian
hope. Does the Christian hope (as symbolized by the kingdom of God) refer exclusively to God's establishment of the kingdom "beyond" or "at the end" of history,
or does it include also present manifestations of the kingdom in relatively more
just social patterns which the church must explicitly support? The importance of
this problem is seen in the fact that it was the central theme of the meeting of the
World Council of Churches in 1954, at Evanston, Ill.

In the discussion in the text, we have sought to restrict ourselves to those general
tendencies of thought which influenced both of these points of view.

To put this in other words, the kingdom of God is not the end product of a progressive "Christianizing" of the social order. That notion of the kingdom was more the reflection of a nineteenth-century evolutionary outlook than of the New Testament hope. The kingdom of God, in the New Testament hope, is wholly *God's* kingdom, not to be established by any human effort but solely at the divine initiative. The responsibility of human beings is not that of "building" the kingdom but of "readiness" for its coming, by repentance and faith. Moreover, the kingdom is not a continuation of historical development. It symbolizes the end of the present age; it stands "beyond" this history.

In this biblical understanding of the kingdom of God, Protestant thinking sees a true parable of the Christian hope and of the meaning of history. Of course, the biblical idea of the kingdom of God is a symbol, for all thinking about the end or the goal of history must be in the form of symbol or picture. But the biblical symbol (which itself includes a variety of detailed pictures of the end) is more adequate to express the Christian understanding of history than any other symbol. It refers to a divine purpose for the whole of history, to an ultimate judgment and fulfillment of individual and social life, to the full "rule" of God. This is not to be separated from the present Lordship of God. Indeed, it is just in the sovereignty of God as manifested in Christ that the hope of the kingdom is founded. Christ is the "center" of history. In him the victory of God is disclosed. In him the kingdom of God is present. So also it is always "at hand," in judgment and promise, confronting us with the claim of God's rule. It may be present in all the partial realizations of God's will in history. But all partial realizations find their meaning and fulfillment in the fullness of the kingdom, which stands always "over-against" or at the "end" of history. This kingdom is the promise of the final victory over evil. The hope of the Christian reaches always beyond the accomplishments or failures of the present to an ultimate fulfillment of personal and social destiny whereby all that is good in history is preserved and completed.

CHAPTER XIII

The Ecumenical Movement

The Problem of Diversity

Nothing has caused more difficulty in the understanding of Protestantism than the problem of diversity and unity. Particularly is this true in the American scene, where well over 250 Protestant denominations may be counted, ranging in size from the more than 13 million members of the Southern Baptist Convention to the mere handfuls of members in those denominations which are composed of only one or two congregations. To the varieties of European Protestantism which have been brought to the United States by immigration there have been added scores of new and divergent bodies, so that often the word "Protestant" seems only a vague catch-all classification for a bewildering mosaic of religious organizations. American Christianity has of course been strongly influenced by the peculiar individualism of the American temper as well as by unique social influences. But the problem of ecclesiastical divisions has been with Protestantism from the beginning, and in order to understand the trend toward church unity (often called the "ecumenical" movement) which has come increasingly to the fore in Protestant thought and action since the beginning of the twentieth century, we need to look more closely at the nature of this Protestant diversity.

The Reformation was neither a simple nor an isolated phenomenon. It was a religious revolution which took place in the midst of several other revolutions: an economic revolution, marked by the breakdown of feudalism, the stirring of the lower classes, the beginnings of modern capitalism, the rise of the middle class, and the discoveries of the fifteenth- and sixteenth-century explorers; a literary revolution wrought by the printing press; a cultural revolution, the Renaissance; a scientific revolution, centering in the discoveries of astronomy; and a political revolution, the rise of national states. All these movements were of profound influence in determining the course of Protestant development. (The growth of national states, for example, contributed both to the success of the original break with Rome and to the ordering of the churches into national units in the case of Lutheranism and Anglicanism.)

Moreover, the Reformation was itself a complex movement, comprising three relatively distinct branches: the Lutheran and Reformed traditions, which were themselves sharply divided at several points; the radical or Anabaptist wing of the Reformation, which included a wide variety of sectarian groups; and the Anglican church, which took its theology partly from the Continent but which had its inception in a quite different complex of causes and preserved the Catholic pattern of church order (see Chs. I–IV). The Reformation was thus not a uniform or homogenous movement. While there were common religious perspectives and principles for the understanding of the gospel, these were expressed with varying emphases in widely different geographical, intellectual, and social contexts. Subsequent development of Protestantism has been characterized by further elaboration of this original complexity of religious elements in relation to novel social situations. This can be seen in the establishment of the Reformed churches in Switzerland, France, the Netherlands, and Scotland. It was most vividly expressed in the appearance of the "free churches" in England in the seventeenth and eighteenth centuries and in the proliferation of denominations in the United States.

Any explanation, therefore, of the internal divisions of Protestantism must take account of several factors. Theological differences have been important, as in the early Lutheran and Reformed dispute over the sacraments, or in the conflicts regarding predestination, or the varying conceptions of proper church government, or the Baptist insistence on believers' baptism and on immersion as the only scriptural pattern. But any attempt to understand Protestant divisions simply in terms of differing theologies or forms of worship is grossly inadequate. Numerous Protestant denominations (e.g., the Methodists) have come out of revival movements which did not spring from any fundamental theological divergence, nor any intention of leaving the established churches, but which led to the formation of separate churches because of the indifference or hostility of church leaders to the new impulses.

Moreover, quite different kinds of social forces were at work,[1] and often quite intermingled with differences of religious understanding.

---

[1] See H. R. Niebuhr's classic study, *The Social Sources of Denominationalism* (New York, 1929).

The influence of nationalism, noted above, was paralleled by racial, economic, and class interests. The issue of slavery in the United States, for example, was one of the main factors which led to the splitting of nearly every major Protestant denomination, the Protestant Episcopal Church being the chief exception. And, in spite of some significant changes in recent years, American Protestantism is still characterized by an almost complete segregation of black and white churches. Economic and social stratification among the churches has been less sharp but equally real. The separation between the Anabaptists and the main Reformation bodies was to a significant degree a cleavage between the "lower" and the more favored social groups. Later Protestantism reveals a tendency for the older communities to become identified with the middle and upper social classes (this is true in America, for example, of the Episcopalians, Presbyterians, Congregationalists, Methodists, and Reformed, and to a lesser extent, of the Baptists and Disciples). New denominations have most commonly appeared among the depressed and "disinherited" social levels, and often represent emphases (e.g., emotionalism and anti-intellectualism) which no longer appeal to the "upper" cultural strata. This is seen today in such groups as the Jehovah's Witnesses and the "pentecostal" or "holiness" sects. Another kind of social source of denominationalism in America was the frontier situation in which Protestantism spread. Problems of frontier life were such as to encourage independent organizations and lay control of the churches. Thus, even the episcopally ordered churches were significantly influenced in the direction of more democratic and congregational church government.

Finally, the multiplicity of Protestant denominations has to be understood in the light of what is vaguely (and not very accurately) called Protestant "individualism." At the center of the Reformation faith was the new acknowledgment of the intrinsic authority of God's self-revelation (i.e., the discovery that faith can begin only as Jesus Christ attests himself to the human soul in which his Word is made alive by the Holy Spirit). Therefore, the Protestant's religious convictions are reached only in personal responsible decision: they are *one's own* response to the Word of God in Christ; they are the convictions which are required of a *self*. This is not the same thing as the "right of private judgment" — for that is not a peculiarly religious conception and suggests a kind of absolute sovereignty of the individual which is quite foreign to the Reformation idea. The Protestant idea of faith does not entitle one to believe whatever one pleases, for everyone must think in accordance with the truth. But the principle of the Reformation is that the truth of the gospel is made known to faith by the inward working of the Holy Spirit. This truth is therefore received only in decision, in personal acceptance, in an obedience to the Word of God which no individual can perform for another.

It is in this sense of complete obligation to the Word of God as it compels the faith of the believer that Protestantism stands for freedom of personal judgment and belief. No finite religious authority (church, creed, or even Scripture) can compel conformity of conviction. Everyone's faith must be *one's own* faith. Such a view involves the risk that Christians might differ widely in their understanding of the gospel. This risk has traditionally seemed intolerable to Roman Catholicism (and often to many Protestants). But it is a risk which cannot be avoided without violating the Protestant understanding of faith and rejecting the religious freedom which is derived from that understanding of faith. Therefore, while it cannot be said that the Protestant understanding necessarily involves church divisions, this understanding does explicitly involve the possibility of differences in belief and practice, and these have in fact led to denominational divisions through the association of like-minded believers into distinct religious organizations. It should also be noted, however, that this process was greatly stimulated by the very different individualism of the Enlightenment, particularly by its doctrine of the complete autonomy of the individual and of the absolute "right" of private judgment. Moreover, Protestantism was slow to accept the consequences of its own implications for religious freedom. The classical Reformation churches held in practice to the notion of an "authorized" religion and denied religious freedom to the left-wing Reformation groups. Not until the eighteenth century did the ideal of religious freedom begin to be generally characteristic of Protestant thought. And, with the exception of the Church of England, Protestant churches generally assumed that there ought to be uniformity of doctrine within each communion. It is fair to say that the denominational divisions of Protestantism have resulted not so much from simple diversity of belief as from the demand for conformity within each institution, with the result that nonconforming groups were forced to organize separately.

It is easy to exaggerate the nature and extent of Protestant divisions. To say, for example, that there are 250 denominations in the United States is seriously misleading unless it is also observed that roughly 80 percent of all American Protestants are included in the membership of thirteen of these denominations, and that 90 percent are included in no more than twenty denominations (if Protestants are grouped by "families" of denominations, for example, all Baptist bodies counted together, all Lutherans together, etc., the concentration is even more striking). More important than this, however, is the fact that religious unity and diversity may be judged not only in terms of unity of organization, but also as regards doctrine, ethics, ritual, and outlook or intention (to say nothing of the sociological aspects of the problem). "Unity" cannot simply be equated with ecclesiastical organization. Completely separate institutions may have very similar theologies and rituals and be essentially one in spirit and intention. And a single ecclesiastical structure may include widely differing points of view. The Roman Catholic church, for example, embraces far greater diversity than is commonly recognized. The differences between Catholicism in Spain, in Germany, in Latin America, in Africa, and in the United States are in fundamental respects greater than the differences between many Protestant denominations; and sometimes the hostility between various monastic orders in the Roman church has exceeded that of all but the most extreme Protestant sects. The Anglican communion may also be cited as an example of a church which finds its unity in a common ritual, in the apostolic succession, and in a minimal doctrinal standard, but which prides itself on including widely differing theologies as well as independent national units. (A secular example of institutional unity with radically different points of view is the American political party.)

We shall be concerned in the final chapter in a more systematic way with the question of the unity of Protestantism, but it should be clear from our previous study that this question cannot be judged simply in terms of organizational unity and diversity. Division in Protestantism has by no means always been accompanied by a divisive spirit. In both the great awakenings and the later revivals, for example, divisions took place in the churches as new societies were established to develop and conserve the results of evangelization. And this was also true of the westward movement of Christianity in America. But these groups were conscious of participating in a common endeavor. Their social and religious divergences, while real, were recognized as subordinate to their common loyalty to Christ, and there was much cooperation between the churches. They felt themselves one "in Christ" and in the invisible catholic church. In American Protestantism particularly, this sense of unity has been more recently expressed in the practical interchangeability of denominations for an increasingly mobile population. Not only millions of church members, but also ministers, have transferred back and forth among denominations (e.g., as early as 1920, Congregational churches accepted as ministers almost as many clergy ordained by other denominations as were ordained in Congregational churches; and between 1921 and 1926, 38 percent of the new Presbyterian ministers came from other denominations). This kind of interchange was made possible by mutual recognition of the denominations as working together in a common cause.

At the same time, the problem of institutional disunity in Protestantism has remained. For mutual recognition has been accompanied by powerful tendencies toward competition and divisiveness. Groups which came into existence to revitalize the life of the churches or to share in the common work of evangelization quickly became self-conscious and concerned with institutional self-preservation. Differing heritages came to seem of more importance than the common task and loyalty to Christ. Each religious society became concerned with extending its own membership and promoting its own particular type of theology, ritual, and methods of evangelization and religious education. Here, also, cultural, racial, national, and economic differences assumed increasing importance. This process occurred after the Reformation and has been repeated again and again in the subsequent history of Protestantism. Indeed, it must be said that every revival of religion, whether in Christianity or elsewhere, has tended to follow the same pattern, the work of reformers being conserved by institutions which become self-defensive and confuse themselves with the ideals they were formed to proclaim (other social institutions, of course, exhibit similar characteristics). But Protestantism has been especially subject to this sort of divisiveness and competition, for this is the peculiar temptation of the Protestant understanding of faith. The recognition of this fact has been of primary significance in the twentieth-century ecumenical movement, which rests on the convictions that, while diversity is not to be denied, the unity of Christianity must be preserved and made explicit, and that unity must be given some formal expression in belief and practice and in institutional order.

The Demand for Church Unity

The term "ecumenical" (from the Greek *he oikoumene,* meaning "the inhabited earth") has in recent Christian thought come to be used as a synonym for "universal." The "ecumenical" church is the universal church, and the ecumenical movement is a movement toward unity or solidarity in Christian life and work throughout the world. This may mean simply interdenominational cooperation or it may mean working toward the merging of all Christian bodies in a single world church. Using the term in its broadest sense, however, we may say that the ecumenical movement (or "ecumenism") includes all aspects of the twentieth-century trend toward the fuller realization of the unity of the Christian church. As such, this is a movement which includes not only Protestantism, but also the Eastern Orthodox churches, the Old Catholic Church, the Coptic Church — and in important ways the Roman Catholic Church. It is concerned with all the breaches in the church. But the problem of division is obviously of particular relevance to Protestantism, and Protestant bodies have been especially active in this movement, both as it involves the major branches of Christianity and as it concerns the internal divisions of Protestantism.

At the root of the ecumenical movement is the sharp contrast between the actual divided state of the church and the affirmation of all Christians that the church is in some sense "one." St. Paul speaks of the church as the one body of Christ, and the Gospel of John records Christ's prayer that his followers "may all be one." Loyalty to Christ, according to the New Testament, means self-sacrificing love for one another and the transcending of those barriers which divide us. "There is neither Jew nor Greek, there is neither slave nor free, there is neither male nor female; for you are all one in Christ Jesus" (Gal. 3:28). There is "one body and one Spirit . . . one hope . . . one Lord, one faith, one baptism, one God and Father of us all" (Eph. 4:4–6). But the actual life of the churches (even from the earliest times, as the New Testament makes clear) suggests division and competition rather than unity. It is a lively recognition of the utter incongruity of this situation which has impelled recent Christianity in the direction of the ecumenical movement. There are those churches, of course, which hold that they alone represent the one true faith and community, and that the division of Christendom is the result of the infidelity and heresy of the rest of the churches. For these groups the unity of the church can be attained only when all Christians acknowledge the validity of a particular church's claim to possession of the fullness of Christian faith and life. The spirit of the ecumenical movement, however, involves recognition that all the churches must share in the responsibility for the disunity of Christianity and that therefore each must learn from the others.

In addition to this aspect of the problem of Christian disunity, there are a number of other more particular factors which have contributed to the demand for greater Christian solidarity. One is the new recognition of the social character of much of the division of the churches, the awareness that many supposed differences of principle are no more than rationalizations of quite different sorts of divisive elements. Another has come from nineteenth-century liberalism's de-emphasizing of theological controversy and its concern for the underlying (and unifying) Christian experience. While the liberal suspicion of theology has more recently been abandoned, it has nonetheless continued to be recognized that theological formulations, while necessary and never to be taken lightly (as if theological differences were really of no consequence), are still not ultimate. Moreover, theological differences among Protestants, since the liberal influence, are much less likely to follow denominational lines.

A third and powerful force contributing to the ecumenical movement has been the experience of the modern missionary enterprise. As was remarked upon in Chapter VIII, the divisions of the denominations were not only largely meaningless to the peoples to whom the missionaries went, but were in the eyes of the non-Christian majorities of these peoples a standing refutation of the claims for the finality of the gospel. Moreover, the difficult decisions which had to be made on social and philosophical as well as religious and ethical questions

were made even more awkward by the lack of unity among the missionary groups. And there was the practical problem of the relative weakness of the mission churches. Thus, the independent denominational
missionary agencies were driven toward increased cooperation. Beginning in 1854, a series of seven interdenominational, international missionary conferences was held, including representatives from the major
churches of the West. These were followed by the World Missionary
Conference at Edinburgh in 1910, which was a primary turning point
in the movement toward unity. At this conference, delegates attended
for the first time from the "younger churches" (i.e., from the churches
established in non-Western nations as a result of the nineteenth-century
missionary activity). An attempt was made at a comprehensive study
of the problems of the missionary enterprise — the missionary message,
the preparation of missionaries, Christian education, the condition
of the church in the mission field, the home "bases" of missions, missions and government, and unity and cooperation.

The results of this conference and its overall analysis extended in
several directions. As concerns the missionary effort itself, it set into
clear focus the problems of divided effort in the mission field — both
the "scandal" of Christian bodies competing against each other and
the sheer folly and waste of duplication of effort. This, and the growing
sense of community among the missionary bodies, led, for example,
to the rapid extension of "comity" arrangements (i.e., agreements
whereby responsibility for missionary work in a specific area was assigned solely to one denomination, so as to avoid duplication and
overlapping). Also, out of this conference came impetus for the formation of the International Missionary Council (1921) and the holding
of world missionary conferences at Jerusalem (1928) and Madras, India
(1938). The latter meeting was particularly significant for the recognition of the "younger churches," not as mere dependencies of the
Western churches but as independent and fully participating bodies.
These younger churches also made a vigorous appeal for unity among
the "older churches"; as they put it, "for you unity may be a luxury.
For us it is a life and death necessity."

Paralleling the move toward missionary cooperation, the Edinburgh
conference also led to recognition of the need for frank discussion
of the theological differences of the churches, with a view to making
explicit the areas of common belief and to mutual understanding of
divergent conceptions. Attempts were made to meet this need in conferences held at Lausanne, Switzerland (1927), and Edinburgh (1937)
on the theme "Faith and Order" (i.e., belief and patterns of church
organization). At both of these meetings, representatives of Western
non-Roman churches and of Eastern Orthodoxy joined in statements
of common faith which revealed an essential unity in many aspects
of Christian belief, the chief exceptions having to do with the nature

of the sacraments and the authority of the ministry (including church organization). These concerns were taken up after 1948 as one of the major foci for the work of the World Council of Churches, through its Commission on Faith and Order. Further world conferences were held at Lund (1952) and at Montreal (1963), and major sessions of the Commission were held at Louvain (1971 — with full membership for the first time of Roman Catholic participants) and at Lima (1982). Another world conference has been proposed for 1988.

A fourth force which has accentuated the demand for Christian unity has been the church's attempt to witness to ethical and social problems of the modern world. The acceptance of the church's responsibility for the redemption of society as well as the individual was the central feature of the social gospel (see Ch. XI). But it was at once apparent that the church's function in society could be effectively exercised only by close cooperation of the denominations. The problems of war, of depression and economic justice, of the rise of totalitarianism, required that the church speak with a single voice if it was to have any influence whatever on their resolution. As noted earlier (Ch. XI), the Federal Council of the Churches of Christ in America was formed partly to meet this need. The demand for unity of ethical endeavor was also recognized at the Edinburgh conference and, in respect of the problem of world peace, in the formation in 1914 of the World Alliance for International Friendship through the Churches. The joint efforts of the Federal Council and the World Alliance were primarily responsible for the origin of what has been called the "Life and Work Movement," an international expression of Christian ethical concern which has developed in a conference at Stockholm (1925), in the formation of the Universal Christian Council for Life and Work (1929), in the Conference on Church, Community, and State held at Oxford (1937), and in the assemblies of the World Council of Churches (Amsterdam, 1948; Evanston, 1954; New Delhi, 1961; Uppsala, 1968; Nairobi, 1975; and Vancouver, 1983). Each of these conferences involved the detailed analysis of major problems of the contemporary world and revealed a large degree of unanimity among the churches with respect to the Christian witness to these problems.

Another contributing factor from the very beginning of the ecumenical trend has been the influence of the various student movements, including especially the World's Student Christian Federation, the Student Volunteer Movement for Foreign Missions, the Christian Endeavor, the Young Men's Christian Association, and the Young Women's Christian Association. In these and similar organizations, students of differing denominations worshiped, thought, and worked together as Christians, and often found there an intensity of Christian experience and a depth of community which made them impatient with denominational divisions. Moreover, in relation to the secularism of the modern universities, the divisions of the church seemed not only senseless but dangerous. It is significant that a large number of the leaders of the ecumenical movement have been participants in the Student Christian movements. That the student concern for ecumenism continues to be strong is evident from the 1985 National Consultation on Ecumenical Leadership Development, held in Washington, D.C., and attended by theological students from every major branch of American Christianity, including Roman Catholicism and Greek Orthodoxy.

A final element in the dynamic of the present ecumenical trend has come from the experience of the churches in the Second World War. The sufferings of the Christians who resisted Nazism, particularly in occupied countries, the awakening of the churches to the necessity of opposing totalitarianism, the "orphaning" of mission churches which had been supported by European churches, the difficulty of communication between Christians across the lines of the conflict, the problems of war prisoners, of refugees, of reconstruction — all of these served to elicit a deepened sense of worldwide community among Christians, as well as concrete joint action for the alleviation of suffering and world reconstruction. Indeed, it has been said that the war revealed the Christian church to be the only actual world community.

Patterns for Unity in the Church

In the broadest meaning of the phrase, the ecumenical movement may be said to include a wide variety of institutional arrangements. It includes a large number of interdenominational and unofficial organizations having specific purposes, such as the Student Christian movements, the World Alliance for International Friendship through the Churches, etc. These groups have been examples of cooperative activity in Christian unity rather than of any formal church union. But, as we saw earlier, precisely such groups foreshadowed and demanded later concrete steps toward ecclesiastical unification.

More directly to the point, ecumenism can be expressed as the movement toward formal or "organic" consolidation of denominations. To many, this process has seemed agonizingly slow and fragmentary. At the same time, however, scores of formal unions have been completed in the twentieth century and many negotiations continue. It has been estimated that negotiations of some sort are under way in nearly one hundred and fifty churches, notably in Africa (The Camroon, Liberia, Malawi, Mozambique, Sierra Leone, South Africa, Tanzania, Zambia) and Asia (India, Malaysia, Sri Lanka), but also in New Zealand, Latin America, the Middle East, and even Western Europe (England, France, Ireland, Italy, the Netherlands, Portugal, Scotland, and Wales).

Generally, the "organic" mergers have been of the same type or "family." Most notable, perhaps, in the American scene has been the series of mergers in the Lutheran tradition (though also with a new split in the conservative Missouri Synod group), culminating in the unification of the American Lutheran Church, the Lutheran Church in America (both the products of a series of prior mergers), and the Association of Evangelical Lutheran Churches, which has been approved and is scheduled for consummation in 1988. Important reunions of northern and southern contingents, to heal the divisions that took place in the nineteenth century, have occurred (e.g., among the Methodists in 1939, with the later incorporation of a closely related group, the Evangelical United Brethren, into the United Methodist Church, as well as the merger of the two wings of the Presbyterians into the United Presbyterian Church, U.S.A., in 1983).

The consolidation of churches of significantly different denominational types has been less frequent, though this is an important phenomenon.[2] A prime example in North America has been the merging of Presbyterian, Congregational, and Methodist churches into the United Church of Canada. Much more dramatic was the formation of the Church of South India (1947), which combined Anglican, English Methodist, Presbyterian, and Congregational churches, representing quite divergent forms of church government and conceptions of the ministry. (It should be noted, however, that this union was vigorously denounced by the High Church or Anglo-Catholic wing of the Church of England.) The Church of South India is a good illustration of the greater pressure for merging different denominations in the "younger churches," where the need for a united front in presenting the Christian witness and the relative smallness of the churches have combined to make unification a more urgent matter than in the "older" churches.

A useful illustration of the difficulties of uniting different denominations is the (so far) quarter-century experience of the Consultation on Church Union, which originated in a dramatic proposal by an Episcopal bishop and a national Presbyterian leader, in 1960, for immediate union of four major American denominations: the Episcopal, Presbyterian, and Methodist churches, and the United Church of Christ. In the following decade, the Consultation grew to include nine member churches. A formal Plan of Union was proposed in 1970, but was rejected (as much because of bureaucratic resistance as because

---

[2] One may recall in passing here the effort of the Prussian ruler in the early nineteenth century to form a united Lutheran-Reformed church — a move that Schleiermacher supported, on the grounds that nothing religiously fundamental separated these two traditions and one could therefore have an inclusive Protestant theology, though Catholic and Protestant piety were so distinct that one could not have for them a unified theological system. But the royal attempt failed, especially because of opposition by the Lutherans.

of theological differences). Attention was then turned to developing a broader consensus and a commitment of the members to "live toward" union. This has resulted in a statement adopted unanimously by the delegates at the 1984 Consultation as an expression of an "emerging theological consensus," articulated in a document called "In Quest of a Church of Christ Uniting." Church union is not envisaged in the immediate future, but as a part of a covenanting process, member churches were called upon to give public recognition to each other as true churches, to "claim" the theological consensus, to recognize each other's ministries, members, and sacraments, thus making possible sharing of clergy, free interchange of members, regular "eucharistic fellowship," engagement in common mission and evangelism, and the formation of "councils of oversight" as bridges "toward a future united church."

Another kind of regional development is represented in the 1971 Leuenberg Concordia, in which Lutheran, Reformed, and United churches in Europe shaped a statement in which areas of agreement included a common understanding of the gospel, a recognition that some of the doctrinal statements in past confessional texts are no longer appropriate, and an acceptance of one another in preaching and in celebration of Holy Communion. Thus it was affirmed that "henceforth the divisions hindering church fellowship ever since the sixteenth century cease to exist."

Paralleling the various steps in organic church union has been the development of federations for joint or cooperative witness, teaching, and action. This was the nature of the Federal Council of the Churches of Christ in America, now joined with parallel missionary and religious education organizations in the National Council of the Churches of Christ in the U.S.A. This is also the nature of the World Council of Churches, formally constituted in a meeting at Amsterdam (1948), and probably the most significant of all the organizations which have come out of the ecumenical movement.

The World Council came into being as a direct result of several of the lines of development noted in the preceding section of this chapter, specifically the Faith and Order conferences, the Life and Work conferences, the international missionary conferences, and the international Christian youth conferences. It is an attempt to synthesize these various aspects of interchurch cooperation and to provide at least a forum for the continued discussion of the problem of the unity of the church. The functions of the World Council are stated in its constitution as follows:

1) To carry on the work of the two world movements for "Faith and Order" and for "Life and Work."
2) To facilitate common action by the churches.

3) To promote cooperation in study.
4) To promote the growth of ecumenical consciousness in the members of all churches.
5) To establish relations with denominational federations of world-wide scope and with other ecumenical movements.
6) To call world conferences on specific subjects as occasion may require, such conferences being empowered to publish their own findings.
7) To support the churches in their task of evangelism.

Both the problems and the meaning of the ecumenical movement are clearly seen in the history of the World Council of Churches. It is emphatically not a "church" and has no authority over its constituent members. It is rather a federation, including more than 250 member churches — Protestant, Anglican, Orthodox, Old Catholic, and Independent, from 90 countries — joining in acknowledgment of the "basis" of the Council as (in the original wording) "a fellowship of churches which accepted our Lord Jesus Christ as God and Savior," and organized for the discharge of stated functions. Even with the addition of a trinitarian reference, incorporated to satisfy the Orthodox churches, the statement of faith which is the "basis" is no more than a minimal affirmation, and the degree of unity indicated by it must not be exaggerated. Some member churches do not recognize some other member churches as fully Christian bodies, because of creedal differences and questions of the validity of the various ministries and sacraments. This mutual nonrecognition is most vividly seen in the inability of some churches to participate in services of Holy Communion with members of other groups. Thus, the Council might be described as simply an institutional framework for discussion and (where possible) joint action, an organization which recognizes both the radical divisions of the churches and the "true" character of the church as "one body," an organization therefore of divided churches looking for unity.

Originally, the World Council was dominantly a pan-Protestant phenomenon, with substantial (though tenuous) participation of Eastern Orthodox churches only after 1961. In its early decades it was informed by a broad consensus on the Protestant biblical theology of the nineteen-thirties, forties, and fifties, on a concern for theological reconstruction and church renewal, and on a general missionary zeal. But the theological consensus has been eroded by fragmentation (see Ch. XIV) and the understanding of the missionary enterprise has been altered, in part as a consequence of the greatly increased influence of the churches of the "Third World." The latter influence also was important in a growing preoccupation with the problems of the developing countries.

A special problem for the World Council has been the fact that the Roman Catholic church is absent from membership. Though Roman Catholics have been present as observers and (particularly since Vatican II) as participants in numerous commissions and committees, the Roman Catholic church as such is conspicuously absent from the Council. The informal and even quasi-formal relations between Geneva and Rome have been open and friendly. But from both sides, formal membership for Rome would be problematic. From the side of the Council, the mere size of the Roman Catholic church, as by far the largest Christian body, would make it an overwhelmingly dominant partner. From the side of Rome, the basis of agreement in the Council is far too narrow for Roman Catholic understanding of the nature of the church (see the following section, "The Impact of Roman Catholic Ecumenism").

Not altogether unlike the problem of the relation of the World Council to Rome has been the relation to the worldwide confessional organizations that have proliferated and grown in influence since the formation of the World Council. As many as seventeen "families" have been involved, including the Anglican Consultative Council, the Baptist World Alliance, the Lutheran World Federation, the World Methodist Council, the World Alliance of Reformed Churches, the Ecumenical Patriarchate, and the Moscow Patriarchate. Even the phrase "Christian World Communions" has been taken up as a designation to replace the former "world confessional families." The interests of such bodies obviously overlap with the interests of the World Council, especially in the concern for a Christian community that transcends national, ethnic, and cultural divisions. Yet they also compete organizationally and by heavy emphasis on their special traditions of faith and life and ecclesiastical self-awareness. Thus the confessional bodies have been particularly interested in bilateral dialogue (e.g., Anglican and Lutheran, Anglican and Orthodox, Lutheran and Catholic, Catholic and Orthodox, etc.) rather than in multilateral discussion and programs like those of the World Council, because in bilateral conversations much greater areas of agreement can be defined.

Both in the World Council and in the world confessional bodies, the question of the nature of unity in the church has come sharply into focus. On one level, this has been a question of structural unity or uniformity. The problem has not been simply that of differing views of the proper ordering of the church (as to creed, sacraments, church government, etc.), but also differing views as to whether there is any single "correct" order of the church. Some groups hold that there are certain indispensable forms for the church, though they disagree sharply as to what those forms are (e.g., the Baptist insistence on believers' baptism and local church autonomy vs. the Orthodox and Anglican insistence on episcopal succession). Others hold that a pluralism in institutions and in forms of ritual, ministry, and church government is quite compatible with the underlying unity of the church — indeed, that the Reformation principles require the allowance for such pluralism. They would see the differences in conceptions of proper church order as variations of emphasis capable of inclusion within a common perspective. One element of that perspective is the recognition that unity does not require uniformity and that there is room (and need) in the Christian community both for the Free Church emphasis on the freedom of the grace of God from all ecclesiastical bondage and for the emphasis of the Anglicans and the Lutherans on the visible "right ordering" of the church. Ultimate unity, which may or may not find expression in organizational structure, is to be found in the mutual recognition of the churches as participants in the one body of Christ. This is not to overlook the great differences between, for example, the Baptist and the Quaker and the Episcopal views of the necessary constitution of the church. But this does mean that such differences exist within a genuine fellowship of Christians who recognize each other as such.

The prolonged discussion of such issues as these in the ecumenical movement has resulted in much clarification of views and mutual understanding. But it has also meant the sharpening of seemingly irreconcilable positions. As we noted, it has led to new interest in the distinctive witness of the particular denominations; thus each group becomes more conscious of its own heritage. Moreover, the churchly kind of ecumenism represented by the World Council and the confessional alliances has come to be challenged by neoevangelical, neopentecostal, and charismatic movements that are transconfessional in nature and on this basis make strong ecumenical claims, but with little contact with the "traditional" structures of the ecumenical movement.

Yet overall the developments we have been describing reveal a significant shift in the central thrust of ecumenism (beginning about the middle 1930s). We may describe this as a shift away from an earlier assumption that unity in the church is primarily something to be achieved by pulling together separate blocks or by bringing fragmented parts into a whole. The spirit of that phase was not unlike the mood of the social gospel's idea of building the kingdom of God.

More recent ecumenical discussion does not begin with the idea of a fragmented organization, asking "how can we get this together?" It begins rather with the affirmation that the unity of the church, however defined, is (and can only be) given by God. The problem is not, therefore, the "achievement" of unity, but the manifestation of the unity of the church which by God's grace *does* exist. The question is "how can we express the unity which must be affirmed?" The World Council, for example, is certainly not itself that unity, just because it is a council of dissimilar churches which disagree in witness, faith, and practice; but it is dedicated to working out the implications of an already given unity. The task of the ecumenical movement is the understanding of the unity of the church as given in Christ. Thus, one of the central decisions of the Conference on Faith and Order at Lund (1952) was to shift the emphasis of subsequent discussion from the comparison of various established doctrines of the church (there is, after all, only so much of this that can be done) to other kinds of questions about the church (e.g., the church in relation to the doctrine of Christ and the Holy Spirit, the churches in relation to tradition, and the social and cultural factors underlying disunity in the church). So also, the Bible has increasingly been emphasized as a source of the unity of the church, and greater stress has been laid on biblical theology.

A further aspect of the new note in ecumenical discussion has been the heightened concern with total renewal of the church. The true unity of the church can be manifested only as the life of the church is deepened in every way. Unity is not a problem which can be dealt with alone. It is but one aspect of the larger problem of the conversion or renewal of church life. In the light of this judgment, attention has been focused, for example, on the problem of professionalism in the church, i.e., the tendency so to separate clergy and laity that the work of the church becomes identified with the clergy, with the consequent loss of the sense of the lay Christian life.

Even more important has been the growth of emphasis (notably in the World Council of Churches) on social questions. Particularly as a result of the influence of Third World representatives and of liberation theologies (see Ch. XV), stress has been laid on the problems of colonialism, economic exploitation, and racism. Sexism, environmental concerns, and the threat of nuclear war have been newly recognized as crucial for the church's life and message. To some, these tendencies in the World Council have seemed a politicization of ecumenism and a relegation to secondary status of the concerns of Faith and Order. But they may also be interpreted as a more vivid awareness of the importance of Life and Work for any valid movement toward church unity. The unity and the holiness of the church are thus inseparable.

A correlative note in the postliberal ecumenical movement has been the renewal of the sense of the church as such as a community that has its existence in an act of God. This sense had been weakened in liberal Protestantism, which had mainly an "instrumental" view of the church, seeing it as essentially a religious institution among other institutions (i.e., a social structure devised for the expression of certain common religious interests and having its origins in human activities). With the general rethinking of the church in ecumenical discussions, reaction against such views was sharp. The church is instead to be conceived as a unique community, *given* its existence by God, not constructed. Here the trend of ecumenical thought was powerfully reinforced by the developments of Protestant theology between the wars (see Ch. XII), particularly the new seriousness with respect to the Bible, revelation, the priority of God's act, and the tradition of the church. The new note in the understanding of the church also came strongly from the Continental Protestant churches, growing out of their experience during the Second World War.

The Impact of Roman Catholic Ecumenism

The Second Vatican Council was without doubt the most important event in the twentieth-century ecumenical movement. Announced by Pope John XXIII as one of his first acts, to the surprise of everyone and with the stated purpose of opening the windows to the world to let in fresh air, the Council convened in Rome from 1962 to 1965 and fundamentally altered the course of ecumenical discussions for Protestant, Catholic, and Orthodox Christians alike. For Protestantism, the questions of ecumenism could no longer be treated in a largely internal or pan-Protestant context (with a nod in the direction of Eastern Orthodoxy), but had to be taken up in a situation in which Roman Catholicism was a full, even dominant, partner in dialogue.

This is not to say that there was no important Protestant-Catholic dialogue prior to Vatican II. The Reformation period itself may be said to be a time of such dialogue. One might also think of the exchanges in the 1830s between Johann Adam Möhler and Ferdinand Christian Baur, of the Catholic and Protestant theological faculties in Tübingen, as a kind of opening of dialogue, at least in the sense that each tried to be fair to the position of the other, in spite of sharp disagreement. But nothing was to come of this and the Catholic "Tübingen school" of Möhler was soon forgotten.

But these are minor exceptions to the prevailing patterns of distrust and recrimination that characterized Protestant-Catholic relations from the sixteenth through the early twentieth centuries.

We should not suppose that the dramatic outcome of Vatican II was without important preparation in Roman Catholicism. At the end of the nineteenth century, Pope Leo XIII had established a Novena for Christian Unity. The January Octave of Prayer for Christianity, which had been begun by American Episcopalians, was approved by Leo's successor, Pius X, and was extended to the whole Catholic church by Benedict XV. In such movements was sounded the note of a hoped-for reunion of Christendom on the basis of mutual repentance for sins. As early as the 1920s, the *Una Sancta* movement, centering in Germany, began to lead to various levels of conversation between Catholics and Protestants in a friendly atmosphere.

Other important preparatory developments were the liturgical movement and the renewal of Catholic biblical and patristic studies in the third and fourth decades of the twentieth century. In the biblical area, Catholic and Protestant scholars became increasingly aware of and influenced by each other's work; critical historical methods were more and more taken up by Catholic students. Patristic scholarship recalled the fluidity and creativity of the thought of the early church fathers, which could be contrasted with the more restrictive categories of the medieval scholastics. The Thomistic patterns of thinking, which had been given the highest seal of approval by Leo XIII and his successors, were reinterpreted in important ways and it was even proposed that other and modern philosophical categories (including existentialism) could be more useful for theology.

Related to these influences were new ways of looking at the nature of the church. From the time of the Catholic reformation, but particularly under the impact of the Enlightenment and through the First Vatican Council (1869–70), Roman Catholic theology of the church was dominated by rationalist and juridical categories, with emphasis on the biblical image of the kingdom of God and on the institutional structures. In the twentieth century, however, the idea of the church as the mystical body of Christ came onto center stage, and the seal of approval was set on it by Pope Pius XII's encyclical *Mystici Corporis Christi* (1943).

Furthermore, new emphasis was placed on the integrity and freedom of conscience. Genuine faith could be elicited but could not be compelled.[3] Thus at least in a pluralistic society freedom for dissenting religion and irreligion must be allowed (in contrast to the older commonplace that "error cannot have the same rights as truth"). And the possibility of true, though invisible, membership in the body of Christ could be affirmed for non-Catholic Christians and even for non-Christians.

Add to these developments the powerful impact on Roman Catholic theologians of the new twentieth-century Protestant thought, especially of the work of Karl Barth, and a whole new level of the Catholic view of the Reformation and of Protestantism was opened up. Catholic interpretations of the Reformation began more openly to recognize

---

[3] For example, Karl Adam, in an influential work first published in 1924, argued on good Thomistic grounds that in cases where human practical reason fails to recognize God's will clearly, or is involved in invincible ignorance, one is not bound to objective law but to what appears to conscience to be God's will, even though the judgment of conscience be objectively false. "Even though in the case of so vital a matter as belief in Christ a man would act wrongly who should profess this faith against the judgment of his (erroneous) conscience." "Even though the judgment of [a man's] conscience be objectively false, and even though it be not in its genesis ethically irreproachable, yet he is bound to follow conscience and conscience alone." *The Spirit of Catholicism* (New York, 1954), pp. 207, 210.

its roots in the scandalous abuses of the fifteenth century. Luther in particular was more sympathetically treated, in respect of both his personal greatness and his religious quest. In such works as Joseph Lortz's studies of the Reformation in Germany and Karl Adam's *One and Holy*, much common ground could be acknowledged between Catholic faith and Luther's theology, and while concessions were not made in matters of faith, the truth that lies at the heart of every heresy could be recognized. Antagonistic attitudes in discourse must therefore be abandoned, matters of discipline can be relaxed, and Rome should recognize the riches that the separated portions of the church can bring — though without the abandonment of the premise that the only basis of reunion is return to Rome.

All these sorts of developments led by the 1950s to a wide variety of informal (sometimes almost clandestine) exchanges between Catholic and Protestant thinkers. Perceptive Protestants could even write of the "evangelical possibilities" of Roman Catholic theology. But one could hardly have predicted the way in which the new forces were to break through in Vatican II. Indeed, in view of the events of 1950 — the reputed discovery of St. Peter's tomb in Rome, the promulgation of the dogma of the Assumption of Mary, and the issuing of the encyclical *Humani Generis* (warning against false irenism, against overly great enthusiasm for the early church teachers and appeals to scripture rather than the teaching of the church, against flirtations with modern philosophies, and against abandonment of the Genesis account of the creation of humanity in favor of evolutionary accounts of a multiple human origin) — it could be felt that official Roman theology was drawing back from ecumenical encounter.

The Second Vatican Council, therefore, came as a great surprise to Catholic and non-Catholic alike. It was, as Karl Rahner has argued, "the first major official event in which the Church actualized itself precisely as a *World Church*." That is to say, it was not a simply Western European-dominated event but a gathering of a worldwide episcopate (Asian, African, Latin American, as well as European and North American) for teaching and decision-making. Thus, Rahner argues, the change with Vatican II is really comparable to the early change from a Jewish church to a Gentile church. And it was important that Protestant observers were invited from the beginning of the Council.

One after another at the Council, the preliminary schemata prepared by the Vatican theologians were sent back for fundamental rewriting. The tone of the Council was pastoral. Its longest and most remarkable document was the "Pastoral Constitution on the Church in the Modern World" (*Gaudium et Spes*), which expressed responsibility to the problems of the whole of humanity. The decree on the liturgy opened the door to the victory of the vernacular in the most central worship of the church, thus to the pluralization of the church's language.

The task of the Council was not to write new dogma. No anathemas were pronounced, and indeed only two of the resulting documents were called "dogmatic constitutions": the Constitution on Divine Revelation (quite conservative in its formulations) and the Constitution on the Church (*Lumen Gentium*).

Of most direct relevance to the ecumenical movement were the Constitution on the Church and the decrees on ecumenism, on the relation to non-Christian religions, and on religious freedom. The Constitution on the Church emphasized the variety of biblical images and took up the idea of the church as the whole new people of God, priests and laity, as sharing in Christ's priestly, prophetic, and kingly work, before turning to a chapter on the hierarchical structure of the church. In the latter section, while maintaining the primacy of the pope, in accord with Vatican I, emphasis was also laid on the collegiality of the whole body of bishops acting with the Roman see in teaching and governance (with some role accorded to regional episcopal bodies).

Most pertinent to the ecumenical question is the way in which reference is made to non-Catholic Christian groups. While maintaining that the church established by Christ is a visible structure, necessary for salvation, and "subsists in" the Roman Catholic church, the Council found it possible to speak not only of individual Christians outside of communion with Rome who have divine gifts and graces, but also of "churches" and "ecclesial communities" in which baptism and other sacraments are received. The result is that these non-Catholic Christian groups are, "in some real way," joined with the Catholic church in the Holy Spirit and sanctifying power works among them.

In the decree on ecumenism, the language of "churches and ecclesial communities separated from the Roman apostolic see" is reiterated, and the new stance is articulated and given practical application. A special place is accorded to the Eastern (i.e., Orthodox) churches, for whom the basic problem is only recognition of the authority of Rome. Other (Western) separated churches and ecclesial communities are recognized as joined to the Catholic church in veneration of the Scriptures and in the sacrament of baptism. Though deficient with respect to the sacrament of Holy Orders and (therefore) lacking in the *full* reality of the Eucharist, they do celebrate the Holy Supper in such a way that dialogue concerning the meaning of the Supper, the other sacraments, and the church's worship and ministry, should be undertaken.

The implications of this partial recognition of Protestant churches as embodying the elements of the true church are spelled out in strong support for ecumenical discussion and common prayer for unity. Meetings of competent theologians are to be encouraged, in which "each can deal with the other on an equal footing" (*par cum pari*). And

Catholic theologians are reminded that they should act in love of truth, in charity and humility, and that Catholic teaching involves a "hierarchy" of truths, some being closer to the foundation than others. Thus in "fraternal rivalry" all can be led to "deeper realization and a clearer expression of the unfathomable riches of Christ."

The brief declaration on the relation to non-Christian religions affirmed both the common humanity of all peoples and the ray of Truth, the "certain perception of that hidden power which hovers over the course of things," which lies in the searchings of other religions, notably in Hinduism and Buddhism. Nothing in these other religions that is true and holy is to be rejected. Special recognition is to be given to Islam and Judaism, particularly the latter, by virtue of their unique relations to Christianity.

The declaration on religious freedom, while maintaining the moral obligation of all to seek the truth, including the moral duty toward the true religion and the One Church of Christ, unequivocally affirmed the right to immunity from coercion in civil society. The question of freedom (for dissent) within the church, however, was ignored.

The enormous consequences of the Second Vatican Council and its aftermath for the ecumenical movement as a whole, particularly for Protestantism, can only be briefly suggested. And what the permanent effects will be is by no means clear, for there have been signs in the 1980s, under the pontificate of John Paul II, of much greater caution on the part of Rome and of a tightening of the lines, a sharp restriction on permissible dissent and thus a broadening of the scope of infallibility. Some see here a major crisis of authority in the Catholic church. But far-reaching changes, at least some of which will be permanent, have obviously occurred.

Among the marks of change, one may note the greater involvement of Rome with the World Council of Churches and its organs. It has not been seriously proposed that the Roman Catholic church should join the World Council, for reasons that we cited earlier, but Roman Catholic theologians have become members of the World Council's Faith and Order Commission and formal joint commissions of Protestant and Catholic thinkers have been established, beginning in 1966 with a commission on Catholicity and Apostolicity.

Along with this direction of development, and to some extent in tension with it, has been a great flourishing of bilateral conversations (e.g., Lutheran-Catholic, Anglican-Catholic, Reformed-Catholic, and Orthodox-Catholic). And this has greatly strengthened the influence of the world confessional federations. The opening to the East (i.e., the Orthodox churches) has been particularly prominent in the Roman agenda, but significant progress has been made in the dialogues with Protestant groups as well, with some corresponding lessening of interest in intra-Protestant discussions. (One minor consequence of the growth of direct Protestant-Catholic relations has been the loss of the earlier role of the Anglican communion as an intermediary between the evangelical and Catholic positions. After all, if one can talk directly to Rome, which represents the strongest Catholic tradition, why bother with a mediating group?)

At another level, Protestant and Catholic theological scholarship and education have become much more collaborative enterprises. In European universities with both Catholic and Protestant faculties, the two faculties no longer just sit side by side, with perhaps an annual tea party for the exchange of new books. Catholic students study with Protestant faculty and vice versa. Especially in North America, there has been increasing interchange. The Roman Catholic theological seminaries have become members of the formerly all-Protestant Association of Theological Schools in the United States and Canada. Protestants have been appointed to the faculties of Catholic institutions. And formal theological consortia, with both Protestant and Catholic members, have emerged in several major centers (e.g., Toronto, Boston, Washington, Chicago, and Berkeley), the most striking and effective of which is the Graduate Theological Union in Berkeley, California, which has brought Dominican, Jesuit, and Franciscan faculties into extensive interrelation with Baptist, Episcopal, Lutheran, Presbyterian, interdenominational, and Unitarian-Universalist faculties.

At the level of scholarship, the Protestant-Catholic lines have become greatly blurred — not only in biblical and historical studies, and in ethics, but also in constructive theology, where such movements as liberation theology and feminist theology are almost completely trans-confessional.

At the community and parish level, such things as exchange of pulpits and common worship have become commonplace. In some places, Reformation Day has seemed to become an integral part of the Catholic calendar of Saints' Days. And on the broader scale, the quincentennial of Luther's birth (1983) and the four hundred fiftieth anniversary of the Augsburg Confession (1980) were widely celebrated in the Catholic world.

The last point suggests a further reflection on the impact of Roman Catholic ecumenism. On the one hand, Luther in particular and the Reformation in general have been extensively rehabilitated in Roman Catholic thinking, with a growing recognition of the responsibility of Rome for the sixteenth-century divisions and with a broad acknowledgment of the extent to which the Reformation emphases were (and ought to be) ingredients in the Catholic tradition. On the other hand, Protestants have been driven back to reconsider the Reformation and the medieval church and have had to recognize much more that the characteristic Reformation themes were not novelties but had deep roots in medieval tradition. Luther's doctrine of grace and faith can be found almost precisely in Thomas Aquinas, rightly understood. And (as even Ritschl had seen a century ago) the notion of *sola scriptura* had been anticipated by Duns Scotus and the Franciscans. Also, many Protestants have come to see the papacy as at least a useful symbol of the unity of the church. Therefore, why not return to Rome? What is it that really divides Protestant and Catholic? Thus Protestants have had to reconsider their whole tradition as a consequence of the twentieth-century ecumenical movement. To this question we return in the final chapter.

Finally, consideration of the recent developments in the ecumenical movement raises the question of whether the most profound divisions in Christianity are not the ecclesiastical ones, but theological and social distinctions that cut across Protestant and Catholic lines — divisions between liberals and conservatives (i.e., between those who accept historical critical method and those who do not), or between the privileged and the oppressed, or between the political and economic liberals and conservatives.

CHAPTER **XIV**

Post-War Directions

For a decade or so after the end of World War II, the Protestant theological world seemed relatively stable. The directions of thought that we summarized in Chapter XII, under the heading "Between the Wars," were still dominant in the theological centers in Europe, America, and the Far East. But by the nineteen-sixties and seventies, the situation was changed radically. The giants of Protestant thought in the preceding time — the Niebuhrs and Tillich and Barth and Brunner and Bultmann — were gone. Their names remained household words in the theological schools and their influence persisted, either positively or negatively, in the work of a host of thinkers, ranging from Pannenberg and Moltmann to Langdon Gilkey and Gordon Kaufman. But the dominance of their thought, the apparent order provided by their common emphases, had vanished.

What has followed in the Protestant scene is not easy to describe or explain. Historical studies have flourished to an amazing degree, with a flood of new studies of all periods in Christian history. Biblical studies have proceeded apace, with such new ventures as sociological interpretations of the life of Israel and of the early Christian community. The study of Christianity, as well as of other religions, has expanded greatly outside the theological school world in the universities and colleges. And one can characterize the *theological visions* of the recent decades by such terms as novel ventures, rich diversity, and creative directions. But one can, and must, also speak of radical pluralism, restlessness and disorder, even confusion and uncertainty (or competing certainties). To use the latter terms is not to say that there have not been striking new impulses, but rather that no coherent pattern is visible in the multiplicity of directions that have been proposed. Hence we can aptly say that for the most recent years, Protestant thinking has been "at sixes and sevens." This diversity, moreover, needs to be seen in the context of great social uncertainties, for example, the anxieties and fears of the nuclear age, the estrangement from tradition and authority in the unrest and protest of the late 1960s (the rise of a "counterculture"), new social activism, the eclipse (particularly in America) of the Protestant establishment, the civil rights movement, and the Vietnam protests.

Our task in this and the following chapter is to give a sketch at least of some of the multiple tendencies that have come to the fore. Among these should be counted the recent developments in the ecumenical movement, which have been discussed at the end of the preceding chapter. Other impulses that might well be identified include new ventures in the relation of theology and science (e.g., in the work of Wolfhart Pannenberg, Ian Barbour, Thomas Torrance, and Arthur Peacock), and the growing sense of the importance of artistic expression (especially in literature and the visual arts) for theological articulation. We shall be primarily concerned here, however, with the following half-dozen kinds of development:

1) new philosophical connections;
2) various sorts of "radical theology";
3) the resurgence of conservatism;
4) the emergence of "theologies of hope";
5) "liberation" theologies; and
6) the growing recognition of religious pluralism and the tentative steps toward interreligious dialogue.

The first three of these strands, which may be said to be responses to questions posed by the immediate past, are treated in this chapter. In Chapter XV we take up the latter three trends, which seem more future-oriented.

New Philosophical Alliances and Critiques

Theology and Process Thought

Process theology is a term commonly used to denote one of the most readily identifiable schools of late-twentieth-century Protestant thought. The roots of the movement go back at least to the work of the French philosopher Henri Bergson, especially in *Creative Evolution* (Eng. tr., 1911), and of the British philosophers Samuel Alexander, in *Space, Time and Deity* (1920), and C. Lloyd Morgan, in *Emergent Evolution* (1923), in which important steps were taken toward conceiving reality fundamentally as process, development, and evolution. But the philosophical hero of the movement is unquestionably Alfred North Whitehead (1861–1947), who was a noted mathematician (teacher and collaborator of Bertrand Russell) and philosopher of science at Cambridge and London before accepting a chair in philosophy at Harvard in 1924 and developing a full-scale metaphysics in *Process and Reality* (1929).

The latter work was to become the touchstone for the theological exploitation of process modes of thought, though Whitehead's earlier *Science and the Modern World* (1925) and *Religion in the Making* (1926) were also welcomed by theologians. Whitehead's thought was at once taken up by two major Anglican theologians, Lionel Thornton, in *The Incarnate Lord* (1928), and William Temple, in *Nature, Man and God* (1934). But it was mainly in the United States that a self-conscious movement of process thought was to develop, and then largely among theologians and philosophers of religion rather than among "secular" philosophers who were much more interested in exploring modes of "analytical philosophy" (see following section, "Theology and Analytic Philosophy") than in revisions of traditional metaphysics.

For two decades after the publication of *Process and Reality* the development of the Whiteheadian impulse was carried on mainly by the theological faculty of the University of Chicago, in such thinkers as Bernard Meland, Bernard Loomer, and above all Charles Hartshorne, who became for several decades the most intense philosophical advocate and interpreter of a Whiteheadian understanding of God. For process theology the work of Daniel Day Williams, especially *God's Grace and Man's Hope* (1949), may also be seen as a landmark, attempting to show how a process view of God and the world is not only more relevant to modern science, and a viable way between naturalism and traditional or neo-orthodox supernaturalism, but also more in accord with biblical understandings. From the 1960s, the employment of process categories has been continued vigorously in such works as Schubert Ogden, *The Reality of God* (1966), and especially in the publications of John B. Cobb, Jr.: e.g., *A Christian Natural Theology: Based on the Thought of Alfred North Whitehead* (1965); *God and the World* (1969); and *Christ in a Pluralistic Age* (1975).[1]

At the heart of process thought is the insistence that time, process, and relationship are more fundamental categories for understanding

---

[1] Both Ogden and Cobb were students of Charles Hartshorne. For a useful collection of essays on various aspects of process theology, see Delwin Brown, Ralph E. James, Jr., and Gene Reeves, eds., *Process Philosophy and Christian Thought* (New York, 1971). See also John B. Cobb, Jr., and David R. Griffin, *Process Theology, An Introductory Exposition* (Philadelphia, 1976). It should also be noted that the highly influential work of the Jesuit paleontologist Teilhard de Chardin is also often counted in the process theology camp, as in Ewert Cousins, *Process Theology: Basic Writings* (New York, 1971), though in Teilhard there is not the specific determination from Whitehead.

reality than "being," whether in the sense of finite, discrete entities or infinite and unchangeable divine being. All reality, for Whitehead, is dynamic and social, a creative process in which all "actual entities" are interrelated, requiring antecedent others as their constituents and being taken up in others in an endless process of new syntheses (i.e., of creativity). In other words, to oversimplify greatly, if we try to start from the idea of independent or static being we cannot account for the reality of time and change, whereas if we begin with process and relationship as fundamental, we can understand actual entities (or "actual occasions") as the final real things of which the world is made up.

The complex structure of Whitehead's argument, and the problems of its special terminology, need not concern us here. What is more important are the consequences that this way of thinking has for the notions of God and of God's relation to the world. Though the doctrine of God was not as such an organizing principle of Whitehead's work, his philosophy was affected from the beginning by a Christian view of reality. And his basic vision of reality, it is argued, is more compatible with essential elements of Christian faith than is the older metaphysics. The idea of God as a simply independent, immutable (i.e., unchangeable and impassable) being, the creator of an utterly dependent world over which God exercises omnipotence and omniscience (even knowledge of the future), will no longer do. That idea, it is alleged, derives ultimately from Aristotle's "unmoved mover," and it is inconsistent both with a modern scientific worldview and with the Christian conception of a loving and responsive God. God must rather be conceived of as, in some real sense, dependent on the world and thus as capable of changing in relation to it. The future is open (i.e., it is really future and cannot be known, even by God, except as a realm of possibilities whose actualizations are yet to be determined). Thus God must be held in a real way to experience and be affected by the concrete entities of the world, hence to be *in* the creative process. God too is in the process of becoming; God's nature is (partly) consequent upon the creative advance of the world, and God and the world are genuinely interdependent. Thus God's nature is "di-polar." In Whitehead's language, God's "primordial" or conceptual nature is unchanging, the original fact of the universe, but as an abstraction or conceptual structure lacking in actualization. The "consequent" nature of God is that in which God as an actual entity takes in and is affected by temporal entities, thus incorporating novelty and being dependent upon the creative advance of the world.

As a way of denoting such a conception of God and the world, Charles Hartshorne has popularized the term "panentheism," to be distinguished from theism and pantheism. Pantheism has generally meant simple identification of God and the world. Theism, as traditionally interpreted in the medieval world and indeed in most European thought before 1800, denoted an utterly self-sufficient divine being, perfect and immutable, and in no sense dependent on the world. As Hartshorne puts it, that kind of theism holds that "there is a being in *all* respects absolutely perfect or unsurpassable, in no way and in no respect surpassable or perfectible." But such a notion, which is coupled with the ideas of omnipotence and impassability, has to be rejected. It is incompatible with human freedom and makes God responsible for evil. Even more, Hartshorne argues, it is a rationally incoherent notion. But the alternative possibilities are not simply pantheism or atheism, or polytheism or a merely finite God. Panentheism is proposed as a view in which God and the world are interdependent and the world is *in* God but not coincident with God, for God surpasses the world in critical respects. God includes the world while transcending it. God is relative to the world in that God changes as the world changes. God is not perfect in every respect but only in some respects and is relatively perfect in other respects (e.g., in power). As the supremely related, God influences and is influenced by the world. God is thus the "self-surpassing surpasser of all." God's being is enriched and enlarged by experience, but just as such cannot be surpassed by anything other.[2]

Conceptions such as this, as Ogden has argued, make the expressions of Christian belief possible. One can say literally, and not just symbolically, that God acts in the world. One can speak both of God's general activity in creation and redemption and of God's special action in unique historical events, notably in Jesus Christ and his suffering love. Thus, as D. D. Williams argues in *The Spirit and Forms of Love* (New York, 1968) — a work that has been called the most fully developed statement of the process movement — the metaphysical structures disclosed in the human experience of love may be applied to God's creative activity (for unless God's love is in some sense like human love, it is simply unknown). Instead of the coercive God of classical theology, to whom human response adds nothing, the biblical God of love seeks only to persuade, in mutual freedom and risk, working in and through creatures who suffer and become occasions for God's suffering, yet without negating the invulnerability and integrity of God, the creative vision which is God's majesty. As John Cobb has put it, traditional thought about God is not distinctively or centrally Christian; it does not square with experienced evil and it works against the attainment of full humanity. Christian faith is not tied to the idea of God as creator, lord of history, lawgiver, and judge. The modern vision requires either drastic reconception of God or abandonment of God

---

[2] See Hartshorne, *Man's Vision of God and the Logic of Theism* (Chicago, 1941), and *The Divine Relativity: A Social Conception of God* (New Haven, 1948).

language. The God of traditional theism is dead and deserves to die.

As noted, process theology has developed as a distinctive school of thought and has grown mainly in America, being actively promoted by the Claremont Center for Process Thought. Yet while it has become the principal contender as a replacement for traditional metaphysical theology and natural theology, and has had influence on a wide variety of thinkers who may not consider themselves "process theologians," its impact has been slight among the professional philosophers, and it has had to share the stage with other personae who question the viability of the "metaphysical" option.

Theology and Analytical Philosophy

Moving in quite a different direction from the process theologians have been those for whom the primary theological dialogue must be with analytical philosophy or language "analysis." Here the question is not one of a better metaphysics, but whether metaphysics and theology are possible at all. What can religious assertions mean, especially statements about God? Not, are religious affirmations true? but what kind of meaning do they have? What logical status do they have? This is the sort of question that has dominated the philosophical schools in Britain and America, though not in Europe, for the past half-century and more. It is signaled by a return (from a blend of theology and idealist philosophy) to common sense as the starting point for philosophy and to "analysis" as its method, or as some would say, to the empiricist standpoint of Locke and Hume. The philosopher here has no business constructing sets of speculative beliefs about the universe, and indeed such beliefs may be judged by philosophy to be either false or meaningless.

For these ways of thinking, one must note the enormous impact of modern science. (That is also true, of course, for Whitehead and those influenced by him — though the analytical philosophers look upon Whitehead as a reactionary.) Given the pervasive doubt about the metaphysical enterprise that goes back at least to Immanuel Kant, the question of epistemology has become dominant. That is, how and about what can we have certain knowledge in a time of moral, religious, and esthetic confusion?

The celebration of science as a bedrock model of knowledge, and the strongest hostility to theology, for example, appears in the movement called Logical Positivism, originating in the program of the so-called Vienna circle. The concerns of this group grew directly out of the impact of relativity physics on the concepts of scientists, whereby any concepts that do not have their place in statements subject to observational or experimental verification are empty of meaning and do not refer to anything. This kind of judgment was extended to the definition of meaning in general, so that "the meaning of [any] statement is the method of its verification." Or, as reformulated, "a statement is meaningful if and only if some sense-experience is relevant to its verification." That kind of "verification principle" was reflected in the classic statement of A. J. Ayer, in *Language, Truth and Logic* (1936), where meaningful statements are divided into three classes: (1) there are logical and mathematical statements, which have no factual content but whose truth is guaranteed by their ultimately tautological character and the definition of their symbols; (2) there are empirical assertions of common sense and science, which can be verified or falsified by some relevant sense-experience; and (3) there are utterances (e.g., value statements in ethics and esthetics), which have no factual meaning but express attitudes and emotions. Metaphysical statements, of which theology is a special case, may be grouped with the third sort of utterances, but since they express neither logical truths nor empirical hypotheses, they are strictly without meaning. To say "there is a God," which sounds like an empirical assertion, is not even a false statement; it is an assertion without any meaning, a nonsensical locution, since its truth or falsity is not subject to verification.

Now anyone with the vaguest familiarity with the history of theology will perceive that the logical positivists did not discover anything new in showing that statements about God are quite different from statements about particular empirical facts. Who had supposed that the question about God can be settled in the same way as the question about electrons? And it was quickly recognized that the verification principle itself does not belong to one of the classes of meaningful propositions, but is a metaphysical assertion of the first order (thus the rules for meaningfulness either let metaphysics and religion in, or they keep science out). But the impact of the positivist critique was a powerful imperative to reflect on the distinctive nature of religious assertions, particularly on the logical status of "God talk." And this was an imperative widely felt among British and American thinkers, so that the primary question could become "what is the meaning of the statement that 'God is' or 'God exists'?"

The decisive turn from positivism to what is dubbed "analytical philosophy" or "philosophical analysis" came from the posthumously published work of Ludwig Wittgenstein, *Philosophical Investigations* (1953). Here Wittgenstein turned his back on his own earlier attempt to say what logical perfection in language would be (an effort that had much in common with the logical positivists), in favor of the view that there are many "language games." The task of philosophical investigation is not to prescribe a single language (e.g., the language that conveys factual information) as the norm, but to explore the uses of ordinary language, to recognize the "prodigious diversity of all the everyday language games" (including guessing riddles, giving orders, thanking, swearing, storytelling, greeting, praying, etc.), and to discover the rules that hold in each game. In other words, the task of analysis is to understand the meaning of an expression by identifying the ways in which it is used with point and purpose.

Here then are possibilities of a more productive encounter with theology, an opening to the "truth" of religion, and a renewed interest by professional philosophers in the philosophy of religion. The question becomes: what is the meaning of religious language, especially of God talk? Subsequent answers to this question have been almost as varied as the schools of analytical philosophy, which have often seemed to have little to do with each other (or even to recognize each other's existence) except for the idea that rules according to which words are used have to be essentially public. Some philosophers of religion have welcomed the positivist attack on the meaning of theological assertions on the (Barthian) grounds that theology is in no way beholden to philosophy (i.e., that religious language is so idiosyncratic that no philosophical account can be given of it). Others, like Anthony Flew, have focused on the problem of "falsification." That is, we can know the meaning of an assertion only if we can say what would count to make it false. For example, what state of affairs would count decisively against the statement "God loves us"? If such a statement of belief is compatible with every conceivable state of affairs, then how is the meaning different from the statement "God does not love us"? Its meaning is evacuated in "death by a thousand qualifications."[3]

Some thinkers, in response, have suggested that religious assertions are not explanations or references to distinctive observable facts, but are an outlook or point of view placed on the facts. For this, R. M. Hare coined the term *blik*. Everyone has a blik, which may be a religious blik or even an insane blik, to which one may be passionately attached. Bliks are not facts but ways of looking at things to which we are committed. And in this sense, bliks are the stuff of religious beliefs. In a related way, thinkers like R. B. Braithwaite have interpreted religious utterances as a kind of moral assertion. They are not statements of fact but expressions of commitment to a policy of action, a way of life. For example, the Christian's statement "God is love" means "I intend to lead a life of love." And what distinguishes religion from morality is the *stories* that belong to a religion, which are entertained in the religious person's mind and which (whether true or false) act as a psychological aid in carrying out the moral intention.

Still others have emphasized that religious utterances cannot be taken in isolation but must be understood in a whole context of religious

---

[3] See the fascinating *University* discussion of Theology and Falsification in A. Flew and A. MacIntyre, eds., *New Essays in Philosophical Theology* (London, 1955).

discourse. And that in turn requires the recognition of particular religions, each of which has its ways of deciding on the authenticity of a belief or practice (i.e., its criteria for determining what religious utterances are authentic). Or, to use the language of "conviction" as a stronger term than belief, we cannot justify any one conviction apart from its connection with other convictions held by the same person or the "convictional community." (See, for example, the work of McClendon and Smith, *Understanding Religious Convictions* [Notre Dame, 1975], which takes up the term conviction from the philosopher Willem Zuurdeeg and develops it in relation to J. L. Austin's "speech-act" theory of religious language.)

Another, much-discussed approach to the meaning of religious language has been than of Ian T. Ramsey, who spoke of situations of "cosmic disclosure" as the way of accounting for the origin of religious language. There are many situations of disclosure or discernment in which suddenly "the ice breaks, the penny drops, the light dawns." What distinguishes the religious from these ordinary situations is that there "occurs a disclosure of such a range and extent that it might be called 'cosmic' " or total, and that it evokes total commitment. In such situations arises belief in God. The language that results, in the attempt to describe the mystery of what is discerned, is a language of stories and particularly of "models" (technically analog models, as in the formulae of chemistry). Models use ordinary language as indicators, though as imperfect or "odd" indicators which must be "qualified" to show the direction in which they are to be developed. For instance, to say that God is a shepherd (i.e., shepherdlike in some ways and not in other ways) needs qualifiers like "infinite" or "ultimate" to indicate the direction for development. Not that the mystery will ever be simply removed, but by expansion of this qualification a discernment can occur which evokes an appropriate commitment. Religious utterances therefore have reference to something other than the attitudes or emotions of the believer, and they can be tested, or justified, by their "empirical fit" with the religious situations in which they arise and to which they lead.

Many other variations in the dialogue between theology and linguistic analysis could be noted, for example, in the work of A. Plantiga, N. Malcolm, Basie Mitchell, F. Ferré, P. Geach, D. Z. Phillips, and A. MacIntyre. But these examples may suffice to suggest the intensity and character of the discussion. While it has been argued that analytical philosophy as a movement has "peaked out" and that other styles of philosophizing (e.g., in neo-Marxist or in hermeneutical studies) have moved to center stage, the effect of the debate has permeated much of Protestant (and Catholic) thought. It is difficult, for example, to find a major theological work of recent decades which does not make at least some reference to Wittgenstein. And at the minimum, theological verbiage has had some badly needed cleaning up and theologians have had to be much more careful in their use of language.

The New Hermeneutic

Another sort of philosophical interest in language, which has been of growing import to the theologian, is represented by developments in hermeneutics. In general, hermeneutics has meant the study of the principles of interpretation, especially of texts and prominently the biblical texts. In what is sometimes called the new hermeneutic, however, the problems of textual interpretation are related to the most general problems of meaning and language, thus to a "hermeneutic of existence." It is possible for a noted theologian to say that "hermeneutics now takes the place of the classical epistemological theory. . . . For theology the hermeneutical problem is therefore today becoming the place of meeting with philosophy" (Gerhard Ebeling, *Word and Faith* [London, 1963], p. 317).

The concerns of the new hermeneutic obviously overlap and intersect with the concerns of analytic philosophy, particularly those of Wittgenstein, but they offer a significantly different sort of substitute for the traditional metaphysical preoccupations of theology. This focus on language gets its impetus from existentialism and the human sciences rather than from the empiricism of Locke and Hume and the natural sciences. Hermeneutics becomes the dialogue partner of theology, so that a hermeneutical philosophy of language comes to have the relevance for theology that metaphysics had for pre-Kantian philosophical theology.

The main line of development in the philosophy of hermeneutics may be said to run from Rudolf Bultmann and Martin Heidegger to Hans-Georg Gadamer and especially (by way of the phenomenologist Edmund Husserl) to Paul Ricoeur.

For Bultmann, as we noted in Chap. XII, "demythologizing" as the proper way of dealing with the mythological worldview of the Bible means "existentialist interpretation." That is, our task is not to reject or simply eliminate the myths about a three-story universe with supernatural beings intervening in the world process, as liberalism sought to do, but to explore what the myths may be saying about the human relation to God in the midst of the world. And what the New Testament offers us is a message about the transition from sin to faith (i.e., from human existence prior to faith to "man under faith") or from inauthentic to authentic existence, a salvation-occurrence announced and made possible by the act of God.

This kind of interpretation involves a further step in hermeneutical theory. There is no "special" hermeneutics for Scripture, for the same hermeneutical principles must apply to the interpretation of all texts, but all hermeneutics needs explicitly to recognize the "interest" of the interpreter. Understanding is never without presuppositions. Questioning arises from a particular interest in the matter referred to in the texts and therefore an understanding of the matter is presupposed. This Bultmann (along with Heidegger) calls a pre-understanding (a *Vorverständnis*), and it involves the distinction between authentic and inauthentic existence. The latter distinction was developed by Heidegger as part of his larger effort (in *Being and Time,* 1927) to deal with the problem of being in general through the analysis of *human* being, which is where being is "lit up" and "unconcealed," so that "man is the guardian of being." Thus Heidegger sought to elaborate the *existentialia* or basic structures of human existence (*Dasein*) as a replacement for Kant's "categories" that had been articulated for a Newtonian scientific world. (Bultmann judged that the possibility of authentic existence and the actual "fallenness" of existence could be adequately stated by an existentialist philosophy, but that the actualization of authentic life emerges only in response to the kerygma.)

More broadly, with respect to hermeneutics, Heidegger described the "hermeneutical circle" as one in which the understanding of the text remains permanently determined by the anticipatory movement of pre-understanding. That is, the meaning of a text always goes beyond its author; its meaning is not just what the author intended, or his perspective, but it is always partly determined by the historical situation of the interpreter. Understanding is thus the interplay of the movement of tradition and the movement of the interpreter. Furthermore, if we ask the question, what does it mean to be human?, Heidegger affirms that "man is language," in the sense that language is the openness of *Dasein* and reveals the relationship to being. Understanding is the original character of the being of human life itself. Thus with Heidegger the problem of hermeneutics gains a universal framework. It becomes a hermeneutic of facticity, an "ontological" hermeneutics, not only posing principles of textual interpretation, but setting forth an interpretation of existence.

In a related way, the pupil of Bultmann and Heidegger, Hans-Georg Gadamer (*Wahrheit und Methode* [2nd ed., Tübingen, 1965], Eng. tr., *Truth and Method* [London, 1975]) writes of the universality of the hermeneutical aspect and of language as the "horizon" of hermeneutical ontology. The world which exists for human beings is linguistic in nature. It is in language that the world presents itself. One speaks of the "linguisticality" of existence, for language is the universal medium of all our thinking and experiencing. It is both the point where "I" and the world show their original unity and the medium through which the difference of "I" and the world is recognized. The object of knowledge and of statements is already enclosed within the world horizons of language. (That is why the meaning of a text always goes beyond its author and why understanding is not only a reproductive but a productive activity.) "That which can be understood is language. . . . For man's relation to the world is absolutely and fundamentally linguistic in nature, and hence intelligible" (*Truth and Method*, pp. 432f.). We grasp being through language.[4]

The attraction of theologians to the hermeneutical approach has become most prominent in relation to the work of Gadamer's "dialogue partner," Paul Ricoeur. This may be particularly because of Ricoeur's attention to religious discourse, to symbolism and the poetic, and even to the hermeneutics of revelation. Ricoeur, too, asserts the basic linguisticality of the process of understanding, for language is the medium in which concrete experiencing and abstract thinking take definite shape and are determined as the experience of something and not another thing. The area of language, for Ricoeur, is where all recent philosophical investigations cut across one another — Wittgenstein, English linguistic philosophy, phenomenology since Husserl, Heidegger, Bultmann and other New Testament exegetes, comparative history of religion, anthropology, and psychoanalysis. Thus, drawing on an enormous variety of sources, including almost every major thinker who has influenced the modern mind, Ricoeur has set out to develop an inclusive hermeneutical theory, a complete ontology of language.

Out of this complex and still developing theory, only a few elements can be noted. One is Ricoeur's critique of Bultmann. As Ricoeur sees it, there were three levels in the program of demythologizing. The first was the elimination of the cosmological form of primitive Christian preaching. The second was the expression of the New Testament meaning in terms of the world of human self-understanding in relation to the foundation and limitations of existence. The third was interpretation that begins with the kerygma, where one speaks as hearer of the Word, as believer, in nonmythological statements about "act of God" and "Word of God," in statements of pure faith where the object of faith and the foundation of faith are the same. But as Ricoeur sees it, having rejected "objectifying" language Bultmann does not carry forward the necessary analysis of language which is no longer objectifying. Bultmann speaks of symbol, image, and analogy in the language of faith but does not analyze this. What needs to be done is to set this in the framework of an inclusive understanding of language, in which comprehension includes "ideality" of meaning and existential signification.

---

[4] Gerhard Ebeling, whom we quoted earlier, also spoke of the linguisticality of existence, but with a more restricted focus on the "word event" as the central category for interpreting the relation between "Word of God" and "word in general." This involves a shift from understanding *of* language to understanding *through* language. "Word" itself has a hermeneutical character, so that the gospel is itself a word event. God can be spoken of in theology only as the *world* thereby comes to expression as event and the world can be spoken of only as *God* comes to expression as event.

Among the most widely cited elements of Ricoeur's developed hermeneutical theory are the phrases "hermeneutics of suspicion" and "second naiveté." Ricoeur's "masters of suspicion" are Marx, Nietzsche, and Freud. (See especially *Freud and Philosophy: An Essay on Interpretation* [New Haven, 1970].) From them we have to learn the necessity of methodical doubt about the contents of consciousness. We have to distinguish between the apparent meaning of our inner states, which is often counterfeit (illusions masking unresolved personal conflicts or social and economic inequities), and the true meaning about human being which lies behind the appearances.

The notion of the "second naiveté" or "second immediacy" is particularly important in Ricoeur's reflections on myth and symbol, which have been a major theme since *Fallible Man* (1965), which is an extended analysis of the dimension of human being that is designated by the concept of fallibility, a concept pertaining to the innermost structure of human reality. The first naiveté is the stage of the self-evidence of symbol and myth and it includes not only the primary symbols (e.g., the Fall), but the theological and metaphysical concepts that reflection on them traditionally led to. The critical consciousness which was particularly the consequence of Kant, however, dissolves that self-evidence of symbolic meaning by the question "how do I know what appears to me is as it appears?" and paves the way for the hermeneutics of suspicion, which unmasks the illusions bound up with the first naiveté by showing the hidden investments of self-interest. The second immediacy, which can only follow upon the stage of critique, is accessible only in hermeneutics, whose task is that of deciphering the double meaning of symbolic expressions. (See *Freud;* see also *The Conflict of Interpretations: Essays in Hermeneutics* [Evanston, IL, 1974].) Symbolism, especially religious symbolism, confronts us with language that is equivocal "not by default of univocation, but by excess of meaning." The task of hermeneutics is to struggle against forgetting by returning to language as richness of meaning, and this can be a way in which modernity overcomes its forgetfulness of the sacred.

Every text, for Ricoeur, has an autonomy by virtue of its having been written, an autonomy that bursts the world of the intention of the author and that removes the reader from the horizon of its original audience. The world of the text is "the sort of world intended beyond the text as its reference." In symbol and myth, this reference is not the same sort of referential function as in ordinary language or scientific discourse. That is particularly important with respect to poetic sorts of texts — including prophecy, narrative (and Ricoeur has been especially interested in the parables of Jesus), legislation, wisdom literature, supplication, thanksgiving, etc. Religious discourse is poetic, and Ricoeur can say "My deepest conviction is that poetic language alone restores to us that participation-in or belonging-to an order of things which precedes our capacity to oppose ourselves to things taken as objects opposed to a subject" (*Essays on Biblical Interpretation* [Philadelphia, 1980] p. 101). To the autonomy of the text, the externality of the work, and the transcendence of the world of the text, there is added a "split reference" to the primordial ground of our existence. Its truth (and this is an areligious sense of revelation) is a manifestation, a "letting what shows itself be."

Though Ricoeur has written only in occasional form about religious language, which he regularly identifies with biblical language, it is easy to see why his hermeneutical approach is attractive to the theologian. Religious texts, beyond the dimensions of self-recognition and of empowering authentic existence, can be understood to present the possibility of an openness for the appearance of God beyond the disappearance of God for thought. The philosopher remains suspended between atheism and faith, but may still dig beneath the surface to a level of questioning that makes possible a mediation between religion and faith by way of atheism.

The interest of theologians in Ricoeur, and in the new hermeneutics generally, also reflects a strong tendency that is present in the other kinds of philosophical alliance described in this section. This is the tendency to define philosophy as the principal dialogue partner of theology. The intimate mutual involvement of theology and philosophy is not of course a new development. From the early centuries, Christian thinking has been informed by numerous philosophies — Platonic, neo-Platonic, Aristotelian, Cartesian, Kantian, Hegelian, existentialist, etc. And sometimes it has been hard to define the boundary between philosophy and theology.

But the relations have been quite varied. Sometimes this involvement has meant simply the use of current philosophical notions as vehicles for the expression of fundamental religious insights. Sometimes, as in Karl Barth, the attempt has been made to avoid any kind of dependence of theology on philosophy. At other times the relation has been one in which a particular philosophical or metaphysical scheme has limited or determined what it is possible for theology to say. The latter view was most extremely described in Ludwig Feuerbach's comment on Hegelian philosophy; namely, that this philosophy only lets religion say what speculation has already said and said much better. Though in a less rigorous way, something of that attitude may be said to be reflected in the recent preoccupations with Whitehead or with analytical philosophy or with the hermeneutical philosophy of Heidegger or Gadamer or Ricoeur. And the attitude becomes intensified again in the flurry of interest in the 1980s in "deconstructing" theology, for which the work of the French philosopher Jacques Derrida is largely responsible (see especially Mark C. Taylor, *Erring: A Postmodern A/Theology* [Chicago, 1984]).

The broader question here, however, is whether the nature and scope of the theological enterprise is determined dominantly, if not exclusively, in debate with contemporary philosophy. For most of the developments so far sketched in this chapter, the answer appears to be affirmative. But other possibilities have also emerged, in which the theological program is to be ordered and tested, not primarily in conversation with philosophy but in relation to the natural or the social sciences, or to literature and the arts, or to the concrete life of persons (particularly the oppressed) in the church, or to the realities of other kinds of religious experience, especially in the non-Christian religions. We need to turn to some of these other directions in Chapter XV.

Theological Radicalism

In the decade of the 1960s a series of new catchwords emerged in the Protestant theological scene: "secular theology," "religionless Christianity," "death of God," "a world come of age," "the alienated theologian," "the post-Christian era," and the like.

Behind such phrases and the tendencies of thought they reflected were broad streams of estrangement and protest that may justly be described as a cultural revolution. These were quite diverse. They included a powerful antitraditionalism, not only with respect to religion but also with relation to social, educational, and political institutions generally, with deep distrust of the competence of existing institutions to overcome the disparity between professed ideal and actual performance. These protests involved a profound questioning of traditional religion, or at least indifference to it, and a growing acceptance of the "secular" as normative for human life. They were marked by widespread dissent by the young against the elders ("no one over thirty can be trusted"), particularly in the educational establishments. Such protests ranged from the "free speech" movement in California to the demand of German students for *Drittelparität* (i.e., an equal share in university governance), and from the creation of "free universities" to the occasional prohibition of the setting of academic requirements by faculties.

There were new impulses of social activism, most dramatically in the United States in the civil rights movement, in the emergence of black militancy, and in the violent outcry against the Vietnam War at the end of the 1960s. Most broadly, they reflected the awful uncertainty of the threat of nuclear holocaust, as well as the growing recollection of the Nazi extermination camps (Auschwitz and Hiroshima alike testified to the self-destructive potential of the human race). There was thus a pervasive moral outrage at a world of astonishing growth in technical capacity which seemed to have neither the will nor the ability to deal with racial injustice or world poverty, or to assure the continuation of the human experiment.

The specific theological radicalisms that emerged in the 1960s may be traced back in a special way — though only in a way — to the late writings of the German theologian and martyr Dietrich Bonhoeffer (who was executed in 1945 because of his participation in a plot on Hitler's life). Bonhoeffer had already been well-known as a promising theologian and the leader of an underground seminary of the "Confessing Church" in the Nazi period, and had launched a vigorous attack on the "cheap grace" which makes no demands on Christians. This, he said, is "the deadly enemy of our Church. We are fighting today for costly grace." (See *The Cost of Discipleship* [London, 1937]; see also *Life Together* [London, 1938].) What made Bonhoeffer most famous, however, were the somewhat enigmatic phrases from his prison writings about a "religionless Christianity" and "a nonreligious interpretation of the gospel" (*Letters and Papers from Prison,* Eng. tr. [London, 1951]).

In part, this language of Bonhoeffer recalls the sharp distinction made by Karl Barth, in his commentary on Romans, between "religion" as the highest projection of the human spirit and the utterly different revelation of God in Christ, which is not a humanly possible attainment, but a divine Yes and No that comes from beyond the world. But Bonhoeffer's point was different. For him, "we are proceeding towards a time of no religion at all: men as they now are simply cannot be religious any more." That is, religion (including traditional Christian religion) for which God is an explanation of the world, or a supplement to human resources, a *deus ex machina* who intervenes to set things right, has come to the end of its time. The kind of God for whom room has to be made is superfluous in a world that has come of age, in which human beings can and must assume responsibility for themselves and their world.

As Bonhoeffer put it, now "the linchpin is removed from the whole structure of our Christianity to date." Metaphysical supernaturalism and individualistic piety, both of which abandon rather than affirm the secular world, must themselves be abandoned. But this did not mean for Bonhoeffer a simple discarding of God or an impossibility for Christian existence. Rather, God is to be spoken of in a different way, "not on the borders of life but at its center, not in weakness but in strength, not, therefore, in man's suffering but in his life and prosperity. . . . God is the 'beyond' in the midst of our life" (*Letters,* p. 93). Indeed, "our coming of age forces us to a true recognition of our situation vis-à-vis God. God is teaching us that we must live as men who can get along very well without him. The God who is with us is the God who forsakes us (Mark 15:34). The God who makes us live in this world without using him as a working hypothesis is the

God before whom we are ever standing. Before God and with him we live without God. . . . God is weak and powerless in the world, and that is exactly the way, the only way, in which he can be with us and help us. Matthew 8:17 makes it crystal clear that it is not by his omnipotence that Christ helps us, but by his weakness and suffering" (*Letters*, p. 122).

If this is the biblical God, who can be met at the center of life, then the Christian life is a "worldly" life of sharing God's suffering in existence for humanity. Christianity plunges us into, not away from, the many dimensions of life.

Bonhoeffer's tantalizing assertions, though never systematized by him, captured the imagination of a host of others. At the minimum, as Paul Ricoeur has put it, "Bonhoeffer has said all that needs to be said against the God of the gaps, whether it be a question of explaining things or of understanding humanity" (*Essays on Biblical Interpretation* [Philadelphia, 1980], p. 97). But beyond that, Bonhoeffer's suggestions have been pegs on which many different theological coats have been hung.

Among those varieties, for example, should be noted the immensely popular work of 1963, *Honest to God*, by the Bishop of Woolich, J. A. T. Robinson. To be sure, what was said in *Honest to God* could cause no particular excitement among the theologically sophisticated who had any familiarity with Bultmann or Tillich or Bonhoeffer, on whom Robinson was heavily dependent. But it did create a public outcry that an Anglican bishop should be propounding the rejection of supranaturalistic ideas of a God "out there" in favor of a Tillichian "ground of being," and a demythologized and "religionless" Christianity, as well as a new morality based on love alone, rather than legalistic prescription, in accord with faithfulness to Jesus as utterly "the man for others." (For a vivid sense of the excitement aroused by Robinson's book, see *The Honest to God Debate* [Philadelphia, 1963], which includes more than a score of reviews and extracts from dozens of letters, as well as further brief essays by Robinson and several other English thinkers.)

In the same year as *Honest to God*, there appeared an American work by Paul M. Van Buren, *The Secular Meaning of the Gospel* (New York, 1963), in which Bultmann and Bonhoeffer also figured prominently, but with the added dimension of an appeal to the work of some of the analytical philosophers. The question whether "God talk" has any meaning comes again to the fore. Van Buren takes it as a consensus of modern kerygmatic theology (Bultmann) and some analytical philosophy that "simple literal theism is wrong and qualified literal theism is meaningless." He opts therefore for a noncognitive, "blik" conception of faith. The language of faith has meaning not as a kind of cosmological assertion but as referring to the Christian way of life. God-statements are translated into "man-statements." Thus statements of faith are to be understood "as statements which express, describe, or commend a particular way of seeing the world, other men, and oneself, and the way of life appropriate to such a perspective" (p. 156). The norm for such a perspective, however, remains the events of the New Testament, centering in the life, death, and resurrection of Jesus Christ. Jesus of Nazareth is the truly "secular man," "a man singularly free for other men, and . . . a man whose freedom became contagious," and thus continues to be central to Christian faith and life. (One wag has commented, though not particularly in reference to van Buren's book, "there is no God and Jesus is his son.")

The theme of "secularity" was sounded in another way by Harvey Cox's popular *The Secular City* (New York, 1965), in which the values of urban life and technology were hailed, in contrast to the Protestant tendency to idealize the rural and simple life.

By the middle 1960s, emphases like those of Robinson and Van Buren were expanded into a so-called death of God theology, which recalled both Nietzsche's proclamation in *Thus Spake Zarathustra* that God is dead and Kierkegaard's attack on the blasphemy of nineteenth-century "Christendom." With this movement the names of Van Buren, of Thomas J. J. Altizer, and of William Hamilton were frequently associated in the popular press. (And see the essays by Hamilton and Altizer, collected in *Radical Theology and the Death of God* [Indianapolis, 1966], on the cover of which was quoted the catchy assertion "God has died in our time, in our history, in our existence.")

In fact, there never was any death of God theology that could properly be called a movement — the authors named were not saying the same things at all — and whatever there was of a theological fad is long gone. But this is not to say that the cultural and religious situation out of which it arose has vanished or that the kinds of assertions being made by these and comparable thinkers were trivial or uninteresting. At the beginning of the 1960s, the nature of the religious crisis had been aptly described in a less-heralded book, *The Death of God: The Culture of our Post-Christian Era*, by Gabriel Vahanian (New York, 1960). On this analysis, the death of God for contemporary culture is not "anti-Christian," as in the case of Nietzsche, but "post-Christian," because current culture has become thoroughly immanental in its outlook, with only the reality of the world as the possible context for human self-understanding. One can speak therefore of a "cultural incapacity for God," a culture impervious to the categories of faith, as well as a "cultural disavowal of God." For Vahanian, the idea of the death of God meant the death of the cultural idol which was the creation of Christendom. For others, the death of God meant the dying of the father-image God that Freud exposed as a projection, or of the *deus ex machina* God of supernaturalism.

More generally, the stir produced by the death of God theology reflected a pervasive sense in twentieth-century culture of the unreality of God as traditionally conceived. Despite the persistence of pockets of conventional inward-looking or ghetto Christianity, and despite the resurgence of conservative Protestantism (see following section, "New Conservatisms"), the experience of the absence of God, both within and outside the church, has to be acknowledged as a dominant characteristic of recent Western European culture. And at a minimum the radical theologians have served to reiterate in the strongest terms the call for honesty in belief and theology.

More or less concurrently with the radical theologies, especially in the late 1960s and early 1970s, came the flourishing, at least in the public mind, of a great variety of the so-called new religious movements. These need be noted only in passing, as for the most part they do not belong to the Protestant story and in retrospect they seem quite ephemeral. Some were movements heavily dependent on Asian traditions, as in the case of the 3HO (Healthy-Happy-Holy) people, the Hare Krishnas, the Divine Light Mission, and the "Moonies" (the Unification Church). Others were quasi-religious movements, like the Human Potential Movement, Synanon, and the Berkeley New Left. More specifically Western in their orientation were groups ranging from the Jesus-centered Christian World Liberation Front to the Church of Satan. In an important sense, such movements as the charismatic renewal, the rise of black theology and feminist theology, and even the new conservatism, may also be counted among the "new" religious movements — but they have proved to be of much wider and more enduring significance and need to be treated subsequently in this volume.[5]

New Conservatisms

If the decade of the 1960s was the time for a new Protestant theological radicalism, especially in America, the following decade was most notably marked by the resurgence of conservatism, both religious and social. Indeed, the year 1976 could be dubbed by America's best-known poll taker, George Gallup, Jr., "the year of the Evangelical."

The early-twentieth-century "fundamentalist" reaction to liberal theology (see Ch. X) had largely lost its momentum in the 1930s, with the failure to capture the power structures of the leading denomina-

[5] Among the many interpretations of the "new religions" see, for example, *The New Religious Consciousness,* ed. Charles Glock and Robert Bellah (Berkeley, 1976), and *Understanding the New Religions,* ed. Jacob Needleman and George Baker (New York, 1978).

tions. As a movement, it never vanished but was pushed to the periphery. Neo-orthodoxy, as the popular name for the new theological directions signaled by the work of Karl Barth and others (see Ch. XII), moved to the center of the response to the felt inadequacies of liberal theology and held that position until well into the decade of the 1950s. After the end of World War II, however, and doubtless as part of the broad religious revival, or at least expansion, that took place then, a new opportunity seemed to open for a resurgence of the fundamentalist cause — though more commonly under the banner of a new "evangelicalism" (neo-evangelicals, some called themselves).

Early theological landmarks in this movement were such works as Cornelius Van Til, *The New Modernism* (Philadelphia, 1946), Carl F. H. Henry, *The Uneasy Conscience of Modern Fundamentalism* (Grand Rapids, MI, 1947), and Edward J. Carnell, *The Theology of Reinhold Niebuhr* (Grand Rapids, MI, 1950). The books by Van Til and Carnell were theologically sophisticated attempts to show that the neo-orthodox theologies were not legitimate defenses of orthodox Christianity against the errors of liberalism but in fact perpetuated those errors.

Van Til was the much more strident in his complaint (and more rationalist in his argument). His book was subtitled "An Appraisal of the Theology of Barth and Brunner," and in this appraisal Van Til concluded that the Theology of Crisis, or the dialectical theology, "is built on one principle and that this principle is to all intents and purposes the same as the principle which controls Modernism." Hence this whole theological program can be properly called "The New Modernism" (p. 364). It is not a recovery of orthodox theology, but is modern in content as well as in form. Barth and Brunner protest against Schleiermacher and Ritschl, but in fact they base their thought on the same theory of knowledge, as developed by modern philosophy, notably by Kant. By the adoption of this critical epistemology, this modern "phenomenalism," Barth and Brunner actually engage in a complete reconstruction of Reformation theology. Despite all the talk of God's transcendence, God is not here rationally *known* at all. This God has nothing to do with the Reformation concept of God as "an absolutely self-contained being," "a God of almighty power and of all-inclusive knowledge," but is only "a useful fiction or ideal by means of which man must order ultimately nonrational existence for himself as best he can" (pp. 370, 372). The orthodox doctrines of creation *ex nihilo,* of providence, of natural law, and of revelation in Christ are not to be found here. Hence the theology of crisis should be recognized not as the friend but as the mortal enemy of evangelical and historic Christianity.

Carnell's treatment of Reinhold Niebuhr was more irenic and appreciative. But in the end, from an evangelical perspective, Niebuhr's theology must be seen as fundamentally flawed in its abandonment of the doctrine of plenary inspiration of Scripture, in its substitution of the symbol of Christ for the absoluteness of the Jesus of history (his qualitative difference from all other historical persons), in its relativistic and pragmatic view of morality, and in its existentialist understanding of Original Sin. Throughout, Niebuhr has given up the claim to final knowledge in Christianity in favor of dialectic and relativism, in which the only finality is the absence of finality. (In his earlier work, *An Introduction to Christian Apologetics: A Philosophic Defense of the Trinitarian-Theistic Faith* [Grand Rapids, MI, 1948], Carnell had argued in a way not unlike Van Til that the only possible metaphysic for Christianity is a pre-Kantian rationalism, which can bring us to a genuine knowledge of God and thus lay the basis for the fulfillment of the system in the special revelation of the Bible.)

Carl Henry's *Uneasy Conscience* marked the powerful introduction of a distinctively new note in the discussion. In this manifesto and other writings, Henry both attacked the temperament of "fundamentalism" and called for the evangelicals to develop a real social ethic. The separatist mood of fundamentalism, its lack of love for fellow believers, and its internal divisiveness and fragmentation do not represent the true evangelical spirit. Instead, there must be cooperation among all evangelicals, a tolerance of differences over less essential points of doctrine, and an informed attitude toward newer elements of liberalism. The antieducational program of the fundamentalists, the anti-intellectualism that had persisted from the 1920s into the 1940s, needs to be replaced by concern for scholarship in all areas, including biblical study and science, and for education at all levels. And most distinctively, Henry condemned fundamentalism's aloofness from social and world problems, its "reluctance to come to grips with social evils," its almost exclusive focus on individual sin. A truly orthodox theology, he argued, must include a thorough system of social as well as personal ethics. Thus, Henry proposed, "contemporary evangelicalism needs (1) to reawaken to the relevance of its redemptive message to the global predicament; (2) to stress the great evangelical agreements in a common world front; (3) to discard elements of its message which cut the nerve of world compassion as contradictory to the inherent genius of Christianity; (4) to restudy eschatological connections for a proper perspective which will not unnecessarily dissipate evangelical strength in controversy over secondary positions in a day when the significance of the primary insistences is international" (*Uneasy Conscience*, p. 76). With this kind of viewpoint, the new evangelicalism was to be sharply distinguished from the separatist kind of fundamentalism which nonetheless continued in the succeeding decades.

Through the 1950s (i.e., until the end of the Eisenhower era), the resurgence of conservative impulses continued to gain strength. A

National Association of Evangelicals had been constituted in 1943 and became one of the leading transdenominational societies for articulation of the evangelical point of view. The evangelist Billy Graham, made famous through his Los Angeles Crusade for Christ in 1949, continued for years to be identified in the public mind as the most prominent representative of the evangelicals' cause (though not without complaint from some that he was too willing to cooperate with nonevangelicals in his crusades). He also was a symbol of the identification of the new conservatism with the American revivalist tradition. Youth for Christ and Campus Crusade for Christ were significant parachurch movements. The biweekly periodical *Christianity Today,* established in 1956 as a counterpart to the well-known "liberal" *The Christian Century* and the Niebuhrian *Christianity and Crisis,* was widely circulated and came to be recognized as an important voice for many of the new evangelicals. Also, as part of the effort to achieve theological "respectability," emphasis was laid on connections not only with the older Protestant orthodoxy and with the classical "fundamentalists" like J. G. Machen and B. B. Warfield, but also with such nineteenth-century critics of liberalism as P. T. Forsyth in Britain and Martin Kähler in Germany. Special stress was given to contemporary European conservative Protestant thinkers, though it is probably only G. C. Berkouwer, of the Free University of Amsterdam, along perhaps with the No Other Gospel (*Kein Anderes Evangelium*) movement in Germany, who properly qualifies as a recent European counterpart to the American evangelicalism. Others sometimes claimed as kindred spirits, like Paul Althaus and Helmut Thielicke, count as theological conservatives but do not have the comparable animus toward liberalism and neo-orthodoxy.

In the 1960s the new conservatives seemed to move off center stage, which (at least in the United States and Britain) was occupied by the radical theological impulses we have noted in the previous section of this chapter. But in the 1970s, evangelicalism, along with various fundamentalisms, began again to flourish — in popular attention, in the volume of publications, in support from a resurgent Pentecostalism and the charismatic movement, in renewed efforts to control denominational structures (e.g., in the Southern Baptist Convention and in the Lutheran Church — Missouri Synod), in the growing establishment of "Christian" schools, and most important in varying associations with the New Right in politics and economics. By the 1980s, evangelicalism and fundamentalism came overwhelmingly to dominate religious broadcasting. Significant attempts have also been made to articulate the "evangelical" position in full-scale theological statements, among which we may note particularly the six volumes of Carl Henry's *God, Revelation and Authority* (Waco, TX, 1976–1983) and the two-volume work by Donald G. Bloesch, *Essentials of Evangelical Theology* (San Francisco, 1978–1979). (And see also Bloesch, *The Future of Evangelical Christianity* [Garden City, NY, 1983], which is a useful summary of the varieties of recent evangelicalism.)

In the new conservatisms of the recent decades, we must recognize both a broad range of commonly held positions and some sharp divergences, which in some cases are so extreme as to cause leaders in the movement to raise questions about its identity and future.

Most generally shared is the claim to represent authentic or historic Christianity, particularly as expressed in classical Protestantism, in opposition to atheism and secularism and to modern religious distortion or abandonment of the faith. At this point the interests of the new conservatives are continuous with those of earlier fundamentalism, as articulated, for example, by J. G. Machen in the 1920s. The opposition, however, is seen not only in liberal (and of course radical) theology, but also in process theology, neo-orthodoxy (usually), relativistic or "situational" ethics, universalism, feminist and liberation theology (sometimes), and of course in "godless Communism" and secularism generally. There is the familiar emphasis on truths of revelation, given in conceptual-verbal form in Scripture, and thus on correct doctrine as essential to Christian life and community. And the important doctrines include the authority of Scripture, the transcendence of the supernatural God, the sinfulness of humanity and redemption understood as vicarious or substitutionary atonement, the deity and exclusive redeeming power of Christ, the virgin birth, and the physical resurrection and return of Christ at the end of the age (which may be close at hand). With these traditional fundamentalist themes is commonly combined a stress on conversion experience (the "born again" Christian) and an emphasis on continuity with earlier revivalism.

Within this spectrum, however, are sharp divisions of opinion. For example, all affirm the importance of the authority of the Bible as the inspired Word of God. But intense debate goes on as to how this is to be understood, and it has been suggested that the basic conflict in the future will be between evangelical biblical rationalism and evangelical mysticism. An effort has been made by some to draw a distinction between infallibility and inerrancy. The idea of biblical inerrancy would mean that the Bible is totally without error (i.e., in the original autographs of the writers), and no biblical critical approach can be allowed except for the textual criticism that seeks the nearest approximation of the original writings. For "detailed inerrantists" like Harold Lindsell and Francis Schaeffer, such a view is the foundation stone and the guarantee of orthodoxy. (At the popular level, this attitude can be extended to include defense of the exclusive authority of the King James translation and even the notes in the Scofield Reference Bible.) Other voices (e.g., Bloesch, Carnell, and perhaps Henry) find it possible to affirm the infallibility of Scripture, in the sense of its being the certain and unfailing rule of faith, while affirming the genuinely human characteristics of the inspired biblical writers, the historical situations and cultural limitations of the authors, and the presence of innocent inaccuracies and discrepancies. There is thus a modified openness to recent patterns of biblical criticism, and also a welcoming of such translations as the Revised Standard Version, the New English Bible, and the Jerusalem Bible, with also an insistence that there are no errors in the heart and substance of what the Bible expressly intends to teach, God's will and purpose for the world.

A related distinction is between the separatist and controversial mood of extreme fundamentalism (which can also lead to divisiveness by elevating sectarian positions such as millennialism, premillennialism, and postmillennialism to the status of essentials) and the more ecumenical or even "catholic" attitude of many recent evangelicals who want to distinguish themselves from "obscurantist" fundamentalists. The latter attitude includes an appreciation for the valid elements in existentialism and in such thinkers as Barth and Brunner, a concern for the unity of the church and for genuine conversation with differing Christian groups, and a more inclusive view of the historical roots of the evangelical position. These are to be claimed in the whole range of Christian history from the early church fathers and creeds through Puritanism and Pietism as well as the Reformers, Protestant orthodoxy, and revivalism. There can even appear, as in the "Chicago Call" of 1977 (by Bloesch and others), a plea for renewal of sacramental understanding of Christianity — though that sort of openness to catholicism has aroused opposition and has not been paralleled by much sympathy for Eastern Orthodoxy.

Within the evangelical camp there have been varying degrees of commitment to rationalism and natural theology of a pre-Kantian sort, as the necessary counter to existentialism, neo-orthodoxy, and subjectivism. This was strong, for example, in the writing of Van Til and the early Carnell, where a philosophical apologetics with a rational knowledge of the existence of God is deemed the necessary presupposition and corollary for the hypothesis of God's revelation in Scripture. The Christian biblical view can be defended as the most rationally adequate explanation of reality. More recently, the appeal to "reason" is strident in the work of Francis Schaeffer, for whom Kierkegaard is the great irrationalist (in Schaeffer, this rationalism is joined with a strict inerrantist view of Scripture — see *Escape from Reason*, 1968). On the other hand, an evangelical openness to existentialism and mysticism (of the nonmonistic sort) is evident in the work of Donald Bloesch.

The rationalist thrust has also been evident in recent evangelical attitudes toward evolution. Alongside a variety of determined attempts, largely unsuccessful, to restrict the teaching of evolution in public schools, on the grounds that evolution is not a "fact" but only a theory and that the biblical account of the origin of humanity deserves at least equal time in textbooks and teaching, there has appeared a "creation science" movement. Creation science, which has found support from a few persons with various kinds of scientific credentials, purports to show on scientific grounds that the Darwinian theory of gradual evolutionary development of species is wrong, and that the evidence points to sudden and cataclysmic changes. Thus it is held that the biblical teaching about the origin of human beings has at least as much scientific legitimacy as the evolutionary view. It should also be noted, however, that some neoevangelicals have shown a clear recognition of the difficulties of relating an infallible Bible to modern science and have reflected an openness to a kind of theistic or "threshhold" evolutionism (i.e., to the idea that God is at work in a process of physical evolution of species within "kinds" and in the subhuman world), though the origin of the human species must be attributed to the special and miraculous act of God.[6]

Apart from the question of biblical infallibility, no issue has been more divisive in the evangelical camp than the issue of the millennium, the thousand-year reign (of Christ?) referred to in the New Testament (Revelation 20:2,3). To what extent are the events of modern Western history enactments of events foretold in the books of Daniel and Revelation? Could the Second Coming happen at any moment? Will the church suffer through the "tribulations" of Revelation? Is the millennium a messianic kingdom inaugurated by the Second Coming of Christ, followed after one thousand years by the last judgment and the end of the world (as the premillennialists contend)? Or are there two returns, a first to the saints, who are taken up to heaven in the "rapture" before the tribulation that befalls the world, and a second in which the millennial kingdom is set up on earth (as the dispensationalists variously contend)? Or is the kingdom of God now present in Christ's rule in the Word and the Spirit, though with an increasing power of the forces of evil and a time of tribulation and persecution for the church prior to the Second Coming (as the amillennialists contend)? Or is the millennium a special time prior to the final return of Christ and the establishment of the kingdom, a time in which the gospel will be preached to all the earth and the Jews (or at least some of them) will be converted (as the postmillennialists contend)? Though the expectation of the personal return of Christ is a staple of doctrine throughout the evangelical world, probably no other doctrine has been the subject of more acrimony or the cause of more separatism within the strict fundamentalist wing of the movement.

---

[6] On the emergence and fortunes of "scientific creationism," see the excellent essay by Eileen Barker in *Darwinism and Divinity*, ed. John Durant (Oxford, 1985).

And it has been argued with considerable force that the historical origins of modern fundamentalism really lie in the premillennial movement in England in the early nineteenth century, which later combined forces with the Princeton theology of Charles Hodge (see, for example, E. R. Sandeen, *The Roots of Fundamentalism* [Chicago, 1970]). At the same time, the more moderate or ecumenical evangelicals now want to hold that this area of controversy is really over minor, nonessential points of doctrine and decry the separatism into which rigid fundamentalism has been led.

Another division of opinion among evangelicals is over the right attitude toward the new charismatic theologies that have emerged from the Catholic and Protestant neo-Pentecostalism of the 1960s. The best-known aspect of this phenomenon is the stress on speaking in tongues, as a manifestation of baptism in the Spirit (recalling the experience of the disciples as recorded in the Book of Acts). But this is part of a larger emphasis on the present work of the Spirit. The gifts of the Spirit are also understood to include healing, discernment of spirits, miracles, prophecy and interpretation of tongues, and sometimes exorcism. Clearly, this charismatic religion is a significant strand within evangelicalism (though not only there), and it has been greeted with mixed feelings by many evangelicals.

A final and most important area of tension within the evangelical ranks is the question of the social relevance of the gospel. The older fundamentalism was essentially individualistic in its ethics, and, with the exception of some extreme groups of social conservatives, decried the attempt to "mix religion and politics" that liberalism and neo-orthodoxy involved. The National Council of Churches had been attacked as much for its social as for its theological stance. But, particularly after Carl Henry's *The Uneasy Conscience,* the newer evangelicalism came increasingly to recognize the social as well as individual nature of evil and the social imperatives of God's law. The events of the civil rights movement, the radicalism of the 1960s, the anxieties over the threat of nuclear war, and the obvious end of the Protestant establishment in America (symbolized by the election of President Kennedy) all served to strengthen this trend. While maintaining the theological priority of evangelism and conversion, the neoevangelicals sought to distinguish themselves from fundamentalism's seeming lack of sociopolitical engagement and emphasized the need for the church to function as an instrument of social reconciliation and reform, and indeed in concert with nonevangelicals. The 1973 Chicago Declaration of Evangelical Social Concern, formulated by Carl Henry and others, confessed the involvement of evangelicals in the racism, sexism, militarism, and economic injustice of American society.

Yet this kind of "social gospel" has remained a minority voice in evangelicalism. Extreme separatist fundamentalism, especially as influ-

enced by dispensationalism, did not develop a social conscience, remaining pessimistic about the world situation. It thus tended to be
thoroughly committed to the status quo or, as in the case of Carl
McIntire and Billy James Hargis, to make "Christian anticommunism"
and conservative political action as important as biblical infallibility.
And by the end of the 1970s, evangelicalism as a whole, commonly
called "fundamentalism" in the media, could seem to be on the side
of the conservative ideology, upholding private initiative and industry,
government decentralization, and nationalism by an appeal to the
American way of life and a preoccupation with national security.

At this point, and particularly in the 1980s, the evangelical resurgence could come to be identified with the political and economic
New Right. The New Right, of course, is not simply (or perhaps even
primarily) a religious movement, but a much broader conservative
political movement, a complex of activists and groups that have been
vigorous proponents of such things as the Human Life Amendment,
increased defense spending, prayer in the public schools, the teaching
of "scientific creationism," and vocal opponents of such things as the
Equal Rights Amendment, the Panama Canal treaty, SALT II, affirmative action, federal social programs, and "liberalism" and "secular humanism" in general.

The ideology of the New Right is a mixture of themes from economic
libertarianism, social traditionalism, and militant anticommunism.
Each of these three tendencies has deep roots in the American tradition
that are not necessarily compatible with each other. For example,
pure libertarianism and pure traditionalism have had little success in
America, but in combination they can flourish. As one interpreter
has put it, "American conservative ideology captures the libertarian
emphasis on material progress and individual success, but envelops
these within an appeal to divine providence, transcendent values, and
collective social bonds. At the same time, it adopts the traditionalist
concern with social stability and spiritual values without the otherworldliness and the pessimism about progress and human values" (Jerome
L. Himmelstein, in *The New Christian Right* [Hawthorne, NY, 1983],
p. 23). Such a merging holds powerful appeal both for special interest
groups (e.g., proschool prayer and antiabortion, anti-gun control and
anti-ERA) and for people generally concerned about social and moral
decay in American society. Support has been particularly sought from
"evangelical Christians."

The success of the appeal of the New Right has been evident in a
host of more or less evangelically oriented activist groups and coalitions,
of which the Moral Majority, led by Jerry Falwell, became the best
known (other major religious groups included the Christian Voice
and the Religious Roundtable). The name Moral Majority was of symbolic importance in recalling that out of the polarization of American

society over such issues as the Vietnam War, student radicalism, black militancy, and feminism, a conviction arose among some politicians in the 1970s that there was a silent conservative majority that could be mobilized — and how better than around evangelical Christianity? Here such themes as profamily, antiabortion, antihomosexuality, and antipornography had obvious appeal, but they could also be coupled with a general antistatism and economic conservatism and a host of other special issues.

As we have noted, the religious Right is not universally representative of recent evangelicalism, and internally the New Right as a whole has many tensions and conflicting interests (and ambitions). But by the mid-1980s it could be widely judged in the press that "fundamentalism" was providing the spiritual power for the new political and economic conservatism, and a television evangelist could entertain ambitions for the U.S. presidency.

CHAPTER XV

Toward the Future

In the preceding chapter we gave attention to recent developments ranging from diverse philosophical approaches to the theological task through the death of God theologies to the new conservatisms. Those varieties of thought, we have suggested, are mainly responses to problems as posed in the more recent past. In this chapter we turn to developments that are groping toward greater independence from past modes of thought and that are also less controlled by philosophical agendas. The theologies of hope and of liberation, together with the new consciousness of religious pluralism and the growth of interreligious dialogue, represent new departures in which the urgencies of the '70s and the '80s define the agenda. The past and its formulations are not forgotten, but they are viewed through fresh and revisionist eyes. Such theologies and approaches are trying to chart the future with a different consciousness of the past and with greater attention to how the present needs to shape the theological forms. In short, these are consciously future-oriented.

Theologies of Hope

In the theologies of Wolfhart Pannenberg and Jürgen Moltmann the concept of hope becomes the fulcrum from which Christian faith is to be understood, an organizing principle that gives a new shape to theology. Historically, "Christian hope" has been associated mainly with eschatology in the sense of a doctrine of "last things" because the final victory of God over the "world" is the content and basis of hope. That victory is manifest in the resurrection of Jesus and, as the New Testament phrase has it, unless Christ has been raised from the dead, our faith is in vain. But the victory is only completed at the end of history.

It is precisely the connection between hope and various views of eschatology that, according to Pannenberg and Moltmann, needs rethinking. On the one hand there were those who thought of the end in apocalyptic terms of historic and cosmic upheaval. One's task was to live in faith and faithfulness, awaiting God's final acts, in which the elect would be saved and vindicated. Such views of the end, held mainly by conservatives, could mean that the intervening historical developments were essentially irrelevant to the final drama. But such apocalyptic views could also be combined with more liberal perspectives, such as that of Albert Schweitzer in *A Quest for the Historical Jesus* (1906), in which it was also held that Jesus thought of the coming of the kingdom in cataclysmic terms. Since such pictures of the end reflect worldviews no longer possible for our time, the message of Jesus, for Schweitzer, must be found elsewhere. And in the wake of Schweitzer, many abandoned all reference to eschatology, relegating it to the thought forms of another age.

For theologians like Barth and Bultmann, however, eschatology became again a central concept. In *The Epistle to the Romans* (1919), Barth contends that without an eschatological understanding of God's raising of Jesus, Christianity loses its center. We live by promise, but in the present as those who through the effective Word addressed to them know the center of their existence. In *The Presence of Eternity: History and Eschatology* (New York, 1957), Bultmann analyzes various and diverse biblical and historical understandings of eschatology, ending however with a demythologized view in which eschatology is the current presence of God through which our lives are reconstituted as those who are free in the present, though hoping for the future. Barth and Bultmann, however different, are joined in thinking of God's revelation as that which constitutes our present life, a present illuminated by history but not dependent upon it.

For Pannenberg and Moltmann, however, the *processes* of history are at the center of the way eschatology and hope are to be understood. Admitting that Jesus must be seen in the context of apocalyptic thought, Wolfhart Pannenberg and Jürgen Moltmann were impressed by the way in which Jesus transformed such visions into an anticipation of "God's future," thus into a whole new way of living, toward the future. Taking that clue, they proposed to think not of the future in pictorial or apocalyptic imagery or of the present as the single context of God's presence, but of a new way of joining the two. We live in a present that is oriented toward the future, in the light of God's promises. Thinking then not of just the present or the future, but of the connection between the two, life becomes a living toward the future in which God is met. We are lured and made accountable by the light of God's future, the first fruits of which are found in the cross and resurrection of Jesus. Hence, hope has to do with what God is doing in the world, and with our involvement in that drama. Hence, history itself is the matrix in which hope is to be understood. Hope does not deal with our individual or communal lives as Christians apart from what is going on in the world, or with a special Christian history, but rather with how history *as a whole* is to be lived in and understood, that is, in terms of its end or telos.

Between 1959 and 1963, Pannenberg, working in association with a group of young biblical scholars, wrote a series of essays in which eschatology was understood as God's future, already given in Christ, and therefore defining our life as hope. Important, however, is not just that the concept was redefined; rather, the reconception of eschatology was nothing less than the redefinition of every phase of theological understanding. Hence, Pannenberg set himself over against the Barthian and Bultmannian approaches, which, while different, seemed alike in their single-minded stress on the Word of God and obedience engendered by it. In the preface to the American edition of *Revelation as History* (New York, 1968), Pannenberg wrote:

> Revelation is no longer understood in terms of a supernatural disclosure or of a peculiarly religious experience and religious subjectivity, but in terms of the comprehensive whole of reality, which, however, is not simply given, but is a temporal process that is not yet completed, but open to a future, which is anticipated in the teaching and personal history of Jesus. To speak of revelation in this way does not involve any irreducible claims to authority, but is open to rational discussion and investigation.

Pannenberg's succinct summary expresses every aspect of a different approach to theology. It is, first of all, synoptic in its accent on the totality of history as the medium of understanding revelation. It is also public in its claim that the Christian faith is not a private disclosure but one that makes sense in a world in which people use their rational and investigative faculties. It is a comprehensive view of history and of the cosmos as the domain and avenue of knowing and of living with God's future. That synoptic, public, and comprehensive view of religion and history, as Pannenberg himself acknowledges, is reminiscent of Hegel's concerns; but the development is more closely tied to a biblical understanding than was the case in Hegel.

For some, this agenda seemed like a return to the older orthodox theologies, with its emphasis on biblical facts and rational coherence. But the approach is far too sophisticated to be seen in such a way. The accent falls rather on the inherent logic in the biblical documents taken in their entirety. For example, the resurrection is to be understood in that context. Thus the accent falls not on proofs of the resurrection but on the fact of its appearance in the sweep of biblical history.

In the resurrection of Jesus, God is seen as providing the first fruits of the future, the "not yet" which is however present in God's act, which shows God's orientation to the future. In the light of God's future, made manifest in Jesus' life, death and resurrection, we can live in hope, for God has not only promised as of old but has already delivered in a proleptic way. Therefore we live toward the future, for we are joined in God's future for us — an openness full of surprises — rather than bound by powers dark and alien.

Biblical history is significant as the context in which God's actions take on new and changing forms, culminating in Jesus, in whom God's future is linked with ours. But if biblical history is the history through which we know God's future and ours, then its meaning is universal. It is a clue not only to all of history but also to the meaning of the cosmos. So understood, theology is not narrowed but expanded, for it represents a total view of the world, one in continuous dialogue with all the perceptions and discoveries in our world. While biblical and church history are the arenas in which we continually appropriate God's initiatives in their many facets, world history is the domain in which these initiatives press for a more comprehensive understanding. It is therefore not by accident that the work of the aged Marxist-atheist Ernst Bloch became important for Pannenberg and Moltmann, for in his writings, primarily *The Principle of Hope* (Cambridge, MA, 1966), the "not yet" uniquely distinguishes the biblical approach from views to be found in literary works other than Scripture. Hence, the claim for an understanding in which the past and the present are understood in the light of the future seems confirmed from an unlikely quarter, giving credence to the contention that the biblical view can enter the world of rational and public discourse.

Pannenberg's work represents a rethinking of the whole of theology from the standpoint of eschatology, not as the end, but as hope, as the future of God, and therefore our future. In that approach, theology is not oriented from the standpoint of a creation to be restored, but, in accord with some of the church fathers, toward a creation that, in spite of the Fall, has a future beyond its alleged original paradisal character. Hence the entire human drama, past and present, is included in the unfulfilled future, of which we have the first fruits. The horizon of theology is as wide as world history and its future.

In Pannenberg, then, the recasting of eschatological understanding through its futuristic dimensions becomes the way in which a total theology was developed. The result is a comprehensive theology, one in which faith is related to all of history. Theology is both Christian and world discourse, and the topics range from the God question to christology to anthropology to the sciences. These themes have been given preliminary form in the series of three volumes, *Basic Questions in Theology* (London, 1970–1973), mainly based on lectures and papers for conferences. Pannenberg's first magisterial volume was on christology, entitled *Jesus — God and Man* (Philadelphia, 1968). In this volume, he focused the christological discussion on the history of Jesus as God's revelation, a history which is at the basis of faith but which will be completed in the future. The christological discussion therefore cannot start with existential questions we may ask about our existence, but with the questions put to us by a history of Jesus itself. Hence, while faith is personal and unique, it is not private, for it concerns a history placed before all of us. And it is from this perspective that Pannenberg deals so fully and irenically with the christological formulations in the history of the church. While Pannenberg is aware that all formulations are provisional, he calls on us to use all the energies and faculties we have to state what we can in our time, as long as it is faithfully grounded in the history of Jesus as seen in the critical use of Scripture and historical understanding.

Equally commanding in their irenic but comprehensive coming to terms with biblical and historical understanding are the two volumes, *Theology and the Philosophy of Science* (Philadelphia, 1969) and *Anthropology in Theological Perspective* (Philadelphia, 1985). In these three major works on christology, science, and anthropology, Pannenberg has marked out a way of working that is free of the flair of popular movements, but enriching for those for whom theological work has an insistent seriousness.

In Jürgen Moltmann, whose *Theology of Hope* appeared in 1964, the necessary openness of God's future and ours continues to be a thread through which he vigorously distinguishes his insights from others. If Pannenberg is comprehensive in his incorporation of the world of human knowledge, Moltmann, in his early writings, is engaged in a dialogue that is more vigorously set over against opponents. The result is that the sharp differences between the theology of hope and other options are also clearer. Moreover, Moltmann, in his early work, more consistently confines himself to the explication of biblical concepts; that is, to a biblical theology, or a theology rigorously based on Scripture.

Fundamental to Scripture are the promises of God — a future that is to be, that is continually being readjusted under its primal focus in the death and resurrection of Christ, where the future of God and our future is expressed. Here, too, the resurrection is critical, for it defines our future. But the resurrection in Moltmann, as in Pannenberg and in Richard Reinhold Niebuhr's book, *Resurrection and Historical Reason* (1957), is a datum to be analyzed in terms appropriate to itself and its meaning, not as an issue of believability or nonbelievability. So Moltmann writes: "The resurrection of Christ does not mean a possibility within the world and its history, but a new possibility altogether for the world, for existence, and for history" (*Theology of*

Hope, p. 179). Just as the world is created out of nothing, so the resurrection presents a new creation, something that does not fit our categories, but sets us in new directions.

In the resurrection of Jesus, God has already shown in one man what will be our destiny in the light of the promises of the resurrection of the dead. But precisely because of that one event, a paradigm of the future, we live toward the future. Moreover, in that event we are joined with Christ as those who anticipate the future and hence act in the light of the future. The world is therefore the place in which new things happen, in which we work and live for the future. In this sense, Christians know the liberating power that sends them toward change and the new in history. But that should not be understood as easy or inevitable progress. Cross and resurrection are joined. Suffering is a part of our existence, for Christ was crucified. That is also our mark, but not without the promise of the future, God's future announced in death and resurrection. Moltmann succinctly writes that the promise of God "contradicts existing reality and discloses its own process concerning the future of Christ for man and the world. Revelation, recognized as promise and embraced in hope, thus sets an open stage for history, and fills it with missionary enterprise and the responsible exercise of hope, accepting the suffering that is involved in the contradiction of reality, and setting out towards the promised future" (*Theology of Hope,* p. 86).

Thus an intimate connection between cross and resurrection is delineated, but in such a way that we are confronted with suffering and rejection, and these are joined with hope for the future, of which we know the first fruits through the resurrection of Jesus. Because of that vision, we are oriented to the future, knowing that God has liberated us in hope and the expectation that new futures can always be formed.

If *The Theology of Hope* accents the future against despair and meaninglessness, Moltmann's *The Crucified God* (New York, 1974) accents rejection and the difficulties and presence of the cross, against all easy hopes, such as the expectation that history will take care of itself. In *The Trinity and the Kingdom* (San Francisco, 1981), Moltmann develops the openness to the future as a history in which God's activity and creativity toward the future can only be understood in appropriate trinitarian terms.

That we are liberated and set in the direction of the future through God's activity in the cross and resurrection of Jesus also provides the base for a politics of liberation. In the light of the future of God and our future, we are not set in the world simply under the presence of God but rather embarked in the struggles that change the present, that offer new possibilities for the future. The present is only interim; the future is our destiny, that to which we are committed. A static politics, a concern with the status quo, is not appropriate to people of the future. An element of radicality is thus endemic to Christian understanding, though never tied with particular programs except as chosen interim measures.

Although some of the accents are different, Pannenberg and Moltmann have reshaped theological thinking in their understanding of eschatology, not as the end, but as the beginning, as the future to which God is committed and to which we are called.

It is obvious that liberation theology, to which we turn in the next section, finds such theologies congenial, particularly that of Moltmann in which the political facets and mandates are clear. But the more conscious appropriation of the work of these theologians for their own theological work is particularly found in two theologians in the United States. In the instance of Pannenberg, one thinks of the writings of Carl Braaten; in the instance of Moltmann, Frederick Herzog. In both cases, the particular accents of these theologians are continued.

Theologies of Liberation

Three distinct theologies of liberation have emerged since the 1960s in response to oppression: black theology in the American scene, liberation theology coming from Latin America, and feminist theology, a movement especially of American women inside and outside the church. Black theology, the first to appear, has been chiefly a Protestant phenomenon, though it should be noted that the masses of blacks throughout the world are mainly Catholic. Liberation theology, arising primarily from Latin America, is predominantly Roman Catholic, though there are Protestant proponents. Feminist theology is both Protestant and Catholic, representing women across a wide spectrum of institutions. While the dominance of Protestant, Catholic, or a mixture of both reflects the respective backgrounds of black theology, liberation theology, and feminist theology and enters into the mode of theological reflection, there is little consciousness on the part of any of the three groups of being either Protestant or Catholic. Their joint agenda is a theology of liberation, born out of oppression.

Common to the three movements is the conviction that only those who have known oppression can genuinely understand their problems, and therefore only they can shape theologies of liberation. This means that theologies born out of the cultures of the oppressors are irrelevant to the oppressed. The sources for theological understanding must be found in the life experiences and context of the oppressed. This is the setting in which biblical and historical understandings must emerge. That is why those outside these three groups are asked, not to try to be of help, but to listen and to learn, for the sake of new understandings which will be liberating to the oppressed and perhaps then also to the oppressor.

Common then to liberation theologies is the necessary task of a revisionist history; that is, reconceiving history in the light of the oppressed rather than accepting existing historical work which, it is alleged, is based on the viewpoints and documents of those who were in power. Apart from the fact that both nonrevisionist and revisionist histories are constantly being reinterpreted, there can be no doubt that the biblical, theological, and historical work among liberation groups is providing us with information and insights that have long lain underground, that will necessarily change the ways in which we understand the past and present.

While the three movements have much in common, their relations to each other have not been easy. In its early phases, black theology expressed rather than attacked a sexist attitude, and the liberation theologies of Latin America stressed economic oppression to the neglect of race and class, while blacks accented the opposite. Blacks and women differed as to which group, given the history of oppression, should receive priority, with blacks claiming that their place in American history should be dealt with first. But within the last decade, the three groups have been reaching out to each other with new understandings about their common problems. Moreover, they have begun to see their plight on a worldwide scale and have sought contact with their compatriots elsewhere.

Black Theology

The debut of black theology on the American scene was traumatic. In the aftermath of the Voting Rights Act of 1964 and the participation of whites in the Selma, Alabama, march, as well as in other events, it seemed that a new era of integration had opened. But the riots which swept cities in the sixties, and the emergence of black power groups and the demands for reparation for the sins of the past, shocked sympathetic white leaders. Their confusion was compounded when blacks with whom they had been working turned inward and away from white communities in order to understand and develop their own religious outlook.

It was obvious to many blacks that integration as it was practiced affirmed equality but in no sense changed the circumstances in which blacks still were the victims and the oppressed. Black theology is the response to that problem, a theology that understands what faith means in the midst of oppression and knows that meaningful change must result in entirely different societal arrangements.

While the first use of the term "black theology" is not known, its first appearance in a publication was the 1969 volume by James H.

Cone, entitled *Black Theology and Black Power,* followed a year later by *A Black Theology of Liberation.* The thesis of Cone, as well as of others in the black theology movement, was that only a black understanding of Scripture and faith could be true and authentic. Cone knew that skin color was not the key, but held that the black person stood in the same place as the oppressed of Scripture, the people with whom God identified. Since the culture that now oppresses is white, black is the key mode of separation and of identification with scriptural witness. So Cone wrote: "Blackness, then, stands for all victims of oppression who realize that their humanity is inseparable from man's liberation from whiteness" (*A Black Theology of Liberation* [Philadelphia, 1970], p. 28). Blackness is thus a symbol of the oppressed with whom God identifies, while whites are the oppressors and hence the Antichrist. The fundamental issue clearly has little to do with the individual attitudes of blacks or whites, but with the structural situation in which blacks have been the victims of oppression by structures which whites control.

Black theology is mainly the appropriation and interpretation of Scripture in the light of the black experience. The conjunction of the two, it is believed, makes black theology the authentic interpreter of Scripture. Blacks know what the Exodus means, for they know what oppression means and they know that God is on the side of those so caught in the world. Likewise, the prophets attack the mighty who oppress the poor and the weak and make unmistakably clear on whose side God is. In the New Testament, Jesus is on the side of the poor, the downtrodden, those who are oppressed.

The lifting of oppression has two facets. First, there is a faith that God will deliver, that God's allegiance is clear, that one can therefore live in hope in the midst of oppression. Indeed, it is said, that is what blacks have always done in American history. Black religion, which to some appeared to be escapist, instead is the expression of hope, a life in the power of the Spirit that survives all oppression.

The second aspect of the lifting of oppression is the unresolved issue of what can and must be done to change the structures that oppress. What are the resources available to blacks in the situation of the predominance of social and economic forces that seem always to place them as a group toward the bottom? Precisely that situation is what is meant when blacks speak of a racist society, for it is a situation in which those who agree that change is essential are still among those who oppress through the structures in which they live. It is in this context that the demand for reparations is to be understood, as a way of helping rectify a history that so extensively oppressed blacks. Blacks, of course, were also aware of the biblical passage with respect to Zaccheus; "If I have taken anything from any man by false accusation, I restore him fourfold" (Luke 19:8).

In addition to Scripture, blacks have sought their own identity and approach to faith through the recovery of their African roots. Gayraud S. Wilmore in *Black Religion and Black Radicalism* (New York, 1982) and Charles Long in a series of essays in *History of Religions*[1] have been concerned to develop that ethos, involving musical and rhythmic styles, and what is known as "soul." Indeed, research in this area is in its infancy, but it promises a rich understanding for both blacks and nonblacks. But while Wilmore is interested in the incorporation of such insights into Christian understanding, Long contends that such discoveries, which have a mystique all their own, must be set over against the Christian theologies of the West. In both, there is a search for "black authenticity in a white-dominated society" (Cone, *For My People* [Maryknoll, NY, 1984], p. 15).

Given the thrust to recover black identity in cultural and social terms in contrast to integration into the life-style and culture of the dominant white world, a distancing between the two cultures was inevitable in order for each to be able to confront the other on new bases. This meant that for many black thinkers, the nonviolent stance of Martin Luther King, Jr., was to be replaced by a new militancy, psychological and sometimes physical in its thrust. Hence, violence, while not sought, was not ruled out as a necessary strategy in the struggle for human dignity and rights in oppressive situations.

All black theologians focus on the need for liberation, with both spiritual and physical ingredients. Indeed, the spiritual and the physical world cannot be separated, for liberation is a total movement. There have been some differences of opinion as to the posture toward nonblacks in the search for the liberation of blacks. James H. Cone, particularly in his earlier writings, is uninterested in a rapprochement with the white world, for such energies would detract from the main thrust toward the development of black theology. While blacks are discovering who they are, they do not have the time or luxury to develop their thoughts in dialogue with an alien world. This does not mean that black theologians had no contact with nonblack theologians. But it does mean that white theologians were no longer seen as the source for theological work; instead, they were asked to listen to the new voices of the black world. Other writers, such as J. Deotis Roberts in *Liberation and Reconciliation: A Black Theology* (Philadelphia, 1971), are equally concerned with liberation, but at the same time call for reconciliation, not as the first word, but as necessary, in the light of the gospel, once the recovery of identity and the commitment to liberation are established.

---

[1] See particularly "The West African High God: History and Religious Experience," *History of Religions*, vol. 3, no. 2 (Winter, 1964), and "Perspectives for a Study of Afro-American Religion in the United States," *History of Religions*, vol. 2, no. 1 (August, 1971). Also see his University of Chicago doctoral thesis, "Myth, Culture, and History: An Inquiry into the Cultural History of West Africa (1962).

The lively debates and fruits of black theology are manifest in persons too numerous to mention. But the pioneering work of C. Eric Lincoln, of which *Race, Religion and the Continuing American Dilemma* (New York, 1984) is an excellent example, as well as his promotion of the works of others in the C. Eric Lincoln Series in Black Religion, deserves special mention. Nevertheless, the future of black theology is difficult to assess. Its early vibrant thrust, manifesting the urgent need for liberation before either Latin liberation theology or feminist theology was on the scene, has been superseded by the constructive consolidation of its early discoveries and scholarly explorations in global terms. It has also had to face the hard reality that the plight of blacks in American society, in spite of advances at many levels, has not improved. While the debates on how to meet poverty and its attendant ills have preoccupied clergy, political figures, and government agencies, the stark fact is that the situation has not changed. Hence it is no small wonder that many blacks cannot escape concluding that such a society is racist at its core and are perplexed by white religious leaders so interested in the poor in Latin America and Africa, but so indifferent to the black poor in American society. And it would be difficult to deny that Latin American liberation theologies and feminist theologies have eclipsed black theology at this juncture in history.

Liberation Theology

While the term "liberation" is used widely today to express the gospel's freeing power against all that oppresses, it emerged in the 1960s in Latin America as a distinct movement among clergy and theologians. Given the predominant Catholic population, it has been largely a Catholic development, though there are Protestant proponents as well. It is estimated that there are approximately one hundred and forty liberation theologians in Latin America. Perhaps best known in the United States is the Catholic Peruvian theologian, Gustavo Gutiérrez, whose book *A Theology of Liberation*, published in English in 1973, has become a standard text. Other prominent Catholics include the Uruguayan Jesuit, Juan Luis Segundo; the Brazilian Hugo Assmann; and the Brazilian Leonardo Boff (temporarily silenced by the Vatican in 1985). Prominent among the Protestants are the Argentinian José Míguez Bonino and the Brazilian Rubem Alves.

Liberation theology stands over against the long history of exploitation and domination of that region, first by European powers and more recently by the United States. It understands its social context in the light of the conquest and colonization by European powers in the sixteenth century, followed by modernization and neocolonialism in the nineteenth, and by dependency on capitalist powers in the twentieth, particularly the United States. That history, these theologians believe, is responsible for a situation in which social, economic, and political life is under the control of the few and has led to the poverty and hopelessness of the masses. Liberation theologians further contend that poverty in Latin America is on such a scale, and conditions are so hopeless, that the situation cannot be compared to that of poverty in capitalist countries. For a long part of that history, the Catholic church was itself allied with and a part of the oppressive powers.

Liberation theology thus arises out of social and political consciousness and these theologians believe that a theology that does not have political consequences is part of the system of oppression that needs to be overcome. In situations of desperate poverty and political suppression, neutrality is not a choice; options must be chosen that change the systems that oppress. Hence, for liberation theologians and for numbers of bishops in Latin America, capitalism is not an option, for the capitalist countries have taken out more wealth than they have created in Latin American countries. Indeed, it is pointed out that the so-called development of underdeveloped countries has actually increased the disparities that have existed. To the argument that underdeveloped countries must go through the same stages of development that capitalist countries have done in order to create a better world, liberation theologians contend that this is too monolithic a view and one that is irrelevant to the Third World. Liberation theologians have no hesitation in using a Marxist analysis of culture, though they are not blind to the nature of Marxist governments. The Brazilian Archbishop Don Helder Camara stated: "I think we can avail ourselves of the Marxist method of analysis, which is still valid, leaving aside the materialist conception of life. . . . But I don't see the solution in the socialist governments that exist today. . . . The Marxist record is awful. . . . My socialism is a special one which respects the human person and turns to the gospel. My socialism is justice" (quoted by José Míguez Bonino, *Doing Theology in a Revolutionary Situation* [Philadelphia, 1975], p. 47). In recent years, the Marxist critique has been used less widely, and accent has fallen on experiences of the church itself as sources of insight on social phenomena.

It is characteristic of liberation theologians that they find traditional conceptions of democracy irrelevant. While lip service was given to democracy in many Latin American situations, the reality was far different. Writes Bonino,

> A free press, free trade, education, politics — all the "achievements" of liberalism — were the privilege of the elite. For the growing Latin American masses, undernourishment, slavery, illiteracy, and later on forced migration, unemployment, exploitation, crowding, and finally repression when they claim their rights — these are the harvest of one century of "liberal democracy.". . . The basic fallacy consisted in understanding

and describing the rise to power and wealth of the North Atlantic countries as a moral achievement due to certain conditions of character
and the principles of democracy, free enterprise, and education. . . .
Latin American underdevelopment is the dark side of Northern development; Northern development is built on Third World underdevelopment. (Bonino, *op. cit.*, pp. 15–16)

Some conservatives in the United States are opposed to liberation
theology because it seems to encourage socialism and to be unaware
of the overriding danger of communism. That difference of opinion
also exercised the Catholic church in Latin America. But at the Latin
American Bishops' Conference in Medellin, Colombia, in 1968, there
was a decided swing toward liberation theology because of situations
of marginality, alienation, and poverty of the masses created by social,
political, and economic structures. Medellin reflected a swing of the
church toward the poor and work in their behalf. Though conservatives
in the church worked hard to throttle that direction, even the conference at Puebla in 1979 came out decisively in behalf of the poor and
human rights in a document that was carefully scrutinized and supported by those present. Hence, facets of liberation theology now
pervade major segments of the institutional church.

The Vatican, as well as conservative bishops, was concerned about
the political role of the clergy in the context of liberation theology.
But the "Instruction on Christian Freedom and Liberation," issued
by the Vatican's Congregation for the Doctrine of the Faith in April,
1986, is notable, not for the strictures it proposes, but for the support
of liberation as standing at the heart of the gospel and for "a love of
preference for the poor," a phrase added at the behest of Pope John
Paul II, though its origin is probably from the widely used Latin
American term, "a preferential option for the poor." While the document calls for a theological understanding of liberation in which social
and economic matters are not as central as for some of the liberation
theologians, it does not sidestep such factors. It calls for changes,
though not through the political power of the church. Violence as a
mode of change, certainly not excluded by many liberation theologians,
is rejected in the 1986 document as a delusion and leading to new
servitudes. Simultaneously, however, the document equally condemns
"violence exercised by the powerful against the poor, arbitrary action
by the police and any form of violence established as a system of
government." Hence, while Pope John Paul II is theologically conservative, he is geared to social change in the world and is acutely aware
of the poverty and oppressiveness that is endemic to much of the
world's population. While the Pope and the hierarchy are opposed
to direct political action on the part of the clergy, they do believe in
the indirect role of the church in forming consciousness among the

poor and in making them aware of the options open to them. Given the large Catholic populations in Latin America and parts of Africa, the long-range consequences of such new awareness are not to be underestimated.

Thus, while the "theology of liberation takes its name from an economic and sociological analysis of the Latin American context" (Claus Bussmann, *Who Do You Say? Jesus Christ in Latin American Theology* [Maryknoll, NY, 1985], p. 11), its theological undergirding should not be underestimated. As in black theology, the concept of liberation is based in biblical paradigms, such as the story of the Exodus, the prophetic denunciations of those who oppress the poor, and the identification of Jesus with the poor. Moreover, in the 1970s, the liberation movement became more theological as it began more consciously to reflect on its role. Gone were the days when protest and political alliances allegedly promised new results, for repression continues in government after government. A more profound analysis was called for, one in which liberation gave hope in a world in which change was difficult and in which discerning the signs of the times was the only avenue toward change, whether short- or long-term. Such theological work may have been responsible in part for the acceptance of so much of liberation thought in the 1986 document when it had appeared that this theology might be rejected outright.

Liberation theology is focused on Jesus, and much of the writings center on spelling out the christological implications of his role as the revealer of God to our world. It is thus a christological emphasis in which God's active role in the lives of people takes precedence over reflections on the nature of God and the world. God's active engagement, that is, God's preferential option for the poor, defines our role as being engaged with the poor, working for their liberation. Hence, orthodoxy, the delineation of what is to be believed, is deemphasized in favor of orthopraxis or praxis; that is, theological reflection that emerges from pastoral involvement. Theology is not the basis of pastoral work, but occurs in the light of it. Such an approach means that metaphysics is replaced by sociological and anthropological analyses as the handmaiden or matrix for theological work. Indeed, theology is then a process, a discerning of the times and of what needs to be done. Claus Bussmann, a German theologian, can thus say, "Liberal theology's interest in Jesus was historical, with dogmatic implications; post-Bultmannian theology's interest in Jesus lies along the lines of systematic theology; and liberation theology's interest in Jesus is in the areas of praxis" (Bussmann, *Who Do You Say?*, p. 49).

Such an approach reorients traditional concepts. Creation is not an event of the past, but an activity that is going on and involves what we are doing as God's people. Its thrust is fulfilled in the resurrection of Jesus and in the meantime we live under the promises of

God. That is the nature of our hope. We live in the kingdom of God, not as its culmination, but as God's presence working in our midst. Utopian thinking is also reborn in that context, not as an expression of what is attainable, but as the contrast to that which is and as the sign of new possibilities on the horizon. While much of liberation theology was initially criticized for its optimism about what was possible, its later utilization of utopian concepts emerged as expressions of hope born in the midst of seemingly intractable structures of a political and social nature.

While liberation theology in its Catholic form continues its accent on liturgical and sacramental realities, its views of the church encourage the creation of "base communities" within the wider context. Such communities study Scripture, not with traditional historical or exegetical eyes, but with the attempt to discern the postures of the prophets and Jesus in real-life situations. That practice raises the consciousness of participants, for they see their plight in analogy to the past and can sense the basis on which hope rests. They know that while God loves all people, God does not love them all in the same way. The poor have a special place.

Latin American liberation theologians have entered into dialogue with European and North American theologians, and some of them have studied in Europe and America. The stress on hope and liberation in such Protestant theologians as Moltmann and Pannenberg and the Catholic Johannes Metz has been welcomed, but not without a critical note. Latin American liberation theologians see the great divide to be that European theologians are finally neutral in the political arena, that their work exists in a vacuum, freed of the necessary option of working with the poor for their liberation.

In the United States, the contextual and revolutionary theology of Paul Lehmann finds a more sympathetic ear. For Lehmann and liberation theologians, the status quo is never acceptable and God is engaging us in prying the mighty from their oppressive places of power. That is the context in which the issue of violence and nonviolence is to be understood. Violence, while not sought, is not ruled out by many; rather, it is seen as the last extremity in the midst of the violence that is perpetrated by the structures of law and order. For some, only suffering is possible, though not without hope of the transformation of the structures of society.

Biblical work in the United States in recent years has focused on the social contexts of both Old and New Testament documents. The result has been an undergirding of concepts of liberation. The most radical of such approaches is that of Norman Gottwald in his *The Tribes of Yahweh: A Sociology of the Religion of Liberated Israel* (Maryknoll, NY, 1979) and in the volume edited by him, *The Bible and Liberation: Political and Social Hermeneutics* (Maryknoll, NY, 1983). Finally, the

most articulate and graceful writing on liberation theology in the
United States is that of Robert McAfee Brown, as in his volumes
Theology in a New Key: Responding to Liberation Themes (Philadelphia,
1978); *Gustavo Gutiérrez* (Atlanta, 1980); and *Making Peace in the Global
Village* (Philadelphia, 1981).

Feminist Theology

Although there has been an emerging consciousness among poor
women of their need for liberation, the feminist movement is mainly
a middle- and upper-class phenomenon, and mainly European and
American. In this respect, it is sharply distinguished from black and
Latin American liberation theologies in which the poor are the center
of attention. One must immediately add that, in contrast to their male
counterparts, women are financially disadvantaged. They, too, suffer
from systems and structures that oppress and deny equality.

Feminist theology shares in a much wider movement for equality
among women in which there is a consciousness that the plight of
women is linked with that of blacks and of the poor striving for new
alignments; that unless all are free, none will be. While some black
theologians contend that attention should center on their plight as
the oldest and most exploited group in the American scene, some
feminist theologians believe that the plight of women is so central to
the total life of humanity that they are the logical choice for winning
the battle of liberation.

The fundamental issue for women is the deprivation of full personhood in a situation of male domination of all phases of life, from
the marketplace to the home, from marriage to the exigencies of the
single life. In short, women understand their situation as oppressed
in all facets of existence, demanding a liberation that touches all segments of life and affirms them as persons of equal worth and status
with males, however distinct women and men are at physical and
psychic levels. Long generations of male domination have inevitably
made women appear of lesser worth and have confined their activity
to dependent roles. While the nineteenth-century women's movements
in the United States led to some advances, such as the exercise of
the ballot, the movement as a whole mainly disappeared, not to re-
emerge in new forms until the 1960s. The current movement, however,
sees itself as the inheritor of that tradition, recalling the leadership
of Elizabeth Cady Stanton in the creation of *The Women's Bible,* of
Susan B. Anthony, Matilda Joslyn Gage, Sojourner Truth, Anna Howard Shaw, Harriet Tubman, and the Grimke sisters in relation to issues
of women in the church. To this group should be added secular writers
of the same period, and in our own time, the impact of Simone de

Beauvoir's *The Second Sex* and Betty Friedan's *The Feminine Mystique* should be noted. Of equal importance in launching the feminist movement in the 1960s was its conscious association with the other liberation movements and with the new perceptions being formed in the culture at large. A consciousness of the power of people claiming their dignity against the alleged oppressiveness of those in positions of power, whether governmental or economic, had become a part of the culture at large. In this context, the struggle is toward sharing power and promoting equality in the marketplace; in civic, public, and religious life; and in personal relations, from friendship to diverse familial settings.

Fundamentally, however, women have been involved in rediscovering their own identity as women. This is considered as the first step toward a new and equal relation with men. Here there is an analogy to black and Latin American theologies, for in all three instances, self-worth must be discovered as the first step toward the possibility of believing that change is possible. That is why women are forming associations with each other and exploring their perceptions of the world around them, including mythology, nature, and history. That need is well expressed by writers such as Nelle Morton, who believes that a transformation of the church is both possible and necessary, and Carol Christ, who believes that Christian theology as we have known it must be abandoned. In *The Journey is Home* Nelle Morton writes:

> All over the world women, rather than reaching up, have begun to reach down, to reach back and to reach ahead. We have begun to articulate our stories, to own our pain and to confront the stereotyped images out of which we have been conditioned to live out our lives. It has required full knowledge of the subtlety and power of sexism. It has involved breaking the images from within by shock, exorcism, and radical repentance — for the change of an image is an infinitely more difficult matter than the correction of a concept. (Morton, *The Journey is Home* [Boston, 1985], p. 81)

It is in this context also that Carol Christ, in her essays "Why Women Need the Goddess" and "Symbols of Goddess and God in Feminist Theology" (see respectively, *Womanspirit Rising: A Feminist Reader in Religion*, ed. by Carol Christ and Judith Plaskow [San Francisco, 1979], and *Book of the Goddess*, ed. by Carl Olson [New York, 1983]), eloquently contends for the reappropriation of all that belongs uniquely to women, their own perceptions of their bodies, their feeling for nature, for those characteristics which belong to women and that could also transform men. Nothing less, she maintains, will lead to authentic personhood for both women and men. Unless that happens, men will continue to read their own religious traditions in androcentric ways, while women make their own quiet, imaginative shifts. Needed are total reorientations. That is why for both Morton and Christ, Goddess concepts need to be explored. It is not a matter of refurbishing such concepts over against male ones, but of reappropriating realities expressed through them. In short, women's liberation depends on recovering the range of women's experiences and delineating those facets as the bedrock of their work and posture.

The special task of feminist theology is understanding and encountering the world of religion, and for our purposes here, the world of the church. While similar issues are present in Judaism, and to a lesser extent in Islam and Eastern religions, feminist theology is focused on Protestant and Catholic understandings, and in some instances, in alternatives to both. Mary Daly, while rooted in the Catholic faith, already rejected that tradition in her book, *Beyond God the Father* (Boston, 1973), and turned to other religious cultures and to the creation of a new language in order to speak of women, as in *Gyn/Ecology* (Boston, 1978) and *Pure Lust* (Boston, 1984). Alternatively, Rosemary Radford Ruether, the wide-ranging Catholic author, draws on many sources for the creation of a Christian feminist theology. Of her many books, *Religion and Sexism: Images of Women in the Jewish and Christian Traditions* (New York, 1974) is a historical study showing how women have been denigrated, while *Sexism and God-Talk* (Boston, 1983) is her systematic construction of a feminist theology. For those working within the Christian context, the question is, are Scripture and church history susceptible to reinterpretation, given that both are primarily patriarchal in outlook, or must one abandon them, except incidentally along with other sources, in order to do theological work? Further, major differences exist among those who believe that the Christian tradition must come to terms with both Scripture and church history.

For Letty Russell, in *Human Liberation in a Feminist Perspective* (Philadelphia, 1974), and Dorothy Sölle, in *The Strength of the Weak: Toward a Christian Feminist Identity* (Philadelphia, 1984), stress falls on the liberating portions of Scripture as the clue to reinterpreting passages and concepts that are not male-dominated — such as Exodus, the prophets, and the identification of Jesus with the oppressed. They share this approach with other liberation theologies. But for some of the feminist theologians, the Exodus itself is too patriarchal with its male warrior-God. They do not find the claim that Israel was less patriarchal than its neighbors as convincing as does Russell.

In contrast to the views of Russell and Sölle, Phyllis Trible, in *God and the Rhetoric of Sexuality* (Philadelphia, 1978), insists that the sexist nature of the Bible cannot be denied and that it must be seen in all its horror, while Elizabeth Schüssler Fiorenza, *In Memory of Her: A*

Feminist Theological Reconstruction of Christian Origins (New York, 1983), and in *Bread Not Stone: The Challenge of Feminist Biblical Interpretation* (Boston, 1984), contends that, without denying the stark patriarchal character of the biblical texts, there are also liberating threads that need to be elaborated. Beneath the texts of both Scripture and church history, she sees the traces of the role of women as prophets, apostles, and leaders. Precisely because they have been suppressed, these hints and subterranean currents need to be developed, while the suppression must be kept before women as a part of their painful history. Essentially, for Fiorenza, a feminist theology must be developed that includes such biblical and church historical sources, together with the experience of women drawn from many sources. That will serve as a special bond for women, a women-church, against ecclesiastical domination. It involves a theology that rejects all sexist texts as having anything to do with divine revelation.

The possibilities in a revisionist history may be illustrated with two examples. The Jewish writers Valerie Goldstein and Judith Plaskow have pointed out that the definition of sin as prideful self-assertion and grace as sacrificial love, as, for example in Augustinian, Reformation, and neo-orthodox theologies, are not the experiences of women, who need to see their sin as the acceptance of self-negation and who need a doctrine of grace that provides them with adequate conceptions of the self. For women, then, other sources within the tradition, such as the mystical one, speak more clearly to their perceptions.

In a paper for the Pacific Coast Theological Society, J. Rebecca Lyman, while agreeing with Fiorenza that the tradition increasingly eclipsed the role of women, also points out that the reading of earlier sources in the light of increasing subsequent patriarchal developments misses facets in which the tradition is not patriarchal. Irenaeus, she points out, saw Adam and Eve in equal responsibility for the Fall, and that on the basis of Genesis itself. Here deceit, seduction, and disobedience belong to both. Only later, she notes, was Eve's disobedience seen in sexual terms and Mary's obedience in terms of virginity. In Irenaeus, Eve and Mary, Adam and Christ, are interpreted spiritually and theologically, not sexually.

Reading the work of feminist theologians one is impressed by its passion and scholarly vigor. Diverse as the viewpoints are on interpretations of Scripture, church history, and non-Christian sources, they reflect work in uncharted territory, with its attendant freshness. But the work is unified in the deep claim of establishing women's identity as the basis for new forms of equality.

While sexist language, ordination of women, issues of abortion and lesbianism are media topics, they need to be understood in the light of the deeper issue of women's identity. The elimination of sexist language is essential and it is hoped that it will be an agent of significant change. But it is also contended that change must be so fundamental that mutual perceptions become different. For example, the ordination of women, important as it is considered to be, must be matched by situations of equality. Whatever progress has been made in both church and public life in providing new roles, women, it must be noted, still suffer from not having full acceptance and incorporation in church and public life. While women themselves are divided on such issues as abortion and lesbianism, they are agreed on the need to be able more adequately to control their own lives. For some women, heterosexuality is the last enslavement of women, while for others, more positive heterosexual relations will result from the liberation of both women and men in new forms of mutuality. In short, it is felt that there are many steps to be taken to introduce change, but that such change must find its fruition in changed perceptions.

The individual women Christian theologians include both Protestants and Catholics. While some differences emerge from these respective orientations, such as the Catholic Fiorenza being less bound to Scripture as a source than, for example, Letty Russell, more pervasive is a common concern, in the midst of which the Protestant-Catholic differences recede into the background. Given that black theology is mostly Protestant and Latin American theology mainly Catholic, feminist theology is a remarkable mixture in which common affirmations are more characteristic than the differences.

* * *

In the seventeenth century, such dramatic reordering of theological thinking in the light of the major motifs expressed in liberation theologies would have led to the emergence of new denominations or churches. Today, denominations and churches themselves reflect a variety of approaches and viewpoints. The realignments do not take institutional forms; instead, they are geared to the goal of the transformation of existing institutions, both the church and society.

Insofar as the goal is change, all of the liberation movements are self-consciously political. Since the gospel demands change in the direction of liberation, neutrality is not a virtue. Hence, faith has a political character. Of course, Christians have always believed that faith makes a difference in life, and in the social gospel this was spelled out in terms of the need for institutional as well as personal change. Today, that consciousness has a new urgency, one in which political action does not have a negative connotation, but is the praxis by which change occurs and is made visible. It is at this point that liberation theologies and the new conservatism meet, each hoping to affect the body politic.

Pluralism and Interreligious Dialogue

Finally, among the future-oriented directions of recent Protestant thinking, we need to take account of the renewed and growing attention to the relation of Christianity to other religions. For many, this is a natural and inevitable extension of ecumenism (see Ch. XIII), a movement toward a *theology* of religions, which overlaps with but is not the same as the study of the "history of religions" or "comparative religions."

An appreciation of the value and inner integrity of other religious traditions had begun to grow in the nineteenth century, with the recognition of Christianity as one religion among others and the beginnings of the modern study of comparative religious history. Partly as a result of the missionary movement, both Hinduism and Buddhism experienced a renaissance in the nineteenth century, and the World Parliament of Religions, held in Chicago in 1893 in conjunction with the Columbian Exposition, stimulated the introduction of Buddhism and Hinduism into the West. As a consequence of all this, many Protestant thinkers were prepared to qualify the traditional claim to the exclusive truth of Christianity, understanding that the Christian religion is part of general religious history. Mostly, however, such interpreters wanted still to maintain that among all the religions, Christianity is the "highest" or the "final" revelation, and they often understood this as the culmination of an evolutionary process in human religious understanding.

These thrusts of interpretation were generally stalled, or sidetracked, by the emergence of the post-World War I dialectical theology or neo-orthodoxy. For such thinkers as Barth and Brunner all emphasis had to be laid on the uniqueness of Christian faith, on the once-and-for-allness of the revelation and reconciliation in Christ, on the utter christocentrism of Christianity (even to the point, especially in the early Barth, of insisting that the encounter with God in Christ is not a religion but a critique of all religion).

With the fading of the Barthian dominance, however, the second half of the twentieth century has seen a powerful resurgence of the question of Christianity and other religions. This has been forced by a variety of factors. Awareness of other traditions has been acutely sharpened by world events, including the Second World War, the establishment of the State of Israel, the Korean and Vietnam wars, the struggles in the Middle East and the emergence of a virulent Islamic fundamentalism, and the flood of Asian refugees into the countries of the West. With the new recognition of other cultures, "inculturation" has become the slogan of all missionary work. And despite the fractious and divided character of the world, some sense of a common human community has begun to grow. One leading contemporary student of religion can even speak of the emergence of a "corporate self-consciousness, critical, comprehensive, global," which means that "the truth of all of us is part of the truth of each of us."[2]

The scholarly study of the world's religions has grown explosively (and not only of the great living religions, but also of primal religion, archaic religions, minor religions, and quasi-religious worldviews such as Marxism). This has led both to new appreciation of the diversity *within* every religion and to recognition of the important periods of historical interactions among the religious traditions (e.g., of Judaism, Islam, and Christianity in the medieval West; of Confucianism, Buddhism, and Taoism in medieval China; and of Christianity and Asian religions in connection with the nineteenth-century missionary movement). Scholars have pointed to common symbols and mythic patterns among the traditions and to specific stories, ideas, and practices that have circulated in different religious contexts and forms (see, for example, Smith, *Towards a World Theology*, pp. 7–11, on the story of Saints Barlaam and Josaphat, which has appeared in Buddhist, Central Asian, and Islamic as well as Christian forms).

The twentieth century has also seen the emergence of "new religions" in Japan and of a powerful Islamic fundamentalism. Various Buddhist traditions have been active in seeking to plant themselves in the West. And many of the so-called new religious movements that began to flourish in the United States have been mixtures of Eastern and Western religion (perhaps most notably the Unification Church, which combines conservative Presbyterian and Korean Confucianist motifs with special insights of the founder, Reverend Moon).

Finally, it is symbolic of the new mood that Ernst Troeltsch has become again a center of intensive study and influence. It was Troeltsch at the end of the nineteenth century who offered a powerful argument for real religious pluralism and relativism, in which the religious experience of (for example) Buddhists had to be recognized as just as valid for them as Christian experience was for Christians (see Ch. X).

All these factors have profoundly affected the Protestant (and Catholic) theological enterprise. Symptomatic of the depth of reconsideration required is the publication by Paul Tillich, after his trip to Japan, of a small book entitled *Christianity and the Encounter of the World Religions* (New York, 1963), in which he argued strongly for Christian self-criticism in light of the encounter and for dialogue instead of conver-

---

[2] Wilfred Cantwell Smith, *Towards a World Theology* (Philadelphia, 1981), pp. 78–79.

sion. Shortly before his death, Tillich asserted in a lecture of 1965 that he would like to rewrite his entire *Systematic Theology* "oriented toward, and in dialogue with, the whole history of religions."[3]

A special case in the new consideration of the relation of Christianity to other religions is the status of Judaism. This has to be special because everyone recognizes that Christianity is a child of Judaism, that the God of Israel is the God of the Christians, that the "Old Testament" is Scripture for Christians as well as for Jews, and so forth. But what of postbiblical Judaism, of the Judaism that continued after Christ? Here the traditional Christian position has been that Judaism is superseded by Christianity, that the expectation of the Messiah has been fulfilled in Christ, that the Old Covenant was replaced by the New (and this even in those theologies, especially in the Reformed tradition, for which the *content* of the New Covenant is the same as that of the Old). The Judaism that continued to exist was thus of no value for Christians, or was only of subordinate value and symbolic of the preparation for Christianity. Jews, or some of them at least, were expected to be converted before the return of Christ, and in some of the worst excesses of Christians, Jews as a group could be blamed as "Christ killers," repudiated and cursed by God.

The twentieth century has seen major changes from the traditional attitude. Particularly in the light of the horrors of the Nazi persecution and extermination of Jews, anti-Semitism has been condemned and Christians have begun to acknowledge the depth of the church's historic complicity in anti-Semitism. This is a first step. The Second Vatican Council deplored all hatred, persecution, and anti-Semitism displayed against the Jews. And in those conservative Protestant groups where conversion of Jews to Christianity is still hoped for, anti-Semitism is rejected and a spirit of love and open dialogue is encouraged.

But the rejection of persecution does not as such imply any abandonment of the supersessionist model, or the acceptance of a view in which the continuing life of Judaism has a positive and permanent validity *for Christians*. A slight opening to such a view (dialectically of course) might be seen in the late writing of Karl Barth, where it was insisted that "in relation to the Synagogue there can be no real question of 'mission' or of bringing the gospel." Barth spoke of "the Jew, even the unbelieving Jew, so miraculously preserved, as we must say, through the many calamities of his history, who as such is the natural historical monument to the love and faithfulness of God, who in concrete form is the epitome of the man freely chosen and blessed by God, who as a living commentary on the Old Testament is the only convincing proof of God outside the Bible. What have we to teach him that he does not already know, that we have not rather to learn

[3] See *The Future of Religions*, ed. Jerald C. Brauer (New York, 1966), pp. 31, 91.

from him?" And Barth could describe Christian treatment of the Jews
as "one of the darkest chapters in the whole history of Christianity."
Yet Barth also went on to say that at the decisive moment "Israel
denied its election and calling" and that the Jew who is uniquely blessed
is also "dreadfully empty of grace and blessing." Thus the Christian
community has a ministry of witness to the Jews by "the life of the
community as a whole authentically lived before the Jews." The Jewish
question stands as "an unresolved problem." (See *Church Dogmatics*,
Vol. IV, Part 3, Second Half, pp. 876–78.)

In his lectures, Paul Tillich was able to go considerably further,
stressing the continuing need of the Christian church for Judaism as
representing the Lord of history in a unique way. The church cannot
supersede the synagogue in the struggle against paganism because
the church itself is subject to pagan distortions. "The Church is always
in danger of losing her prophetic spirit. Therefore the prophetic spirit
included in the traditions of the synagogue is needed as long as the
gods of space are in power, and this means up to the end of history."
Thus, "it is important that there always be Judaism. It is the corrective
against the paganism that goes along with Christianity. . . . Synagogue
and Church should be united in our period in the struggle for the
Lord of time."[4]

Dialogue between Christians and Jews has subsequently become
more intense, with serious attempts to understand each other's traditions and present tendencies. A complete departure from the supersessionist view has appeared among Catholic and Protestant writers alike.
As a result both of the historical recognition that the kingdom has
not *finally* arrived and of reconsideration of the New Testament witness
to Jesus, it has become more difficult for Christians simply to claim
that the Jewish hope for the Messianic Age was realized in the death/
resurrection of Jesus. The differences between Judaism and Christianity are viewed not as contradictory but as complementary. The two
religions need each other. For some, this is interpreted by the idea
of two covenants that are complementary to each other, not competitive
or successive. Or, as in Eckhardt and Van Buren, Judaism and Christianity may be seen as embraced by a single covenant, which in Christianity is extended to the non-Jewish world (whether there is any
difference other than this "extension" is an open question).[5]

---

[4] See the discussion in A. Roy Eckhardt, *Christianity and the Children of Israel* (New
York, 1948), pp. 146f.

[5] See A. Roy Eckhardt, *Elder and Younger Brothers* (New York, 1973); Paul M. Van
Buren, *The Burden of Freedom* (New York, 1976), and especially *Discerning the Way:
A Theology of the Jewish Christian Reality* (New York, 1980). For a brief identification
of other Protestant and Catholic writers who articulate these new perspectives, see
Paul F. Knitter, *No Other Name?* (Maryknoll, NY, 1985), pp. 159–63. Knitter's book
is a most useful survey of many views on the relations of the religions.

Judaism as a living tradition, we said, presents a special case for Christian self-understanding. Apart from this, the new consideration of Christianity's relation to other great living traditions has focused especially on Buddhism and Indian religions (Hinduism, Sikhism), and in different ways on Islam, Taoism, and Confucianism. And in relation to these traditions we can distinguish several positions and attitudes toward the basis and character of interreligious dialogue.

One position is that of Christian absoluteness or exclusivism. This is of course the traditional Christian view, viz., that the revelation/ salvation in Jesus Christ is alone valid and that all other religious claims, while there may be elements of truth and salvific power in them, are fundamentally wrong, or even pernicious. This view empowered the older missionary attitude, in which the goal was to convert the "heathen," including even Jews and Muslims. It is generally a church-centered view, classically expressed in the slogan *extra ecclesiam nulla salus* (outside the church no salvation). And this exclusivism is still powerful in both Catholic and Protestant circles, even though it may be accompanied by serious efforts at sympathetic understanding. On the Protestant side, this is the dominant view among fundamentalists and the new evangelicals. In one of the more extreme expressions of the exclusivist view, it was declared by the Congress on World Mission in 1960 at Chicago that of the billion souls which had passed into eternity since the war, more than half went to the torment of hell because they did not know who Jesus Christ was or why he died on the Cross. While many of the new evangelicals would be hesitant about condemning to hell every person who had never heard of Christ, widespread support has been given to the "Frankfurt Declaration" of 1970 that salvation is possible only through participation in faith in the sacrificial crucifixion of Jesus Christ, which occurred once and for all and for all humankind, that the non-Christian religions are not in fact ways of salvation similar to belief in Christ, and that the idea of a "give-and-take dialogue" must be rejected in favor of proclamation that aims at conversion. And this uncompromising position was reaffirmed by a large gathering of evangelicals from all over the world at the International Congress on World Evangelization, held in Lausanne, Switzerland, in 1974.

The Christian absolutist position has in recent years been subject to attack from a variety of directions, reflecting views that have distinguishable emphases, though also common elements. All of these new views recognize some kind of relativity in all religious claims (though not an unqualified or indifferent relativism) and they focus on the meaning of "salvation" as authentic present human life and fulfillment more than some "future state." Christian "imperialism" of the old sort is rejected and a mutual learning is sought. With a heightened appreciation of other traditions, both common elements and real differences are identified.

One form of the attack on Christian absolutism is a revival of the view, common in the nineteenth century, that finally all religions are in some sense the same. We do not mean here the vulgar popular idea that differences are simply irrelevant, all religions being equally valid ways to salvation, but much more sophisticated ways of saying that at bottom all religions have something in common, a fundamental religious experience which is articulated in varying ways. Some of these rely on the influential argument of Rudolph Otto that religion roots finally in the sense of the "numinous" (a view that in turn is related to Schleiermacher's idea of religion as a "feeling" of utter dependence). Others emphasize the psychological commonality (e.g., along the lines of C. G. Jung's idea of archetypes). Or, in the language of Mircea Eliade, stress is laid on similarities of "hierophanies." Still another way of putting the sameness, which has deep roots in Eastern thought, is in terms of the "perennial philosophy," a term popularized some years ago by Aldous Huxley in *The Perennial Philosophy* (New York, 1945). Variations on this theme have been put forward by several interpreters of Hinduism (Ananda Coomaraswamy and René Guenon) and of Islam (Seyyed Hossein Nasr) and in recent writings of the Protestant Huston Smith (see *Forgotten Truth: The Primordial Tradition* [New York, 1975], and *Beyond the Post-Modern Mind* [New York, 1981]). Fundamental to the perennial philosophy is the idea that the core of all religion lies in the mystical, or esoteric, experience of the ultimate unity or "nonduality" of God and the self. Mystical experience is judged to be the wellspring of religion and is basically the same in all religions. The differences arise at the secondary or exoteric level of belief and practice and are to be understood as functions of differing historical and cultural contexts.

A quite different way of pointing to sameness in the religions, impressive and subtle in its argumentation, may be seen in the series of works by the distinguished historian and philosopher of religion, Wilfred Cantwell Smith, which has culminated in *Towards a World Theology: Faith and the Comparative History of Religion* (already noted above). To be sure, Smith expressly rejects the idea that all religions are the same, or even that one religion is the same. Even more vigorously, he has rejected the notion of an essence of religion, arguing in *The Meaning and End of Religion: A New Approach to the Religious Traditions of Mankind* (New York, 1963) that even the word "religion" should be abandoned. Religion is useless and misleading as a category of interpretation because it is a wholly Western and modern term that has no equivalent in other traditions, it does not correspond to the way premodern Christians have looked upon themselves, and it always suggests some unchanging essence, an objective systematic thing.

Instead of the undifferentiated and blanket term "religion," Smith holds that we should speak of "faith" and "cumulative tradition." Faith is an adjectival quality of a person's living, "an inner religious experience of involvement of a particular person; the impingement upon him of the transcendent, putative or real." Cumulative tradition is "the entire mass of overt objective data that constitute the historical deposit, as it were, of the past religious life of the community in question: temples, scriptures, theological systems, dance patterns, legal and other social institutions, conventions, moral codes, myths, and so on; anything that can be and is transmitted from one person, one generation, to another, and that an historian can observe" (*Meaning and End*, p. 141).

With respect to the cumulative traditions, Smith's work has been remarkably fruitful in identifying ways in which the traditions have in fact historically interacted with each other, so that their histories can only be understood in terms of each other "as strands in a still more complex whole." "The unity or coherence of humankind's religious history" is both an "empirical fact" and a "theological truth," and we now see indeed a world process of religious convergence (*Towards a World Theology*, pp. 3, 6, 44).

But faith, understood not as a fixed something but as an existential quality or psychological act or spiritual state of personal existence, does seem to be the same for Smith in all the traditions (and Smith's descriptions seem regularly to draw on Christian ideas of faith). The contents of faith may take myriad forms, to be sure, but the human activity which the term "faith" denotes is a reality common to all "religions." And Smith also appears to hold that there is a commonality in the reference of faith to some transcendent level or reality. Thus in the end it seems fair to view Smith as a representative of the claim that despite all the differences in their histories, there is a sameness in the religions. And on the basis of this commonality, as well as their historical interactions, and especially the growing convergence, Smith can urge that we pass beyond "dialogue" to "colloquy."

A second major departure from the Christian absolutist view, and one that has been winning widespread adherence among both Protestants and Catholics, has been called "inclusivism" (e.g., by such interpreters as Hick, Race, and Kittner). Here one can speak of a shift from the church-centeredness of the exclusivists to a new sort of Christ-centeredness.

On the Catholic side, some see this view as a legitimate extension of the pronouncements of Vatican II. Without abandoning the dictum that there is no salvation outside the church, and while maintaining that the true Church of Christ *subsists in* the visible institution of the Roman Catholic church, the Council moved beyond the earlier efforts to open the door to participation of non-Christians in God's universal salvific love, which included such notions as "baptism by desire" or "implicit faith," through which individual nonbelievers could be said to belong to the "soul" of the church or to be imperfectly or "tendentially" members of the church. In the Declaration on the Relationship of the Church to Non-Christian Religions, Vatican II could speak appreciatively of the strivings in other religions and could recognize that they "often reflect a ray of that Truth which enlightens all men" and that Hinduism, Buddhism, and Islam do contain what is true and holy. Thus prudent and loving dialogue should be encouraged. Yet the Council remained ambiguous on the question of how effective the Truth and Grace in other religions are for salvation, since Christ's Catholic church is the all-embracing means of salvation, where alone the fullness of the means of salvation can be found. And in the decree on missionary activity, the Council treats dialogue as a means to conversion.

A much clearer and bolder Catholic expression of the inclusivist view is found in the highly influential theology of religions of Karl Rahner, who was himself one of the shapers of Vatican II. Starting from the basic Christian assertion that God desires to save all humankind, and the corollary that God will act on this desire, Rahner presses to the idea that human existence is constituted by openness to infinite mystery and is infused by Grace. Thus revelation is universally a part of human existence, and the experience of God is inherently salvific. It follows that Grace cannot be excluded from other religions and that non-Christian religions can be "a positive means of gaining the right relationship to God and thus for the attaining of salvation, a means which is therefore positively included in God's plan of salvation." As Christianity understands salvation to be worked out in community, so Hindus and Buddhists work out their salvation in their religions. This is not, for Rahner, a denial of the Christian claim that the event of Jesus Christ is the final cause of all saving Grace (i.e., the goal and norm of the entire process of universal Grace). So Rahner was led to the much debated idea of "anonymous Christianity," a hidden reality of Grace and Truth outside the visible church which is grasped in a clearer, purer, more reflective and explicit way in Christianity. It may also be argued, of course, that this idea rests on an epistemological limitation, an aspect of the relativity of points of view: from a *Christian* standpoint one may say that the Buddhist is an anonymous Christian, yet the Buddhist could similarly say that the Christian is an anonymous Buddhist.[6]

A somewhat comparable Catholic view was expressed by Hans Küng in the idea of the "ordinary" way of salvation in the world religions and the "extraordinary" way in Christianity. This early view of Küng

---

[6] See Rahner, "Christianity and the Non-Christian Religions," in *Theological Investigations,* Vol. V (Baltimore, 1966).

seems to allow for a permanent validity in the non-Christian religions but at the same time asserts that Christianity is the essential "critical catalyst" for other faiths, the full realization of the revelation they possess.

What we see at work in this sort of "inclusivism" is a commitment to the centrality of Christ as the final definition of Truth and salvation, but without the "church-centeredness" that holds all salvific action to be mediated through visible connection with Christianity. The Truth and Grace that are genuinely found in other religions, and that make real dialogue possible, are thus (for Christians) included in Christ.

Such a view is not far from that of several influential Protestant interpreters (Knitter even calls this the "mainline" Protestant position). For thinkers like Paul Althaus and Emil Brunner, for example, we must affirm a general or universal revelation in humanity, an "original revelation" or "creation revelation" which comes to expression in the other religions. While this revelation may not have the full redemptive character of God's act in Jesus Christ, it is nonetheless the work of the same God who spoke in Jesus and is the basis for the genuine striving and searching, the sense of the need for fulfillment, and the care for other persons, that we see in other religions. In the language of Tillich's *Systematic Theology,* all religion is a state of being grasped by an ultimate concern, and the "question" of the meaning of existence is raised independently of the "answer" of the New Being in Christ. (As we noted earlier, toward the end of his career, Tillich seemed ready to go further in the direction of a mutual criticism among religions and of a dialogue among the answers.) At a minimum, then, there is for such thinkers a positive connection with the apprehensions in other religions, a preparation or point of contact for the gospel of Christ, which remains of course the final norm for interpretation.

More recently, Wolfhart Pannenberg has put the matter in terms of the historical and future-oriented character of human existence. Full revelation can come only at the end of history, yet the history of religions is "the history of the appearing of the divine mystery which is presupposed in the structure of human existence." Respect for the immediacy of the other religions to the divine mystery is required. Pannenberg thus eschews the description of non-Christian religions simply through Christian glasses, while at the same time holding that in Jesus the coming reign of God is known by anticipation and that Jesus' pointing away from himself to God and his self-sacrifice of his individual existence for the sake of his mission "is a decisive condition for the infinite God becoming revealed through him." Christians can thus learn from other religions and assimilate their truth, though in the end it is the Christian understanding of the God of the Future which provides the norm.[7]

---

[7] See *Basic Questions in Theology,* Vol. II (London, 1971), esp. pp. 114–17.

In the work of M. M. Thomas, of the Church of South India, the language is closer to that of the Catholic inclusivists, particularly to that of Karl Rahner's anonymous Christianity. For Thomas, it is only in Christ that human self-centeredness and self-justification can be overcome. But the Christ who is the one savior is a cosmic Christ, whose work is not restricted to the church but is to be found in all history, including especially the history of Hindus and Buddhists. Christ both relativizes and affirms all religions, including Christianity, and cannot therefore be confined to one religion. This is not to say that all religions are equally manifestations of the truth, but if Christianity has in Christ the universal ultimate truth, Christians are to seek in dialogue the positive responses of faith to the cosmic Christ in other religions.

A final important example of an inclusivist perspective, though one that may also go beyond it, is the process theologian John B. Cobb, Jr. In *Christ in a Pluralistic Age* (Philadelphia, 1975), Cobb developed a position intended to incorporate both the spirit of mutual recognition and the essential Christian commitment to Christ as "truly supremely important." All beliefs and attitudes are relative, not in the unqualified sense that any notion is as good as any other, but in the true sense that every view is historically and culturally conditioned. How then to accept the integrity and achievements of another religious tradition (e.g., Buddhism in particular) and maintain the centrality of Christ? Cobb's way of solving the problem is to interpret the idea of Christ as the power of creative transformation, which is apprehended through Jesus but is not bound to any particular religious system. Christ is the Logos (in the traditional language) and the Logos is literally incarnate in Jesus. But Christ is not simply a name for Jesus. Christ is the creative transformation that, in Whiteheadian language, transcends all particular instances but is present in all in varying ways and degrees. Thus Christ, for Christians, is "the Way that excludes no Ways" (p. 22).

In *Beyond Dialogue: Toward a Mutual Transformation of Christianity and Buddhism* (Philadelphia, 1982), Cobb seems to go further. "Beyond dialogue" means not only abandonment of all Christian absolutism but conversation in which each partner is truly open to learning from the other and therefore to being transformed by the other. Convictions are not absent but are subjected to the light of criticism and radical questioning. For Christians this includes the ideas of Christ and of divine transcendence. Cobb is chiefly concerned with the mutual criticism and transformation of Mahayana Buddhism and of Christianity. Both see themselves as universal traditions, yet both must be recognized as constantly changing movements. Thus "a Christianity which has been transformed by the incorporation of the Buddhist insight into the nature of reality [e.g., Nirvana] will be a very different Christianity from any we now know. A Buddhism that has incorporated Jesus Christ [e.g., Amida is Christ] will be a very different Buddhism from any we now know." Christians will not abandon Christ and Buddhists will not abandon Emptiness. Differences will not be obliterated, but "the lines that now sharply divide us will increasingly blur" (p. 52).

In *Beyond Dialogue* Cobb verges toward a third major line of critique of Christian absolutism. This we may call a still more pluralistic view of dialogue among the religions (or perhaps, as some have suggested, "theocentric" in contrast to "Christo-centric" and "inclusivist"). In the inclusivist approach, dialogue is theologically essential because of the recognition of full, authentic human life in others' religions, yet ways are found of attributing this authenticity and salvific power to the work of Christ, who remains unique and normative. In a pluralistic approach, on the other hand, the claim for the finality of Christ is recognized as precisely the obstacle to mutual appreciation and understanding. This claim has thus to be suspended, or, to put it another way, Christology becomes an open question.

From this perspective, we have doubtless the strongest rejection of Christian imperialism. And we may see forerunners of such an attitude in Ernst Troeltsch and especially in the "confessional" approach of H. R. Niebuhr, for which any claim of the Christian religion to universal empire or sovereignty is utterly incompatible with the sovereignty of God and the real meaning of revelation (see Niebuhr, *The Meaning of Revelation* [New York, 1941], pp. 38–42).

The English theologian John Hick, of Birmingham, England, and Claremont, California, is a well-known representative of this pluralistic view.[8] Arguing that the universe of faiths centers on God rather than any religion, he has proposed that each of the world religions has served as a means of revelation and (following the philosopher Karl Jaspers' suggestion of an "axial period" in human history beginning about 900 or 800 B.C.) that independent "seminal moments of religious experience" occurred in each of the four centers of civilization: in Greece (Pythagoras, Socrates, and Plato); in the Middle East (the Hebrew prophets and Zoroaster); in India (the Upanishads and the Bhagavad Gita); and in China (Confucius and the Taoist scriptures). In each of these cultures and their subsequent histories one is to see the Divine Spirit at work. With this emphasis, Hick incorporates the theme of "sameness" in the religions. In each of the great traditions we see a distinction between the Real in itself (or his or her self) and the Real as humanly experienced (i.e., between a higher Reality and a human relation to the Real). And by shifting from a Christianity-

---

[8] See *God and the Universe of Faiths* (London, 1973); *God Has Many Names* (London, 1980); and "Religious Pluralism," in Frank Whaling, ed., *The World's Religious Traditions* (Edinburgh, 1984).

centered or Christ-centered model for viewing the universe of faiths to a God-centered model, we see the great religions as "different human responses to the one divine Reality, embodying different perceptions [e.g., the concepts of ultimate reality as personal or impersonal] which have been formed in different historical and cultural circumstances."

In Christianity, Hick argues for thorough reconsideration of the traditional idea of Christ as the unique incarnation of God. That idea, properly speaking and in terms of our understanding of the nature of religious language, is mythological, or poetic imagery. And it is important to recall the widespread doubts among biblical scholars that Jesus ever claimed even to be the Messiah. This reconsideration does not require Christians to abandon the reverence for Jesus as the one through whom they have found a saving and effective contact with God. But it does require giving up the negative conclusion that there are no other saving contacts and experiences. Whether it can be established from historical evidence that Christ is the final or supreme disclosure is an open question. And the goal of conversation among religions, of a "world ecumenism," is not a single world religion but mutual enrichment and a "mutually interactive system" based on common humanity, common ethical ideals, and the search for transformation (salvation/liberation) by a higher spiritual reality. There must be cooperation "in face of the urgent problems of human survival in a just and sustainable world society."

With Hick in such a generally pluralistic view we may associate the names of the Anglicans Ninian Smart and Alan Race, Catholic thinkers Raimundo Panikkar and Paul F. Knitter, Stanley J. Samartha from the Church of South India, and perhaps the German theologian Jürgen Moltmann. From the Catholic side also, the recent large work by Hans Küng, *Christianity and the World Religions* (1985, Eng. tr., New York, 1986), shows a partial openness to this more radically pluralistic view. He speaks of a "global ecumenical consciousness," which will include the community of the great religions, and he seeks a way beyond absolutism and relativism, rejecting a standpoint of superiority, which rates one's own religion, a priori, as better. Thus real dialogue aims at "mutual critical enlightenment, stimulation, penetration, and enrichment of the various religious traditions." Yet Küng is not ready to surrender the normative definitive role of Christology, which he thinks would alienate him from his faith community, and thus finally seeks a presentation of Christianity in the light of a detailed examination of its relations to Islam, Hinduism, and Buddhism.

Ninian Smart, of Lancaster, England, and Santa Barbara, California, writes primarily from the standpoint of a historian of religions. In the Gifford Lectures, *Beyond Ideology* (San Francisco, 1981), he argues (vs. W. C. Smith) for a "plurality of patterns of basic religious experience," and proposes to speak of "worldviews" so as to be able to take account of secular ideologies such as Marxism, nationalism, and scientism. While dealing with a broad range of worldviews, he focuses particularly on the Christian and Buddhist types of experience. Emphasizing the subtle internal complexity of these great traditions (e.g., five distinct forms of Christianity), he suggests that Christianity and Buddhism have different dynamics in their alternate ways of representing the Transcendent. There are real divergences, so that worldviews are not reducible to one another. Yet there are also convergences of experience, so that one can speak of Christianity and Buddhism as in important ways mirror images of each other and of a genuine complementarity of Eastern and Western views and of religious and secular ideologies generally.

Raimundo Panikkar writes from the unique position of a Roman Catholic priest who was born of a Spanish Catholic mother and an Indian Hindu father and who grew up in both traditions. While continuing to affirm the "universal Christ" as "a living symbol for the totality of reality: human, divine, cosmic," for a dynamic "nondualistic" yet "nonmonistic" unity of God, humanity, and the world, he has come to reject any exclusive identification of Christ with Jesus or any single historical embodiment. Christians believe that Jesus is the Christ, but this Christ can go by many historical names, as many as there are authentic forms of religiousness. No historical form can be the full and final expression. Thus what is needed is "dialogical dialogue" in which the partner is considered as another human subject whose convictions can be understood only by somehow sharing them. And so Panikkar can speak of a "double belonging": "I 'left' as a Christian; I 'found' myself a Hindu; and I 'return' as a Buddhist, without having ceased to be a Christian."[9]

In Jürgen Moltmann, the relativization of the Christian claim is perhaps less clear than in Hick and Smart, but he too is adamant in rejecting any Christian absolutism and will let the plurality of religions remain. It is just because of the suffering of God in Christ, which is for the reconciliation of the whole world and from which no one is excluded, that Christians must be open and vulnerable in dialogue with other religions. And because Christianity's particular vocation is to prepare the messianic era among the nations (the theology of hope), "the dialogue with the world religions is part of the wider framework of the liberation of the whole creation for the coming kingdom." Thus Christianity can come to be a Buddhist, a Hindu, a Moslem, an animist, a Confucian, and a Shintoist Christianity. And all religions can be "charismatically absorbed and changed in the power of the Spirit,"

---

[9] See Panikkar, "Faith and Belief: A Multireligious Experience," in *The Interreligious Dialogue* (New York, 1978), pp. 1–23; also the revised edition of Panikkar's *The Unknown Christ of Hinduism* (Maryknoll, NY, 1981).

not by being Christianized or ecclesiasticized but by being given a messianic direction toward the kingdom."[10]

It is evident even from the brief sketches we have given that the lines of distinction between the various attacks on Christian absolutism are often blurred, and any attempt at classification must be tentative. Panikkar, for example, is at points close to Huston Smith. Hick's vision of a "mutually interactive system" is not far from W. C. Smith's idea of convergence in the great traditions, or Smart's notion of complementarity. Nearly all of the views are future-oriented and look for *mutual* transformations.

It is equally evident that we see here a major theological shift under way, perhaps what Hick calls a "Copernican revolution" in Christian thinking. For all these ways of dealing with the plurality of religions, it is no longer possible to do Christian theology except in dialogue with other religious traditions. Every religion is involved in constant change and in the modern world each is increasingly confronted by the others. Just as Protestantism and Catholicism need each other, so Christianity needs the other great traditions in a way not hitherto realized.

[10] Moltmann, "Christianity and the World Religions," in Hick and Hebblethwaite, eds., *Christianity and Other Religions* (Glasgow, 1980), especially pp. 208–209. For other thinkers mentioned above, see Paul Knitter, *No Other Name? A Critical Survey of Christian Attitudes Toward the World Religions* (Maryknoll, NY, 1985); and Alan Race, *Christians and Religious Pluralism: Patterns in the Christian Theology of Religions* (Maryknoll, NY, 1983).

CHAPTER XVI

What Is Protestantism?

The Point of View

We have been looking at the development of Protestantism with a view to understanding both its continuities and its varying responses to a changing world, its self-understanding in faith and its role as a social phenomenon open to analysis.

Our task now is to ask the question "what is Protestantism?" in a more systematic way, and to suggest a perspective from which all these elements of the Protestant development can be viewed as an intelligible whole.

Several commonly suggested answers to this question must be rejected at once as at best half-truths. One such answer is the simple description of those groups willing to call themselves Protestant. Impressed by the variety and complexity of Protestant history, those who make this answer would only point to certain institutions and communities and doctrines and say "here it is." That is, Protestantism *is* simply the sum total of Lutherans, Calvinists, Methodists, Baptists, Quakers, perhaps Anglicans, etc.

Protestantism is indeed a complex of histories and principles and structures. This serves to warn us against arbitrary selection and oversimplification. But along with the assertion of variety and multiplicity must also be placed the conviction of Protestants that they are bound together in a profound unity. Breaches within the community have been recognized as occurring *within* a real community, and sharp theological disagreement within a broad consensus. At times the bonds of community have been strained to the breaking point, but again and again appears a sense of a common loyalty and purpose. Institutional divisions have sprung largely from the motive of reform, not of separation. Individual denominational developments have been paralleled by movements cutting quite across institutional lines (e.g., Pietism, the missionary movement, biblical criticism, the social gospel, and the ecumenical movement). The story of Protestantism, as we have seen it develop, can be understood only from a perspective which recognizes both diversity and unity in this historical movement.

A second misleading way of answering the question of the nature of Protestantism interprets this movement as essentially opposition to Roman Catholicism. Protestantism and Roman Catholicism do exist in a continuing tension with each other. Whenever Roman Catholicism or Protestantism try to interpret themselves as bearers of the Christian gospel, they must necessarily take account of each other, both negatively and positively. The Reformation, "Counter Reformation," and the First Vatican Council (1870–1871) were points of extreme opposition. In spite of differences that continue to exist, the Second Vatican Council (1962–1965) and its aftermath have marked a period of positive tension.

But neither Protestantism nor Roman Catholicism can be understood primarily in terms of the tension which exists between them. Attempts to do this overlook the common history and loyalty which Protestants and Roman Catholics share. Their loyalty is to the gospel of Jesus Christ, mediated through Scripture and centuries of Christian witness. Their common history includes not only the Bible and the ancient and medieval church, but also the four centuries in which Roman and Protestant groups have stood over against one another, since in the latter period each has been continually influenced by the other. What separates Protestantism and Catholicism is precisely the *positive* character of the understanding of the faith which each represents. Each claims to be a faithful interpreter of the common loyalty and history. Just because of its understanding of the meaning of the gospel, Protestantism has had to be critical of Roman Catholicism. The Reformation break with Rome, the negation or revolt, was the by-product and result of what the reformers affirmed. There is truth in the understanding of Protestantism as a protest against Roman Catholicism, for that protest springs out of the heart of the Protestant witness to the nature of the Christian faith. But it is this positive confession which must be made central in any statement of the "nature" of Protestantism.

The duality of protest and affirmative witness can be seen in the term *Protestant* itself. The word first had reference to the "Protestation" of the German evangelical states in the Diet of Speyer (1529) (see Ch. IV). Here the meaning was partly that of protest, but from the standpoint of affirmed faith. Few churches ever adopted the name "Protestant." The most commonly adopted designations were rather "evangelical" and "reformed" (these terms continue to be used, especially in the European churches and in Latin America). On the other hand, when the word *Protestant* came into currency in England (in Elizabethan times), its accepted signification was not "objection" but "avowal" or "witness" or "confession" (as the Latin *protestari* meant also "to profess"). And for a century the English "Protestant" church was the Church of England, making its profession of the faith in the Thirty-nine Articles and the Book of Common Prayer. Only later did the word "protest" come to have a primarily negative significance, and the term *Protestant* come to refer to non-Roman churches in general.

A third inadequate way of understanding the nature of Protestantism is by exclusive appeal to the Reformation. Here the norm for the interpretation of what Protestantism means and ought to mean is simply the great principles of the reformers (e.g., justification by faith, the right and duty of personal judgment in matters of faith, the sole authority of Scripture, and so forth). In this view, Protestantism means "classical" Protestantism, an outlook which should determine the patterns for all subsequent Protestantism.

Certainly an indispensable truth is embodied in this appeal. Protestant Christianity cannot be understood apart from the Reformation and it is at least a necessary touchstone and guide for all interpretations of the nature of Protestantism. Yet the whole course of our analysis of Protestant development shows clearly that the Reformation cannot be made the exclusive source of understanding. Indeed, which Reformation group would we choose? Moreover, Protestantism has been more than the patterns of its historical origins (even these, of course, cannot all be identified with the Reformation). Nor would it be true to the intention of the reformers to fix upon their patterns as final and unchangeable norms. They rather sought forms of thought and institution which would give expression to a gospel which laid claim upon them. Their witness was not to themselves but to the God whose reality they had grasped afresh. And they were quite conscious that they stood in a historical situation which shaped the forms of their witness.

In contrast to all three of these views, we must say that Protestantism, like every other historical movement, can be understood only through the whole of its development. Thus, a recent church historian wrote:

No historical movement can be so interpreted that the character which distinguished it as unique among other historical events is once for all fixed in the understanding. Just as the character of a person can be known only in connection with his acts in concrete situations, so the nature of a movement in human history can be comprehended only by a constantly fresh attention to the inner and outer circumstances in which it has unfolded itself. And just as the character of a person does not only impress itself upon concrete life situations but is also shaped by them, so the nature of a movement in history is conditioned by the living realities through which it proceeds. Thus Protestantism, which was born in the Reformation and then received the prophetic, dynamic character which set it in contrast to Roman Catholicism, can be fully understood only in terms of the transformations and adaptations of its nature which it effected and underwent in the course of its development.[1]

We must insist on a perspective which is inclusive. In effect, we have to say that the answer to the question "what is Protestantism?" appears only in the entire history with which we have been concerned in the first fifteen chapters of this book.

We can, nevertheless, draw together various aspects of the understanding of Protestantism to which we have been led and set forth certain formal judgments regarding the dynamics or informing principles, of the Protestant movement. We cannot attribute finality to any such summary interpretation; but we can offer it as a perspective from which the Protestant development can be more adequately understood.

A Historical Community of Faith

Protestantism is a movement within history. Its existence is observable by all in certain events and institutions which can be located in time and space. As a historical phenomenon, Protestantism began in the early sixteenth century with certain events in the life of the Christian church in Western Europe. This was not an isolated event, but a very complex religious development which was interrelated with a variety of other movements — social, economic, and political. So also the history of the Protestant movement has been intimately bound up with subsequent history in general, particularly in the West but also in the East. In this sense Protestantism means certain concrete institutions, patterns of thought and statements of faith, ways of worship, groups of persons bound together in a certain geographical contiguity and historical continuity. Such groups have shared to a greater or lesser extent not only in a common religious community but also in economic, social, and political communities. This we may call the "outer history" of Protestantism. It is a history open to the inspection of everyone, subject to sociological and historical analysis as is any historical movement. It is that history which meets the eye of the nonparticipating observer.

But it is also a movement that must be understood in terms of its inner dynamics. This community sees itself as a part of that total

[1] W. Pauck, *The Heritage of the Reformation* (Glencoe, IL, 1950), p. 131.

community which is the Christian church. Its history is the history of the church. It holds in memory the story of Israel — the story of patriarchs, of bondage in Egypt and liberation, of Moses, of great prophets, of law given of God, and of the promise of a Messiah. It holds in memory the story of a "new covenant" — of Jesus of Nazareth, of preaching of the kingdom of God, of demand for repentance and faith, of teaching and healing and forgiving of sins, of crucifixion and resurrection, and of the living presence of the crucified and risen One with the community he founded. It holds in memory the story of apostles and martyrs, of the development of creeds and liturgies and church organization, of councils, of great leaders and missionaries and theologians, and of the whole company of Christians from New Testament times to the present, of the church in its glory and in its weakness.

In other words, this is a community in which it is affirmed: "All this is *our* history. The Bible is in our history. The history of the Hebrews is part of our story. Jesus Christ is an event in our past. The story of the church is our story."

At the center of this history is the gospel: the good news that in the life, death, and resurrection of Jesus Christ, God was reconciling the world. It is characteristic of Protestantism to hark back continually to this gospel, to recall always, as of first and decisive importance, the events of the New Testament witness and to warn against placing anything else at the center.

Thus Protestantism is marked by continual going back to the gospel, recalling the church to its central memory and loyalty. We have seen in the development of Protestantism how this concern has shown itself again and again. We found it in the Reformation. The reformers were quite clear in their intention to reaffirm the apostolic witness. Theirs was not a new gospel but the old gospel newly declared. This was why they placed the authority of the Bible above that of council or creed or pope, because in the New Testament they found the gospel of God in Christ freshly disclosed. So, too, Luther could assert that Christ was Lord even over the Scriptures. And in some Reformation groups (e.g., the Anabaptists) the concern for going back to the gospel was expressed in the attempt to reinstate the earliest forms of worship and church organization.

We have seen also how this intention has shown itself in the subsequent history of Protestantism. Pietism sought to recover the warmth and fervor of the message of salvation, which had seemed to be obscured in the creedalism and theological controversy of Protestant orthodoxy. The missionary movement recalled the command of Christ to his followers to go into all the world. The theme of Ritschl was "back to the New Testament by way of the Reformation," and the goal of biblical criticism and of "liberalism" was a clearer view of him who was the gospel, Jesus of Nazareth. Dialectical or neo-orthodox theology was directed toward the recovery of the wholeness of the gospel from the partialities and distortions which had come with liberalism. Liberation theologies now see a different thrust to be necessary in order to reclaim the gospel message.

If this be true, Protestantism cannot be understood as an isolated movement of reform, begun in the sixteenth century; it must be seen as continuous with reform movements of all the previous centuries. The reformers were quite conscious of their debt to those who had gone before, and we know that the way to the Reformation was prepared by numerous tendencies in the medieval church. The Reformation was not merely protest against the Roman church; it was the ripe fruit of central tendencies within the church.

Thus the Protestant community understands its history as belonging within the history of the whole church. It remembers the story of that church as its own story. And it remembers especially the gospel of Jesus Christ, the foundation of the church, seeking always to make this gospel central in memory and to hold this One Lord at the heart of its loyalty and hope. This community thus stands in the "apostolic succession" of the gospel. Its claim to apostolicity is its maintenance of the apostolic witness. It lives in conscious continuity with all those who have sought to recall that gospel. The members of this community understand themselves as speaking for a succession of renewed comprehensions of the gospel.

Much of the Protestant faith is shared with Roman Catholic and Eastern Orthodox Christians, and in seeking to delineate the Protestant perspective we must always keep in mind that this is a point of view which appears *within* the common history and faith and worship of the church. Here, however, we are interested in laying bare the distinctive elements of the way in which Protestant Christians receive and understand the gospel. These are the qualifications in the light of which Protestants view the whole of the faith.

Protestants claim no historic monopoly on this view of Christian faith. On the contrary it is the Protestant conviction that this understanding has been characteristic of the church wherever it has been at its best. It is the concern of Protestants that this understanding should be recognized by the whole church as integral to the true reception and proclamation of the gospel, and therefore should mold the common loyalty and worship and memory of Christians. This is not just a "Protestant" perspective, but more importantly a Christian perspective, which has repeatedly been lost and recovered in the church.

The elements of this understanding are not uniformly present in all Protestant groups at all times. The process of loss and recovery, of continual renewal of memory and understanding, is characteristic of Protestantism as it is of the whole of the Christian community.

Indeed, it is of the essence of the Protestant perspective that this should be so. The characteristic themes of Protestantism are dynamic elements which appear in varying forms and with varying emphasis, sometimes dropping out of sight, but continually coming again to the fore in the Protestant witness.

A basic element of the Protestant understanding has sometimes been called the "Protestant Principle." It is the spirit of prophetic criticism, or creative protest, which springs from the acknowledgment of the sovereignty of God and of the living character of the revelation in Jesus Christ. This is certainly not the sole Protestant principle, but it is truly a viewpoint which influences the whole of this community's witness. However often this spirit has been lost, it must be made central in any interpretation of Protestantism. The understanding of the dynamic character of revelation, the notion of the sole authority of the Word of God, the understanding of sin and forgiveness, the idea of the church, the principle of continuing reformation, and the actual pattern of recovery and reform which has characterized the development of Protestantism — all these are bound up with this creative and critical principle.

This principle is a dual one. On the one side, it is a principle of criticism and protest. In the name of the sovereign God who transcends all the limitations and distortions of finite existence, this principle requires the rejection of every human claim to finality and absoluteness. This is the truth in the interpretation of Protestantism as protest against Roman Catholicism. For the Roman church precisely claims that it is infallible and irreformable and has absolute authority in matters of faith and morals (i.e., by virtue of the guidance and protection of the Holy Spirit). Even in the more open stance represented by the decrees of Vatican II respecting such matters as religious freedom, the question of freedom and dissent within the church was bypassed. Against every such claim to absoluteness (whether religious or social and political) Protestantism must protest. Every religious institution, every creed, every pattern of worship, shares in the limitations and distortions (i.e., sin) of human existence. No religious pattern or form can be exempt from criticism in the light of fresh apprehension of the truth. Though our apprehension of God in Jesus Christ may be an apprehension of ultimate truth, it is still *our* apprehension and subject to the limitations of our perspectives as historically conditioned and as sinful human beings.

The principle of criticism in Protestantism must also be directed against Protestantism itself. Where Protestantism is true to the principle it is open to God's judgment and therefore *self-critical*. Protestantism protests against itself. Though the development of Protestantism shows repeated claims of finality, that development also shows the presence of continual protest against such claims and thus of continuing reformation and rebirth. Because Protestantism is ultimately committed to

the principle of criticism in the light of the Word of God, there is
always the possibility of inner renewal. Protestantism is able to see
itself as standing under the judgment of God, and needing to be
reformed. This is both the strength and the peril of Protestantism —
strength because of the possibility of rebirth (the hope of resurrection),
peril because of possible uncertainty and confusion.

But this principle is not primarily negative, or simple protest. The
demand for criticism is prophetic and creative. The protest springs
from the positive Protestant understanding of the gospel, of the sovereignty of the God who was in Christ, and of the dynamic character
of that revelation and gospel. It is the acknowledgment that God in
Christ continually meets us in new historical situations. Therefore
the knowledge of faith must ever be expressed in relation to new
situations. The witness of the Christian community to the gospel springs
from a *dialogue* between God and persons who respond in faith out
of their particular place in history. The gospel is directed to us where
we are. The gospel itself judges and demands continual reinterpretation in terms of the world in which it is to be proclaimed. The gospel
remains the same, but the forms in which it is expressed are diverse
and continually changing.

This is the reason why no single form of Protestantism can be simply
identified with the essential nature of the movement. There can be
no unchanging "essence" of Protestantism. Protestantism is a movement calling attention to a reality which transcends itself. The central
elements in the Protestant witness do not appear in fixed forms which
can be taken as normative and final. No system or ecclesiastical organization can rightly claim to embody the Protestant witness fully, though
many Protestant groups have claimed to do so. Protestantism is a
spiritual attitude which recognizes that faith in the living God expresses
itself in new ways of life and thought in response to the new situations.

Thus the breaking down of old patterns and claims to finality which
characterizes the development of Protestantism is not simply a protest
against partialities and distortions. It is precisely the appearance of
new and creative forms which demands the rejection of forms which
have become irrelevant and therefore false and misleading. It is the
renewed apprehension of the gospel which calls forth criticism and
self-criticism. The gospel of God in Christ is a dynamic reality which
makes impossible the enclosure of the Christian witness in any finally
fixed and unchangeable form.

This aspect of the Protestant principle or perspective is intimately
related to several others. Indeed, we can really see the meaning of
the creative protest only as we see it in the context of the other Protestant motifs.

1) We have made reference to the sovereignty of God, which needs
to be understood less in terms of a statement of the Godhead and

more with respect to what God means vis-à-vis all human activity, inside and outside the church. For example, the protest against claims to infallibility and absoluteness in religious or cultural forms is launched in the name of the lordship of God. It is a protest against the deification of the finite and the historical. The recognition of new and creative forms stems from the acknowledgment of the freedom of God to work outside the established patterns and institutions; it is a confession that God can and does make truth known in new ways.

The sovereignty of God is given most vivid expression in the writings of the reformers, especially in their theme of *sola gratia*. The doctrine of salvation by grace alone is in part a confession of the inadequacy and perverseness of all human claims to righteousness before God. But this doctrine is also and primarily a testimony to the utter priority of God's action. Wherever we turn in relation to God, we find that God has preceded us. All human seeking after God, all faith, all obedience, is perceived to be a response to God's gracious dealing with us. Thus, the doctrine of predestination has occupied such a large place in Protestant theology. Thus, a modern interpreter of Luther could summarize the reformer's thought in the demand "Let God be God!"[2] So too the liberalism of the nineteenth century was quick to understand evolution as the means by which God worked to achieve the sovereign purpose of bringing into existence responsible selves in community with each other and with God. And a social gospel and liberation theologies could appear to apply the word of judgment and redemption to social processes and structures as well as to individuals.

The renewed acknowledgment of the sovereignty of God has been a source of the variety of Protestantism. To be sure, there have been many other causes of Protestant differences: social stratification, economic and political conflict and controversy, human perversity, arrogance and conceit, individualism, rigid insistence on uniformity of belief and practice within the religious community, etc. But these differences are also the result of the consciousness that God alone is wholly sovereign and free. This has brought into Protestantism a persistent spirit of dissent and nonconformity which can call into question every apprehension of God and every attempt to restrict God's Spirit to unchangeable forms. It is a spirit which acknowledges that God is Lord even over religion, over the church, over Scripture, over creeds. It is a spirit that can even take the form of a "God is Dead" theology as a critique of all traditional ideas of God.

2) A second way of affirming God's role has been the insistence on the living Word of God, Jesus Christ. We have remarked on the persistent concern in Protestantism to return to the gospel, to make

[2] Philip Watson, *Let God be God* (Philadelphia, 1949).

unmistakably central in the memory and loyalty of this community the act of God in Christ and to let this gospel speak freely and directly to people in their own concrete situations.

This was the motive of the reformers in appealing from church and council to the authority of the Bible. The forms in which the gospel had been cast by much of the development of the Middle Ages seemed to stand in the way of the living presence of Christ and the word of forgiveness. But in direct confrontation by the witness of the Bible, people could again come to know for themselves the full power of the gospel of God's act in Christ. Thus, the churches of the Reformation sought to make the Bible accessible to everyone and rejected the hierarchical and sacramental forms of the medieval church.

So also, the biblicism of Protestantism, as the symbol and means of the concern to recover and be faithful to the gospel, continued to nourish the understanding of the living lordship of Christ. In Protestant scholasticism, rigid doctrines of verbal inspiration tended to circumscribe the living Christ within the pages of the Book. But devotion to every word and line of the Bible could result not only in intellectualism and pride in "right belief," but also in the recovery of the sense of the immediate personal presence of Christ in Pietism and the Wesleyan Movement and in the resurgent vitality of the awakenings and the missionary movement. In the liberalism of the nineteenth and twentieth centuries, criticism tended to reduce Christ to a figure of the historical past. But that very criticism was informed by the desire to recover again the Jesus of the gospels, whose real humanity had often seemed obscured in christological doctrine. And that same concentrated and diligent historical interpretation of the Bible led in turn to the discovery that this "Jesus of history" could not be separated from the apostolic witness — and thus to a renewed awareness of the Christ who is not only a figure of the past but the living Lord who encounters us in every present.

Though in quite diverse ways, these movements within Protestantism revolve around the acknowledgment of the living presence and sufficiency of Christ, who as revealer, reconciler, and judge is the expression of the sovereignty of God. Christ alone is Head of the church.

This understanding of Christ has implications also for the meaning of forgiveness. Christ is a Word of Grace, of reconciliation, of forgiveness. For Protestantism, this means that forgiveness is a personal act of God in relation to us, and the restoration of personal relationship between ourselves and God. It cannot mean the infusion of a character or virtue, of a substantive Grace channeled by sacramental means. Grace and forgiveness are rather terms descriptive of the new situation in which one stands and to which one responds in faith.

3) The human side of the sovereignty of God and the living authority of Christ is the response in faith, however it occurs. Protestants acknowledge God's freedom to create or use any means whatsoever to bring us to the knowledge of God's love in Christ. God is not coerced or bound to doctrinal form or good deed or rite. "The Spirit bloweth where it listeth." In Christ, God's revelation and reconciliation comes to men through finite forms, but at the same time directly and freely.[3]

The classical Protestant insistence on "justification by faith" is not only a warning against the inadequacy and perversity of human attempts to win the favor of God. It is even more a recognition of the priority of God's gracious act of forgiveness and an indication that reconciliation is actualized in human life by the intensely personal response of faith. Faith is the act in which the sovereignty of God and the living lordship of Christ are truly acknowledged. In faith God becomes God "for me." This is a response which can be made only by me. As Luther put it: "Every one must do his own believing as he will have to do his own dying."

This conception has been the subject of perennial misunderstanding, both outside and within Protestantism. Faith has sometimes been reduced to so-called right belief or sound doctrine. Or, as in Pietism and some forms of liberalism, the emphasis has been turned away from God who is the object of faith and toward the subjective attitudes and emotional state of the believer. Or, and this is an almost universal stereotype of the Protestant perspective, the demand for faith has been misinterpreted as individualistic and as meaning simply "the right of private judgment."

But the central theme of the Protestant view of faith is none of these. It is the confession of the intrinsic and immediate authority of the Word of God, which can come fully alive in the human spirit only as by the Holy Spirit this Word is received in the responsible decision of faith. This is not the suggestion that everyone has a right to believe whatever one likes, for one has the obligation to believe what is true. But Protestantism views this truth as given only in the believer's personal acknowledgment that this is what God leaves that person no alternative but to affirm. Christian convictions can truly be held only by one who personally judges them to be true. There is here the peril of freedom and of difference in belief, which has been fully exhibited in the development of Protestantism. But this is a risk

---

[3] The great temptation in Protestantism has not been the idolatry of particular forms, but the opposite, viz., the lack of concern for all religious forms and the consequent weakening of the sense of the sacred. A religious perspective which rejects all finite claims to ultimacy runs the risk of failing to see that the ultimate is known only through finite vehicles. This risk is taken, however, in order to maintain the freedom and spontaneity of the human encounter with God.

which Protestantism accepts, in the assurance that only so can the gospel truly be received. All individuals, though standing in the midst of the community of believers and bound to them by the demand of the gospel, must acknowledge for themselves the truth of that gospel.

Here lies a deep root of religious freedom, an implication of the reformers' witness which they themselves were loath to recognize. It appeared in some groups of the Reformation and later came to be almost universally affirmed by Protestants as an inevitable corollary of their understanding of the gospel. So, too, this view militates against every effort to reduce persons to mere items in the collective whole, against all tendencies to the "mass man," whether religious or economic or political.

The understanding of response in faith is expressed also in the classical Protestant doctrine of the "priesthood of all believers." As we saw in our study of the Reformation, this phrase did not mean that everyone is his or her own priest, but was a recognition of the *community* of faith and of the opportunity and responsibility of the believer toward the neighbor. The commandment is not only to "love God" but to "love your neighbor as yourself." The universal priesthood means that each person is a priest to every other; one can, in Luther's words, be a Christ to the neighbor. No believer can exist merely unto self; the believer always stands in the church, which is a "mutual ministry of believers."

Perhaps no principle of Protestantism is more thoroughly exhibited in its institutional development than this one. The Protestant "minister," "preacher," "pastor," or "rector" is set apart for the performance of certain functions in the church, but is only one among equals in the community of faith. For the sake of discipline, and perhaps of tradition, there may be a hierarchy of authority in the church, but the distinction is essentially functional. "Clergy" and "laity" are on one level in their responsibility to the gospel and to each other. Each is bound to wrestle with the gospel and to be servant of the other. Emphasis on the role of the ministry can be made only with full consciousness of the equal status of all Christians before God. (Even the Anglican view of the "priesthood," except perhaps for some Anglo-Catholics, differs radically from the Roman view of the distinction of clergy and laity and of the role of the hierarchy.)

The Protestant perspective as it comes to focus in the understanding of faith and the mutual responsibility of believers has led in several further directions. In services of worship, it has meant the use of the language of the people, and the creation of hymns and liturgies, so that all might share fully in the common worship. It has meant the revival of preaching, the proclamation of the Word assuming a central place in Protestant worship. It has meant a continuous emphasis on the translation of the Bible, that all might be confronted directly

with the biblical witness, and the production of a vast religious literature. It has led also to a profound concern for public education, as
the means of creating a literate and informed constituency.

4) Equally important has been the Protestant revaluation of the
common life. Indeed, it has been argued (e.g., by Albrecht Ritschl)
that the concept of a new style of life was more distinctive of the
Reformation than even the ideas of biblical authority and of justification
by faith. For Protestantism there can be no sharp separation of vocations into "religious" and "secular," as if the former had a higher
level of dignity than the latter. God is the Lord of the whole of life
and is to be served just as truly in the "earthly" as in the so-called
religious life. The daily round of work can be fully a means of glorification of God and the expression of love for the neighbor. Any
honest and useful activity, acknowledged as the place in which one
is called to responsibility to God and pursued with concern for the
common good, has a religious meaning and significance quite on
a par with the functions of ministry or with formal acts of worship.
The service of God in the ordinary life is no substitute for public
and private worship, but the common life is given a new dignity and
status.

Thus the idea of the "calling," whether in the sense of the call to
serve God in whatever kind of work one found oneself or in the
sense of a call to some specific vocation, was greatly widened. This
means responsibility as well as opportunity. The Christian is obliged
so to perform daily work as to make it an expression of faith and
love. We have seen how this awareness was developed in the ideals
of honest and faithful labor, of discipline and simplicity in life, of
thrift and sobriety, and of earnest stewardship (especially in Calvinism).
We saw how this moral and religious purpose served as a stimulus
to a youthful capitalism, yet at the same time sought to apply checks
to acquisitiveness and injustice — rejecting wealth as an end in itself
and insisting that all must be used for the glory of God and with a
view to the common good. We also saw how, when the inadequacy
of that method of christianizing the economic order became obvious,
the social gospel appeared as a call to restructuring the order itself.
And most recently, in the various liberation theologies, the question
is sharply raised whether one can responsibly serve God within the
patterns of work and status determined by an oppressive socio-economic order. Thus the traditional concept of vocation itself seems
called into question — yet precisely in the interest of the common
life of the oppressed, which is lived in response to God.

5) Many of the aspects of the Protestant perspective that we have
delineated could be summed up as elements of the understanding

of the church. The principle of creative protest in response to the reappropriation of the gospel, the sovereignty of God and the sole headship of Christ, the understanding of faith and of the mutual ministry of believers, the estimate of the common life — these inform the Protestant view of the Christian community. Indeed, it could be said that what is uniquely Protestant is its view of the church.

Protestants vary widely in the precise ways in which they define the church. But implicit throughout the Protestant development, and continually becoming explicit, is the dialectic between loyalty to the historic community with its traditions, and persistent protest against absolutizing the forms and institutions of that tradition.

The tradition in which we stand cannot be abolished or rejected so long as we remain in the church. It is the history of which we are a part, which shapes us, and to which our witness and worship contribute. The Christian engages in continual conversation with the past as well as with other present members of the community and seeks to be loyal to the One who is Lord of the community. In general this has meant for Protestantism a continuation of the central patterns of the church's belief and ritual (though Quakers, for example, feel no need of external sacraments). But these are affirmed in the conviction that loyalty to the gospel not only permits but often requires reformation in the church. The tradition is shaped both by the living activity of God in Christ and by response in particular historical situations; the tradition is not irreformable.

Thus, Protestant Christians understand the church broadly as a historical community of faith. It has its existence from God. It is a community which has its reason for being in the act of God in Jesus Christ. Christ is central in its memory, loyalty, and hope, in its worship, belief, and work. It seeks always to bear witness to the gospel. When it is affirmed that the church is the congregation of believers in which the Word is truly preached and the sacraments rightly administered, the reference is centrally to God's gracious act in Christ. The preached word and the sacraments set forth that act.

The church is not only a community of the proclamation of the Word; it is a community of Grace. It is a community which is being redeemed and is at the same time a means of redemption. It is a fellowship of those who confess their faith, forgiven sinners who have been led to a new life of growth in Grace. It is a mutual ministry of believers, who are means of Grace to each other and to all. Yet sin remains, and the church is forbidden to claim infallibility or absolute authority. It must always point away from itself to the One who is the source of its life. It finds its unity in common loyalty to that One, a loyalty which may be expressed in a rich variety of ways. It finds its continuity in maintenance of witness to the gospel. Its life is in God, and its historical existence is preserved as it remains open to

God's judgment and redemptive activity. It looks to a transcendent gospel which judges all human claims to finality and calls for reaffirmation and new response.

A Gospel for Every Present

We have sought to indicate the nature of Protestantism as a historical community which stands in the history of the whole Christian community and seeks always the recovery of the gospel, a community which is also informed by certain themes for interpretation of that gospel. To these two aspects of Protestantism must now be added a third, which has its rationale in the Protestant perspective. This is the peculiar relation of Protestantism to culture.

Frequently in our study of the Protestant movement, we have seen how developments in Protestantism, particularly in Protestant thought, had to be interpreted in intimate relation to the changing social, intellectual, and economic patterns of Western society. Protestantism cannot be understood simply as a self-contained unit, or by reference to a purely internal principle of authority, of theological tenet or spirit. To be sure, there is in Protestantism, as we suggested earlier in this chapter, an inner memory, loyalty, and hope which binds these Christians together in genuine religious community. And every description of institutional and theological developments tends to exaggerate differences and discontinuities, and thus to obscure the basic unity and continuity of the faith and piety of the body of believers. But the varieties of the Protestant development are truly symbolic and expressive of something which is essential to the life of this community.

Protestantism by its nature exists in a give and take with the cultural whole. So long as Protestantism continues to exist, its history *must* be marked by constant re-relation and readjustment to varying human situations. This is required by the Protestant understanding of the historical limitation and distortion in every religious expression. Equally important — and this we saw to be but the other, positive side of the principle of protest — is the Protestant impulse to maintain the vitality of the connection between the witness of faith and a changing culture. This is an understanding of the ways of God with human beings, which sees a relevance of the gospel to every human situation. The response of Protestantism to cultural change can never be simply negative; it must always bear witness to the presence of God's redemptive activity as well as God's judgment.

Thus, in spite of obvious failures to maintain its own perspective, Protestantism has been able to be open to the flux of the world in which it exists. Though Melanchthon opposed Copernicus, it was only in the Lutheran schools that the new astronomy early found a welcome place. Though its proponents may seem now to have gravely weakened the substance of Christian faith, the natural religion of the eighteenth and nineteenth centuries was an attempt to communicate the gospel in the new philosophy and science of the Enlightenment. Thus, also, Schleiermacher saw in Romanticism a means for the expression of depths of the religious life not realized by Rationalism or orthodoxy. The same pattern appears in the nineteenth-century acceptance of biblical criticism and of the findings of the sciences, especially of the theory of evolution. Subsequent Protestant thought was marked by the recovery of classical Christian perspectives and the concern with the analysis of modern culture. Liberalism and the social gospel may have been too shallow in their view of evil, but opened us to more social views of both sin and community, facets featured and made central in liberation theologies. One also finds the openness to culture in the various statements of the faith in terms of existentialism, process philosophy, and secularity. The whole of our survey of the Protestant development shows the presence of this pattern.

The same point can be expressed in another way in the assertion that Protestantism has no culture of its own. Though it is always expressed in cultural forms and influences culture, it cannot be found bound to any one form — not even to Western civilization as a whole. Though the history of Protestantism has been intimately related to the Western world of the last four centuries, even in its Asian and African forms it is characteristic of the Protestant movement to be finally free from these or any other cultural form. Protestantism cannot be content with the perpetuation of the cultural patterns of any given epoch, nor can it absolutely reject such patterns in the development of its own ritual, theological, and institutional life. Rather, the inner dynamics of Protestantism are in constant interrelation with the dynamics of the social whole — and this is not accidental but a matter of principle, as Protestantism seeks to give expression to God's redemptive activity in every present world. The continual return to the past which characterizes the Protestant perspective is paralleled by a continual openness to the present.

Let no one suppose that this understanding has been uniformly expressed in Protestantism. We have seen departures from this perspective in two directions. The openness to a present world has again and again led to a dissolving of the substance of the faith into the thought forms of a contemporary culture (e.g., in the individualism and natural religion of the Enlightenment and in the scientism of some "liberalism"). On the other side, the impulse to maintain the truth of the gospel has led recurrently to false absolutisms: thus Protestant orthodoxy in its creedalism and rigorous biblicism, and in our own time the extreme fundamentalist effort to perpetuate not only an outworn view of biblical inerrancy but the social and economic patterns of a past era.

But this very duality compels us to recognize the continuing operation of the dual motif of protest and creative renewal in the Protestant movement. The weaknesses of Protestantism are the weaknesses of its virtues. Protestantism recognizes within its own history the Christian theme of resurrection. That history is marked by recurrent dissatisfaction with dead ends, with "orthodoxies" and conventionalism — whether of medieval sacramentalism and moralism, of Protestant forms of scholasticism, of Rationalism, or of reductionist liberalism. And protest against these is for the sake of renewal, as in the Reformation, in the evangelical revivals, in Romanticism, in the missionary movement, in evangelical liberalism, in the social gospel, in the ecumenical movement, and in liberation theologies. Yet each kind of revival may in turn become a static form which must be broken down for the sake of renewed apprehension of the gospel. It is the Protestant conviction that this process can be given no simple historical or sociological explanation, however much such factors may be operative, but that ultimate explanation must have reference to the continuous and living activity of God, which works in the forms of life and thought in the church but always transcends them. For Protestantism, the church itself is seen as the object of Christ's injunction, "whoever would save his life will lose it, and whoever loses his life for my sake will find it."

Protestantism thus represents a faith direction that eschews both absolute certainty and absolute uncertainty. Its life is found in the flux and conflicts of historical existence, with confidence that in those living encounters, life will in fact be found. It represents a common quest that includes much diversity and that is full of mistakes. But Protestantism is also characterized by the continuous reforming of its own life, in the conviction that more will be disclosed of God's way in and with the world. Protestantism is not without boundaries; yet its boundaries are not definitive and infallible. Thus it is no ultimate problem that the Protestant witness in the ecumenical movement or in the encounter with other religious traditions can be seen to be merging with other forms of witness, or that questions can emerge about the viability of any kind of language about God, or there can be profound uncertainties about how far the distinctive emphases of Protestantism can be stretched without losing their distinctiveness. With respect to such questions, Protestants can be said to be at sea, but safely at sea in the confidence that land will be reached.

At the end, then, we must return to the assertion made earlier in this chapter, that no form or epoch in the life of Protestantism can be taken as finally definitive for the nature of Protestantism. What Protestantism is can be seen only in the light of its development. The dynamics of Protestantism have been operative both in terms of biblical literalism and in the criticism of that view in the name of historical analysis, both in the Calvinist reinforcing of the spirit of capitalism and in the sharp critique of capitalism and the structures of oppression by the social gospel and by liberation theologies. Protestantism is a life in community which expresses itself in a variety of forms and yet points to a gospel that both creates and transcends those forms. It is a continual reappropriation of Christian faith by a community which lives always in interaction with the whole human community. Thus it is a community which can only understand itself and its past, and the whole history of the church, in a critically appreciative way. Thus it expresses its faith in the God who is ever creating, judging, and redeeming.

Index